Bloomsbury's Prophet

G. E. Moore and the Development of
His Moral Philosophy

Bloomsbury's Prophet

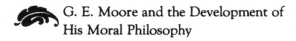 G. E. Moore and the Development of
His Moral Philosophy

Tom Regan

WIPF & STOCK · Eugene, Oregon

Wipf and Stock Publishers
199 W 8th Ave, Suite 3
Eugene, OR 97401

Bloomsbury's Prophet
G. E. Moore and the Development of His Moral Philosophy
By Regan, Tom
Copyright©1986 by Regan, Tom
ISBN 13: 978-1-62032-460-8
Publication date 8/15/2012
Previously published by Temple University Press, 1986

To
Bob Bryan

Teacher and Friend

*"the more completely rational
is also the more beautiful."*

G. E. Moore

Contents

	Preface	xi
	Acknowledgments	xvii
1.	The Sacred Book	3
2.	The Wages of Reason	29
3.	A Youthful Idealism	63
4.	A Cambridge Platonist	93
5.	The Right to Believe	121
6.	Art as Salvation	153
7.	The Autonomy of Ethics	183
8.	The Liberator	217
9.	The More Beautiful	251
	References	291
	Index	303

Preface

Every student of Bloomsbury knows something of the role the philosopher G. E. Moore played in its history. Opinion may be divided over how great his influence was or why he had the influence he did. But that he was an influential figure in the larger reality known as Bloomsbury no student of that phenomenon would deny.

The situation of students of Moore the philosopher is different. Here it is not the exception, it is the rule, to receive a large dose of Moore's philosophy without learning a thing about his connection with Bloomsbury. Why students of Bloomsbury should all know something about Moore the philosopher while most students of Moore the philosopher should know nothing of his historical association with Bloomsbury is an interesting question in the sociology of knowledge. Possibly Moore himself is partly responsible. In the autobiographical sketch he contributed in 1942 to *The Philosophy of G. E. Moore*, Moore does not minimize his involvement with Bloomsbury. He does not even mention it. Or its denizens. Bertrand Russell is mentioned, as are Henry Sidgwick and Ludwig Wittgenstein, for example: philosophers all. But not Lytton Strachey. Not John Maynard Keynes. Not Clive Bell or Virginia Woolf. Not any member of Bloomsbury, not even Moore's closest friend, Desmond MacCarthy. Perhaps Moore thought it inappropriate to mention his Bloomsbury connections in a volume about his philosophy. And modest man that he was, he may have regarded it as unseemly to parade the names of the great and near great he had influenced. But the absence of any mention of Bloomsbury has not been entirely salutary. Later generations of philosophers who study and teach Moore's philosophy independently of his Bloomsbury connections have been encouraged to suppose that they are living up to his high example.

But Bloomsbury was, and Moore did influence it. That much in the end must be conceded. What remains open to dispute is how and why he did, and whether our findings here should make any difference to our interpretation and assessment of his moral philosophy. Clearly, if there is nothing philosophically important or new to be gained from reading Moore's ethical writings, especially his *Principia Ethica*, against the backdrop of his influence on Bloomsbury, then the neglect of that influence by philosophers would need no apology. Students of Moore the philosopher would be justified in ignoring what students of Bloomsbury now know or might discover.

As it happens, there is more than a little of philosophical importance to be gained from reading Moore through the eyes of a student of Bloomsbury. *Principia* in particular had a liberating effect on the Cambridge-core of Bloomsbury and, through them, on Bloomsbury generally. Unless we assume (what seems unreasonable) that his followers accepted radically different merchandise from what Moore offered, we are right to assume that *Principia*'s message and spirit are cut from the same cloth. If so, then, like Bloomsbury, that work should itself celebrate the liberation of the individual and not, as is commonly supposed, demand that the individual unquestioningly conform to existing social customs and moral rules— conventional morality, so-called. That students of Moore the philosopher do not read *Principia* in this way is no answer to asking whether they should. Possibly his Bloomsbury disciples saw philosophical themes that his philosophical commentators and critics, in their rush to reconstruct or demolish his views, continue to miss.

The present work takes this possibility seriously. Its major thesis is that Moore, especially in *Principia*, does offer a moral philosophy that for its time and place is a radical defense of the freedom of the individual to judge and to choose. The foundation of this defense is to be found in Moore's conception of what he calls the "Science of Morals" ("Ethics"). It is because of what this Science can and cannot do that individuals in his view have the extensive liberty they enjoy, a liberty he both celebrates and seeks to defend. The chief (but certainly not the only) lesson Moore's Bloomsbury followers learned was that reason, in the guise of a truly scientific Ethics, is on the side of the individual and against the oppressive demands of society. Once having learned this, Keynes, Strachey, Leonard

[margin note, handwritten]: Reason is on the side of the individual and against the demands of a repressive society.

Woolf, and the others set about the task of living it. Moore's influence was that deep.

To understand its depth presupposes that we understand Moore's distinctive views about the Science of Morals. And to understand his views here requires an examination of his thought before *Principia*'s publication in 1903. *Principia* is the culmination of a process that begins at least as early as an unpublished paper dating from 1894, one of scores of unpublished essays that pre-date *Principia*'s appearance. These essays, together with other early work, both published and unpublished, help place *Principia* in a new light and go some way toward explaining the fierce passion burning between its lines. As we shall see, nothing less than Moore's own liberation as a moral philosopher and as an individual are at stake in that work. The reason for his uncommon influence on others regarding the importance of individual freedom is due, then, not only to the power of his ideas but also to the inspiring demonstration he himself gave of their importance.

The interpretation of Moore's ideas advanced here encounters the dissenting voices of both students of Moore the philosopher and students of Bloomsbury. Sometimes (or so it seems) it encounters the noisy opposition of members of Bloomsbury itself. Each critical constituency will be heard and answered. With so many informed sources against it, the view that Moore offers a radical defense of individual liberty itself has some title to the claim "radical." The hope is, it has greater title to the claim "true." To the extent that it does, both students of Moore the philosopher and those of Bloomsbury will be required to reconsider their received opinions about the man and his ideas. To force this reconsideration is the present work's principal objective.

Because the interpretation of Moore's thought offered here was occasioned by the attempt to read him through Bloomsbury's eyes (so to speak), Bloomsbury's cast of characters, something of their "corporate" identity as the Bloomsbury Group, and a few representative occurrences in which they played some role figure in the pages that follow. Students of Bloomsbury might find this wearisome, but students of Moore the philosopher might be surprised to learn some of the ideas and events in which *Principia* and its author were implicated. I can only hope that the former group of students will be tolerant of my attempt to illustrate what it means when we talk about "the depth of Moore's influence on Bloomsbury."

Indulgence from students of Moore the philosopher also is solicited.

Moore was always in at least two different places at the same time, one of which usually was academic philosophy. His connections with some of this and the previous century's most illustrious philosophers, those he influenced and those who influenced him, cannot be omitted from an account of how he came to have the views in Ethics he did. If the telling of this story sometimes retraces steps familiar to academic philosophers, perhaps it will impart something new to others. My aim is to be a student of Moore the whole man, and this sometimes necessitates mentioning parts that, while familiar to some, are not familiar to all.

That aim certainly is less than fully realized in some respects. Neither Moore nor Bloomsbury developed in a vacuum, and scholars of the post-Victorian and early Edwardian periods almost certainly will discern major influences that have eluded me. Moreover, because my major interest concerns how and why Moore influenced Bloomsbury, I doubtless have overlooked obvious instances where the dynamics of cause and effect worked the other way. Moore was a strong-willed and independent man, even in his youth. But it is unlikely that anyone who knew the likes of Lytton Strachey or John Maynard Keynes as well as Moore did could have failed to be influenced by them. Perhaps Moore was no less a Bloomsberry than the Bloomsberries were Moorites. If I emphasize Moore's role in shaping the lives of others, I do not mean to imply that no one helped shape his.

A second aspiration has sustained me during researching and writing this book. I hoped to craft a work about a philosopher unlike any other previously done. I wanted to create a book at once literary and entertaining, but one that did not fall short of the highest demands of philosophical scholarship. How well I have realized my ambition it is of course impossible for me to say. Here I wish only to make my aspiration explicit so that the conception and style of the present work might be better understood. The vignettes with which most of the chapters begin and end, for example, though in many ways imaginative constructions, are rooted in fact. They are intended to add a sense of psychological and social reality to discussions of the sometimes austere and other-worldly ideas of particular interest to philosophers.

Earlier, *Principia* was characterized as the end of a process. In one sense this is true; in another, false. It is true because we can see how and why *Principia* answers certain questions—some for the first time—that Moore had been asking for a number of years. It is false because, having given his answers in *Principia*, he did not stop there. Ahead lay the publication of his *Ethics* (1912), a number of essays on moral topics, and that portion of *The Philosophy of G. E. Moore* in which he replies to critics of his published work in Ethics. Various aspects of his post-*Principia* work, both in and outside moral philosophy, are alluded to in the following pages to illustrate the direction in which his thought sometimes moved and some episodes from his later life are sketched. Fundamentally, however, the present work is concerned with understanding the development and nature of Moore's moral thought, and the influence it had both within and (especially) outside academic philosophy, up to and as a result of *Principia*.

There is a vastly different book—a number of them, in fact—waiting to be written about the development of Moore's thought before and after the publication of *Principia*. How this early period bears on his later views about analysis and perception, for example, or his defense of common sense, are questions no less deserving of close attention than those explored on this occasion. And whether and, if so, when and why any of Moore's ethical beliefs are true, or any of his moral arguments valid— these, too, are legitimate queries calling for extended treatment enriched by a close reading of the pre-*Principia* material, both published and unpublished. These questions have not been explored in detail here because others have claimed pride of place. It is to be hoped that my peers in philosophy will add to the growing body of Moorean scholarship by doing the work that needs to be done. My deepest wish is that the publication of this book will quicken the pace.

Tom Regan
Raleigh, North Carolina
May 28, 1985

Acknowledgments

Books require the labor, cooperation, and skill of many hands. In the present case, as in previous ones, I am pleased to acknowledge the support of both my department and my university, without which I would not have had the time away from teaching that was necessary to write this book. I am particularly grateful to my department head, Robert S. Bryan, and to the Dean of the School of Humanities and Social Sciences at North Carolina State University, William B. Toole. Their confidence in and enthusiasm for my work have helped sustain me in my own confidence and enthusiasm. I owe both men much.

I am no less pleased to be able to express my gratitude to the staff of the National Humanities Center, where it was my great good fortune to be a Fellow during the academic year 1984–1985. I cannot say enough about the professionalism, competence, and support I received from every member of the Center's staff. There have been other Fellows before me, and some after, but none, I think, who is more grateful for having had the opportunity to spend time there. I only wish all those other scholars who are no less deserving than I was could be as lucky.

While at the Center I was assisted in my research by other Fellows, among whom the following should be mentioned: William Bousma, Donald Greene, Leon Kass, Lucinda MacKeithan, William Rowe, Larry Temkin, and Jack Wilson. Each read all or part of the manuscript and, along with John O'Connor, a member of the Center's staff, made helpful suggestions. Whatever shortcomings this book may have, it is the better for the time and trouble my associates at the Center gave to it.

The same is true of those beyond the Center who read the manuscript at various stages of completion and who gave me the benefit of their suggestions and criticisms. To the names already mentioned, therefore, I am pleased to add those of John Bowker, David Falk, George Pitcher, James Rachels, and David Ring.

Part of my research was carried out at the University of Cambridge, and it is a pleasure publicly to acknowledge the always courteous professional help I received there, both from Timothy Hobbs and the staff at Trinity College Library, and from A. E. B. Owen and the staff of the Rare Books and Manuscripts division of the Cambridge University Library. All of G. E. Moore's unpublished work alluded to in this book is to be found in these two libraries, and I thank the Syndics of the Cambridge University Library for the opportunity to read and quote from these unpublished sources.

But it is G. E. Moore's son, Timothy Moore, to whom I owe most in this regard. For it is Timothy Moore who retains the copyright to all of his father's written work, both the published and the unpublished. The sort of book I aspired to write, and which I have tried to produce here, simply would have been impossible if I had not been able to quote from G. E. Moore's work, especially his unpublished papers, letters, and the like. Not only did Timothy Moore give me the necessary permission to do this; he also granted me permission to assemble ten of his father's early published essays, none of which had ever been republished during his father's lifetime. I refer here to the recently published G. E. Moore: The Early Essays (Temple University Press, 1987). I profoundly hope that the fruits of my labors on that collection and on the current book are adequate to repay Timothy Moore for the trust he has placed in me. I can assure him, I've done my best.

One other denizen of Cambridge I should mention—and Timothy Moore would be the first to remind me of the need to do so—is Casimir Lewy. It was only after consulting with Professor Lewy that Timothy Moore granted me permission to quote from his father's unpublished work and to anthologize his early essays. My debt to Professor Lewy is therefore both real and deeply felt. I thank him.

Whatever the explanation may be, whether it be God's wisdom or an ungenerous store of genes, the world does not contain many outstanding editors. How blessed I have been, therefore, to have had the benefit of not one but two. The first is Jane Cullen, Senior Acquisitions Editor at Temple University Press. Jane Cullen encouraged my work every step of the way and, as before, lent her great ability to every aspect of the project. The second is Doris Braendel, Managing Editor at Temple, who served as my copy editor. Doris Braendel is, quite simply, the finest copy editor with whom I have ever worked; in my experience, she has no equal.

Sustained work on a book requires a single-mindedness that others can easily misunderstand. One does not love one's family or friends the less for working on a book the more. My children, Karen and Bryan, always have understood this, and so has my wife, Nancy. I do not think that I have done anything to deserve this uncommon love from them. I think it's their gift to me. I want them to know how very much I value their gift, and how much I love and value them for giving it. Theirs are among the "many hands" who have made this book, and certainly not the least important ones.

Bloomsbury's Prophet

G. E. Moore and the Development of His Moral Philosophy

1

The Sacred Book

 The place: 38 Brunswick Square, London. The time: A Thursday evening in November 1911. These are the facts. The rest we may imagine. On one of the couches in the large sitting room are the two Stephen sisters. Vanessa, at thirty-two the elder by three years, is the more youthful and radiant in appearance though less attentive to the pulse of life around her. Calm and serenly detached, she absently strokes the arm of her sister Virginia, who is engaged in taut conversation with the moustached man leaning forward in the chair opposite. Large oval eyes dominate Virginia's gaunt face; the skin, pulled thin across fine bones, seems almost translucent. Her fragility gives her an incomplete, ethereal beauty. Speaking through tight lips, she savors the nuances of her words, quietly relishing their power to insult and unnerve. In the decades ahead she will reshape our language, stretch both her imagination and her sanity beyond their breaking points, seek and find the watery release of Ophelia. But on this evening there is a mixture of sarcasm and satisfaction in her smile which, when she tilts her head toward her sister, elicits a gentle absent-minded nod, as of approval. "It's all in the mind," Virginia says.

Leaning further forward, almost rising out of the chair, John Maynard Keynes wags a finger to emphasize his point. Virginia, disdainful of speculation, has no need for theory. Keynes is filled by it. Truth. Beauty. Goodness. Although it is owing largely to his contributions to economics that he will one day be most remembered, and although in the ensuing years he is destined to dine with royalty and plan with generals, his is a temperament drawn to philosophy first, the world later. Virginia's barbed wit he allows without allowing it to deter him. Truth, he will always believe, is *not* "in the mind."

The high-pitched voice demanding attention is unmistakably Lytton Strachey's. Strangers think it pretense, but the "Strachey voice" is genuine, as authentic as his lanky, incompetent frame, his newly acquired black, broad-brimmed hat and cape, his too-small silver spectacles and audacious beard. Burdened by frequent illness and constant hypochondria, he makes a vocation of being publicly unwell. At thirty-one he laments missing the fame he believes is his due. When, before the first world war is over, fame comes with the publication of *Eminent Victorians*, he will take possession of it, incorporating it into his identity as naturally and completely as the black cape and beard. But on this occasion his point concerns the identity of aesthetic and sexual experience. He flaps his arms in imitation of a bird in flight, a pair of gold Etruscan earrings jangling from his pierced ears. His black shape sporadically collapses and expands, like the burnt lung of a mythical beast. He is Icarus, he tells his listeners, challenging the sun to preserve the identity of art and sex.

Noisy opposition is the immediate response from two of the three men who have been listening. Each disagrees with Strachey. Neither agrees with the other. Both talk at once. Vanessa's husband, Clive Bell, is the least congruous of the room's inhabitants. More likely as a young man to be in the fields shooting wild game than in his room reading the classics, he is the product of new wealth from a family lacking notable blood lines. His tangled red hair, large oval face, flushed complexion, and unrefined bearing create the impression of an overdressed farmer on his wedding day. Yet it will be Bell who will surprise them all when, with the publication of his slender volume *Art* in 1914, he becomes the first of the group to achieve wide notoriety, a development Strachey is never to understand nor quite forgive. Here and now, however, he simply refuses to listen to the objection Bell puts forward.

At forty-five Bell's mentor and senior by fifteen years, Roger Fry has stopped talking but continues to shake his head. Fry's work in aesthetics, especially his 1920 *Vision and Design*, will surpass the scholarship but lack the popularity of his younger protégé's. An art critic and historian of immense energy and organizational brilliance, Fry, with the "Art-quake" of 1910 behind him, already has introduced the English to post-Impressionism. A second post-Impressionist show will follow in 1912. In 1913 he will found the Omega workshops in neighboring Fitzroy Square. The members will decorate every aspect of interior design, from dinnerware to wallpaper, eschewing any assertion of personal authorship, having been persuaded by Fry that a collective identity—the Omega trademark—

would motivate as it fulfilled the creative impulse. Vanessa will be an energetic contributor until the workshops are discontinued in 1919, combining her intense though transient love for Fry, with whom she has recently begun an affair, with her belief in his doctrines. Clive Bell, "a gay and amiable dog," in Keynes's words, will not so much forgive as he will quietly acquiesce before the passion currently fusing his revered mentor and his wife of four years.

As Strachey's voice rises again, refusing to make room for Bell's tenacious objection, the third member of his audience sits down on the back of the couch, brushing against Vanessa's shoulder as he does. Lacking the Cambridge background of the other men, Duncan Grant at twenty-six is the youngest person in the room. Throughout his ninety-three years he will lack the inclination to theorize about art but not the urge to practice it, securing by the volume of his work a permanent position among the most important British painters of the twentieth century. The pacifist son of a career major in the British army, Grant will spend World War I laboring as a farmhand in lieu of military service. Since 1907—and over Strachey's strenuous objections—he and Keynes have been lovers. Strachey felt doubly betrayed, since it was he, Lytton, who had "discovered" Grant, a cousin who lived in the Strachey household for a time, and it was he, Lytton, who had gushed over Duncan's innocence and beauty to his own chosen confidant and counselor, Maynard. But Strachey will endure his dual rejection, and Grant will in time find Vanessa a more companionable presence than Keynes. Her affair with Fry behind her, her marriage to Bell no more than a formal reality, Vanessa will join Grant at the Charleston farm in 1916 and live with him until her death, at eighty-two, in 1961. Their daughter, Angelica, will marry the novelist David Garnett, Grant's fellow conscientious objector and wartime lover. Bell and Mary Hutchinson, one of Clive's many mistresses, will be frequent guests at Charleston, Clive taking an active interest in his two sons by Vanessa, Julian and Quentin Bell. Grant will welcome Bell always. But mainly he will paint. He is never so filled with life as when he works at his chosen vocation. Idle conversation he finds "bad for morale." His interest in Strachey's identity theory spent, he remains silent, arms folded across his chest, a look of honest boredom on his face.

Leonard Woolf is laughing. Leaning against a wall, he is listening to Desmond MacCarthy recount the critical outrage that had greeted the first post-Impressionist show. Fry had persuaded MacCarthy to serve as secretary of the Grafton Gallery's exhibition, an exhibition that included major works by such then unknown (to the English) painters as Van Gogh, Cezanne, Gauguin, and Matisse (no English painters were exhibited). MacCarthy's sharp Irish wit and sonorous, fluid voice recreate the critics' reactions: "pretension and imposture," "a bloody show," "absolutely skeptical as to [the paintings'] having any claim whatever to being works of art," this last opinion voiced by no less a figure than Vanessa's former teacher, John Singer Sargent. With mocking pomposity MacCarthy recalls the image of the show penned by Sir William Richmond, who pictured Fry out front leading a pack of asses— "exactly his right place!" The future literary editor of the *New Statesman* and the *Sunday Times*, and the general editor of the ill-starred but highly praised *Life and Letters*, MacCarthy, by the force of his judgment and the power of his position, will play a major role in directing the course of twentieth-century English literature, with results hardly detrimental to Bloomsbury's writers. Yet he will be the one person among those in the room whose promise of greatness never will be realized. The monumental book everyone expects will not come, even as his longevity (he will die in 1952, aged seventy-five) will deprive both him and his wife Mary of the excuse of an untimely end. "Imagine Roger," he says, "in front! Leading a pack of asses! Where he belongs!"

Leonard Woolf is laughing. He has been in London only since June, having come home to England after more than six years as a colonial civil servant in Ceylon. During his student days at the turn of the century he had been a contemporary of Bell, Strachey, and Keynes at Cambridge. Fry is a new acquaintance, but already Woolf feels drawn to his energetic complexity; Woolf, at Fry's invitation, will serve as secretary for the second post-Impressionist show, which will include works by Vanessa, Grant, and Fry himself, as well as a portrait of Strachey by the non-Bloomsbury painter Wyndham Lewis. The fire of Woolf's youthful friendships with Keynes and Strachey will rekindle in the coming years, while his relationship with Bell will remain steady if less warm. And yet unlike Strachey, who will stay on in Cambridge past the point of good taste in the hope that he might be named a Fellow of Trinity, and unlike Keynes, who will be named a Fellow of Kings, Woolf, like Bell before him, looked to opportunities beyond Cambridge's boundaries. But the selection of the Colonial Service was a choice made to fill the void in his life created by his graduation. Despite the promise of a governorship were he to return, replete with all the trappings of Kiplingesque power and position, he understood that his work in Ceylon, distinguished as it had been, was not expressive of his deeper aspirations. That will come later, both in his fiction, beginning with *The Village in the Jungle* in 1913, and in his political and social writings. He will move into 38 Brunswick Square in December, joining Virginia, Keynes, Grant, and Virginia's brother, Adrian. In January 1912 he will propose to Virginia. She will ask for more time. He will resign from the Colonial Service. In August of that year they will marry. Together they will found the Hogarth Press and through its friendly offices publish notable fiction and poetry, some of it (T. S. Eliot's *The Waste Land*, for example) of enduring importance. From a devotion born of love and friendship Leonard will successfully mother Virginia through the horrors of her tempestuous nervous breakdowns until, her plot this time too subtle to be gauged, she will take her life by drowning at the age of fifty-nine. In her last letter to Leonard she will write, "Everything has gone from me but the certainty of your goodness. I can't go on spoiling your life any longer." But that letter's message is thirty years hence, thirty years of as yet unlived and unimagined history. For now, Leonard Woolf is laughing.

The Bloomsberries

Such a room as this once was. Peopled with Virginia and Vanessa, Duncan Grant, Desmond MacCarthy, and the others, this evening in November 1911 is an imaginary microcosm of the larger reality know as Bloomsbury. That world began in 1905, when, after the death of their father Leslie, the Stephen children—Virginia, Vanessa, Thoby, and Adrian—moved from Kensington to 46 Gordon Square in the London area known as Bloomsbury, where Thoby introduced his Cambridge friends to his sisters at their weekly "at homes" on Thursday evenings. It lasted until 1920, when, with the founding of the Memoir Club, the people who had been the Bloomsbury Group began to meet weekly—and this they did for the better part of two decades—to exchange their recollections about what Bloomsbury had been. Perhaps others will insist on finding Bloomsbury shadows before 1905 and after 1920. The debate about Bloomsbury's age (or the other familiar one about its "true" list of members) will not be rehearsed here. Recognizing what Bloomsbury was is what is important. An uncommon collection of highly creative, disciplined, productive artists and thinkers, the Bloomsbury Group was a powerful force in the artistic and intellectual avant-garde of post-Victorian England, pioneering new

forms of expression in fiction and biography, forging new theories in economics and aesthetics. They were the harbingers of "the new," being
everywhere—and often contemptuously—against "the old," not only in
art and theory but also in their day-to-day lives. As a matter of deliberate,
conscientious decision they chose to live apart from both the very poor
and the very rich. Though they seldom lacked money they were not con-
sumed by the desire to accumulate wealth—though Keynes managed to
succeed well enough. An intellectual aristocracy in the truest sense, the
Bloomsberries (the name given to the group by Mary MacCarthy) may
have existed in the ordinary world, but they lived in their own. And they
made no effort to conceal and offered no apology for their shared sense of
superiority, their spiritual elitism. They rather enjoyed parading it.

Many of those on the outside took another view. The Group's sexual
permutations, real enough in their own right, were magnified in the popular imagination and press. Perhaps only the public's appetite for the newest
escapade exceeded its expressions of disgust and shame. Other members
of the British artistic community were no less censorious. Because of the
control MacCarthy and Fry had over what was reviewed (and by whom)
and what was exhibited (and where and when), Bloomsbury exercised a
degree of power in the artistic world that was disproportionate to the
Group's size. Bloomsbury reviewed and exhibited Bloomsbury. With the
founding of the Hogarth Press, Bloomsbury even published Bloomsbury.
Few of their artistic contemporaries thought so well of them as they did of
themselves. Critics, including F. R. Leavis, would grieve over such large
power wielded by undeserving men and women of such small talent.
And Leavis, himself a professor at Cambridge, would repeatedly lament
Bloomsbury's roots in the Cambridge of Keynes, Strachey, and Woolf.
The "Cambridge-Bloomsbury milieu"—this "ethos"—had, Leavis complained, destroyed the best of Britain's intellectual empire decades before
the death watch of its political counterpart.

Uncommon in their collective power, the Bloomsberries were unusual
also for the intensity and depth of their shared passions, for their loves
and loyalties, the latter often challenged by the former. Strachey loses
Grant to Keynes. Clive Bell loses Vanessa to Fry. Fry loses Vanessa to
Grant. Vanessa shares Grant with David Garnett. As an anonymous wit
has said, in Bloomsbury "all the couples were triangles." Yet through it all,
deeper than the surface of physical attraction, more powerful than the
requirements of jealousy and anger, the friendships endured. As Clive Bell

[handwritten marginalia, left margin top: This maybe the ordinary world but I live in my own.]

[handwritten marginalia: ha!]

[handwritten marginalia, left margin bottom: Erotic Geneology of Bloomsbury] would be a welcome guest at Charleston, so Keynes's affair with Grant would not rupture Strachey's friendship with either. They had been friends for so long, Strachey wrote to Keynes, that he saw no reason "to stop being friends now." On this occasion Strachey spoke for all who belonged to Bloomsbury. Those who did belong varied somewhat over time (Thoby would be lost when he died tragically in 1906, for example) and members could and often did live elsewhere than in Bloomsbury itself. Like Augustine's City of God, Bloomsbury was less a place and more a shared way of life.

Differences there were, both real and apparent. Bell and Grant, as a matter of conscience, refused to serve in the military or to cooperate with the government during the war. Strachey, too, protested on principle and would have joined them as a conscientious objector except that, like Woolf, he was exempted from service for medical reasons. But Keynes, while also objecting to a military role, served the cause of victory in the Treasury, with distinction. Again, Woolf gave generously of his time and energy to political causes, while Virginia and Roger Fry, for example, seem never to have been even tempted to contribute to the larger world of social justice. As for Strachey, politics was, as Keynes observed, only "a fairly adequate substitute for bridge" and so divorced from the political world was Vanessa that on one occasion she asked H. H. Asquith whether he was interested in politics. Asquith as it happened was then the prime minister. To see only the surface similarities among those who were Bloomsbury is to see a myth and miss the reality.

That complex reality refuses a simple explanation. We shall not find it in the members' educations (which varied greatly), nor in their genealogies (there was no Leslie Stephen in Clive Bell's past, for example), nor in their socio-economic positions (one has only to consider Leonard Woolf's status compared with, say, Strachey's). The rivers of biography run deep; the currents are subtle; when joined in the lives of many, perhaps they are non-navigable. Still, it is not unreasonable to listen to Bloomsbury voices when they speak to the question of Bloomsbury's origins and character in the hope of finding, if not the first cause, at least explanatory tributaries, hints of major influence. When given the opportunity to speak, these voices express common themes: Ideas, not just feelings, held Bloomsbury together; beliefs, not just passions, helped form it. And these ideas, these beliefs, expressed concretely in the complex weave of Bloomsbury's uncommon marriage of creativity and hard work, of friendships and sexual proclivities—these ideas and beliefs, the voices say, came from a source outside Bloomsbury itself. Bloomsbury had its prophet. And its sacred book.

To Be a Brother

The room is dark except for the dull light of a lamp on the desk. An ashtray is filled to overflowing with burnt tobacco and the remains of wooden matches. On the floor are torn and crumpled sheets of paper. The man seated at the desk, his head propped up by his left hand, a pipe clenched tightly in his mouth, bends fiercely over the paper before him, the pen in his right hand hesitating after every word. Beads of sweat glaze his broad, receding forehead; the unloosened buttons of his vest, already a size too small for the weight he carries, press hard against his chest and abdomen. Muttering aloud, he goes back to the beginning of a sentence, crosses out the words "The meaning of what we say is," and adds "If we deny this, what exactly can we mean?" More changes will soon be made, and many of these in time will be altered until the page becomes a jumble of scratches, arrows, and insertions, the remaining words barely legible. One of his teachers had told the young George Edward Moore, "Das Denken ist schwer" ("Thinking is hard"). Even before this Thursday evening in August 1911, Moore, who is now thirty-seven, had confirmed the harsh truth of his earlier instruction.

The source of Moore's present difficulty is the meaning of the word 'could.' What exactly do we mean when we say "we could have done something we did not do"? Words adequate to express his thought come slowly. There will be more deletions and additions, more crumpled, more fresh pages until, after an hour's struggle with his private daemon, he will allow the following.

Let us begin by asking: What is the sense of the word 'could', in which it is so certain that we often *could* have done, what we did not do? What, for instance, is the sense in which I *could* have walked a mile in twenty minutes this morning, though I did not? There is one suggestion, which is very obvious: namely, that what I mean is simply after all that I could, *if* I had chosen; or (to avoid a possible complication) perhaps we had better say 'that I should, if I had chosen'. In other words, the suggestion is that we often use the phrase 'I *could*' simply and solely as a short way of saying 'I *should*, if I had chosen'.

And in all cases, where it is certainly true that we *could* have done, what we did not do, it is, I think, very difficult to be quite sure that this (or something similar) is *not* what we mean by the word 'could'. The case of the ship may seem to be an exception, because it is certainly not true that she would have steamed twenty knots if *she* had chosen; but even here it seems possible that what we mean is simply that she *would, if the men on board of her* had chosen. There are certainly good reasons for thinking that we *very often* mean by 'could' merely 'would, *if* so and so had chosen'. And if so, then we have a sense of the word 'could' in which the fact that we often *could* have done what we did not do, is perfectly compatible with the principle that everything has a cause: for to say that, *if* I had performed a certain act of will, I should have done something which, I did not do, in no way contradicts this principle.

This night will find Moore laboring over additional permutations of the meaning of 'could.' Different words with no less intransigent meanings will occupy his time in the days ahead. By the end of August the manuscript on which he is working will be finished and, in 1912, published under the title *Ethics*. Except for a few technical essays and replies to criticisms, this will be Moore's last contribution to moral philosophy. In the ensuing years he will become increasingly preoccupied with questions of meaning and analysis, with "analytic philosophy" broadly conceived. Concepts of knowledge and perception will demand more and more of his time. "The Status of Sense Data," "Some Judgments of Perception," "Are the Materials of Sense Affections of the Mind?," "The Nature of Sensible Appearances"—the titles of the papers he will write and the symposia in which he will participate themselves map the severe analytic turn his work will take over the next four decades, a turn that will lead him to narrow the focus not only of his largely critical published work but also of his future teaching. Throughout the Fall term in 1922, for example, he will devote his Tuesday, Thursday, and Saturday morning lectures to analyses of propositions of the form "This is a pencil." His work will enshrine the quixotic spectacle of the mind's ability to concentrate on the minutiae of thought. The machinery of his intellect ground fine. Under the pressure of his rapacious appetite for finding error and confusion, the robust but malformed ideas of others will fall to the page as dust, lifeless and inert.

As the century unfolds and the middle-aged lecturer in philosophy at

Trinity College, Cambridge, becomes the treasured professor emeritus, Moore will emerge as the very paradigm of a philosopher's philosopher. He will speak only to matters of specialized concern, including questions about the analysis of propositions of the form "This is a pencil," for example, without arousing the informed interest of the general public. Among those who share his concerns he will be canonized, elevated to a status of esteem perhaps unequalled by any other philosopher in the twentieth century. But the knowing audience that will express its adulation and surround the elder Moore with the glow of idolatrous affection will always be small, comprised almost exclusively of fellow professionals in philosophy. Moore, the philosopher's philosopher, was little known or appreciated beyond the cramped borders of his chosen profession.

Toward the end of his life Moore was obliged to address a difficulty at the heart of his philosophical work, the so-called "paradox of analysis." On Moore's view we give an analysis of the concept Brother if we say "To be a brother is the same thing as to be a male sibling." For this to be so, however, it would seem that Brother and Male Sibling must be identical concepts. And if this is true, then it would seem that we may substitute the words "male sibling" for the word "brother," and vice versa, whenever they occur, without changing the status of what is said. The paradox of analysis arises for Moore because, if we carry out this substitution, the putative analysis of the concept Brother—namely, "To be a brother is to be a male sibling"—becomes "To be a brother is to be a brother." And this last statement, whatever else we may want to say of it, certainly is *not* an analysis of the concept Brother. Hence, the paradox: If Moore's view of what it is to give an analysis is correct, then the analyses he offered must be mistaken, whereas if any of his analyses are correct, then his view of what analysis is must be erroneous. Moore's comments on this paradox in his "A Reply to My Critics" are characteristically honest. He does not know how precisely to solve the paradox, he writes, because it involves the notion of identity, and he does not understand that notion well. "I do not know, at all clearly," he says, "*what* I mean by saying that 'x is a brother' is identical with 'x is a male sibling,' and that 'x is a cube' is *not identical* with 'x is a cube with twelve edges'" (p. 667). Uncertain of his precise meaning, he is equally uncertain how to address let alone pacify the virulent paradox threatening to consume the very body of his analytical philosophy. Like Socrates, Moore could—and did—inspire the awe and love of others by the sincere expression of his own ignorance. He knew that he did not know. Sometimes he thought he knew why. But that was no solution to the problems that claimed his attention in later life, including the paradox of analysis. He knew that too.

The Greater Paradox

However enervating the paradox of analysis may have been for Moore, it is a mere shadow when compared with the paradox of the man himself. For more than four decades, dating from his appointment as lecturer in Moral Sciences at Cambridge in 1911, Moore filled his life with the daily ritual of private worries over the analysis of "could," of "identity," "reality," "knowledge," "existence," and other well-worn coins in the currency of Western philosophical thought. He became a philosopher's philosopher in the clearest, narrowest sense, one who spoke in the language of the specialist and who aspired to satiate different appetites from Bloomsbury's thirst for new forms of expression in painting, literature, biography, and letters, bold theories in aesthetics and economics. No less a distance separated Bloomsbury's raucous sexual instabilities from Moore's marriage to Dorothy Mildred Ely in 1916, a union that lasted until Moore's death in 1958 without the slightest hint of scandal or waning of affection. Moore, the philosopher's philosopher, appears to be as far removed from Bloomsbury, both temperamentally and in terms of substantive convictions, as Vanessa was from H. H. Asquith. As Paul Levy remarks, "one could hardly choose a more unpromising prophet or invent a more unlikely inspiration than G. E. Moore" (p. 258). How paradoxical it is, then, that Bloomsbury voices identify Moore as their prophet and inspiration. Leonard Woolf's recollections in *Sowing* are representative:

> Mrs. Sidney Webb once said to me: "I have known most of the distinguished men of my time, but I have never yet met a great man" . . . "I suppose you don't know G. E. Moore." No, she said, she did not know G. E. Moore, though she knew, of course, whom I meant, and the question of human greatness having been settled, we passed to another question.
>
> The author of Ecclesiasticus probably agreed with Beatrice Webb, for he asked us to praise not great men but famous men—a very different thing. The conversation in Grosvenor Road took place forty years ago, but I still think despite the two impressive authorities that I was right, that George Moore was a great man, the only great man whom I have ever met or known in the world of ordinary,

real life. There was in him an element which can, I think, be accurately called greatness, a combination of mind and character and behaviour, of thought and feeling which made him qualitatively different from anyone else I have ever known. I recognize it in only one or two of the many famous dead men whom Ecclesiasticus and others enjoin us to praise for one reason or another. (p. 131)

This same theme is replayed in a later work, *The Journey Not the Arrival Matters*, where Woolf remarks that "[his] purity, moral and mental, was the most remarkable of Moore's qualities; I have never known anything like it in any other human being."

Whether Moore was unique in the way Woolf supposes is both uncertain and unimportant. What is clear is that Moore had a powerful, galvanizing personality, one that attracted minds and wills not lacking in power of their own. All who knew and were drawn to him understood that he lacked the native brilliance common enough among his contemporaries; he was not "quick," not "witty" (Woolf remarks in *Sowing* [p. 134] that he could not recall Moore's ever having said a witty thing), not even very learned. What he was, was *passionate* about his determination to get things right, or at least as right as the nature of the case allowed. Clarity was to be purchased at any cost to patience and time, and this requirement extended to questions, not only answers. Those within Moore's inner circle, Keynes recalls in his memoir, practiced "Moore's method, according to which you could hope to make essentially vague notions clear by using precise language about them and asking exact questions. It was a method of discovery by the instruments of impeccable grammar and an unambiguous dictionary. ('What *exactly* do you mean?' was the phrase most frequently on our lips. If it appeared under cross-examination that you did not mean *exactly* anything, you lay under a strong suspicion of meaning nothing at all." (p. 88) As Leon Edel suggests (pp. 35-36), "Gertrude Stein was perhaps echoing Moorism when she was asked, 'What is the answer?' Her reply is well known: 'What is the question?' "

That question took on near-mythic proportions. Writing in the *Times of India* (April 26, 1922) an unidentified writer refers to it as Moore's "famous poser." Once that "poser" is asked by its fabled inventer, it turns out "that any question of which the average human brain would think proves to be six questions instead of one. Such is the logico-analytic method: first you analyse the universe into nuts and ball bearings and then, if you can, construct." How good Moore was at putting the nuts and ball bearings of the universe back together again is less important than his resolute determination not to confuse the one with the other. Moore cared about clarity because he cared about truth. "When [he] said: 'I simply don't understand *what* he means,'" Leonard writes in *Sowing* (pp. 135–136), "the emphasis on the 'simply' and the 'what' and the shake of his head over each word gave one a glimpse of the passionate distress which muddled thinking aroused in him." He had a "passion for truth," but not just any truth, not truth "dead from the waist down," only important truth. It was this almost visceral, unrelenting, and consuming desire to possess some part of truth, however small, that both drove Moore and attracted others to him. His "passion for truth was an integral part of his greatness, and purity of passion was an integral part of his whole character."

But Moore's magnetism grew out of much besides his passion for truth. Incapable of deceit, he was a man of almost saintly innocence. As Virginia observes in her *Diary*, Moore's "moral eminence [was] comparable to that of Christ or Socrates." Throughout his mature life he was whole, of a piece: what he seemed to be, he was. And was so incorruptibly. That passion, that lack of pretense were inseparable from Moore's fierce independence of mind. Even Virginia, who had a stern antipathy toward intellectuals—"How I hate intellect!" she writes in a letter to Violet Dickinson (July 20, 1907), adding in a letter to Clive Bell (February 19, 1909), "I detest pale scholars"—even Virginia, like her husband Leonard, saw Moore as "a great man." More than "an intellect" or "a scholar," Moore was a full human being, an aspect of his personality Sir Roy Harrod perhaps captures best in the following passage:

His devotion to truth was indeed palpable. In argument his whole frame was gripped by a passion to confute error and expose confusion. To watch him at work was an enthralling experience. Yet, when the heat of argument died down, he was the mildest and simplest of men, almost naïve in unphilosophical matters. He was friendly to the young, approaching them on natural and equal terms. Despite his naïveté, he seemed to have understanding. In human questions he had none of that intolerance or crabbedness which so often marks the academic man of thought. He was happy and at ease in discussions beyond his proper range. There was no question of his being shocked, and the young had no inhibitions in his presence. When Strachey made one of his subtle, perhaps cynical, perhaps shocking, utterances, the flavour of which even his clever undergraduate friends did not at first appreciate at its full value, Moore was seen to be shaking with laughter. If the veneration which his young admirers accorded him almost matched that due to a saint, we need not think that they were mistaken.

The Power of Ideas

As important as the force of Moore's character was on the members of Bloomsbury, the substance of his teachings was not less so. Those formative teachings are to be found not in *Ethics*, but in Moore's first book *Principia Ethica*, published in October 1903. Never one to be self-conscious about his enthusiasm, Strachey admits to being "carried away" in his reaction to *Principia*. "I have read your book," he writes to Moore on October 11, 1903,

> and want to say how much I am excited and impressed. I'm afraid I must be mainly classed among 'writers of Dictionaries, and other persons interested in literature', so I feel a sort of essential vanity hovering about all my 'judgements of fact'. But on this occasion I am carried away. I think your book has not only wrecked and shattered all writers on Ethics from Aristotle and Christ to Herbert Spencer and Mr. Bradley, it has not only laid the true foundations of Ethics, it has not only left all modern philosophy bafouée —these seem to me small achievements compared to the establishment of that Method which shines like a sword between the lines. It is the scientific method deliberately applied, for the first time, to Reasoning. Is that true? You perhaps shake your head, but henceforward who will be able to tell lies one thousand times as easily as before? The truth, there can be no doubt, is really now upon the march. I date from Oct. 1903 the beginning of the Age of Reason.
>
>   . . . Dear Moore, I hope and pray that you realize how much you mean to us.

In *Sowing*, Leonard Woolf describes the impact of Moore and *Principia* in only somewhat less effusive terms:

> The tremendous influence of Moore and his book upon us came from the fact that they suddenly removed from our eyes an obscuring

accumulation of scales, cobwebs, and curtains, revealing for the first time to us, so it seemed, the nature of truth and reality, of good and evil and character and conduct, substituting for the religious and philosophical nightmares, delusions, hallucinations, in which Jehovah, Christ, and St. Paul, Plato, Kant, and Hegel had entangled us, the fresh air and pure light of plain common-sense.

It was this clarity, freshness, and common-sense which primarily appealed to us. Here was a profound philosopher who did not require us to accept any "religious" faith or intricate, if not unintelligible, intellectual gymnastics of a Platonic, Aristotelian, Kantian, or Hegelian nature; all he asked us to do was to make quite certain that we knew what we meant when we made a statement and to analyze and examine our beliefs in the light of common-sense. Philosophically what, as intelligent young men, we wanted to know was the basis, if any, for our or any scale of values and rules of conduct, what justification there was for our belief that friendship or works of art for instance were good or for the belief that one ought to do some things and not do others. Moore . . . answered our questions, not with the religious voice of Jehovah from Mount Sinai or Jesus with his sermon from the Mount, but with the more divine voice of plain common-sense. (pp. 147–148)

Keynes's portrait of the power of *Principia*'s teachings remains *the* classic among classics. "The New Testament is a handbook for politicians," he writes in "My Early Beliefs,"

compared with the unworldliness of Moore's chapter on 'The Ideal'. I know no equal to it in literature since Plato. And it is better than Plato because it is quite free from *fancy*. It conveys the beauty of the literalness of Moore's mind, the pure and passionate intensity of his vision, *un*fanciful and *un*dressed-up. Moore had a nightmare once in which he could not distinguish propositions from tables. But even when he was awake, he could not distinguish love and beauty and truth from the furniture. They took on the same definition of outline, the same stable, solid, objective qualities and common-sense reality. (p. 94)

Love. Beauty. Truth. These were bound up with the pure intrinsic goods Moore extolled and whose resonance attracted Keynes, Strachey, and the

Love, Beauty and Truth intrinsic goods.

others. The love of these great goods formed the basis of what Keynes calls "Moore's religion." "Broadly speaking," he writes, "we all knew for certain what were good states of mind and that they consisted in communion with objects of love, beauty, and truth" (p. 86). It was, Moore writes in *Principia*, "in order that as much of [such goods] . . . may at some time exist . . . that any one can be justified in performing any public or private duty." The values of friendship and the enjoyment of beauty are, he writes, "the *raison d'être* of virtue," forming "the rational ultimate end of human action and the sole criterion of social progress." These and other substantive moral convictions, not only the power of Moore's passionate character, attracted adherents at the time of *Principia*'s publication and in the years that followed. To be a follower of Moore, a disciple, one did more than insist on clarity in those questions to be considered. One also subscribed to certain answers. In *Beginning Again*, Leonard Woolf once again captures well what Moore meant to Bloomsbury:

> There have been other groups of people who were not only friends, but were consciously united by a common doctrine and object, or purpose artistic or social. The Utilitarians, the Lake poets, the French Impressionists, the English Pre-Raphaelites were groups of this kind. Our group was quite different. Its basis was friendship, which in some cases developed into love and marriage. The colour of our minds and thought had been given to us by the climate of Cambridge and Moore's philosophy, much as the climate of England gives one colour to the face of an Englishman while the climate of India gives quite a different colour to the face of a Tamil.

Keynes agrees, adding that the influence created by acceptance of Moore's teachings "was not only overwhelming; . . . it was the extreme opposite of what Strachey used to call *funeste*; it was exciting, exhilarating, the beginning of a new renaissance, the opening of a new heaven on a new earth, we were the fore-runners of a new dispensation, we were not afraid of anything" (p. 82).

[handwritten margin note: funeste - phoon-est / - fatal, catastrophic, ffc]

Dissenting Voices

This happy adoration of *Principia* was not contagious much beyond the circle of Moore's friends. Among the reviews the more enthusiastic include "a clever, interesting, and stimulating volume" (*Literary World*) and "eminently ingenious and acute" (*The Saturday Review*). The unknown author of this latter review also registers his displeasure with Moore's "acute but narrow mind," while a reviewer in the *Scotsman*, finding the style "clear and untechnical, if somewhat pedestrian and unillumined," warns readers that the author has "a scholastic habit of mind," a "tendency to logic-chopping" which manifests itself in "an excessive multiplication of distinctions which lead to no very definite result."

Keynes's enthusiasm would not be chilled by banal reviewers. "It is *impossible* to exaggerate the wonder and *originality* of Moore," he writes to Strachey on February 21, 1906. "People are beginning to talk as if he were only a kind of logic chopping eclectic. Oh why can't they see. How amazing to think that only we know the rudiments of a true theory of ethics; for nothing can be more certain than that the broad outline is true."

People had been saying more than Keynes acknowledges. Keynes's most recent biographer, Robert Skidelsky, reminds us that *Principia* was written with a "vehemence of utterance," a characteristic that, however much it may have been admired or ignored by Moore's followers, generally was found offensive by others. The reviewer in the *Scotsman* notes "a tone of undue condescension towards previous thinkers." "One has to regret certain faults of manner and temper which are quite gratuitously provoking," the reviewer in the *Saturday Review* observes, adding that Moore displays "a profound contempt for his predecessors." The author of a review in the *Guardian* is less sparing, chastising Moore for his "arrogant dogmatism." In style and content not untypical of the dominant reception *Principia* received, this same reviewer writes the following:

> Few things are so depressing as a man with a mission. Mr. Moore's mission is of the intellectual type, and takes the modest form of assuring almost all other philosophers since the world began that they have never even conceived the problem of ethics correctly, much less succeeded in solving it. And so he sweeps the gross absurdities of Aristotle, Kant, and other triflers into the waste-paper basket, tosses Christianity on to the top of them, and finally leaves no one outside that useful receptacle except a fragment of Henry Sidgwick and himself, a result which may be gratifying to the University of Cambridge but must be distressing to the rest of the world.

But there was a different, deeper critical note struck by some of the early reviews of *Principia*. So far was that book from supplying, in Keynes's words, "the rudiments of a true theory of ethics," that some who reviewed *Principia* were "disposed to pronounce Mr. Moore's book of immoral tendency" (*Oxford Magazine*). "If Mr. Moore's [views] . . . were ever to have the slightest chance of currency," another reviewer urges in the same vein (*Notes on British Theology and Philosophy*), "ethics would be in danger of becoming a science of the visionary, imaginary, and unreal." Moore's basic moral teachings, we are told, "give an irrational cast to ethics which is hardly to be commended."

Opinion, it is safe to say, was divided concerning *Principia*'s merits or lack of them. Although the first fifty pages may create the impression of "a bare and bleak book, a little low in tone, not nearly as exciting as it [was] to the young Keynes," Leonard Woolf assures us that "the cumulative effect becomes tremendous" (*Times Literary Supplement*). That "cumulative effect" not only was not experienced by the majority of *Principia*'s reviewers; they found the book even less than "bare and bleak," the tone even less than "a little low."

The Eyes of the Beholder

However "immoral" its "tendency," *Principia* was read by members of Bloomsbury who were not part of its Cambridge-core. Virginia in her letters relates her slow progress through its narrow conceptual corridors. We first encounter her ordeal with *Principia* in a letter to Clive Bell dated August 3, 1908: "I am climbing Moore like some industrious insect, who is determined to build a nest on the top of a Cathedral spire. One sentence, a string of "desires" makes my head spin with the infinite meaning of words unadorned" (p. 340). A week later she writes to Saxon Sydney-Turner that she has been "reading an immense number of books, and look forward to my nightly 10 pages of Moore, when the bells have done tolling and my landladies [sic] children are in bed, with something like excitement. Well—there are numbers of things in the world which I don't know—numbers I shall never understand. I sent myself to sleep last night by thinking what I feel at the prospect of eating an ice; and woke this morning thinking Moore is right." Her confidence and enthusiasm have slackened in a second letter to Sidney-Turner on August 14: "I have been reading a good deal, and make some way with Moore, though I have to crawl over the same page a number of times, till I almost see my own tracks. I shall ask you to enlighten me, but I doubt that I can even ask an intelligent question" (pp. 352–353). Five days later, in a letter to Clive Bell, the mood is still heavy: "I split my head over Moore every night" (p. 357). Ten days later, however, in a letter to Vanessa, the cloud has lifted: "I finished Moore last night. . . . I am not so dumb founded as I was; but the more I understand, the more I admire. He is so humane in spite of his desire to know the truth; and I believe I can disagree with him, over one matter" (p. 384).

What that matter is we do not know. What we do know is that *Principia* was woven into the fabric of the lives of those denizens of Bloomsbury who were neither students with nor students of Moore at Cambridge. Virginia, who gave praise as easily as a possessive parent parts with a child on the first day of school, who hated "intellect," was perhaps the most difficult person to be won over. She might easily have asserted her own independence by scowling at his bleak prose, the "infinite meaning of words unadorned." Significantly, she does not. The more she understands, the more she admires. That ungrudging expression of admiration speaks volumes for Moore's uncommon powers.

More than admiration bound Virginia to Moore in Leonard Woolf's view. Though the two met infrequently, Woolf maintains that Moore had a significant influence on Virginia's work. Virginia, he writes in *Beginning Again*, was

> deeply affected by the astringent influence of Moore and the purification of that divinely cathartic question which echoed through the Cambridge Courts of my youth as it had 2300 years before echoed through the streets of Socratic Athens: "What do you mean by that?" Artistically the purification can, I think, be traced in the clarity, light, absence of humbug in Virginia's literary style.

Virginia even paid Moore the compliment of finding a place for him in her first novel, *The Voyage Out*, published in 1915. The dark brown binding of the first edition of *Principia* was assumed by Virginia to be so familiar that she thought she could refer to the book by the color of its cover without bothering to mention its title.

Her sister, Vanessa, seems never to have read *Principia* and met Moore personally only once when, much to the surprise of both, they found themselves alone in the house at the Charleston farm. Neither could think of anything to say. Even so, Vanessa was representative of Bloomsbury's philosophy and optimism. "A great new freedom seemed about to come," she writes of the period before the outbreak of World War I. Frances Spalding, her recent biographer, has suggested that "Moore's insistence on the precise definition of meaning may have indirectly encouraged Vanessa's use of elemental shapes [in her painting] and the extreme openness and honesty of her abstract style."

Spalding's speculations about Moore's influence on Vanessa's art, like Leonard's in the case of Virginia's, are provocative. They are also difficult of proof. Perhaps there is an understandable though regrettable profligate tendency to find Moorean influences where none exists. Whatever we do or should decide regarding Moore's role in the artistic development of the Stephen sisters, we can agree with Clive Bell when, looking back on the time and place that once was Bloomsbury, he observes that it is doubtful "whether either of the Miss Stephens gave much thought" to Moore's theoretical constructs. And we can say this without having to conclude that only Moore's style, not the substance of his thought, influenced the two young women. Virginia and Vanessa swam in pools deeply affected by the strong currents that flowed from Moore's character and teachings. Though they were not directly touched by Moore, the Cambridge student and Fellow, they were intimately linked to him by those who were. And that linkage helped consolidate, even if by itself it did not create, the phenomenon of Bloomsbury. Virginia's solitary journey through *Principia* made her a part of that "new renaissance" of which Keynes spoke, the "great new freedom" her sister sensed and whose Moorean spirit bound the members of Bloomsbury together, perhaps sometimes in spite of themselves. Roger Fry, it has been claimed, dismissed the tenets of *Principia* as "sheer nonsense." And yet Fry's own aesthetic theories accord with Moore's insistence that aesthetic contemplation is intrinsically good. It is difficult to see how Fry's teaching in this regard could be any less nonsensical than Moore's.

An Amusing Fabrication?

Not all who embraced Moore's teachings, especially as these were set forth in *Principia*, recall embracing the same things. In his discussion of Moore's influence Leonard Woolf voices his partial disagreement with Keynes's account. In "My Early Beliefs" the latter characterizes "religion" as "one's attitude towards oneself and the ultimate," while "morals" he defines as "one's attitude towards the outside world and the intermediate."

Morals concerns "the general rules of correct behavior." Speaking for all those who fell under Moore's spell, Keynes writes that "we accepted Moore's religion . . . and discarded his morals" (p. 82). "We had," he continues, "no respect for traditional wisdom or the restraint of custom" (p. 99). Woolf thinks Keynes misremembers, writing in *Sowing* that "it is not true that we recognized 'no moral obligation' . . . or that we neglected all that Moore said about 'morals' and rules of conduct" (p. 148).

Whom shall we trust? All the obvious evidence seems to support Keynes. For the Bloomsberries were nothing if not contemptuous of convention. With their myriad sexual dalliances, their eccentric dress (Virginia, for example, going about in a veritable collection of rags held together by safety-pins), their haughty aloofness, their insatiable appetite for the outrageous and the irreverent—wherever one looks one finds the tangible outpouring of that absence of respect for traditional wisdom and the restraint of custom of which Keynes speaks. "Moore's morality was jettisoned from his religion," Noel Annan assures us, echoing Keynes's distinctions, "and the undergraduates who were to form the Bloomsbury circle went on to deny that there was any close connection between *being* good and *doing* good, or that there existed any moral obligation to consider the effect of one's actions on other people. Moore's precept that the rightness of actions depended on the eventual good which they produced, seemed to them to be a relic of utilitarian orthodoxy" (p. 125).

The correctness of Keynes's recollection and the fallibility of Woolf's seem to be further corroborated by the now standard interpretation of Moore's *Principia* account of right conduct, the topic of that work's fifth chapter. We are to follow the existing rules of our society, according to this interpretation, even when we think the results would be better if we were to make an exception in our case. And we are to do this because the probability of our being mistaken in making an exception is greater than the probability that our judgment is correct. Thus do we find Skidelsky writing that Principia's fifth chapter "was in the main, a justification of accepted rules of conduct, a position which was anathema to Keynes" (p. 152). Moore's position, given the standard interpretation, appears to be nothing so much as, in Gertrude Himmelfarb's telling phrase, a "feeble concession to conventional morality" (p. 49). When Keynes recalls that the members of Bloomsbury "discarded Moore's morals," it is natural to suppose that they simply refused to accept the blind obedience to the moral status quo demanded by Moore, according to the standard interpretation. Bertrand Russell speaks well for this interpretation when, in his letter to Moore congratulating him upon the publication of *Principia*, he adds that he finds "some of your maxims in Practical Ethics . . . unduly Conservative and anti-reforming."

For all its apparent plausibility, Keynes's memory cannot be altogether right. To begin with, there is the conflicting evidence of his own life, as recently illuminated by Skidelsky (pp. 147 ff.). In an unpublished 1905 outline for a treatise on ethics entitled "Miscellanea Ethica," Keynes earnestly sets forth his conception of both speculative and practical ethics. The concerns of practical ethics dominate a second, unpublished paper entitled simply "Egoism," dating from 1906, where Moore's views concerning right conduct are examined at length in the course of Keynes's attempt to fashion a theory of obligation which, though Moorean in spirit, is Keynesian in letter. Even as early as 1904 Keynes authored a paper whose very title—"Ethics in Relation to Conduct"—casts doubt on the reliability of his memory in 1938. It cannot be quite true, then, that Keynes and the others who became Bloomsbury neglected *everything* that Moore had to say about "morals."

To think about what Moore says is different from accepting his injunctions, and it may be thought that it is the latter, not the former, that Keynes recalls discarding. How else square Bloomsbury's behavior with the standard interpretation of *Principia*? Part of the answer lies in rejecting the standard interpretation. It is true that Moore is not a moral reformer (in one sense), true that he is a utilitarian of sorts, and true that he offers a defense of everyone's always abiding by certain socially accepted and sanctioned rules of conduct. But it is not true that he is not a moral reformer (in another sense), not true that his brand of utilitarianism requires habitual concern with how the general welfare will be affected by what we do, not true that he makes a "feeble concession to conventional morality" by demanding uncritical obedience to socially accepted and sanctioned rules. On the contrary, what Moore teaches about right conduct is the very sort of thing that most typifies Bloomsbury's collective behavior: we are to have the courage to act on our own, by our own lights, without being dominated by the oppressive demand to conform to widely accepted but unwarranted expectations about what is "proper" and "right." The moral nerve of Moore's teaching is to free oneself from unreflective acceptance of tradition and custom in the conduct and direction of one's life. Moore's ethic, in short, is essentially an ethic of individual liberation, a point Strachey recognized immediately. Writing to Leonard Woolf just after *Principia*'s publication, Strachey enthuses about

[margin note, handwritten:] freeing one's self from unreflective acceptance of tradition

"the last *two* chapters" (emphasis added), proclaiming "glory alleluiah!"
The last chapter is the setting for Moore's famous exposition of "the
Ideal." In the next to last chapter we find his position regarding right
conduct. It is scarcely conceivable that Strachey could have been smitten
by a chapter whose purpose was to defend conventional morality. Or by a
chapter that was little more than "a relic of utilitarian orthodoxy." Or by
one that failed to display appropriate disrespect for "traditional wisdom
and the restraint of custom." On this point Keynes could not be further
from the truth. (Those who were Bloomsbury did not discard Moore's
morals. They lived them.)

This view of the nature and scope of Moore's influence has the testimony of many experts against it. Some, such as F. R. Leavis, would have us
believe that Moore played an influential role in spite of himself. "A disinterested, innocent spirit" in Leavis's view, Moore gave to the Cambridge-
core of Bloomsbury "the very sanction [they] needed." That he didn't
know the ill he had wrought was what made him all the more innocent and
his sanction "[all] the more irresistibl[e]." Bertrand Russell's account in
his *Autobiography* repeats the theme of Moore the Innocent at Home:

> The tone of the generation [at Cambridge] ten years junior to my
> own was set mainly by Lytton Strachey and Keynes. It is surprising
> how great a change in mental climate those ten years had brought.
> We were still Victorians; they were Edwardians. We believed in
> ordered progress by means of politics and free discussion. The more
> self-confident among us may have hoped to be leaders of the multi-
> tude, but none of us wished to be divorced from it. The generation
> of Keynes and Lytton did not seek to preserve any kinship with the
> Philistine. They aimed rather at a life of retirement among fine shades
> and nice feelings, and conceived the good as consisting in the pas-
> sionate mutual admiration of a clique of the elite. This doctrine,
> quite unfairly, they fathered upon G. E. Moore, whose disciples they
> professed to be.

The accuracy of Leavis's assessment and Russell's account of Moore's
influence on the Cambridge-Bloomsbury milieu can only be challenged
after that influence has been charted in some detail. And the same is true
of the varying accounts of those who claim that Moore's ideas, not just
his "innocence," made a difference to what Bloomsbury was. Among these
thinkers there is unanimous agreement that the values Moore celebrated

in his discussion of the Ideal were incorporated into the fabric of Bloomsbury life, as they earlier had been in Cambridge. Disagreement enters
when Moore's views regarding moral obligation are considered, the standard interpretation teaching that Moore's followers rejected this, the present interpretation maintaining that this, too, became a part of their life.
The case for this latter interpretation remains to be presented. Once it
has, many of the apparently irreconcilable differences between Keynes's
and Woolf's accounts will be explained away without having to take the
route Hugh MacDonald might suggest. In a letter to Moore calling the
latter's attention to the publication of Keynes's two memoirs, MacDonald
writes that "the second seems to me the better. All the Bloomsbury folk
—including J. M. K.—are unreliable on public affairs. They never were
much given to telling the truth if some fabrication was more amusing."
Our problem is to determine which, if any, parts of the "amusing" story
are not "fabrications."

More Than a Gesture

This much said, it remains true that Moore's disciples did not agree
on everything, and it is perhaps largely owing to the diversity of views we
find among them that Paul Levy is led to diminish the importance of
Moore's ideas on the lives of his followers and to emphasize the powerful
influence of Moore's character. "Those who proclaimed themselves his
disciples," he writes,

> were devoted not so much to his ideas as to certain aspects of his
> character. Everyone agrees his character was remarkable, and some
> agree with Leonard Woolf that it was unique. My claim is that what
> Moore's followers had in common was admiration—even reverence
> —for his personal qualities; but that as their hero happened to be
> a philosopher, the appropriate gesture of allegiance to him meant
> saying that one believed his propositions and accepted the arguments
> for them. Had the great man been a poet, they would no doubt have
> showed their fealty (as others have) by reciting his verses; if a com-
> poser, by singing or playing his music. This is a radical view to
> espouse, for one does not often encounter the 'cult of the person-
> ality' in the history of philosophy. . . . It is tantamount to saying
> that in professing belief in Moore's 'philosophy' his Bloomsbury

disciples were, for the most part, gesturing in order to demonstrate their loyalty. However, this does not make the profession of belief in his philosophy a trivial thing: the gesture of allegiance in no way *excludes* the possibility that the belief is sincerely and genuinely held, or even well-grounded.

I think this perspective greatly helps to explain the selectivity of . . . Bloomsbury in taking only as much from *Principia Ethica* as suited their needs, discarding—but not denying—the bulk of the book which deals with the traditional ethical topics of duties and obligations, and which is chiefly concerned with explicating the meaning of the concept 'good.' (p. 9)

Levy, whose biography of Moore is to be commended to every person interested in his life, thought, and influence, seems here to want it both ways. On the one hand, he would have us accept the view that it was not belief in Moore's ideas, but rather the magnetism of his character, that attracted others to him. If we object that his followers after all *did* affirm their belief in what he said, or in what they thought he said, then Levy responds, on the other hand, that of course these beliefs may have been "sincerely and genuinely held." But if these beliefs *were* "sincerely and genuinely held," as they were in the case of Woolf and Keynes, for example, then we distort rather than illuminate the extent of Moore's influence if, in Levy's words (p. 9), we "discount the importance of his ideas *as ideas.*" Without disputing Levy's assertion that "Moore's followers regarded him as a sort of intellectual saint," we are right to look for the explanation of Moore's influence in the power of his ideas, ideas that include his considered views about "the traditional ethical topics of duties and obligations," not just in the power of his personality.

Religion Without God

A place to begin is with Keynes's choice of the word 'religion' to characterize certain aspects of Moore's teachings. What mattered most, Keynes writes were certain "states of mind. These . . . were not associated with action or achievement or consequences. They consisted in timeless, passionate states of contemplation and communion, largely unattached to 'before' and 'after.' . . . The appropriate subjects of passionate contemplation and communion were a beloved person, beauty and truth, and one's prime objects in life were love, the creation and enjoyment of aesthetic experience and the pursuit of knowledge. Of these love came a long way first" (p. 83). That was the substance of Moore's "religion."

Keynes goes on to observe that Moore's disciples would have been "very angry at the time" with the suggestion that they had a "religion": "We regarded all this as entirely rational and scientific in character" (p. 86). Moore, too, we may be sure, would have looked with disfavor on the suggestion that he had propounded a "religion." Even before he began his studies at Cambridge in October of 1892 at the age of nineteen, he was, Moore writes in his autobiography, "a complete Agnostic." That may be so. But Moore was hardly done with thinking about God during his philosophically formative years. While there is very little explicit discussion of religious belief in *Principia*, Moore wrote a not inconsiderable amount on these topics elsewhere. A close reading of these sources reveals how very similar ethical and religious beliefs are in his view: the basic ethical propositions he sets forth in *Principia* belong in the same family of propositions as propositions about God. The suggestion to be examined is that Moore's ethical precepts, including his views about both the right and the good, offered, and were offered by him as, a cognitively and emotionally satisfying substitute for the discarded belief in a supernatural deity—offered, that is, a religion without god.

How close to the truth this suggestion is remains to be determined. For the present we may recall the charged ambience of 38 Brunswick Square on that Thursday evening in November 1911. Dedication. Wit. Knowledge. Industry. Creativity. Companionship. Love. The main room is filled with qualities both rare and greatly to be prized. Feelings of communal optimism and affection, of boldness and courage, of cultural aloofness and shared superiority envelop the separate conversations, bind the separate selves. Alone in his rooms at Cambridge Moore labors on with his private conceptual obsessions. The road between Cambridge and London is shorter than the distance between the pale fixedness of his solitary study of the meaning of 'could' and the sometimes bawdy, sometimes austere fellowship at 38 Brunswick Square, Bloomsbury. To cover that distance with understanding requires mapping the godless religion *Principia* offers and, before that, surveying Moore's religious exercises, including his earlier days at Cambridge, where, in a variety of ways, he slew the gods.

2

The Wages of Reason

A Meeting of Minds

Books dominate the room. On the tables. In stacks on the floor. Crammed into the sagging shelves lining the walls. The gold-embossed names of eminent authors and titles—Sophocles, Gibbon, Plutarch, Descartes, LaPlace, *The Origin of the Species*, *The Critique of Pure Reason*, *The Aeneid*—declare that this is no ordinary personal library. In a space heavy with an atmosphere of severe erudition small etched portraits of Spinoza and Leibniz are the only concessions to decoration. Dressed stiffly in a black, close-fitting wool suit, high starched white collar, and maroon and silver ascot, the young Bertrand Russell blends with his surroundings, a thin reed of dry intellect at home in arid lodgings. Lighting his pipe, he looks alternately to the door, then to the clock on the mantel, then to his disheveled companion who, sitting hunched up on the front edge of a wooden chair, hands folded in his lap, toes turned awkwardly in, head sunk down on his chest, stares vacantly at the floor, his dark, bulbous eyes unblinking. Steadfast in his silence and immobility, he joins Russell in waiting.

Even as a child John McTaggart Ellis McTaggart was—different. Throughout his life he had an unusual gait. Whether walking or running he moved forward sideways, like a crab. Prone to stopping at unpredictable intervals, he became riveted to the ground, as if the power of the ideas in his mind had taken possession of his body. Sometimes he talked aloud to himself. The sight of the young boy sidling across the countryside, abruptly stopping and starting in apparently random fashion, wandering privately among the darkest abstract mysteries of thought (by thirteen he already had made a close study of Kant), was familiar to his neighbors in Weybridge; among the children it earned him the nickname

29

"Loonie." In adult life his eccentricities were accepted more supportively. His Sunday morning at-homes were legendary. Those of his students who came to the "breakfasts" he hosted on those occasions soon learned the prudence of bringing their own food; McTaggart himself was too preoccupied with his thoughts to remember the needs of the body. Pleased to have them come, he greeted his students with warmth and affection and saw them off with sincere regrets. But as likely as not he would spend the greater part of their visit reclining on a couch, eyes fixed on the ceiling, never speaking a word, at apparent peace with himself, his immediate surroundings, and the world at large. It is the same blank appearance of serenity he gives now as, sitting in silence in Russell's rooms in Whewell's Court, the two men wait.

At twenty-four McTaggart is the elder by four years. Having been named a Fellow of Trinity in 1891, he will be appointed lecturer in 1897, a position he will fill with distinction until his retirement in 1923, just two years before his unexpected death—at fifty-eight, at the height of his philosophical powers—from complications brought on by blood clots in his legs. Recognized in his youth as a remarkably gifted speculative thinker, he will more than fulfill his promise, publishing ingenious (if, according to informed scholars, implausible) interpretive studies of the philosophy of Hegel as well as other works of bold originality, most notably *The Nature of Existence*, on whose third and final draft he will be working when he dies. In a field justly renowned for their absence he will bring clarity and rigor to his professional writings in metaphysics, combining his unwavering insistence on precision and proof with the same contagious passion and optimism friends and students found in him (when not withdrawn in contemplation) in day-to-day life. To his students, his biographer and friend Goldsworthy Lowes Dickinson relates, he gave the impression of "one who had found the secret of the world," one whose ideas seemed "not only inspiring but *true*" (p. 55). The philosopher C. D. Broad, himself a former student, observes (in language as revelatory of the biases of the age as it is of McTaggart the man) that the "intellectual standards [of his students] were exalted and refined, until slovenly thinking and loose rhetorical writing in themselves or in others began to evoke the same reaction of disgust as dirty finger-nails or bad table-manners or a Cockney accent" (p. xxix). To his closest friends he gave by all accounts much more than he took. "The truth of his philosophy," Dickinson observes, "many philosophers would deny, many men doubt, and most be unable to estimate; but true or no, his pilgrimage through life was directed from beginning to end by the twin stars of truth and love. Like all the great philosophers he not only thought but believed his philosophy; and whatever may be the fate of his ideas his memory in the hearts of his friends is secure. He was their dear, their faithful, their never-changing Jack" (p. 123).

That constancy of affection would disappear in the case of his friendship with Russell. McTaggart was a man of fierce loyalties, to institutions as much as and sometimes more than people. Unlike E. M. Forster, who remarked that "if I had to choose between betraying my country and betraying my friend I hope I should have the guts to betray my country," McTaggart put loyalty to country above loyalty to Russell when, after the outbreak of World War I, Russell wrote a pamphlet in which he argued on behalf of conscientious objection. He was convicted of "hampering recruitment" and, in no small measure because of McTaggart's leadership, but with the unanimous vote of the College Council of Trinity, was removed from his post as lecturer on July 11, 1916. In fact their friendship had been dissolved earlier. As Russell records in his *Autobiography*, McTaggart previously had asked him "no longer to come and see him because he could not bear my opinions" (p. 84). There is no evidence that they met or spoke thereafter. On this afternoon in March 1893, however, the two are united by their shared expectations. When there is a knock at the door, McTaggart looks up and the two exchange hopeful glances.

Russell has described the young man who enters:

> In my third year [as a student at Cambridge] I met G. E. Moore, who was then a freshman, and for some years he fulfilled my ideal of genius. He was in those days beautiful and slim, with a look almost of inspiration, and with an intellect as deeply passionate as Spinoza's. He had a kind of exquisite purity. (p. 85)

Because he had been visiting his mother in New Zealand, McTaggart was meeting Moore for the first time. How Russell explained to Moore his intention of having McTaggart join them for tea we do not know. Certainly it must have seemed at least a little unusual for a nineteen-year-old freshman studying classics, as Moore then was, to be invited to have tea with one of Cambridge's most distinguished philosophical minds. Whatever pretext Russell may have used to make the introductions seem natural, the actual reason for the meeting is well established. It was to secure McTaggart's blessing for Moore's election to the Cambridge Conversazione Society, a semi-secret society of whose existence Moore was at the time richly ignorant.

The preliminaries must have been strained. For all his displays of affection toward his friends, McTaggart was not easily approachable by those who did not know him, and though Russell knew Moore the relationship was then superficial. Moore, moreover, was intensely shy. And so we can imagine the trio of future greats fumbling with pipes and matches, passing sugar and cream, exchanging lacquered inquiries, each feeling his way along the reason for their being together at this time and place. For McTaggart the timing had to be just right; for Russell each man had to be put at his ease; and for Moore, what expectations he had had presumably already had been fulfilled by the mere fact of the occasion itself. But as they talked, Moore writes in his autobiography,

> McTaggart . . . [was] . . . led to express his well known view that Time is unreal. This must have seemed to me then (as it still does) a perfectly monstrous proposition, and I did my best to argue against it. I don't suppose I argued at all well; but I think I was persistent and found quite a lot of different things to say in answer to McTaggart. (pp. 13–14)

Moore's memory may here be colored by the direction his philosophy took in his maturity, when he became the defender of common sense. The youthful Moore seems to have been of a different mind. Writing in his contribution to an 1897 symposium on the topic "In What Sense, If Any, Do Past and Future Time Exist?," Moore answers this question as follows: "If I need, then, . . . to give a direct answer to our question, I would say that neither Past, Present, nor Future exists, if by existence we are to mean the ascription of full Reality and not merely existence as Appearance." Time, in other words, is unreal, a position Moore reaffirms in a paper published the following year where certain arguments in favor of the unreality of time are said to appear "perfectly conclusive." We do the elder Moore no injustice by noting the youthful Moore's espousal of that "perfectly monstrous proposition" he and McTaggart discussed during their first meeting. Whatever the details of the "different things" he said on that occasion, Moore's promise as a critical, speculative thinker must have been obvious to McTaggart. As the most influential member of the Society at the time, his approval assured the freshman's candidacy. On February

10, 1894, Moore officially became a member. It would change his life, as it had changed the lives of others before him.

The Apostles

In existence over seventy years by the time of Moore's arrival in Cambridge, the Society was a select group of curious intellectuals, limited in size to twelve active members at any one time (hence the aptness of its other name, "The Apostles"). Members met every Saturday evening during academic terms to discuss whatever topic had been chosen at the previous meeting. An essay was prepared and read, spirited discussion followed, and a vote was taken, for and against, the merits of the controversial proposition that was the occasion for that week's meeting and debate. Stephen Toulmin observes that "from 1820 on, the Apostles had . . . a remarkably consistent record of co-opting to itself the most brilliant Cambridge undergraduates of each generation; and it did so with most notable effect during the decades immediately before World War I." In addition to the philosopher Alfred North Whitehead, the mathematician G. H. Hardy, and the poet Rupert Brooke, "just about all the [male] members . . . of Bloomsbury" were formally associated with the Society: Strachey, Keynes, MacCarthy, and Woolf. (Roger Fry was a member from an earlier period—1887–1891). The members during Keynes's years (1903–1910), his recent biographer Robert Skidelsky writes,

> with one or two exceptions, were distinctly deficient in charm and beauty, the qualities which tether people to society. Not only were they lacking, as Virginia Woolf later remarked, in 'physical splendour'; they had no small talk; they were arrogant, prickly, withdrawn. They compensated by the brilliance and fearlessness of their cerebration to each other. . . . They were men whose lives tended to be devoid of feminine company, except that of female relations. This was a common Cambridge, even Victorian, pattern in young adulthood; but it was exaggerated by precisely those features which cut off the Society from the world. (pp. 119–120)

Members of the Society referred to the Apostolic world as "noumenal," while the non-Apostolic world was "phenomenal"; *their* world was "real," the world of ordinary mortals was "appearance." When to everyone's surprise McTaggart married in later life, he spoke well for these Apostolic traditions by reassuring the brotherhood that nothing *really* had changed; Mrs. McTaggart was merely a "phenomenal wife." Insulated from the workaday world by their secrecy, elitism, and traditions, the Society, Skidelsky goes on to observe,

> functioned as a 'protective coterie' for members who were too shy or awkward or clever to be fully comfortable in the world and who needed each other to sparkle or for social therapy. At the same time, one must not ignore the positive power of the unworldly ideal for clever men bred both in the classics and gentlemanly ideals, to whom much of Victorian life seemed ugly and oppressive. (p. 120)

That "unworldly ideal," understood as the unwavering commitment to search for truth, was to become inseparable from Moore as it had before in the case of one of his teachers, Henry Sidgwick, who describes "the Spirit" of the Apostles and his devotion to it in the following terms:

> This spirit—at least as I apprehended it— . . . absorbed and dominated me. I can only describe it as the spirit of the pursuit of truth with absolute devotion and unreserve by a group of intimate friends, who were perfectly frank with each other, and indulged in any amount of humorous sarcasm and playful banter, and yet each respects the other, and when he discourses tries to learn from him and see what he sees. Absolute candour was the only duty that the tradition of the Society enforced. No consistency was demanded with opinions previously held—truth as we saw it then and there was what we had to embrace and maintain, and there was no proposition so well established that an Apostle had not the right to deny or question, if he did so sincerely and not from mere love of paradox. The gravest subjects were continually debated but gravity of treatment, as I have said, was not imposed though sincerity was. In fact it was rather a point of the Apostolic mind to understand how much suggestion and instruction may be derived from what is in form a jest—even in dealing with the gravest matters. (pp. 34–35)

Russell in his *Autobiography* states that "the greatest happiness of [his] life at Cambridge" (p. 91) was as a result of his association with the Society; in this he echoes Sidgwick, who continues his Apostolic psalm as follows:

After I had gradually apprehended the spirit as I have described it, it came to me that no part of my life at Cambridge was so real to me as the Saturday evenings on which the Apostolic debates were held; and the tie to the Society is much the strongest corporate bond which I have known in my life. I think, then, that my admission into this society and the enthusiastic way in which I came to idealize it really determined or revealed that the deepest bent of my nature was towards the life of thought—thought exercised on the central problems of human life. (p. 35)

In 1942, looking back almost fifty years after joining, Moore describes the Society in his autobiography in a characteristically restrained style. But the description is no less full of appreciation in substance:

Towards the end of my first year, I began to make the acquaintance of a set of young students—most of them a year or two my seniors, both in age and academic standing*—whose conversation seemed to me of a brilliance such as I had never hitherto met with or even imagined. They discussed politics, literature, philosophy and other things with what seemed to me astounding cleverness, but also with very great seriousness. I was full of excitement and admiration. My own part in these discussions was generally merely to listen in silence to what others said. I felt (and was) extremely crude compared to them; and did not feel able to make any contributions to the discussions which would bear comparison with those which they were making. I felt greatly flattered, and rather surprised, that they seemed to think me worthy of associating with them. . . . At Dulwich [the school Moore attended before going up to Cambridge] I never became really intimate with any of the clever boys I met there. At Cambridge, for the first time, I did form friendships with extremely clever people; and, of course, this made an enormous difference to me. Until I went to Cambridge, I had no idea of how exciting life could be. (pp. 12–13)

---

*Moore here is referring to Eddie Marsh, Charles Sanger, Ralph Wedgwood, Crompton and Theodore Davis, and Russell, among others. A brief sketch of each is offered by Paul Levy in *Moore*, chap. 4.

Moore's memory very likely is unreliable when he says that "[his] own part in these discussions was generally merely to listen in silence to what others said." From the beginning he occupied a position of immense power and influence within the Society, a fact Russell captures in the following letter to Alys Pearsall Smith, Russell's first wife:

> Yesterday Moore made his début in the Society, and the scene was so perfectly wonderful and unprecedented that I would give anything to be able to describe it adequately. He spoke perfectly clearly and unhesitatingly. . . . He looked like Newton and Satan rolled into one, each at the supreme moment of his life. . . . At one point he said: scepticism cannot destroy enthusiasm, there is one which will always remain, and that is the enthusiasm for scepticism. And to see him say it no one could doubt his utter conviction of the truth of what he was saying. We all felt electrified by him, and as if we had all slumbered hitherto and never realized what fearless intellect pure and unadulterated really means. If he does not die or go mad I cannot doubt that he will somehow mark himself out as a man of stupendous genius.

During his seven years as an active member Moore wrote more than twenty papers for the Society, delivering some more than once, and continued, we may assume, to play an active role in the discussions. If it was McTaggart's blessing that Moore's candidacy required in March of 1893, it would be Moore's blessing that future candidates increasingly would need up until the time he "took wings" and resigned in January 1901. If anything, however, his influence was to increase after his resignation; for the next generation of Apostles included "just about all the [male] members . . . of Bloomsbury," whose Moorean views about Truth, Beauty, and Goodness they were to carry with them to London.

A Philosopher Is Born

Moore was a student at Cambridge from 1892 to 1896. The son of Daniel Moore, a physician, and Henrietta Sturge, a descendant of the Sturge family prominent in Quaker history, he entered Cambridge with the intention of preparing for a career as a teacher of classics in the public schools. Those of his translations that remain reveal a young classicist of considerable promise, one who would not have disappointed the hopes of his instructors at Dulwich College. But circumstances were not to cooperate with Moore's early intentions. Although he studied classics during each of his four years at Cambridge, taking a First in Part I in 1894 and a Second in Part II in 1896, the passion of his mind found a new object in philosophy, a subject which as a student he studied formally only in 1894–1896, taking a First in Moral Sciences. By the time he finished his formal studies, if not before, his righteous dedication to philosophy had taken root. The question for the young Moore was not so much whether but how that dedication would find its expression.

The change from Moore the student of classics to Moore the disciple of philosophy must have been gradual. When he began his studies at Cambridge, Moore was a shy, lanky, inexperienced, and, as Russell saw him, beautiful boy of nineteen making his first physical break from a home that breathed the heavy air of religious fundamentalism. Family prayers and Bible study were compulsory daily rituals, and the local Baptist church in the South London neighborhood in which Moore was raised, near the Crystal Palace, where Moore and his three brothers and four sisters played, found the entire Moore family in attendance twice every Sunday. It must have been during his early teens that Moore, himself a recent convert to an evangelical form of Christianity, took to the streets to distribute religious tracts "to try to convert other people." This he did "out of a sense of duty." "And my conviction that this was my duty," he relates in his autobiography,

> led to one of the most painful continued mental conflicts I have ever experienced. I did make efforts to do what I conceived to be my duty in this respect, but I had to fight against a very strong feeling of reluctance. There seemed to be something utterly inappropriate and out of place in trying to persuade my school-fellows, for example, to love Jesus. I did drive myself to distribute tracts along the promenade at the sea-side (and this was not the hardest thing I actually drove myself to do), though I positively hated doing it, and all the more because there happened to be at the same place the family of two other boys from Dulwich, whom I greatly admired, and I was greatly unwilling that they should see me distributing tracts. But I constantly felt that I was not doing nearly as much as I ought to do. I discovered that I was very deficient in moral courage. (p. 11)

Moore characterizes this period of his life as an "intense religious phase," a phase he says "cannot . . . have lasted more than about two years." Well before he went up to Cambridge, we are told, his "religious beliefs gradually fell away, and so quickly that . . . I was, to use a word then popular, a complete Agnostic" (p. 11). Moore does not acknowledge the price he paid for his agnosticism. The emphasis is on the immensely liberating atmosphere he encountered at Cambridge. A young man who, as we learn from his letters home, found it acutely difficult even to mention *dancing* to his parents let alone discuss controversial philosophical ideas with them, Moore, especially after his election to the Apostles, must have been genuinely dazzled by the breadth and freedom of undergraduate intellectual life. It was philosophy, manifesting itself through "the immensely clever people" he met in the Apostles, that called Moore—not Moore, the shy, inexperienced lad from a rigid religious background, who knowingly set out to find philosophy.

Moore would have been the first to agree with this account. "Until [1893]," he recalls, "I had in fact hardly known that there was such a subject as philosophy" (p. 13). It is Russell who is given credit by Moore for "urg[ing] me strongly" to study philosophy because, in Moore's words, "Russell came to think I had some aptitude" for the subject (p. 13). Russell came to think this, Moore relates, on the strength of the abilities he displayed in his discussion with McTaggart regarding the unreality of time and on "other occasions." Knowing what we now know of the Apostles, these "other occasions" surely must have included Moore's contributions to their Saturday evening meetings. It must have been what was *said* on these occasions that Moore found both puzzling and intellectually invigorating. His discussion with McTaggart about the "perfectly monstrous proposition" that time is unreal, Moore writes, was

> typical of what (if I am not mistaken) has always been, with me, the main stimulus to philosophise. I do not think that the world or the sciences would ever have suggested to me any philosophical problems. What has suggested philosophical problems to me is things which other philosophers have said about the world or the sciences. (p. 14)

While in time it would be what other professional philosophers said that would command Moore's attention we cannot be far from wrong in supposing that a large part of his initial impetus to do philosophy came from the swirl of Apostolic ideas in which he found himself. Like his mentor and fellow Apostle Sidgwick before him, Moore's "admission into this society and the enthusiastic way in which [he] came to idealize it [probably] determined or revealed that the deepest bent of [his] nature was towards the life of thought."

Modest Beginnings

Moore's earliest papers for the Apostles reveal just how richly naive he was, both philosophically (however prodigious his untutored talents may have been) and in the ways of the world. They also reveal just how painfully honest and far removed from Bloomsbury's sexual permutation he could be. In his third paper, for example, entitled "Shall we take delight in crushing our roses?" (dated December 8, 1894), Moore ashamedly confesses (without naming the activity) to having masturbated and then goes on to bare his innocent soul even more, writing:

> Another point which may help you to judge whether I am speaking from prejudice or rationally, is my ignorance till a very recent date. When I came up to Cambridge, I did not know that there would be a single man in Cambridge who fornicated; and, till a year ago, I had no idea that sodomy was ever practised in modern times.

Unlike the young Strachey and Keynes, for example, the youthful Moore is a stiff Puritan even when in possession of this new knowledge. He condemns sodomy, arguing that lust for intercourse without intending propagation "appears to be the greatest evil upon earth"; we ought not, then, "take delight in crushing our roses"—ought not, that is, violate the virginity of "our women" in the name of satisfying "our carnal lust." A less solemn tone is struck in his maiden effort, "What end?" (dated May 12, 1894), a free-for-all "history of the world" that features appearances by the Devil, God, and something like Hegel's Absolute. There are, besides, stirring declarations on behalf of hedonism and ethical egoism.

These earliest papers, aside from offering glimpses of a more carefree, less plodding, and considerably more humorous prose writer than the one with whom most of his readers are familiar, contain little worthy of note. Beginning with Moore's first effort, however, and continuing throughout his Apostles papers during the next seven years there are recurrent themes, themes that are more or less amplified in his published writings. Among the more amplified are his protracted worries over the meaning and nature of goodness; among the less, his views regarding God and immortality. But even granting the comparatively modest amount he published on these latter topics, A. J. Ayer grossly overstates the case when he writes that "almost all that Moore thought it necessary to say about the grand metaphysical questions of God and Immortality is contained in one short paragraph of the essay, 'A Defence of Common Sense,'" published in 1925. In point of fact Moore published a number of early reviews of books that deal with these "grand metaphysical questions." One of his earliest published essays, "The Value of Religion," which appeared in 1901, is a sustained critical examination of the rationality of religious belief, while his "Mr. McTaggart's 'Studies in Hegelian Cosmology'" of this same year includes a lengthy critical discussion of McTaggart's views on immortality. The former essay will be examined in detail below. For the moment it is sufficient to note its existence and to correct Ayer's misperception of the public record of Moore's interest in God and immortality.

Paul Levy is even more unreliable when it comes to the private record previously locked away in the Ark of the Apostles. In 1897, for example, Moore read three successive papers to the Society on religious questions ("What is belief in God?," February 26; "Was the epistle of straw?," May 14; and "What is it to be wicked?," November 13, read again on November 15, 1902). Other of Moore's papers accessible to Levy but not to Ayer also touch on the questions of God's existence and immortality. Yet Levy minimizes the importance of Moore's consideration of these questions, suggesting that the topics of the 1897 Apostles papers, for example, "may well have been urged upon Moore [by others] *because* of his lack of genuine interest in religious questions"(p. 193, emphasis in original). This is an interpretation of Moore that will not bear up in the face of the public and private record of his thought, especially between 1897 and 1901, when in addition to the three Apostles papers presented in 1897 Moore wrote and delivered two other lengthy essays on religious topics, one entitled "Religious Belief," and the other, "Natural Theology," both of which he presented to the Trinity Essay Society, a group that met on Sunday evenings for the discussion of subjects connected with religion. "Natural Theology" was read on November 5, 1899, "Religious Belief" a year earlier on November 13, 1898. This latter essay, moreover, after it was revised and expanded, was presented to the London School of Ethics and Social Philosophy; it is the paper published in 1901 under the title "The

Value of Religion." On June 3, 1900, Moore also presented a paper entitled "Immortality" to the Sunday Essay Society. Furthermore, Moore gave a series of lectures on ethics during the Fall of 1898, and though these "Elements of Ethics," as the course and lectures were called, touched on much more than ethical questions; religious questions, including inquiries into the rationality of belief in God, were examined. And as for immortality, Moore's philosophical concern for this topic can be found at least as early as his Apostles paper "What is matter?," read before the Society on May 24, 1895. It is scarcely credible to maintain, in view of the available evidence and notwithstanding Moore's professed agnosticism, that he lacked "genuine interest in religious questions."

The Price of Unbelief

How deep Moore's interest was is painfully apparent in a pivotal Apostles paper, "Vanity of vanities," which he delivered to the Society on April 29, 1899. Moore poses the principal question he examines in two different ways. He wonders at the outset "what, on earth, people do live for," adding that "there is no question to which I am half so anxious to obtain an answer." Toward the end of the paper this question becomes "whether things are good or bad." "This question," he writes, is "the most important of all [questions] and indeed the only one of any importance." In Moore's view what people live for, what gives their life meaning or purpose, are those things they think are good. It is only if people know what things *truly are good* (if any things are) that they can know what *truly makes life worth living* (if anything does).

Moore sees two options. There is, first, a "cheerful view" that rests on steady convictions about what things are good, a view that gives meaning or purpose to human life. Second, there is "the utterly desperate view" that nothing is really good (or bad), so that we "live for nothing." The former view is hospitable to happiness; the latter not. For a happy person is one who "whenever the question arises, whether things that we have or can get are worth having . . . [answers] . . . that they are," whereas a person is unhappy "when, on that question arising, [he has] to answer No." Unhappily Moore is obliged to confess that he belongs in the latter category. He finds that he does not believe in the value of anything: "The more calmly and dispassionately I look at things in general—the more I look at them merely with an eye to what is true about them, the more plain it seems to me that they are worthless." Quite apart from the pleasures he currently enjoys and the pains he presently escapes, Moore is unable to avoid the harsh verdict: His life is not worth living. He "lives for nothing."

Now, Moore despondent is not the Moore his successors have come to know, and some might be tempted to suppose that he is being disingenuous. Few will find this explanation attractive. Sincerity, not disingenuousness, is at the heart of the Apostolic tradition, and Moore is hardly one to flaunt that tradition for an evening's amusement. Besides, the content of the paper, the despondency to one side for the moment, is recognizably Moorean; it is not as if, for example, Moore reaches the conclusions he does by arguing from premises based on Nietzsche's "Will to Power." Moore's letters at this time provide additional evidence for reading "Vanity of vanities" as genuinely descriptive of his mood. "In all that matters most," he writes to Desmond MacCarthy on June 19, 1898, "it does seem that nothing can be known and nothing done. I have no better philosophy than that and smiles: but they cannot satisfy. I wonder, as always, whether the rule of thumb people can be right? I envy them, and yet I would not be them." In a second letter to MacCarthy, written just a few days before (April 26, 1899) he delivered "Vanity of vanities," Moore writes that "I don't know how to get anything worth having. The only way seems to be to drown the consciousness that you haven't got it; and to that I cannot make up my mind." A third letter to MacCarthy, this one dated February 18, 1900, reveals that Moore is still despondent and that his will to do philosophy is being affected: "Silence, timidity, incapacity for work; but perhaps I shall find my corner some day." And a fourth letter (February 24, 1900) reaffirms his depression: his paper on "Necessity" is due in two weeks; his progress is more labored and slower than usual; he is "even encouraged in the idea that I will not try to finish it."

The relevant available evidence confirms, then, that the Moore who speaks in "Vanity of vanities" is the Moore who was, and this not for one Saturday night only. There was a period of his life, between the years 1898 and 1901, when the deeper logic of his melancholy would not be satisfied by the abundance of superficial pleasures that then fell his way. There were fundamental questions to be asked: What things are good? What makes life worth living? *Principia*'s answers, with their power to change and invigorate the lives of others, lay in the future. For Moore himself the answers he offered now were impotent to lighten the burden of his personal despondency.

There are two ways to escape the melancholy in which he finds himself, he declares in "Vanity of vanities," neither of which in his view is rationally acceptable. First, one may administer to one's self "the common remedies that are prescribed against unhappiness": "Live virtuously and you will be happy; work hard and be unselfish and take regular exercise and be temperate, and relax yourself with those amusements which are generally held to be innocent: do all these things and you will be happy." Moore concedes that one who follows this advice—one who abides by "the rules of common sense morality"—will or is likely to attain happiness. But there is a "difficulty" with this approach. What *reasons* are there for believing that the values associated with this "cheerful view" are the correct ones? What reasons do we have for believing that the values affirmed or assumed by "common sense morality" are true? "If there are reasons," Moore insists, "then you ought to be able to convince yourself that it is so [i.e., that the things valued by common sense *are* valuable] by direct consideration": you ought to be able to give an *argument* that confirms the reality of these values *before* embarking on common sense's road to happiness. Because he finds no rationally compelling argument either at hand or in the offing, Moore feels "a strong repugnance against the idea of attempting by any means, however infallible, to produce in myself the conviction that the cheerful view is true." So much for the escape from melancholy offered by common sense morality.

A second avenue of escape is to join the ranks of religious believers who, Moore thinks, "can be happy, however much pain they may suffer." These believers *do* have a steady conviction about what is good—namely, heaven. Believing that they will one day get there, they believe they have something to live for. But for Moore the door is closed: "That I could pass from unhappiness to happiness, that, by deliberately refusing to take a rational view, I might come to believe that [heaven exists] or something similar, I do not doubt. But I don't believe we have the right to do so."

In both cases, then—in the case of both common sense's and religion's remedy for melancholia—Moore is obstinate in his unhappiness. His dilemma is clear: *Either* he may purchase his happiness (but only at the price of sacrificing his rationality) *or* he may retain his rationality (but only at the price of sacrificing his happiness). He cannot have it both ways—cannot be *both* rational *and* happy. Faced with the need to choose, Moore in "Vanity of vanities" opts for the life of reason. He will not "deliberately refuse to take a rational view" though it promises more unhappiness: "I do not believe we have the right to do so." The price of unbelief is melancholia.

Principia Ethica is Moore's sustained attempt to avoid this dilemma.

Its power lies in its gospel of rational moral faith: Happiness can be achieved without sacrificing one's rationality. It is not easy. But neither is it impossible. That is part of the neglected message of Moore's major work, a message that helps explain *Principia*'s overpowering influence on his Bloomsbury disciples. A defense of these claims will be offered in the pages that follow. For the present a number of preliminary matters require attention.

Moore brings several assumptions to the dilemma he poses. Some concern what things are and are not good; others concern what is and is not rational. Among the former is Moore's rejection of hedonism—the view that pleasure and pleasure alone is good in itself. Its rejection is implied because Moore thinks the question of what makes life worth living is to be answered *apart from* how much pleasure (or pain) we experience.

A second major assumption is that belief in God is not rational. If it were, Moore could escape from his melancholia, or so he assumes, by choosing to believe in the heaven God promises. Since the irrationality of belief in God is not argued for in "Vanity of vanities" we do well to assume that that position is argued for elsewhere. This is an assumption we can now confirm, postponing until Chapter 7 a survey of Moore's objections to hedonism.

The Ethics of Belief

In "The Value of Religion" Moore proposes to "re-discuss [the] ancient controversy . . . : Ought we to believe in God?" (p. 81). In times past people have been killed or persecuted depending on how they answered; for his contemporaries, Moore notes, how one answers "is of little practical importance" because both believers and non-believers usually are of one mind concerning what things are good and what ought to be done. Nevertheless he goes on to note that

> so long as many say, "There is a God," while others answer, "I see no reason for thinking that there is," it remains a possible danger that hostile action should result. This difference, I remind you again, has in the past been a large cause of violence and persecution: and so, not probably, but possibly, it may become again. (p. 82)

To his examination of "the ancient controversy" Moore brings a theory about the nature of belief. At the most abstract level he divides beliefs into two categories: (*a*) those we cannot help believing and (*b*) those we can help believing. The former are psychologically necessary (the believer is psychologically unable not to believe; psychologically, he cannot not believe); the latter lack this necessity (the believer can and does choose to believe, and could have chosen not to). The truth of any belief, Moore maintains, is logically independent of its classification as psychologically necessary or otherwise. That a person cannot help believing something does not guarantee the truth of what is believed. Truth depends on the content of what is believed, not the psychological state of the believer.

The above is true even in the case of those beliefs that are universally psychologically necessary—beliefs no rational person can doubt. Beliefs about "the facts of common life" belong in this category: "We all believe that we are here, between four walls, alive and able to move; nay, more, thinking and feeling. . . . In these things we all do believe; we cannot help believing them, whether we like it or not" (p. 88). What we *can* help believing is what is alleged to *follow* either strictly or probably from such beliefs. For example, our beliefs about the facts of common life (our common sense beliefs) are the basis "from which the Natural Sciences infer their laws" (p. 88); whether we *should* choose to believe in certain laws depends on whether the arguments given in their support are rationally compelling. If they are, then as rational beings we should choose to believe in them; if not, not. Our choice in such cases ought always to be guided by reason. But those beliefs that are universally psychologically necessary are incapable of proof: "[We] cannot prove" them because any premise from which we might attempt to derive their truth would be as doubtful as the conclusion we sought to establish and so would not establish it. All we can do is let reason guide our choices regarding *what else* to believe about the world. The "ancient controversy" about God's existence requires such guidance. To inquire into the rational grounds of belief in God's existence is to ask whether we are able rationally to infer his existence given the same point of departure from which the several sciences must begin: common sense beliefs.

It is against this backdrop that Moore sees the question of belief in God as a *moral* question. As rational beings he assumes that we *morally* ought to believe the conclusion of an argument if and only if (*a*) the argument is valid, (*b*) the premises are themselves psychologically necessary, or (*c*) the premises, though not themselves psychologically necessary, can be validly supported by other premises that are. For Moore it is a *moral*, not merely an intellectual, failure to accept the truth of a belief whose only known support is a shoddy argument. To ask whether we ought to believe in God is thus to ask whether any argument for his existence satisfies the canons of rational proof. To the extent that the question of God's existence is a question to be decided by rational argument, to that extent, in the absence of such a proof, we are morally obliged *not* to believe. As Moore puts this point in "Vanity of vanities": "we have not the right" to believe, when proof is lacking, even if it costs us our happiness. This same melancholic theme is echoed in "The Value of Religion." "For some," Moore notes, disbelief in God, "though it makes no difference to their conduct, to their happiness it may make much" (p. 82). At least for one period of his life Moore was one of those for whom disbelief contributed much to his own unhappiness.

It is out of respect for the requirements of morality that Moore proceeds to examine the arguments for God's existence. As a preliminary to his examination he distinguishes between two questions he thinks others frequently confuse. First, there is a question of fact: Is it a fact that God exists? Second, there is a question of value: What, if any, morally desirable effects are associated with belief in God? The two questions are logically distinct. Belief in what is false can have desirable effects, and the effects of true belief can be undesirable. It is just as fallacious to infer that a belief is true because the belief causes good results as it is to infer that a belief that causes bad results is false. Whatever reasons there are for believing that God exists, the valuable effects that result from believing cannot be among them. Which is not to say that assessing the value of these effects is unimportant. Moore in fact assesses them and what he says in his assessment is essential for understanding the ties that bind his religious and ethical writings. But first his treatment of the factual question, "Does God exist?," requires attention.

An affirmative answer to this question, when the Deity is understood to be a personal God, as wise, good, and powerful "as any Christian is likely to imagine" (p. 85), may either be supported by argument or accepted on faith. Moore begins with a critical examination of some of the standard proofs of God's existence, reserving until later his discussion of faith. His criticisms of the arguments are borrowed from his predecessors, Kant and Hume in particular. Persons familiar with the body of critical literature devoted to the proofs will not find anything new in Moore's discussion or in the following summary.

The Inadequacy of the Proofs

Moore makes short work of the First Cause argument, dismissing it in one sentence: "Even if some First Cause were necessary, it would yet remain to prove that this Cause was intelligent and good: it must be both, you remember, to come within our meaning of personal God" (p. 90). Moore's point is the following. The First Cause argument starts with some fact of common life—for example, the fact that Ronald Reagan exists now (in October 1984) and has not always existed. From this we are able rationally to infer that he was caused to exist by his parents, who also have not always existed and who in turn were caused to exist by *their* parents, and so on. Proponents of the First Cause argument allege that this regressing causal series cannot be infinite; there must be a First Cause, a being that was not caused to exist by anyone or anything else. Without such a being proponents contend that neither President Reagan, nor his parents, nor their parents, nor anything else could have existed.

Critics frequently dispute the necessity of inferring the existence of a First Cause, arguing that there is no demonstrable reason why there cannot be an infinite regress of causes stretching back in time, however emotionally unsatisfactory some people might find the vision of an eternal sequence of causes and effects. Obviously familiar with this criticism Moore does not even raise it, concentrating instead on another major weakness.

Let it be assumed that the argument establishes the existence of a First Cause. All this can guarantee is that there once existed a being who was not caused to exist by anyone or anything else. Was this being intelligent? Stupid? A little of both? Was this being good? Evil? A combination of the two? Was this being great in power? Weak? Great in some respects but weak in others? The First Cause argument, Moore insists, is absolutely incapable of offering a rationally compelling basis for choosing between these options. Since the Deity whose existence is under examination is supposed to be a personal God, as good, wise, and powerful "as any Christian is likely to imagine," the First Cause argument in Moore's view fails to provide a rational proof of the Deity's existence.

The Design argument attempts to succeed where the First Cause argument fails. Moore sketches this argument as follows:

> From the nature of the world, as it appears on observation, we can infer that it or parts of it were or are caused by a being immensely intelligent, wise or good. . . . We assume that useful and beautiful objects we find in the world were made by man—had for their cause a being of some intelligence and goodness. By these useful and beautiful objects I mean houses and drains, hospitals and works of art— if you like, a watch—and I call it an assumption that they were made

by man, in order not to overstate my case. We have as our premise, then, that certain objects, which I am far from denying to be either useful or beautiful or sometimes both, had for their cause some tolerably good people. Then, says the Natural Theologian, we may infer that anything useful or good we find in the world, that is not a work of man's designing—man himself, above all, the most useful and beautiful of all—had also for its cause a person of intelligence and goodness. (p. 90)

Moore's main criticism of the Design argument takes the form of a dilemma. In order for the argument even to get under way one must assume that *some* natural events have natural causes; for example, one must assume that the local hospital was caused by the acts of human beings. Now, suppose the Design argument did succeed in establishing the existence of a Designer-God. Ought we to conclude that the Deity is like one sort of natural cause (the humans who built the hospital)? Or ought we rather to conclude that this Deity is more like some other sort of natural cause (more like the acorn that grew into the oak tree in front of the hospital)? Both? Neither? Who is to say? Certainly the Design argument in Moore's view provides us with no rational basis for choosing one option rather than another. *Even if* we were to allow that the argument establishes the existence of some sort of Designer, we could not rationally say *what* that Designer is like. The Designer's *nature* would be unknowable. That is the first horn of the dilemma Moore poses.

The second is this. If we describe the nature of the Designer so that he resembles *one* sort of natural cause, then Moore allows that we might understand the Designer's nature. The Designer is, let us suppose, more like humans than acorns: very good, very intelligent, very powerful. Only now we cannot prove *that the Designer exists* from our study of natural causes. We are rationally unable to prove that a Deity exists who is more like us and less like an acorn. So either we can know (perhaps) God's nature but not be able rationally to prove God's existence, or we may (let us assume) prove the existence of a Designer-Deity but not be able rationally to say what the Deity's nature is. This is the dilemma that in Moore's view is fatal to the Design argument's aspirations.

"We cannot then," Moore writes by way of summing up his critical discussion of these two proofs, "make a single step towards proving God's existence from the nature of the world, such as we take it to be in common life or such as Natural Science shows it. That we are here to-night, that we were not here this morning, that we came here by means of cabs or on our feet: all facts of this sort, in which we cannot help believing,—these facts, with all the implications, which Science or Philosophy can draw from them, offer us not one jot of evidence that God exists" (p. 92).

The First Cause and Design arguments are the inventions of philosophers and theologians. Other familiar arguments have less scholarly homes. Moore moves quickly to demolish them. The argument from general belief infers God's existence from the fact that most people have believed or do believe in "a God of some sort." Moore allows the assumption but disputes the reasoning, noting that there are many erroneous beliefs that were once accepted as true by most people (for example, that the sun revolves around the earth). Moreover, Moore reminds us that religions tend to flourish in times and places where the natural sciences do not and where the fallacies involved in arguments for God's existence go undetected. The plausible inference is hardly theistically propitious:

> You can therefore hold that belief in God will persist undiminished, while other beliefs disappear, if you maintain the continued triumph of ignorance and fallacious reasoning. But a belief which persists from causes like these has surely no claim to be therefore considered true. (p. 93)

The so-called historical proofs are the last arguments Moore considers. One such argument attempts to prove God's existence on the ground that miracles occur, where by a 'miracle' one means an event that occurs without a natural cause. Moore denies the rationality of belief in miracles when understood in this way, claiming (without clearly explaining why) that if *any* miracle *ever* occurred it could then be that *every* event is miraculous; this is a consequence he thinks too presposterous to need further refutation. If, however, all one were to mean by 'miracle' is that people sometimes perform remarkable feats, then Moore concedes that miracles occur but denies that one rationally can infer God's existence from their occurrence. "That a man can perform astonishing feats is no proof either that he knows the truth or that he tells it" (p. 94).

"The facts of common life, then," Moore concludes, "the facts with which natural science and history deal, afford no inference to God's existence. If a man still believes that God exists, he cannot support his belief by any appeal to facts admitted both by himself and the infidel. He must not attempt to *prove* that God probably exists; for that is impossible" (p. 94, emphasis in original).

Having criticized a variety of arguments for God's existence, Moore does not conclude that belief in God is false. His position is that of the infidel: "I do *not* believe that he [God] does exist, but I also do *not* believe that he does not exist" (p. 88). Why Moore does not believe the latter is not explained in "The Value of Religion" or elsewhere in his writings, both published and unpublished. We must assume, given what we know of his considered views, that he did not find the arguments against God's existence rationally compelling and so concluded that he was morally obliged not to be an atheist; he "had not the right" to deny God's existence.

When Belief in God Is Justified

Although Moore is adamant in his claims about the rational inadequacies of arguments for God's existence, and although he counts himself among the infidels, he nonetheless allows that some people are justified in believing in God. His explanation of this possibility is given in tandem with observations he makes about certain logical similarities between (a) religious beliefs and (b) moral beliefs about what things are good-in-themselves. He observes, first, that neither sort of belief can rationally be inferred from "the facts of daily life." Just as we cannot infer God's existence from these facts, so we cannot infer *what ought to be* from our knowledge of *what is*. This same view is set forth with equal force in "The Elements of Ethics," where Moore also notes "that religious faith and moral faith are on a level in this [further] respect, that the truth of neither can possibly be proved by an inference from any scientific fact" (p. 313). Moore's use of the word 'faith' here, in referring to moral beliefs, is not a slip of the pen. "Any ethical view," he declares in "The Elements," "no doubt, is a mere matter of faith" (p. 312). "There is, therefore," he thinks in "The Value of Religion," "no more evidence for moral than for religious belief" (p. 96). Read in this light the moral nihilism that characterizes Moore's "Vanity of vanities" may be interpreted as the outer sign of Moore's inner loss of moral faith. And his examination of religious belief in "The Value of Religion" may be viewed as symptomatic of his desire to reassure himself that this loss of moral faith cannot be restored by resurrecting his discarded belief in God. Sometimes nails must be driven into coffins before a new birth is possible.

At this juncture in "The Value of Religion" Moore anticipates an objection. Given that moral and religious belief both lack factual evidence, the religious believer "may be tempted to say, 'I have as much right to my belief that God exists, as you have to any of your moral beliefs' " (p. 96). Moore thinks this inference is illicit, and his reason for thinking so is characteristic of the moral cast of mind he brings to the whole controversy over God's existence. In Moore's view anyone who claimed that he had as much right to believe in God as other people have to their moral beliefs would be making a moral judgment—namely, about what people have a right to believe. This same point is made in "The Elements," where Moore states that "the question whether you should have religious faith is simply one among other particular moral questions" (p. 315). So despite the crucial logical similarity between moral and religious beliefs Moore insists upon, there is also a crucial logical dissimilarity: There is one moral belief —the belief about what people have a right to believe, or what they are morally justified in believing—that is and must be logically more fundamental than any religious belief, including the Christian's belief in God. For one cannot even begin to discuss whether one should or should not have this belief, given Moore's position, without presupposing that *whatever* answer one gives will itself stand in need of ethical justification. There is at least one commitment that is logically more fundamental than every religious one.

In view of the foregoing it would be natural to assume that in "The Value of Religion" Moore would deny that belief in God can be justified. He does not. Like moral beliefs, belief in God, though not demonstrable by reason, need not be irrational. Assuming that the believer understands that his belief cannot be inferred from any "fact of common life" or science, understands, further, that it is logically inappropriate even to try to make this inference and so does not *ask* that supporting "facts" be adduced— assuming that a believer understands all this and, what is more, assuming that the believer finds it psychologically impossible to doubt God's existence, *then*, on Moore's view, and *only* then, is the believer morally (and therefore rationally) justified in her belief. "It is mere faith, not proof, which justifies your [the believer's] statement: God exists. Your belief is right, because you cannot help believing: and my unbelief is right, because I have not got that intuition. We both are justified by mere necessity" (p. 95). And so it is that despite his lengthy criticisms of belief in God Moore does not conclude that religious belief must be irrational, must go beyond what respect for the requirements of morality will allow, must be false. If one has faith, understood as the psychological inability to doubt or deny God's existence independently of any "fact of common life" or science, then—and only then—is one's belief rationally and morally justified. Of such a man "[who] really cannot help believing in God" there is, Moore allows, "nothing [that] can be said against him" (p. 96).

"But I very much doubt," he goes on immediately to observe, "whether this is often the case." Almost all believers *lack faith*. Professing a belief that lacks psychological necessity for them, they then try to "prove" its truth in one sham way or another. It is the same kind of mistake frequently made by those who try to "prove" that various things are intrinsically good by appeal to scientific facts or "the facts of common life." In both cases the type of error is the same: Attempts at proof are made in the case of propositions for which no proof is possible. And for which no proof ought to be required. Faith, whether religious or moral, must know its silence.

Immortality

Moore's views regarding life after death, set forth in his Sunday Essay Society paper "Immortality," exactly parallel his views concerning belief in God. His quarrel is not with those who have faith in immortality; it lies with those who aspire to prove or render probable the object of that faith. The arguments in favor of immortality (which we shall not explore) he contends are demonstrably inadequate. As for those "religious believer" who "merely assert that we are immortal and do not attempt to urge that this can be proved," they are unaffected by Moore's criticisms. "It is certain," he writes, that immortality is "neither probable nor improbable," though in his view it would be "desirable." No good reason can be given in its favor; and none against. Nor ought any to be sought.

That this last sentence is normative, concerning what *ought* to be, is vital. To believe or not to believe in God or immortality are *moral* questions for Moore because they ask what a rational being *ought* to believe. Unless we find belief in God or immortality psychologically necessary (and very few people find it so in his view) we cannot be morally justified in believing, whatever price we must thereby pay in terms of our own happiness. This recurring theme in Moore's writings—that the requirements of morality may and often do conflict with what is conducive to our happiness—is strongly Kantian in flavor and is suggestive of Kant's powerful influence on Moore's thought. The nature and scope of that influence will be examined below (see, especially, Chapter 3). Here we may note that it already has asserted itself in another place in the preceding. The logical independence of moral propositions from scientific truths and the truths of "common life" is a thoroughly Kantian tenet. In any event the Moore of "The Value of Religion" does not find it psychologically necessary to affirm God's existence; true to the spirit of "Vanity of vanities," he "has not the right" to believe in God. The Moore of that earlier essay also found that he lacked any confident *moral* beliefs. Recall the somber passage: "The more calmly and dispassionately I look at things in general—the more I look at them merely with an eye to what is true about them, the more plain it seems to me that they are worthless." It remains to be asked whether the Moore of "The Value of Religion" is equally nihilistic in his outlook.

A New Home for Old Values

Moore's views are positive but sketchy, set forth in a short final paragraph in which he addresses the second question remarked on earlier, the question of value: What, if any, morally desirable effects are associated with religious belief? He thinks there are two. First, there is the comfort belief in God affords, or is supposed to afford, to those who have faith; second, there is "that valuable element in religious emotion, which proceeds from the contemplation of what we think to be most truly and perfectly good" (p. 98). Essential to a proper understanding of Moore's thought is the recognition that the value of the effects he mentions are never denied by him. On the contrary his ongoing challenge, touched on only briefly in "The Value of Religion" but resolutely pursued in other places, is to explain how these old values can find a new home once they have been removed from their religious lodgings. The values of religion are retained. Only their philosophical foundation and material manifestation change.

This interpretation will be defended more fully in subsequent chapters. Here attention must be confined to Moore's discussion of religion's values in the essay under examination. Taking the value of comfort first, Moore argues that (*a*) the comfort associated with religious belief lacks a rational basis and that (*b*) it is in any event psychologically unobtainable. Such comfort lacks a rational basis in Moore's view because, as he has argued earlier, it is irrational to believe that God can miraculously intervene in the course of nature; similarly irrational is the belief that God can *do* anything to comfort anyone. As rational beings we are deprived of the belief that a Deity can offer us any help or solace. Moreover, those who aspire to find comfort in the belief that God at least *cares* about our plight are embarked on a "fruitless endeavour." For in order to increase their comfort in the knowledge that God cares about their plight, they must first believe that God exists, whereas in order to embrace this belief, they must first increase their comfort in the knowledge that God cares about their plight. As for his second criticism—the psychological one—Moore claims that the motivational situation is hopeless. "That this difficulty is a real one," he notes, from firsthand experience we may fairly assume, "I think most people for whom the present question has been raised, will acknowledge" (p. 97). There is, Moore believes, no true comfort to be obtained by believing in God.

Should we therefore deny the belief in the great value of comfort? Or ought we rather to look for the source of comfort and the ground of its value beyond the pale of religious belief? As we shall see momentarily, Moore chooses the latter alternative.

Concerning the "valuable element in religious emotion" Moore again affirms the value while at the same time denying that religious belief is necessary for its realization. This emotion "proceeds from the contemplation of what we think to be most truly and perfectly good" (p. 98). Because the object of our contemplation is an *ideal*, concerning what *ought* to be, it need not be what *is*. We can conceive of the most truly perfect as an ideal but nonexistent object or state of affairs, and we can find great value in the emotion we experience as we contemplate it. The crucial logical point is that our conception of something ideal does not require our belief in its actual existence. "The effects of literature," Moore notes by way of example, "show how strongly we may be moved by the contemplation of ideal objects, of which we nevertheless do not assert the existence" (p. 98).

In "Vanity of vanities" Moore, finding all things "worthless," could find no exit from his acute unhappiness. In "The Value of Religion" he remains mindful of the connection between belief in the reality of valuable things and his sense of well being. It is not enough that all worthwhile things be ideal objects—fictional creations, for example. Fictional characters can no more sympathize with our lives or act to help us than can a nonexistent God. "That some good objects should be real, is indeed necessary for our comfort" (p. 98). The cloud of his nihilism of "Vanity of vanities" lifted, Moore here declares that "we have plenty" of really existing "good objects":

It surely might be better to give up the search for a God whose existence is and remains undemonstrable, and to divert the feelings which the religious wish to spend on him, towards those of our own kind, who though perhaps less good than we can imagine God to be, are worthy of all the affections that we can feel; and whose help and sympathy are much more certainly real. We might perhaps with advantage worship the real creature a little more, and his hypothetical Creator a good deal less. (p. 98)

In these brief remarks Moore makes it clear that he continues to accept a set of values originally part of his early religious instruction and that he seeks a nonreligious basis for them. Comfort in the knowledge that one will find help and sympathy from another: that value remains. Only the identity of "the other" is not God but "those of our own kind," not "the hypothetical Creator" but "the real creature." And as the lessons of "Immortality" make clear, the temporal emphasis is altered too, from a "desirable" but hypothetical eternity to the certainty of our earthly existence. Moreover, the value of the emotion derived from contemplating "what we think to be most truly and perfectly good" remains, only now the object of our contemplation, given its status as an ideal, need not be believed to exist in fact in order to be contemplated and so is available for contemplation by people who do not believe in the existence of God—is available to Moore and his fellow infidels. We can have the best that religion has to offer without believing in God's existence. Mindful that "we have not the right" to choose to believe in God we may yet affirm the reality of the valuable things such belief affords, or is supposed to afford. We need not do something wrong in order to believe in what is good. That is the optimistic note struck by Moore's sketchy remarks about religion and value at the conclusion of "The Value of Religion," remarks that contrast sharply with the mournful mood of "Vanity of vanities."

A Promissory Note

But while the spirit of the man in the former essay is far less dreary than what we find in the latter, we cannot fail to ask whether the letter of the latter essay has been met. Recall the dilemma traced there by Moore: Happiness is possible but only at the price of compromising our commitment to reason. It is not enough to believe that some things are good; reasons must be given to support one's judgments. The value of comfort is a case in point. In a sensitive letter from Moore to Desmond MacCarthy's mother, dated August 22, 1900, he sympathizes with her loss of comfort and bemoans his (and Desmond's) lack of it. "I do sympathize with you," he writes, "but I'm afraid you think I'm better off than I am. Desmond

and I have got nothing in place of religion; and we do feel to need something. . . . [And] as for wanting comfort, that we do; and we don't at all
see how to get it." But wanting comfort is no confirmation of its value.
The "ought to be" of what is good in itself is not guaranteed by the "is"
of desire. That is at the heart of Moore's teachings, even at this time. The
more hopeful tone of the conclusion of "The Value of Religion," where
Moore states that "we have plenty" of really existing "good objects," must
be read as little more than a promissory note. Reasons remain to be given
for thinking that there are even a few things that are good, let alone
"plenty" of them. The passionate certainty Moore gave to Bloomsbury
must first overcome the heavy burden of his own acute scepticism.

Thus is Moore's challenge clear. With belief in a God both wise and
good, one seems able to guarantee the objectivity of fundamental values.
Man, whether individually or collectively, is not the measure of all things.
Our judging something good or beautiful does not make it so, even if we
all judge with one voice. Things *are* good, they *are* beautiful, independently of our judgment and awareness. They are what they are because
God has made them so. Deprived of a Deity on whom to rest one's belief
in the objectivity of fundamental values, Moore must find an adequate
philosophical substitute. We do not find this in "The Value of Religion."
Knowing something of the character of the man, we should not be surprised to find that he does not shirk his duty in this regard. *Principia* is his
major attempt to do what duty requires. But not the only one.

The Logic of Growth

What Moore would count as a philosophically adequate replacement
for the religiously grounded ethic he sought to supersede obviously depends on what determines a theory's philosophical adequacy in his view. It
would be implausible to suppose that Moore had an unalterable conception
of adequacy; more plausible is the conjecture that his understanding of a
theory's adequacy evolved in the course of the theories he developed.
That this is so will be borne out in the chapters that follow. The suggestion
made here is that Moore's development as a moral philosopher may be
interpreted by asking how well his own views measure up to a set of
criteria that in time he himself quite consciously endeavored to satisfy. His
two most sustained works in moral philosophy—*Principia* and *Ethics*—
offer the best insight into what these criteria are. In introducing these
criteria now, as an heuristic, interpretive device, the claim is not being

made that Moore *consciously* set about the task of satisfying their demands from the beginning of his quest. Even less so is it being claimed that he *unconsciously* set out to do this. The suggestion, rather, is that if we consider the theories Moore sets forth in *Principia* and *Ethics* we are able to identify a set of criteria he sought to satisfy in these works, criteria we may then in turn use as a means of interpreting the major developments in his moral philosophy both before and after *Principia*'s publication. In this way we can understand something of the logic of Moore's growth as a moral philosopher.

What follows is a brief description of six of the most conspicuous criteria of adequacy Moore uses to assess his own work, and the work of others, in and after *Principia*.

1. *The Objectivity Criterion.* No ethical theory can be adequate if it fails to recognize the objectivity of intrinsic value. Those things that are intrinsically valuable, or that are good-in-themselves or good as ends, have their value independently of anyone's believing, hoping, recognizing, etc. that they do. The intrinsic value of those things that are intrinsically good is as objective to them as the shape of a rectangle is objective to it. The objectivity criterion does not specify what else may be said about intrinsic value over and above its objectivity; it only requires that any adequate ethical theory must recognize the objectivity of value of this kind.

2. *The Universality Criterion.* No account of intrinsic value can be adequate if it fails to account for the universality of this kind of value. Once good, always good. Given that something is intrinsically good at one time, it follows that it must be good, and just as good, at any other time it exists, whether in the past or in the future. How this can be so is a question the universality criterion does not itself attempt to decide; it only requires that any theory of intrinsic value must recognize that it is so.

3. *The Natural Goods Criterion.* No ethical theory can be adequate if it fails to affirm both that (*a*) some things that actually exist in the natural world are intrinsically good and that (*b*) some things that actually exist in the natural world are intrinsically better than other things that actually exist. What things these are is an open question given this criterion. All that it requires is that an adequate ethical

theory must include positive propositions about "the good," in the
sense specified in (*a*) and (*b*).

4. *The Ideal Criterion.* No ethical theory can be adequate if it fails to
account for the validity of ideals, understood as conceivable states of
affairs that are intrinsically better than some things that actually exist.
This criterion does not itself specify what these ideals are (that is, what
conceivable states of affairs are better than some of the things that
actually exist), only that an adequate ethical theory must recognize
that ideals have the properties they do.

5. *The Conduct Criterion.* No ethical theory can be adequate if it fails to
offer a standard for deciding which acts are morally right or morally
wrong and to give guidance for its proper application. Again, this criterion does not itself say what this standard is or how it is to be
applied; it only requires that an adequate ethical theory must offer a
standard and illustrate its application.

6. *The Method Criterion.* No ethical theory can be adequate if it fails to
offer a method that we may use to decide what things are intrinsically
good. Like the other criteria, the method criterion does not specify
what this method is, only that some method must be offered.

These criteria, by no means exhaustive of the criteria Moore uses, are
not sufficient conditions of adequacy in his view, whether taken individually or collectively. They are necessary conditions. A theory is *not*
adequate if it fails to pass one or another of these tests. A fully adequate
theory would have to do a great deal more.

A Pilgrim's Progress

Embarked as he soon will be on his quest for an ethical theory that
will be a philosophically adequate replacement for the abandoned theistic
ethic of his youth, Moore's growth and development as a moral philosopher may be gauged by how well his own work measures up to the criteria
of adequacy he himself will use to challenge the views of others. In the
future some of his earliest speculations will fail these tests and wither
away. Others will pass and endure. For the present we can imagine the shy
teenager only recently up from Dulwich College making his way passed

the fountain in Great Court. Russell is waiting—Russell, whose religious background and development were in some ways like Moore's. "Alongside with my interest in poetry," Russell recalls in his *Autobiography*, "went an interest in religion and philosophy," adding:

> My grandfather was Anglican; my grandmother was a Scotch Presbyterian, but gradually became a Unitarian. I was taken on alternate Sundays to the Episcopalian [sic] Parish Church at Petersham and to the Presbyterian Church at Richmond, while at home I was taught the doctrines of Unitarianism. It was these last that I believed until about the age of fifteen. At this age I began a systematic investigation of the supposed rational arguments in favour of fundamental Christian beliefs. I spent endless hours in meditation upon this subject. . . . I thought that if I ceased to believe in God, freedom and immortality, I should be very unhappy. I found, however, that the reasons given in favour of these dogmas were very unconvincing. . . . Throughout the long period of religious doubt, I had been rendered very unhappy by the gradual loss of belief, but when the process was completed, I found to my surprise that I was quite glad to be done with the whole subject. (pp. 46–47)

Moore, too, found these reasons unconvincing and like Russell was never to renew his faith. But unlike Russell, whose sense of well being and of the meaningfulness of life seem to have happily survived his loss of religious belief, Moore's religious infidelity sometimes was at least part cause of his acute unhappiness. It is no more reasonable to view Moore's religious unrest as settled by the time he went up to Cambridge (despite his telling us that he was "a complete Agnostic" well before he arrived) than it is to believe that he was throughout his life ill disposed to that "perfectly monstrous proposition" that time is unreal. The elder Moore's recollections are not always the most reliable guide to the younger Moore's beliefs and aspirations. Religious belief may have lost an adherent before Moore left Dulwich College. But not a uniformly happy one.

McTaggart was more fortunate. Like both Russell and Moore he had examined "the reasons given in favour of [religious] dogmas" and found them wanting. "At a very early age," by which Goldsworthy Lowes Dickinson presumably means by about the age of ten, "[McTaggart] was sent to a preparatory school at Weybridge. Here he was reported to have argued against the Apostles' Creed and even to have announced that he did not believe in God" (p. 7). Even before that tender age McTaggart had squarely faced life's great mysteries. "At the age of six, he is reported to have remarked to one of his uncles, who was trying to console him for a death which he felt, 'we know nothing beyond the grave' " (p. 6). Again, a clergyman who knew him at this time in Weybridge describes him as running about on the heath, suddenly stopping, running on, falling down, starting off again, and again standing still, and when he was asked what he was thinking of as he stood thus in meditation he replied "he was thinking about God" (p. 7). Those precocious thoughts led him to reject belief in God but not belief in immortality. For though we know on his view little or nothing "beyond the grave," McTaggart at an early age came to believe that death was but a passage to continued life, though not to the heaven of the faithful, a belief he retained throughout his life and one that enabled him to face his own death with uncommon equanimity. Having abandoned belief in God, McTaggart was yet able to achieve that "cheerful view" Moore describes in "Vanity of vanities," and it is McTaggart's optimistic presence we find unmistakably embodied in the words "or something similar" when Moore affirms his own fidelity to reason at the price of his unhappiness: "That I could pass from unhappiness to happiness, that, by deliberately refusing to take a rational view, I might come to believe that [heaven exists] *or something similar*, I do not doubt. But I do not believe we have the right to do so" (emphasis added).

McTaggart, too, is waiting in Russell's rooms, and the three young men are, we may suppose, only minutes away from that famous discussion of time's unreality. Each in his own way emancipated from the uncongenial dogmas of the Christian faith, their similar religious backgrounds and questions will help consolidate their friendship over the next decade. Russell will wander prodigiously over the philosophical landscape, changing his mind on virtually every question he examines, only to change it again. But not McTaggart, who by the time of his introduction to Moore, according to C. D. Broad, (p. xlvi), already had decided upon his two fundamental convictions: "that man is immortal, and that the love of one man for another is of infinite value and profound metaphysical significance." The object of his future philosophical writings will be not to discover whether but to prove that these fundamental convictions are true.

And Moore? Moore was the composite of these two tendencies. With Russell he shared that restless intellectual energy and honesty that force one to think new thoughts, thoughts that sometimes are inconsistent with those previously held and that therefore can require abandoning former opinions and theories, though dearly held, as a snake abandons an old skin. But like McTaggart Moore had some convictions which he could never permanently surrender and which in his view, as in McTaggart's, it was the task of philosophy to illuminate and not confirm. For Moore some of these convictions were moral in nature, concerning the objective reality of certain values, and both the inventory of these values and their genesis in Moore's thought can be traced to his early religious instruction. If as Paul Levy suggests McTaggart's speculative philosophy is "a near-paradox" because its apex is "Christian love without a godhead" (p. 106), Moore's is no less paradoxical for the same kind of reason. For the values Moore cannot for long abandon are the very ones that he himself attributes to religion, or modest mutations of these values. And the central object of *his* moral philosophy is to offer a nonreligious basis for his faith in the objective reality of these values. Gilbert Ryle is on firm ground when he "speculate[s]" that Moore must have "felt a homesickness not so much for the theistic beliefs as for the moral certitudes of his former days" (p. 101). For Moore, "Good is, though God is not." When Moore enters Russell's rooms—when that meeting, in Paul Levy's words, "so momentous for the subsequent history of philosophy" (p. 124) takes place—Moore's religious pilgrimage begins in earnest.

3

A Youthful Idealism

A Passage to America

His body is unimposing, inclining toward the portly. Seated during the introduction, his frame seems to have sunk into itself, creating the appearance of a man considerably shorter than he actually is. The thin, silver-grey hair, receding at the forehead; the deeply creased, sunken cheeks; the wrinkled brow; the small, somewhat glazed eyes—every feature of his face testifies to his sixty-eight years. As he stands and walks to the lectern, however, those who have come to hear him—and many have —sense in his stride and posture the vitality synonymous with his name, so that when, the generous applause abated, he begins to read his prepared remarks, it surprises no one that the voice is strong, young even. From the outset the intensity of his intellect is more palpable than the gnarled hands with which he turns the pages of his lecture. Those who listen expect him to speak on behalf of the plain man and against the philosophical skeptic, to raise concern about the commonplace to a level of uncommon seriousness and importance. He does not disappoint them. "I am at present," he begins,

> as you can all see, in a room and not in the open air; I am standing up, and not either sitting or lying down; I have clothes on, and am not absolutely naked; I am speaking in a fairly loud voice, and am not either singing or whispering or keeping quite silent; I have in my hand some sheets of paper with writing on them; there are a good many other people in the same room in which I am; and there are windows in that wall and a door in this one.
>
> Now I have here made a number of different assertions; and I have made these assertions quite positively, as if there were no doubt

whatever that they were true. That is to say, though I did not expressly say, with regard to any of these different things which I asserted, that it was not only true but also *certain*, yet by asserting them in the way I did, I *implied*, though I did not say, that they were in fact certain—implied, that is, that I myself knew for certain, in each case, that what I asserted to be the case was, at the time when I asserted it, in fact the case. And I do not think that I can be justly accused of dogmatism or over-confidence for having asserted these things positively in the way that I did. In the case of some kinds of assertions, and under some circumstances, a man can be justly accused of dogmatism for asserting something positively. But in the case of assertions such as I made, made under the circumstances under which I made them, the charge would be absurd. On the contrary, I should have been guilty of absurdity if, under the circumstances, I had *not* spoken positively about these things, if I spoke of them at all. (p. 223)

Pausing momentarily, looking up from his text and scanning the stilled room, he continues.

Suppose that now, instead of saying "I am inside a building," I were to say "I *think* I'm inside a building, but perhaps I'm not: it's not *certain* that I am," or instead of saying "I have got some clothes on," I were to say "I think I've got some clothes on, but it's just possible that I haven't." Would it not sound rather ridiculous for me now, under these circumstances, to say "I *think* I've got some clothes on" or even to say "I not only think I have, I know that it is very likely indeed that I have, but I can't be quite sure"? For some persons, under some circumstances, it might not be at all absurd to express themselves thus doubtfully. Suppose, for instance, there were a blind man, suffering in addition from general anaesthesia, who knew, because he had been told, that his doctors from time to time stripped him naked and then put his clothes on again, although he himself could neither see nor feel the difference: to such a man there might well come an occasion on which he would really be describing correctly the state of affairs by saying that he *thought* he'd got some clothes on, or that he knew that it was very likely he had, but was not quite sure. But for me, now, in full possession of my senses, it would be quite ridiculous to express myself in this way, because the circumstances are such as to make it quite obvious that I don't merely think that I have, but know that I have. For me now, it would be absurd to say that I *thought* I wasn't naked, because by saying this I should imply that I didn't know that I wasn't, whereas you can all see that I'm in a position to know that I'm not. But if *now* I am not guilty of dogmatism in asserting positively that I'm not naked, certainly I was not guilty of dogmatism when I asserted it positively in one of those sentences with which I began this lecture. I knew then that I had clothes on, just as I know now that I have. (pp. 223–224)

A pause again. A glance around the room. And then a return to the text which he will continue reading during the next hour. Referring to this paper, entitled "Certainty," in the Preface of his *Philosophical Papers*—the year is 1958, seventeen years after the essay's initial presentation and only a month before his death—Moore will confess that "there are bad mistakes in it which I cannot yet see how to put right" (p. 9). That at eighty-five he should have cared enough about his "youthful" work openly to confess to its shortcomings is a remarkable testimony to his equally remarkable intellectual honesty.

Moore read "Certainty" in his capacity as the Howison Lecturer at the University of California in 1941. With his wife, Dorothy, he was embarked on a series of visiting appointments and lectures at universities throughout the United States, which lasted from 1940 to 1944. After the German bombing of England started in earnest during World War II, friends and students convinced Moore that he owed it to his profession to go abroad so as not to run unnecessary risks. He was by then retired from Cambridge, having stepped down in September 1939, and the trans-Atlantic sojourn gave him an unexpected and much cherished opportunity to visit America, where he was welcomed with a respect bordering on reverence. Well before his arrival he had attained a position of eminence within a "school" of academic philosophy whose very existence owed much to the power of his example. He came as a saint. And a hero. The voice of the plain man. The defender of Common Sense. "I am one of those philosophers," Moore had written in his classic 1925 paper, "A Defence of Common Sense" (reprinted in *Philosophical Papers*), "who have held that the 'Common Sense view of the world' is, in certain fundamental respects, *wholly* true (p. 32)." He even offered a "list of truisms,

every one of which (in my opinion) I *know*, with certainty, to be true."
Here is a sample from that now classic list.

> There exists at present a living human body, which is *my* body. This
> body was born at a certain time in the past, and has existed con-
> tinuously ever since, though not without undergoing changes; it was,
> for instance, much smaller when it was born, and for some time
> afterwards, than it is now. Ever since it was born, it has been either
> in contact with or not far from the surface of the earth; and, at every
> moment since it was born, there have also existed many other things,
> having shape and size in three dimensions (in the same familiar sense
> in which it has), from which it has been *at various distances* (in the
> familiar sense in which it is now at a distance both from that mantel-
> piece and from that bookcase, and at a greater distance from the
> bookcase than it is from the mantelpiece); also there have (very
> often, at all events) existed some other things of this kind with which
> it was *in contact* (in the familiar sense in which it is now in contact
> with the pen I am holding in my right hand and with some of the
> clothes I am wearing). Among the things which have, in this sense,
> formed part of its environment (i.e. have been either in contact with
> it, or at *some* distance from it, however *great*) there have, at every
> moment since its birth, been large numbers of other living human
> bodies, each of which has, like it, (a) at some time been born, (b)
> continued to exist for some time after birth, (c) been, at every
> moment of its life after birth, either in contact with or not far from
> the surface of the earth; and many of these bodies have already died
> and ceased to exist. But the earth had existed also for many years
> before my body was born; and for many of these years, also, large
> numbers of human bodies had, at every moment, been alive upon it;
> and many of these bodies had died and ceased to exist before it was
> born. (pp. 32–33)

One can almost hear Russell extolling Moore's remarkable ability to
embolden by the sheer power of his personality. "To see him say it no one
could doubt his utter conviction of the truth of what he was saying. We
all felt electrified by him, and as if we had slumbered hitherto and never
realized what fearless intellect pure and unadulterated really means" (p.
127). Moore never lost this power, even when his task was to give an
inventory of those pale truths he knew with certainty.

Mythology

Such certainty about so much does not always characterize Moore's thought. In one of his Apostles papers ("What is belief in God?," February 26, 1897), for example, he offers two criteria of knowledge: "Firstly, we cannot hold a proposition to be known when it conflicts with the logical law of contradiction. . . . All we hold for known must be consistent with itself. . . . Secondly, I propose as a positive criterion [of knowledge] the inconceivability of the opposite or absolute universality. If there is anything so involved in the nature of all propositions that it cannot be denied without asserting it, this also must be held for truth." These ungenerous conditions exhaust Moore's analysis of knowledge on this occasion, and though their implications will not be explored in any detail here it should be reasonably clear that there is not a single proposition on his later list of truisms that meets the criteria he sets forth on this earlier occasion something Moore himself understood. "A proposition that is true by this latter test" (that is, by Moore's second criterion), he writes, "seems to me to be that 'There is'; and by applying our former test we can also see it to be true that 'There is not' is false." Knowledge, it seems, begins and ends here since "if pressed," Moore concedes, "I don't know that I could admit myself to know much more than this." The robust confidence of "Certainty," of "A Defence of Common Sense," of "A Proof of an External World," and of the other essays in which Moore defends the views of the plain man against the philosophers—that robust confidence is not to be found here. But the myth is so much the man that it was perhaps inevitable that we would not so much fail to recall as we would habitually ignore Moore's shadowy past, lost as it was in the glow of his adulation as the patron saint of Common Sense.

G. J. Warnock speaks well for the mythological Moore when he writes the following:

> Among the immediately operative factors contributing to the decay of Absolute Idealism, special notice should be paid to the *character* of Moore. The word may [seem], perhaps, curiously chosen; but it was chosen deliberately. For it was not solely by reason of his intellectual gifts that Moore differed so greatly from his immediate predecessors, or influenced so powerfully his own contemporaries. He was not, and never had the least idea that he was, a much cleverer man than McTaggart, for example, or Bradley. It was in point of

character that he was different, and importantly so. He seems to
have been, in the first place, entirely without any of the motives that
tend to make a metaphysician. He was neither discontented with
nor puzzled by the ordinary beliefs of plain men and plain scientists.
He had no leanings whatever towards paradox and peculiarity of
opinion. He had no particular religious or other cosmic anxieties;
and he seems to have felt that in aesthetics and morality (not, of
course, in moral or aesthetic *philosophy*) all was as well, at least, as
could reasonably be expected. He thus did not hanker for any system
on his own account. But secondly, he had the great force of character
that was necessary to resist the temptation to conform himself with
his environment. He soon overcame, if he ever had, the desire so
natural in any clever young man, to excel in the same line of business
as his admired elders. He did not borrow a modish metaphysical
idiom to make up for, or to conceal, his own real lack of relish
for any such thing. And thirdly, he seems never to have had the
slightest difficulty in causing his views to be taken seriously. It was
always clear that his opinions, however unorthodox or naïve they
may have been or seemed, were not those of one who could safely
be disregarded.

Some of this is true, but most is false. It is true that Moore was not, and
that he did not ever think that he was, "cleverer" than such early contemporaries as McTaggart and F. H. Bradley. And it is also true that people did take his views "seriously . . . , however unorthodox or naïve they
may have been or seemed." But it is not true that "he was entirely without
any of the motives that tend to make a metaphysician," not true that "he
did not borrow a modish metaphysical idiom to make up for, or to conceal, his own real lack of relish for any such thing," not true that "he soon
overcame . . . the desire so natural in any clever young man, to excel in the
same line of business as his admired elders" (if "soon overcame" means
"overcame in a few years"), and not true that "he had no leanings whatever towards paradox and peculiarity of opinion." The later Moore, the
revered defender of Common Sense, may, perhaps, fit this description.
But not the early Moore, not the Moore whose work we can read up to
and including *Principia*. Of that Moore the very opposite of Warnock's
description is the more accurate.

How far Warnock is from capturing the early Moore is illustrated by
Bernard Bosanquet's response to Moore's Second Dissertation, which

earned Moore a Prize Fellowship in 1898. Moore had encountered Bosanquet before and the history of their relationship was not always favorable to Moore's apparent interests. In a February 18, 1896 letter to his mother, Moore relates the following:

> We had a grand meeting of the Moral Science Club last Friday, at which Bernard Bosanquet, of Oxford, who is to be one of my examiners, read a paper. Stout [G. F. Stout, one of Moore's teachers] made me speak, as he has done at all the last meetings, and then supported me. I think I was a good deal in the right. I was the only student who took part.

One cannot help wondering how well Bosanquet took this challenge from Stout's favorite son and what if any lingering effects it may have had. In any event, Bosanquet served as the outside reader of Moore's Second Dissertation, and to say that his estimation of the Dissertation's quality is lukewarm is to overstate the case. Himself an adherent of the view that there is only *one* true individual, the belief in our separate individuality proving to be illusory—himself an adherent, then, of a view that has some claim to the title "paradoxical"—Bosanquet finds Moore's views more than he can rationally tolerate. "The theoretical point of view which the author has adopted," he affirms in his "Report," "appears to me to lie beyond the limit of paradox which is permissible in philosophy." Not that Moore lacks ability or that he fails to display his knowledge and ingenuity. "As a piece of controversial pleading," Bosanquet allows, "his work would do credit to any living author." "But it is my duty to point out," he writes, "that I have never met with a stronger case of the paradox that a man may be exceedingly able and devoted, and yet, for some inexplicable reason, may fail to take up a sound position in his science." Bosanquet frankly acknowledges that his judgment "is based on a difference of philosophical opinion between the author and myself," noting further that "I feel a difficulty in regarding . . . as serious" the paradoxical views Moore sets out.

To help the Board of Electors understand his deep reservations Bosanquet ends his "Report" by indicating how he would react to Moore's work if it had been sent to him for review by *Mind*. "I should have treated it respectfully as a brilliant essay by a very able writer," he declares, "but should have endeavoured to point out that its positive stand-point and consequently its treatment of the subject were hopelessly inadequate." According to Bosanquet, that inadequacy lies, *not* in Moore's repudiation of all metaphysics but in *Moore's* metaphysical position, a position (as we shall see below) richly deserving the name "paradox" and one that shows, contrary to Warnock's assessment, that Moore was no more lacking in those "motives that tend to make a metaphysician" than he was in the desire "to excel in the same line of business as his elders." Moore wanted to do what his elders did, only better.

To challenge Warnock's description of Moore by citing Moore's Second Dissertation and Bosanquet's "Report" might seem unfair since these sources have only recently become accessible to interested readers. But the challenge does not rest only on these sources. To begin with, the greater part of that portion of the Dissertation Bosanquet judges "to lie beyond the limit of paradox which is permissible in philosophy" was published in *Mind* in 1899, under the title "The Nature of Judgment." That paper, together with a number of other papers published by Moore before *Principia* and, indeed, *Principia* itself, show how very deep were Moore's metaphysical aspirations. The inaccuracy of the Moore-myth, in short, can be verified by consulting the public not just the private record of his early philosophical writings. The painful demythologizing process must begin with an examination of Moore's first serious love in philosophy. The object was not the warm promiscuity of Keynes and Strachey. It was the cold inflexibility of metaphysics—idealism in particular.

Such Poor Idealistic System

Moore's unstable affair with idealism makes its first appearance in the fifth paper he presented to the Apostles, "What is matter?," read on May 24, 1895. Near its end he writes that the "chief interest [of the paper] is for myself . . . that it signifies my departure from the materialism which I once thought I could uphold, and sets out (I fear not even plainly) such poor idealistic system as I can construct in its place." The materialism that earlier had attracted Moore never was argued seriously by him in writing. The closest he comes to setting forth his materialist vision of the world is in his first Apostles paper, "What end?" (May 12, 1894). He writes:

> In the beginning was matter and then came the devil. First we have gases, minerals, chemical combinations: of these I have nothing to say. Next we have vegetables, possessed of what is called life, and having needs which must be satisfied else death comes. Of this kind of life I am not speaking in this paper. Next comes the first animal

organism and with it appears God; whom we find to be a dual not a trinal unity. God is life, and his two indivisible components are consciousness and will. His presence is shewn by the movement of the whole of his own body or by internal causes undiscoverable to science. The lowest animal I conceive [has] both will and consciousness, and one thing which puts them into connection is two abstractions—pleasure and pain. Either pleasure or pain or both are always to be predicated in some degree of every state in which consciousness is; and *will*, without which life cannot go on, is always being prompted by desire to avoid pain and seek pleasure.

Whatever attraction Moore may have felt toward the materialist metaphysic soon waned under the force of McTaggart's influence. Moore was a student of McTaggart's during the academic years 1894–1896. Referring in his autobiography to his four tutors in philosophy—Sidgwick, James Ward, G. F. Stout, and McTaggart—Moore makes it clear whose influence in his opinion was the greatest:

But of the four men, whose lectures I attended for the Moral Sciences Tripos, I think I was undoubtedly most influenced by the youngest, McTaggart. This may have been partly due to the fact that I saw a good deal more of him outside the lecture-room, and partly also, perhaps, to the fact that he was nearer to me in age. He produced the impression of being immensely clever and immensely quick in argument; but I think that what influenced me most was his constant insistence on clearness—on trying to give a precise meaning to philosophical expressions, on asking the question "What does this mean?" That he himself, in his own philosophical works, did not by any means always succeed in being perfectly clear, has, I think, been conclusively shown by Broad, in his *Examination of McTaggart's Philosophy*; but how clear he was, as compared to the majority of philosophers! and what immense pains he took to get clear, even though he did not always succeed! (p. 18)

At least part of Moore's opportunity to see McTaggart outside the lecture-room is attributable to the meetings of the Apostles, whose existence Moore himself is careful not to reveal in his autobiography. In acknowledging his debt to McTaggart for the latter's unflagging insistence on clarity, moreover, Moore reveals how far those Apostolic Brothers who thought they were practicing "Moore's method" were from paying proper homage to the "method's" ancestry. The corporate memory of the Apostles evidently was short-lived.

McTaggart's lectures were on Hegel and, as Moore recalls,

> these lectures . . . took place in McTaggart's own rooms at Trinity; but, instead of sitting down at the same table with us, as Ward and Stout did, McTaggart preferred to stand up and walk about while he was lecturing. He, however, like them, did not simply read his lectures, though I think perhaps he followed his notes more closely. I think it can fairly be said that what McTaggart was mainly engaged with was trying to find a precise meaning for Hegel's obscure utterances; and he did succeed in finding many things precise enough to be discussed: his own lectures were eminently clear. But I think most Hegelian scholars would agree that many of the comparatively clear doctrines which he attributed to Hegel were very unlike anything which Hegel could possibly have meant—certainly Hegel never meant anything so precise. After these two years in which I was obliged to read some Hegel, I never thought it worth while to read him again; but McTaggart's own published works I have thought it well worth while to study carefully, and have both written and lectured on particular points in them. (p. 19)

Moore may be correct when he says that he did not read Hegel after 1896. We would risk serious misunderstanding, however, if we supposed that the influence of Hegel's idealism, filtered through the sieve of McTaggart's draconian interpretations, ended when Hegel's books began to gather dust on Moore's shelves.

In that "poor idealistic system" Moore first constructs, however, at age twenty and after less than a year of formal study in philosophy, the "system" is not yet settled enought to mark him as a disciple of any particular thinker. "Search as far as I can," he writes in "What is matter?," "I cannot find anything which is outside myself." Of his own existence he is quite certain, and even has a fair conception of what he is: "I am, then, properly all that I perceive or think or feel, and only the more so in that I try to separate these things from me: since that very act of setting up a part of me as another being shows the greatness of my unifying activity." There is "a manifold in space and another manifold in time" which Moore perceives, but *what* he perceives "immediately" is *in him*: "We know of nothing immediately but our own perceptions, and . . . these are in us."

How, then, can Moore avoid the solipsist's position that the only things he can know to be real are his own perceptions, which are in his mind? How can the case be made for knowledge of a world external to his perceptions and for the reality of other minds in addition to his own? These are the two main questions Moore proceeds to explore.

Noting first that "we do actually believe in the existence of things, which we cannot see to be dependent on us," Moore goes on to express his dissatisfaction with the eighteenth-century Christian idealist Bishop George Berkeley's treatment of this belief:

> Berkeley points out, with admirable clearness, what I have tried to repeat, that we know of nothing immediately but our own perceptions, and that these are in us. Now, there is a fountain in Great Court. The being of that fountain, says he, consists in its being perceived: its esse is percipi. I am willing to admit that there is much truth in this. When I look at the fountain, all the qualities which I see directly, or which its appearance leads me to infer in it, are of a kind that could only be perceptions of my mind. . . . But these perceptions do *not* constitute all the being of the fountain for me. . . . There is certainly something else in the fountain, which makes me say that it is. One thing is the fact that my perception of it belongs to an ordered system: that my perceptions and sensations at this moment are such as I have often observed to have a fixed connection with the perception of the fountain.

Moore illustrates this last point by noting that he has "found, by experience, that upon certain sensations in my legs and body, which may accompany the perception of this yellow-walled room, there may follow the perception of a door being opened, of a going down stairs, of a passing by several buildings and over a street, until at last occurs the perception of the fountain itself." For all Moore actually *perceives*, however, given that his perceptions are "*in him*," the place of the fountain within such a system of perceptions is perfectly compatible with solipsism. For it could be that the perceptions which the solipsist perceives, and which constitute his sole reality, are (sometimes) systematic. Clearly, then, the being of the fountain must involve more than noting that perception of it occupies a regular position within an orderly series or system of perceptions. We are not surprised, then, when Moore quickly adds further meaning to his belief in the fountain's existence: "But I do mean much more than this when I say that the fountain is. . . . I cannot help believing that the fountain is in the Great Court now, though I do not perceive it." Berkeley, when he sought to account for the belief in the present existence of things not now perceived by any human being, hypothesized that an omniscient God must be thinking of them else they would slip out of existence. Moore is not buying: "Nor am I satisfied by the answer that, may be, someone else is perceiving it; for I can perfectly imagine its being there without anyone perceiving it."

Berkeley is not the only one whose views are dismantled. Moore is no less dissatisfied with "the accepted view of philosophy" on this matter, which he attributes to John Stuart Mill. On this view the fountain is "a permanent possibility of sensations": *If* we were to go out through the door, down the stairs, etc., *then* we would have sensations/perceptions of the fountain. Moore objects:

> But this existence, again, can only be understood either as the validity of the law that perceptions will recur in a certain order, which is no real existence at all but only an abstraction from the content of our minds; or else possibility must mean "condition" for possibility, that is, some real existence, which, by coming into certain relations with us, causes our perceptions, but is itself quite different from the content of those perceptions.

Moore's objection to Mill, then, is that Mill *either* adds nothing new to the view that our sensations tend to follow one another in an orderly fashion, in which case his view is idle, *or* he does add something new, implying that the fountain, for example, *is* a "real existence" distinct from our perceptions of it, but fails to explain *what* it is or even what it is like, in which case his view is futile.

At this juncture one would naturally expect that Moore would offer his own way out of the solipsist's trap he seems to have set for himself. Evidently he does think he has managed to escape since he writes later that "the course of my discussion has led me to see a probability that other things, of whose dependence on myself I am not conscious, do exist." However, when we inquire into the grounds of this "probability," we are likely to be disappointed. For this probability rests on the fact that

Moore *cannot help believing in* the reality of objects that exist independently of his awareness: "the order of my perceptions and the combining power of the percipient have *somehow forced upon me* the belief" in such "independently existing objects" (emphasis added); more, they have combined to force him to believe that "there persists through time an infinite ordered universe, independent of my perception of it, and made up of qualities, which I only know as capable to exist within a mind—namely—the qualities which I perceive."

This belief of Moore's is an example of what he will later call a psychologically necessary belief (see Chapter 2, pages 44–45). We do not choose to have such beliefs; they are forced upon us; we cannot choose not to believe them. But whereas Moore was later to maintain that the psychological necessity of a belief is no evidence for its actual or probable truth, the younger Moore is not as logically diligent. One feels that he has not so much met the solipsist's challenge as avoided it.

In any event Moore understands the need to say something about what such objects as fountains are, assuming they are something:

> Of the nature of this that is I have not much to say. It cannot be matter, in the sense of something extended in space, since extension in space is only in my mind. It cannot be a mere possibility of sensation, since possibility is an abstract term. . . . It is certainly something which is able to be perceived by me, but is not always so perceived: and this something is not explained by Berkeley's crude notion, that it is the perception of an infinite mind, external to my own.

The reality of the fountain, it would appear, is a something-Moore-knows-not-what even while it is true that he knows, or thinks he knows, a few things it is not. Most significantly, it is not matter, a denial we find in the passage just quoted, which is why the "system" Moore traces here has claim to the title "idealistic." Moore exists, in this system, as a unifying mind. And things exist. But matter does not. Even Moore's body appears to be neither more nor less than "a thing composed of sensible qualities similar to those which constitute my other perceptions," though, as Moore notes, "if my probable argument for the real existence of something able to be so perceived by me is at all valid, there must be some real existence corresponding to the perceptions which constitute it [i.e., Moore's body]; since I cannot help believing that it too is permanent."

In addition to his mind and body, his perceptions, and whatever it is that "corresponds" to the latter, Moore also recognizes the reality of other minds. He supports his belief in their existence by means of an argument from analogy. Upon perceiving the bodies of others, Moore perceives "signs, such as I am conscious of producing in my body and which are directly connected by will with my thought that is with myself, whose existence, actually such as I know it, I cannot doubt. And I have no reason for doubting that these signs may be produced by a self similar to my own." That self, Moore proceeds to explain, because it is distinct from the body, could survive the body's death:

> All this world of colours and sounds, figures and motions is, we have seen, only the manifold, which it, this spirit, unifies. Now there comes a time when it ceases to declare itself to other similar spirits through these appearances. It is said to die, because that body disappears through which it makes these communications and through which in turn it receives the perceptions which declare to it the existence of other spirits and of that other unknown existence. But this fact is no proof that it itself ceases to exist. We have no reason for thinking that every being need declare itself through our perceptions: no being is in space and therefore we need not look for a place in space wherein this disembodied spirit may be. It may still exist, though we with our forms of perception can get no knowledge of it.

Though Moore does not here affirm belief in immortality, and notwithstanding the fact that he subsequently became highly critical of philosophical arguments in its support, this passage together with his request, at the end of this paper, for further discussion of the idea of immortality, show that his interest in this matter, like his interest in God's existence, did not quite "fall away" as completely as his autobiography might lead one to suppose.

· The significance of "What is matter?" clearly does not lie in the merits of its "poor idealistic system." It lies, rather, in the first place, in the role it can play in helping us take the measure of Moore's philosophical development. Idealistic in its brusque denial of the reality of matter, it is nonetheless an idealism closer to the one idealist explicitly criticized—namely, Berkeley—than it is to Hegel's, Bradley's, or McTaggart's. As in Berkeley's work, there is in it no hint that the world we perceive is in any way an inferior world, no intimation that the world available to our senses is (mere) Appearance, the (true) Reality forever concealed from our sight and touch, accessible only to our reason. The Moore of "What is matter?" is a young man who stumbles into his "idealistic system," not because he wishes to repudiate the ordinary world of tables and chairs but because he wants to understand how he can know what he thinks he does know about that world—for example, that there is a fountain in Great Court or that other people have a mental life in fundamental respects like his own. The "system" Moore offers in reply to these questions thus is more epistemologically than metaphysically motivated. It is offered as a reply to questions about human knowledge; it is not constructed independently of such concerns by appeal to some abstract ontological principle. The details of the metaphysic, one might say, remain to be worked out *in the light of* how epistemological questions, questions about the possibility and validity of human knowledge, are answered. In this respect "What is matter?" displays a tendency in Moore's approach to philosophical problems that remains more or less constant throughout his life, a tendency that will have especially important implications for his moral philosophy. As his conception of the Science of Morals grows clearer, he will see its principal task to be that of illuminating how it is possible to know what he usually assumes we know about good and evil, right and wrong, duty and obligation. Moore's metaphysic of morals is built on the sometimes insecure ground of his convictions about moral knowledge.

"What is matter?" also is significant because it shows how fully Moore himself at one time accepted a position he was later to attack with acid vehemence. "We know of nothing immediately but our own perceptions," he writes, adding: "and . . . these are in us." From that bland starting point solipsism is all but impossible to avoid. Moore manages to avoid it in this paper only by having expedient recourse to his psychological inability to doubt that a world exists beyond and independently of his perceptions. Concomitant with his dismissing appeals to psychological necessity as constituting any evidence of a belief's truth (as in "The Value of Religion"), Moore abandons the starting point that prompted this appeal in the present case. In his 1904 paper, "Kant's Idealism," for example, we find that he now thinks that "certain *objects* of sensation do really exist in a real space and really are causes and effects of other things. . . . Colours and sounds are *not* sensations; . . . space and time are *not* forms of sense. . . . All these things are . . . things *of* which we are conscious; they are in no sense parts of consciousness." We cannot be far from wrong in assuming that among the reasons Moore had for abandoning his earlier, Berkeleian idealism is his coming to believe that its starting point leads one to a solipsistic dead end.

The True Kantian

Moore's attraction to idealism intensified during the years 1896–1897, while he worked on and submitted his First Dissertation in the hopes of receiving a Prize Fellowship. He read part of this work before the Aristotelian Society in November 1897, later publishing it as "Freedom" in *Mind* in 1898. The nature and direction of his growing interest is intimated by his opening remarks in that essay. Stating that he intends to concentrate on Kant's notion of Freedom, Moore adds that he has "chosen to deal with him at such length mainly because I think that reference to the views of the philosopher, with whom you are most in agreement, is often the clearest way of explaining your own view" (p. 179). What Moore's own view is remains to be explained, as does the profound but little noted influence Kant's thought had on Moore's moral philosophy. A hint of that influence is suggested by the view that Moore sees himself as out-Kanting Kant—as setting out, that is, a view of Freedom that is true to the Kantian philosophy. In Moore's view Kant was not Kantian enough.

Though Moore's differences with Kant are real, there are two points of fundamental agreement that help make these differences more intelligible. The first is their mutual rejection of empiricism. That view, as classically expressed by John Locke, holds that the human mind is a *tabula rasa* at the time of our birth. It is only as we begin to experience the world through sensation that we come to know anything about it, and what we first come to know is what the world imprints upon our mind through sensation. We are at birth passive recipients of data about a world external to and independent of our internal mental life, and all of our knowledge about this world, both at the levels of the most naïve common sense and the most sophisticated science, is based on the ideas or sense impressions we first passively receive in our sense perceptions and which we assume "copy" or "represent" external reality.

Kant, with his so-called "Copernican revolution," denies this model of the origin and nature of human knowledge. The human mind is not an empty receptacle to be filled with data forced upon it from without. On the contrary, it is highly structured from within, bringing to experience a set of organizational categories that instead of being generated out of the data of sense experience actually serve to determine the very nature of what we perceive. Kant calls these categories the pure categories of the human understanding. They are, he says, *a priori*, meaning that they are not based on or formed out of the contents of our experience. Included in the set of categories are substance and attribute, which may be used to illustrate the difference between Kant's theory of human knowledge (his epistemology) and that of an empiricist such as Locke.

According to the empiricist we must learn that the various ideas of color and shape we perceive when we look at a chair, for example, represent the properties of the same object: that chair. In other words, we must construct the notion that a particular chair is a unity of various properties out of our different, distinct perceptions of our ideas of these different, distinct properties. Kant views the situation in a dramatically different way. In order for us even to have the sort of experience we have when we perceive a chair, we must bring to that experience the categories of substance and attribute. The chair *for us* is perceived as a unified object because that is how our minds structure the contents of our perceptions. Rather than our different, distinct perceptions of the chair's several properties generating the idea that one and the same object (that chair) has those properties, our minds are so constituted that we cannot perceive the chair except as the union of these properties. Just as Copernicus brought a revolution to our thinking about the place of the earth in the orbits of the planets, theorizing that the earth revolves around the sun, not vice versa, so Kant would have us enter into an analogous revolution in our thought about the mind's role in the acquisition of knowledge. Rather than the structure of the mind being the product of experience, experience itself is structured by the mind.

At the time of the publication of "Freedom" Moore seems fully to accept the main outlines of Kant's epistemology. He applauds Kant for "the enormous services which he did to epistemology" (p. 199), adding that "he supplies, as seems to me, more materials for a true view than any one else, and those, too, in a wonderfully forward state of preparation" (p. 200). If in Moore's view Kant's fault lay in his failure to abide by the major principles of his revolutionary philosophy, his great merit was to be found in discovering and systematizing those principles in the first place. At least that is the opinion of Moore as late as November 1897. That in time Moore outgrew these principles is a crucial development in his own philosophical growth. But even as he rejects the letter of Kant's philosophy, much of the spirit remains. Moore, like Kant before him, will stead-fastly repudiate the empiricist epistemology.

At the time of "Freedom" Moore is no less influenced by Kant on a second, related matter. Essential to Kant's epistemology is the thesis that the structure of our experience is a function of the *a priori* categories of the understanding. What we perceive, therefore, is always the world as it appears to us through the mediating filter of the categories. In the nature of the case we never do and never can perceive the world apart from and independent of the organizational structure of our minds. What things are *in themselves*, as distinct from how they appear to us, must forever remain a mystery. All that we can know is that there must be a thing-in-itself (a *Ding an sich*) that serves as the ground or basis of its appearances to us, and that this *Ding an sich*, unlike its appearances, transcends the temporal and spatial dimensions of the world of appearances. In addition to the world as we perceive it in space and time, which Kant regularly calls the phenomenal world, or Appearance, there is a second, more fundamental world, called the noumenal world by Kant, or Reality. It is this two-tiered conception of existence—itself, ironically enough, part of the standard nomenclature of the Apostles—that Moore accepts with enthusiasm both in "Freedom" and throughout the First Dissertation. The world of Ap-pearances, he writes in true Kantian fashion, includes "matter as treated in Physics and mind as treated in Psychology" (p. 182). The objects and processes studied in both sciences, physical in the former case and psychi-cal in the latter, are *not fundamentally real*. Both "may not be considered as fundamentally real," Moore explains, "because [they are] inconceivable except as taking place in time" (p. 202). And the unreality of Time, that "perfectly monstrous proposition" abjured by Moore in 1942, is here endorsed with no lack of fervor:

> That time itself cannot be conceived to be fundamentally real is always admitted by Kant himself, and indeed he has attempted a proof of it. How far his proof is satisfactory, and whether, if unsatis-factory, any other proof is forthcoming, is too large a question to be fully discussed here. I can only state that the arguments by which Mr. Bradley has endeavoured to prove the unreality of Time appear to me perfectly conclusive. (p. 202)

Like a contagious disease Time's unreality infects the ontological status of everything it touches. Physical and psychical processes are not immune. Both physics and psychology are sciences of Appearances, not Reality.

It remains for the science of philosophy, metaphysics and epistemology in particular, to determine, as far as this is possible, what Reality is. And is not.

This Kantian theory of Appearance and Reality has implications both clear and explosive for that "poor idealistic system" Moore offered in "What is matter?" In that paper Moore claimed that "we know nothing immediately but our own perceptions, and . . . these are in us." Because these perceptions themselves occur in time they can only be categorized as Appearances, a finding in perfect harmony with Kant's teaching but not with Berkeley's, and one that leaves unresolved the problem solipsism poses for Moore's earlier position. Moore must have been aware of this, especially since, as we shall shortly see, his major criticism of Kant is that he (Kant) looks to Appearance for a confirmation of Reality, a move that is absolutely forbidden by Kant's principles. The idealism we find Moore endorsing in "Freedom" and throughout the First Dissertation is a much different variety from what we find in "What is matter?" In that earlier paper he was a closet Berkleyeian. In the latter he is an enthusiastic Bradleian.

At this point Moore does not look back to his own "poor idealistic system" nor yet ahead to the major criticisms of idealism he will develop in his Second Dissertation. Instead he focuses his attention on Kant's view of Freedom or, in any event, what he takes to be Kant's view. Moore endeavors to show that Kant is thoroughly confused about what Freedom is, about how its existence can be confirmed, and about what its relation to human volition is. All this confusion, moreover, is attributable to Kant's failure to be consistent with his own principles. Though the details of the argument are more than a little esoteric, the main outlines are reasonably clear.

Kant views the world of Appearances—of tables and chairs, perceptions and emotions—as wholly deterministic. Every event that occurs in this, the phenomenal world, has a cause, and every such event, he believes, occurs as the result of the operation of some natural law. It is the task of the empirical sciences, physics and psychology in particular, to discover these laws. As Kant conceives Freedom, there is no place for it within a wholly deterministic universe. If every event has a cause, then our choices, conceived as events, must have causes also; and if every event falls under the provenance of some natural law, then the same must be true of our choices. Thus, just as falling objects are not at liberty to fall or not to fall but are, rather, controlled by the power of the law of gravity, so it is that our choices would likewise be controlled by the operative physical or psychological laws. Within a wholly deterministic universe we are no more at liberty to choose to do one thing rather than another than a falling object is at liberty to decide whether to fall or rise. Viewed in this light, Freedom must be seen as a *contra-causal* power. That is, if there is such a thing as Freedom, it must be a power to choose which is not itself controlled by causal laws. It must, so to speak, stand outside the world of causal determinism, free of the control of natural laws. Given the Kantian categories, this Freedom must be Transcendental, a manifestation of the noumenal, not the phenomenal world.

Moore has no quarrel with the Transcendental part of Kant's position. He writes approvingly that "Transcendental Freedom is the relation in which the world as it really stands to events as we know them. It is the relation of Reality to Appearance" (p. 183). Where Moore parts company with Kant concerns, in the first place, the latter's attempt, according to Moore, to offer an empirical confirmation of the reality of Transcendental Freedom. Such a confirmation, based on considerations about what we are aware of in human volition, clearly is ill-starred given Kant's principles, since human volition *as it appears to us* occurs in time and thus lacks the kind of ultimate reality Transcendental Freedom, if it exists, must possess. By attempting an empirical proof of Transcendental Freedom, Moore asserts, "Kant betrays the too psychological standpoint above which he seems never to have completely risen in treating epistemological questions" (p. 199). Reality neither is nor can be the object of experience, neither 'outer' experience [e.g., sights and sounds] nor 'inner' experience [e.g., introspection or volition]. Whether Kant in fact attempts a confirmation of the sort Moore attributes to him must be left for Kantian scholars to decide. What is of interest here is a second correction Moore makes to Kant's position, as Moore understands this.

This concerns Kant's apparent intention to limit Transcendental Freedom only to rational beings. Now, it is true that Kant conceives of Freedom as being logically presupposed by morality; without Freedom morality is impossible. We cannot be morally obligated to do something if we lack the power to decide between doing it or not doing it. For Kant the only individuals who have this power, and thus the only ones who have moral obligations, are rational beings. Moore rejects this limitation of the range of Transcendental Freedom. *Every* appearance, not simply human volitions, requires some noumenal ground. As Moore expresses this point, "for every 'appearance' we must suppose an intelligible ground (the Ding an Sich)" (p. 203). In the case of human volition that ground is identified by Kant as Transcendental Freedom. Following Bradley, Moore contends that Kant should have said the same thing about the ground of *every* appearance: *all* are "equally . . . results of 'transcendental freedom'" (p. 204). Indeed, *everything* that happens in the world of Appearances, according to Moore, is the logically necessary result of the operations of Reality. Because the latter transcends our powers of perception, however, we are unable to form a clear conception of the details of how this exchange between the two worlds occurs. "The relation of reality to appearance, or the inter-relation of realities, must be conceived as that of logical necessity," he writes, "changed (in a way which we cannot understand, because we have no intelligible intuition) by the fact that it there holds between things" (that is, between things rather than between statements or propositions) (p. 202). For every event that occurs in the phenomenal world, then, it is true that (*a*) it has a phenomenal cause and occurs in accordance with a law of nature, such as those discoverable by physics or psychology, and that (*b*) it has a Transcendental ground, identifiable as Transcendental Freedom, and occurs as a matter of logical necessity because of the expression of this Transcendental Reality. Viewed in this light, Moore contends, one may infer that Transcendental Freedom has "not even so much connexion with volition as to deserve the name of 'Will'" (p. 204). For "Transcendental Freedom is the relation in which the world as it really is stands to events as we know them." Transcendental Freedom is neither more nor less than "the relation of Reality to Appearance" (p. 183).

Moore concludes "Freedom" on a tantalizing note, remarking that once Kant's notion of Freedom is seen to have no essential connection with volition we can then recognize "clearly the problem which remains for Kantian Ethics—how to establish a valid connexion between the notion of Transcendental Freedom and that of End or Good" (p. 204). Kant had thought the connection was to be found in the Good Will. Because he thinks that Kant is untrue to his own philosophy when he limits Freedom to Volition, Moore believes the essential missing link must be found elsewhere. Readers of "Freedom" would have been justified in wondering where that is. Those who have read the entire First Dissertation, from which "Freedom" was extracted, can discover where Moore locates it. His remarkable discovery remains to be explained.

The Missing Link

In the First Dissertation Moore characterizes Ethics as a "science," meaning that it is or, in any event, aspires to be a systematic body of knowledge. The essential task of the moral or ethical philosopher is to systematize our moral knowledge. "The direct aim of Ethics is to know . . . and not to do" the good, Moore contends, adding that, properly conceived, Ethics is "pure theory and [so] subordinate to the general conditions of knowledge." What makes Ethics different than other sciences is not the systematization it seeks but *what* is systematized. Fundamentally considered the object of this science is Good,* where by Good we understand an "abstract notion" which, like "Being," "is always identical with itself and different from every other predicate." We can no more say what Being is by saying what things exist than we can say what Good is by saying what things are good. This "abstract notion," Good—the predicate which attaches to all (and only) those things that are good in themselves, or that are ends in themselves—this "abstract notion" must be understood transcendentally, Moore thinks, if Ethics is to succeed in the task of systematizing our knowledge of good and evil. While there may well be things which exist in space and time that are good, the predicate itself— Good—does not and cannot exist in the phenomenal world. "There is a real object or relation corresponding to" our notion of goodness, Moore claims, but that "object or relation," though real, though it has being, is not itself a piece of furniture in the world of Appearance. Good is not in space and time, and the notion Good "must have some meaning of its own, apart from any reference to empirical concepts." This is why there is a "fallacy involved in all empirical definitions" of Good. Like Being, Good cannot be *identified* with anything empirical, with anything that exists in time. Moreover, since what the word 'good' refers to, when used in its transcendental sense, is necessarily an "object or relation" that is not empirical, it follows, Moore argues, that propositions declaring that one or another thing is good cannot be empirically verified. Such propositions are "not of the nature of empirical or scientific propositions, which uniformly include some particular phenomenon in a larger class—but a class of *phenomena* only: e.g. when we say man is an animal, where the two

---

*Whenever Moore's meaning makes it clear that he is referring to an abstract notion (or an abstract concept, idea, or object) by the word 'good,' the referent of the word will be indicated by capitalizing the word thus: Good. This same device will be used in similar cases. For example, when he refers to an abstract notion (concept, idea, or object) by the word 'red,' this will be indicated by capitalizing the word thus: Red. If it is the abstract notion referred to by the word 'rose,' this will be indicated by capitalizing the word thus: Rose. And so on. A fuller explanation of the logic of this device is given in the following chapter.

notions conjoined are both of them defined by directly given empirical characteristics." Because the "object or relation," Good, is a Transcendental, not a phenomenal, object or relation, we cannot taste or smell, see or feel, or in any other way have Good as an object of our sensory experience. Good must be grasped by the mind, not the senses.

Convinced as he is of the Transcendental status of Good, the reasons for Moore's attraction to Kant's philosophy in general and to his moral philosophy in particular should be clearer. From the former he takes the basis for distinguishing between Appearance and Reality, while from the latter he secures much guidance for his own attempt "to give a 'transcendental' meaning to [G]ood." For "it is Kant," Moore declares, "who seems most clearly to have recognised" the transcendental character of goodness (that is, Good), and to have done more than any other philosopher "towards a systematic exploration of" its nature. Up to Moore, that is. For while he acknowledges Kant's many accomplishments and the debts he owes to him, Moore believes that Kant wanders off the Transcendental path when he argues that the supreme principle of morality must make essential reference to the will of rational beings, an error that in turn is traceable to Kant's mistakenly assuming, on Moore's view, that Transcendental Freedom is essentially restricted to the will of such beings. As soon as we recognize that this latter assumption is erroneous, we should see that we have no good reason to accept the former one either. Or so Moore implies.

Mistaken on these matters, Kant is nonetheless correct, according to Moore, when he maintains that the "Moral Law" must be universal and objective. But these conditions can be met, Moore insists, without requiring that the Law take the form of a command. The "primary form [of the Moral Law] is 'This is good' or 'this is an end-in-itself' or 'this ought to be'; the command, 'do this' is no more than a corollary from such a judgment. It is a 'law', because such a judgment, if true at all, expresses a universal truth." And it is objective because what is good in itself is so apart from human judgment. Things are good (if they are) whether we think so or not.

For Moore, then, the fundamental principle of Ethics is propositional in character. "That principle amounts merely to this, that there is an objective 'end,' something which ought unconditionally to be, an absolute good." And the proposition which declares what this is, having no essential reference to the wills of rational beings, leads Moore to "give up the precise connection, which Kant found, between ethics and [the] freedom [of the will]." Thus arises the question Moore poses but does not answer at the end of the article "Freedom": "How to establish a valid connexion between the notion of Transcendental Freedom and that of End or Good." The two, Moore insists in the First Dissertation, "must be somehow connected. Only the connexion must be sought directly, discarding the irrelevancies which made the transition seem easier to Kant." Moore's own bold attempt to say what the missing link is takes the following form:

> We have a supersensible reality, which Kant calls 'free', and we have a notion 'good', which bases Ethics, and the problem is, taking them as they stand, reduced to their simplest terms, to justify their connection. The connection which it is desired to establish is this: That, that which is ultimately real, appearing to us as the reason of whatever happens, is also necessarily 'good', and alone absolutely good . . . [from which] . . . we should be entitled to declare that the world is 'good'.

Elaborating on this theme later in the Dissertation, Moore squarely faces the apparent incomprehensibility of evil, given the thesis that the world is good:

> For that which is nothing but good does not seem to supply a reason for the existence of evil. We have here the result that since the intelligible character [that is, the noumenal *Ding an sich*] is necessarily good, and also the sole reason of everything that happens, everything that happens is necessarily good.

Thus do we have the true antimony of practical reason: "[The above result] seems to conflict with the actual fact that some things are evil. They can be evil [however] only in so far as Freedom is their reason; and yet freedom is unable to supply a reason for evil."

Moore's proposed solution of this dilemma shows him at his Kantian best. "The solution," he argues,

> lies in the fact that the objects of experience are not Things-in-Themselves; and hence that though the Thing-in-Itself, i.e. the Free Cause, cannot be both good and bad, yet when the character of goodness, which properly applies to it only, is transferred, as it must be, to those things of which it is the reason, it is found equally

necessary both to affirm and to deny it of them. Evil thus appears to be absolute, only when appearances are taken to be real.

Evil, in short, is unreal. For nothing can *be* at all save that which is good — which, however, does not entail that everything is equally good. "Appearance," Moore contends, "may partake more or less of Reality" and thus of Good.

His Own Views?

Edward Caird, the distinguished Kantian scholar, served as the outside reader of Moore's First Dissertation. In his lengthy critical remarks (twenty-one handwritten pages) he praises Moore for his "power of following out his ideas to their ultimate results," says that Moore has "shown himself to be a thinker of no ordinary power," and—somewhat ambiguously—adds that "he has established his claim to any reward that is given for such work." He does lament, however, Moore's lack of clarity in general and in particular the frequent difficulty he encountered in deciding "whether Mr. Moore is interpreting Kant, or expressing his own views." This last worry of Caird's is one any reader of the First Dissertation must share. Moore himself certainly seems to be enamored of the positions sketched in the preceding. At the same time he does remark in one place that the view most recently discussed—namely, that everything that exists is good and is so necessarily—"whether true or not, is, I think, a fair deduction from Kant's connection of Freedom with Ethics." If we were to assume that Moore would not be content with a view that *may or may not be true*, then the "deduction" he offers, summarized in the previous section, should be read as a summary of his interpretation of Kant's views, not as a statement of a position to which he himself would subscribe. On the other hand, it is difficult to see how Moore himself could avoid the position in question since he does accept (*a*) the fundamental distinction, understood in Kantian terms, between Appearance and Reality, (*b*) the view that Reality, in its guise as Transcendental Freedom, expresses itself in each and every appearance, not only through the 'free' will of rational beings, and (*c*) the identification of Reality with what is ultimately good. Given this much, Moore himself seems committed to the position he ascribes to Kant—namely, that everything that is, is good. It cannot be far from wrong, then, to read Moore as offering more than an impartial interpretation of Kant's thought. The major claims he makes in the First Dissertation, concerning the nature both of Reality and of Good, express his own considered views at that time.

Promise, Not Performance

The truth of these views is not our concern. What is, is their relative adequacy given the criteria we are using to interpret Moore's efforts to find a philosophically adequate ethical theory, one to fill the void created by his rejection of the theistically grounded ethic of his youth. That alternative, to be viewed as adequate by Moore, must meet the criteria set forth near the end of Chapter 2. For reasons now to be advanced the ethical position we find in the First Dissertation arguably meets some but not all of them.

To be adequate an ethical theory—and here and throughout "ethical theory" is being used to cover the metaphysical and epistemological presuppositions of an ethical system—must assure both the objectivity of intrinsic goodness and the universality of judgments of the form 'This is good-in-itself.' The metaphysical basis of the ethical theory advanced in the First Dissertation seems to satisfy both these criteria. By severing the ties that bind Transcendental Freedom to the wills of rational beings, Moore certainly offers a theory that liberates what is good-in-itself from any essential connection with human volition, thereby removing one possible obstacle to assuring the objectivity of intrinsic value. And by interpreting intrinsic value transcendentally he provides, at one stroke, a metaphysical basis for the universality of such judgments: Once good, always good. (And what *is* good certainly is so independently of human thought or awareness.) Moreover, the third criterion of adequacy set out earlier— namely, that there are *natural* goods, or goods *in the world*—this criterion, too, arguably is met by the ethical theory offered in the First Dissertation. Indeed, since *every* expression of Reality in Appearance is the expression of what is good, *every* natural object is good to one degree or another. So far, perhaps, so good.

The First Dissertation's ethical theory fares less well when tested against the remaining criteria of adequacy. Not only must an adequate theory make the existence of natural goods intelligible; it must also explain the intelligibility of ideals, understood as nonexistent but conceivable states of affairs having intrinsic value, states of affairs which, given their status as ideals, must be *better* than some actually existing states of affairs. It is unclear whether or, if so, how the ethical theory offered by Moore in the First Dissertation could satisfy this requirement. If, as his theory seems to imply, this is the best of all *possible* worlds, it must be obscure how it *could* be any better. But that things *could* be better than the way things actually are is precisely what is embedded in the concept of ideals. So long as we aspire to have a theory that will make sense of this concept, the ethical theory we find in the First Dissertation must ultimately disappoint not only us but Moore as well.

Equally if not more unsatisfactory is the assessment of the First Dissertation against the requirements of the conduct criterion. An adequate ethical theory must offer both a standard for judging the morality of our acts and guidance concerning how this standard should be used. Whatever else might be said about it, any theory that entails that nothing that we do is or can be any better—or any worse—than anything else we might have done fails to satisfy the intent of the conduct criterion. Yet this appears to be the unhappy fate of the theory Moore offers in the First Dissertation. If this *is* the best of all possible worlds, then it follows that there is nothing that we could possibly do to make it any better. There is no "standard" of right conduct and no need for guidance regarding how to apply it. Along with the illusoriness of natural evil the First Dissertation also entails the unreality of moral evil: *Whatever* is, is good. Noumenal Reality cannot have it any other way. Moore in time will.

An adequate ethical theory must also offer an intelligible method on which we may rely in approaching questions of intrinsic value. Such a theory must answer the questions, How may I rationally decide what things are good and, among those things that are, how may I rationally decide which of them are better than others? The First Dissertation fails to offer such a method. True, that work implies that everything we encounter in the world of Appearance, given its status as an expression of what is absolutely good, is itself good to one degree or another. So we do know *what* things are good—namely, everything. But what in the nature of the case we cannot know is *how good* different things are. To know that would require our knowing the degree to which different things express or embody their metaphysical ground—the Ding an sich. And that is something we not only do not, it is something we cannot, know. The First Dissertation, therefore, offers no intelligible method for rationally deciding what things are better-in-themselves than others. To the extent that for Moore an ethical theory's adequacy depends on its offering such a basis, to that extent the ethical theory we find in the First Dissertation must be judged inadequate.

This is a judgment presumably shared by both Caird, in his capacity as outside reader, and Sidgwick, who represented the philosophy faculty on the Fellowship Electors. Caird is especially distressed by the lack of clarity in Moore's writing: "Mr. Moore has not sufficiently studied how to be clear to those who are not looking at things at his precise angle; he is extremely difficult to understand. It has cost me much trouble to do so, and I do not think the fault is entirely mine." A lack of clarity was to plague Moore throughout his student years at Cambridge; he had lost an earlier scholarship competition, in 1893, when, he relates in a letter to his mother, one of the examiners "complained, as usual, of my English style." As early as 1883, when Moore was only ten, his brother Tom (later the poet Sturge Moore) had criticized the writing Moore was doing for the *Boomerang*, the record of their club. Tom, who was then thirteen, writes (the punctuation is in the original): "I wish to say that I would like to see better writing by G. E. Moore, at present it is most disgraceful, he has the least to write and does the worst." That clinical, plodding, repetitious, unadorned, humorless but eminently clear prose style we have come to regard as synonymous with Moore's name clearly was an acquired, not a natural skill.

Worse than Moore's style and lack of clarity, in Caird's view, is his Kantian scholarship. Or lack of it. "Kant," he protests, "is read so much through the eyes of Bradley and Lotze." Sidgwick, too, is less than enthusiastic. While allowing that "the Dissertation seems to me of a high order: quite first-rate in respect of critical acumen and dialectical vigour, and independence of thought," he concludes by saying that "on the whole, the merit of [the final] part of his work seems to me to lie in promise rather than performance: but I judge it to be very promising." In this Sidgwick displayed a prescience about Moore's future that Moore himself is unlikely to have equalled in his wildest dreams. Though Moore's first attempt to secure a Prize Fellowship was unsuccessful, he would not be a friend of failure for long.

Though Moore was never one to feel satisfied with his work, his sense of dissatisfaction with his First Dissertation was especially acute. "I shall indeed be relieved when I have given up my dissertation and got away from here," he writes to his mother on August 26, 1897. "It is not so much that I have overworked, but rather that it is difficult to force myself to work as much as the approach of the necessary end seems to demand. It is a constant preoccupation that there is more to do than would take up all my time, and a temptation to do less than could be done, because all that should, cannot." The disorganized state of the First Dissertation and the hurried pace of the critical Appendix on Sidgwick's hedonism are the products of one who has given in to the "temptation to do less." In the Second Dissertation he would do more.

A Window in the Roof

Moore lectured on certainty at a number of different universities during his years in America. The catalogue of bland propositions with which "Certainty" begins, listed at the outset of the present chapter, is as far removed from the First Dissertation's enraptured speculations about the Ding an sich as common sense is from Hegel. Unless those in his audience had somehow escaped the pervasive mythology about Moore's philosophical development they would never have supposed that he had idealistic skeletons in his closet. And few did escape this mythology. Moore, the story had it, was born with a defense of common sense in his mouth.

But all was not well for this defense. There was much we could be certain of, Moore supposed; the problem was to understand certainty itself—to give an analysis of the concept. On this score there was much to be uncertain about. Ward was right: "Denken ist schwer!" But at least there was a solid base of certain knowledge from which to begin.

Or was there?

Included in Moore's tour of American university campuses was a visit to the University of Michigan in Ann Arbor. In his *Commonplace Book* he relates (p. 193) that during his lecture he had pointed to the ceiling and declared, by way of illustrating what he knew with certainty, "There is a window in the roof." To emphasize the importance he attached to this particular example, he had then declared "that if I didn't know this, when I said it, I never know anything of the kind" (p. 193). The entire weight of the common sense view of the world hung by the thread of this one example.

It could not have come as good news to Moore, therefore, to learn that there was no window in the roof. "What looked like a window," he was informed later, "merely covered an opaque portion of the dome" (p. 193) Ever resourceful in his convictions concerning what he knew with certainty, Moore was troubled by the absence of a window but not dissuaded from his cause. In his *Commonplace Book* we find the following record of his later musings on this matter.

> When I said "There's a window" I certainly *thought* there was; but did I *feel* sure there was? or did I *think* it was certain there was?

> When I said that other thing *later*, I can be said to have thought *then*
> that it was certain there was. But when I said "There's a window" I
> don't think I did feel sure—if anyone had said at once "that's not a
> window", I should have been surprised . . . but I shouldn't have
> refused to admit I was mistaken: I shouldn't have asserted "I feel
> sure there is". But does this prove I didn't feel sure? No: how about
> Cook Wilson's slap on the back? Here the man would have said "I
> *felt* sure it was my friend"; but I doubt if I should have said here, I
> felt sure it was a window: only, I *thought* it was. (p. 193)

Somehow, in short, the common sense view of the world remains intact.
Though the fabric of certainties is pulled, it does not tear. Once enthroned
as the Defender of Common Sense, Moore was forever reluctant to give
up his seat.

But the conversion to the gospel of common sense did not come without a struggle. In the First Dissertation "the common point of view," the
view that "takes the world of experience as ultimately real," is denounced
as lacking the stuff of which Truth and certainty are made. In that work,
and at that time, it mattered little if there was a window in the roof. Even
if there was, windows and roofs were then viewed as tarnished Appearances, not Reality. This was a most uncommon sense of the nature of
things that Moore was still some years from giving up, one that was light
years away from providing a stable philosophical basis for the *this*—
worldly values that are inseparable from Bloomsbury.

4

A Cambridge Platonist

The Perpetual Hopefulness of His Inquiry

"Yesterday I finished my investigations," the letter begins, "all except Bridport." These investigations, it continues,

> [are] not disagreeable when the subjects of inquiry live in well-situated country houses and ask one to lunch; one feels, in fact, that one is making the best of two worlds. But when (as on Wednesday) one travels from 7 A.M. to 10 P.M. in abnormal heat, on the day of the fair in the neighborhood, on railways where the regular practice is to stuff the (heated) 3rd-class passengers into 2nd-class carriages, the case is altered, and one has to remind oneself of the sacrifices made by other scientific investigators in the cause of truth. (p. 388)

His sacrifices were too few, he thought. The demands of his regular work seemed always to come before his scientific research, even while he felt that his research "*ought* to be my work more than it is. One effect of growing older (he is forty-six at the time) is that I cannot really give my mind to more than one thing at once" (p. 387). Convinced that the results of his research promise to be "profoundly more important to mankind" in comparison to "sound views on the evolution of political ideas," which are "a luxury easily dispensed with, I am," he confesses, "ashamed to find how much more interested I am in the latter than in the former" (p. 387). Fifteen hours on a crowded, stuffy train was not enough, not even when multiplied by days and months of similar sacrifices for the cause of truth. Henry Sidgwick was a man never easy on himself.

The research referred to is psychical research, research into the occult and paranormal, from telepathy to ghosts. Sidgwick had a deep interest in

93

this area throughout the greater part of his adult life and was instrumental in forming the Society for Psychical Research in 1882, twice serving as its president before his death, at sixty-two, in August 1900. His interest was not merely scientific. Throughout his life he was preoccupied with those grand metaphysical questions: Is there a God? Is the soul immortal? Eight days after his mother's death, on January 17, 1879, for example, he writes the following letter to F. W. H. Myers, himself a pioneer in the field of psychical research:

> I have been wishing to write to you since we came back [to Cambridge] on Wednesday; but I find it difficult to write, not from painfulness of feeling—for this actual end, now that all is over, seems really a release—but from perplexity and mingledness. I feel as if I had reached the summit of the Pass of Life; behind the old memories from infancy, unrolled like a map, and before the strange world of "the majority," near though in a mist, at which I am forced to gaze. And more than ever the alternatives of the Great Either-Or seem to be Pessimism or Faith. (p. 340)

Sidgwick came to his calling as a part-time investigator of the paranormal because he thought that the scientific confirmation of psychic phenomena had a logical bearing on which of the two alternatives a rational person should choose. He profoundly hoped it was not Pessimism.

Pessimism was a state of mind seemingly ill suited to Sidgwick's predispositions. Moore, in a letter to his mother dated April 30, 1895, during his first year as a student of philosophy, reveals that in a social setting "the professor [that is, Sidgwick] is immensely interesting and amusing; he always has plenty to say, wandering on gently from topic to topic, with shrewd remarks and plenty of witty anecdotes." Beneath the wit and humor, however, there lurked a disquieted heart, one that perhaps reaches the nadir of its despair in January of 1887. After more than a two-week lapse in his diary we find the following entry:

> January 28.—This is a long interval, but I have been passing through a mental crisis which disinclined me for self-revelation. I have been facing the fact that I am drifting steadily to the conclusion—I have by no means arrived at it, but am certainly drifting towards it—that we have not, and are never likely to have, empirical evidence of the existence of the individual after death. Soon, therefore, it will

probably be my duty as a reasonable being—and especially as a professional philosopher—to consider on what basis the human individual ought to construct his life under these circumstances. Some fifteen years ago, when I was writing my book on Ethics [his *Methods of Ethics*], I was inclined to hold with Kant that we must *postulate* the continued existence of the soul, in order to effect that harmony of Duty with Happiness which seemed to me indispensable to rational moral life. At any rate I thought I might *provisionally* postulate it, while setting out on the serious search for empirical evidence. If I decide that this search is a failure, shall I finally and decisively make this postulate? Can I consistently with my whole view of truth and the method of its attainment? And if I answer "no" to each of these questions, have I any ethical system at all? And if not, can I continue to be Professor and absorb myself in the mere erudition of the subject—write "studies" of moralists from Socrates to Bentham— in short, become one of the "many" who, as Lowell says,

> Sought truth, and lavished life's best oil
> Amid the dust of books to find her,
> Content at last for guerdon of their toil
> With the last mantle she hath left behind her.

I am nearly forty-nine, and I do not find a taste for the old clothes of opinions growing on me.

I have mixed up the personal and general questions, because every speculation of this kind ends, with me, in a practical problem, "What is to be done here and now." That is a question which I must answer; whereas as to the riddle of the Universe—I never had the presumption to hope that its solution was reserved for *me*, though I had to try. (pp. 466–467)

Sidgwick did not just talk of conscience when it came to doing what he thought duty required. In 1869 he had boldly resigned his Fellowship at Trinity because he found that he could no longer sincerely assent to the Thirty-nine Articles, a profession of faith then required of Fellows. His doubts about the truth of the doctrines of Anglicanism were overshadowed by his doubts about the truth of Christianity generally, and even a friend of Sidgwick's would have to concede that there is an element of sad truth in Keynes's observation, quoted by Charles H. Hession, that Sidgwick "never did anything but wonder whether Christianity was true and prove that it wasn't and hope that it was" (p. 55). What doubts he had, however intense, could never quell his longing for belief. And so he lived unsettled in his faith, and uncertain in his doubt, something he came in time to accept in himself. "Faith must give the last word," he writes in an 1895 letter to Tennyson's son,

> "but the last word is not the whole utterance of the truth: the whole truth is that assurance and doubt alternate in the moral world in which we at present live, somewhat as night and day alternate in the physical world. The revealing visions come and go; when they come we *feel* that we *know*; but in the intervals we must pass through states in which all is dark, and in which we can only struggle to hold the conviction that
>
> > . . . Power is with us in the night
> > Which makes the darkness and the light,
> > And dwells not in the light alone.
> > (*In Memoriam* xcvi) (p. 542)

Sidgwick was bowed but not defeated by the darkness. Speaking at a memorial meeting of the Synthetic Society, held on the occasion of Sidgwick's death—the speech is included in A *Memoir*—Canon Gore first recalls Sidgwick's joining the Society two years earlier, and then goes on to add the following observations:

> The object of the Society was to bring together people of quite different points of view in order that they might see how far they could arrive at any basis of agreement with regard to those matters which underlie our life—the great principles of philosophy and religion; or if it was plain that an agreement could not be reached, how far they could contribute anything by way of discussion to the mutual understanding of one another's position. At once he became the life and soul of that Society, so much so that his death makes us wonder whether we had not better die too. . . . It was extraordinary the difference which appeared in the treatment of questions by Henry Sidgwick. There is a passage . . . in the *Phaedo* of Plato, in which, after he had been speaking sadly of the unsatisfactoriness of the arguments for the immortality of the soul, he yet declares that unless some Divine word . . . should give us a better basis of security, at least we must make the best of all the human arguments we can get,

and never relax the earnestness of our inquiry until death. That was what was so remarkable in Henry Sidgwick—the perpetual hopefulness of his inquiry. He always seemed to expect that some new turn of argument, some new phase of thought, might arise and put a new aspect upon the intellectual scenery, or give a new weight in the balance of argument. There was in him an extraordinary belief in *following reason*—a belief and a hopefulness which continued up to the last. (pp. 556–557)

It was this quality of "perpetual hopefulness" that had led Sidgwick to embark on his investigations of psychic phenomena. The results, arrived at scientifically, promised to "put a new aspect on the intellectual scenery" surrounding the grand metaphysical questions of God and immortality. It was in the hope of moving these phenomena from the status of appearance to that of scientifically verified reality that he labored. Such was the temperament of the man that the destination he sought seemed always to recede just over the horizon, however much he quickened his pace.

But Not Without a Struggle

Though Moore's debts to Sidgwick are many, the two men seem not to have found one another's company particularly enjoyable. Of his five teachers Moore observes in his autobiography that he "gained least from personal contact with Sidgwick. His personality did not attract me, and I found his lectures dull. . . . [They] were, I think, too formal to be very interesting: he simply read out to us, not in a very stimulating manner, things that he had written in finished form, fit for publication as they stood. I think I could have gained more by reading them to myself than by hearing him read them" (pp. 16–17). Moore is less sparing in a letter to his mother dated April 30, 1895. Sidgwick's lectures "generally seem to be three times as long as any body else's, and are very difficult to follow." There is an almost comic irony here, since as a teacher Moore himself was initially inclined to emulate Sidgwick's "formal" methods. And this is not the least of Sidgwick's dispositions Moore was to acquire. On matters of personal influence, in any event, Moore gives Sidgwick a mixed review. On matters of philosophical influence, Sidgwick's vital role is duly acknowledged. "From his published works," Moore recalls in the autobiography, "especially, of course, his *Methods of Ethics*, I have gained a good deal, and his clarity and his belief in Common Sense were very sympathetic to me" (p. 16). Moore's memory arguably is overly selective on this occasion. For although he did in time come to have sympathy for Sidgwick's belief in Common Sense, it was not always so. Initially Moore reacted quite negatively to Sidgwick's teachings. And Sidgwick responded in kind.

The scene of the early conflict is Sidgwick's course of lectures in the Fall of 1894. Among the papers Sidgwick assigned was one on the topic "The Relation of Reason to Moral Action, and of Ignorance to Moral Responsibility: The Intellectual Virtues." Moore's paper, complete with Sidgwick's marginal comments, has survived. We understate the case if we say that the student is not in complete agreement with the teacher.

One of Moore's theses is that "reason can only determine truth or falsehood; good only has meaning as the content of will." "Do you mean," Sidgwick writes in the margin, "that whatever is willed is good?" The seeds of Moore's First Dissertation already had been set. In a second paper on this topic, subtitled "An Attempt at Explanation in Answer to Prof. Sidgwick's Criticism," after noting that "Mr. Sidgwick drew from one of my statements the conclusion that I must hold whatever is willed to be good," Moore declares that "this does follow and I do hold it." He then adds that he also holds that "whatever is willed is evil." This apparent paradox allows of a subtle resolution, Moore maintains, one that relies heavily on the views of "Mr. Bradley." The longer the paper goes on, the more is Moore's debt to "Mr. Bradley" acknowledged. And the more frequent and strident are Sidgwick's marginal intrusions. By page 7, when Moore asserts that "will must determine its content," Sidgwick interjects, "I do not see the demonstration." On the last page, after Moore claims that Hume had used Moore's sense of "efficient causality" and had "maintain[ed] the view which we have above maintained," Sidgwick parries with "I doubt it very much!" "From this point of view," Moore continues in his summary, "will must be sole cause of everything, and a timeless cause; and the final cause is its object, as opposed to it before realisation," to which Sidgwick pens, "Unproved assertions again." As we have had opportunity to observe before, the belief in Common Sense, which Moore says was "very sympathetic" to him, certainly did become so. But not without a struggle. The views of "Mr. Bradley" and other idealist metaphysicians were a formidable obstacle to Sidgwick's—and Common Sense's—having any appreciable influence on Moore. When Moore writes to his father on January 30, 1895, that he has "almost dropped . . .

Professor Sidgwick's Ethics" we sense how wide the gap between the two men could be.

Beyond the Bounds of Permissible Paradox

Moore submitted his Second Dissertation for a Prize Fellowship in 1898. The Second bears the same title as the First: "The Metaphysical Basis of Ethics." The greater part of the second chapter is missing but there is strong evidence for supposing that the missing parts form virtually the whole of his paper "The Nature of Judgment," published in *Mind* in April 1899. The evidence is twofold. First, the second chapter breaks off with the same quote from Bradley's *Logic* with which "The Nature of Judgment" begins. Second, there is the testimony of Moore himself who, writing in his autobiography, relates the following:

In my second year's work [1897–1898] I got on to what I think was a much more profitable line of inquiry, though one which had a much less direct connection with Kant's Ethics—had, indeed, a more direct connection with the *Critique of* Pure *Reason* than with the *Critique of* Practical *Reason*. It seemed to me that it was extremely difficult to see clearly what Kant meant by "Reason." This was a term which occurred not only in the title of both these works, but also frequently in the text, and, as it seemed to me, in a very mystifying manner. What on earth did Kant mean by it? He must be referring, more or less directly, to something which was to be found in the world, and which could be described in other terms. But to what exactly? This was what I set myself to think about; and it led me to think first about the notion of "truth," since it seemed to me that, in some of its uses at all events, Kant's term "Reason" involved a reference to the notion of "truth;" and, in thinking about truth, I was led to take as my text a passage from the beginning of Bradley's *Logic*, in which after saying that "Truth and falsehood depend on the relation of our ideas to reality," he goes on to say that the "meaning" of an idea consists in a part of its content "cut off, fixed by the mind, and considered apart from the existence" of the idea in question. It seemed to me, if I remember right, that the meaning of an idea was not anything "cut off" from it, but something wholly independent of mind. I tried to argue for this position, and this was the beginning, I think, of certain tendencies in me which have led some people to call me a "Realist," and was also the beginning of a break-away from belief in Bradley's philosophy, of which, up till about then, both Russell and I had, following McTaggart, been enthusiastic admirers. I remember McTaggart once saying of an occasion when he met Bradley at Oxford that, when Bradley came in, he felt "as if a Platonic Idea had walked into the room."

I added what I had written this year about "reason" and "ideas" as a concluding chapter to what I had written the year before, and submitted the whole at the Fellowship Examination in 1898. . . . The substance of the new chapter was published soon afterwards in *Mind* under the title of "The Nature of Judgement;" and though I am sure that article must have been full of confusions, I think there was probably some good in it. (pp. 21–22)

It was Ward's task to represent the philosophy faculty on this occasion. But Sidgwick's behind-the-scenes role may well have proven to be decisive. Ward, Moore recalls,

told me that in the next year [1898], when he had taken Sidgwick's place on the Board of Electors, Sidgwick spoke to him just before the final meeting of the Electors and warned him that he must be careful not to ruin my chances of election by failing to speak sufficiently favourably of my work. (p. 21)

We do not have the benefit of a public record of either Ward's or Sidgwick's estimation of the Second Dissertation. Moore, however, offers a humorous account of what he himself thought Sidgwick's opinion was:

I expect that Sidgwick . . . must have felt about my dissertation much the same as he is said to have felt about the dissertation on Hegel by which McTaggart won his fellowship a few years earlier. Sidgwick is reported to have said about McTaggart's dissertation (and I believe this is authentic): "I can see that this is nonsense, but what I want to know is whether it is the right kind of nonsense." I think he must have decided about my nonsense, as he had decided about McTaggart's, that it was the right kind. (p. 21)

Ward must have followed Sidgwick's instructions more than adequately. Moore received a Prize Fellowship in September 1898. For the next six years he resided in rooms at Trinity, dining in Hall without cost, the recipient of a £200 annual "dividend": in his words, "a very pleasant place and a very pleasant life."

Bosanquet's acid assessment of the Second Dissertation, offered in his capacity as outside reader, already has been mentioned. Moore's substantive claims in Bosanquet's view appear to "lie beyond the limit of paradox permissible in philosophy." "The intellectual motive of the Dissertation, as I read it," he adds, "is to dissociate Truth from Knowledge, and Good from the nature of Will, so as to free Metaphysic from all risk of confusion with Psychology." We have already seen how Moore endeavored to dissociate "Good from the nature of Will." That is the principal aspiration of the First Dissertation. It remains to be seen how in the Second he sets out to complete a comparable project in the case of Truth and Knowledge, a project that he chastises some of his contemporaries for overlooking. Writing in his review of Leon Brunschvicg's *La Modalité du Jugement* Moore observes that "intellectual activity, *qua* activity, seems to be merely a form of conation, and is therefore a subject matter for psychology, not philosophy." Brunschvicg's "fallacy," Moore claims, is due to his failure to recognize the division of labor between the two sciences: philosophy and psychology. "It is not the *process* of cognition or judging, but knowledge or judgment, in so far as they are true, which offer to metaphysics that point of departure, which justifies itself, and so distinguishes this from every other study." The challenge of metaphysics is to understand the nature of the objects of knowledge, not to examine the process of knowing.

The same "fallacy" Moore finds in the little-known Brunschvicg he also finds in the well-known Kant. Commenting on part of Moore's supporting arguments, as we find them in "The Nature of Judgment," Gilbert Ryle declares that "Moore here seems to have gone temporarily crazy" (p. 99). That diagnosis, coupled with Bosanquet's grim appraisal, more than guarantees that Moore's views at least will prove interesting.

The Possibility of A Priori Knowledge

One question Moore considers in both dissertations concerns *a priori* knowledge. Such knowledge is not based on evidence gained from experience, and the propositions that are the objects of such knowledge are necessarily not contingently true (or false). The truths of mathematics and logic frequently are cited as examples of knowledge of this kind.

Kant held this view, adding that the fundamental principles of morality also are known *a priori*. Moore concurs. So the question Moore poses is not whether we have *a priori* knowledge; it is how to account for its possibility, given that we have it. In the First Dissertation Moore's answer proceeded along the well-trodden Kantian path. Kant's Copernican Revolution teaches that as knowers we bring to our knowledge a set of *a priori* categories which rather than being generated out of, actually structure and are presupposed by, our experience. On Kant's view, then, as understood by Moore, *a priori* knowledge is possible because of the structure of the human mind. We know that every event has a cause, for example, because we could not have the kind of experience we have if this were not true. Moore uncritically accepts Kant's view of *a priori* knowledge throughout the First Dissertation. The opening sentences of the Preface to the Second alert us to the presence of "an important change of view": "The greater part of the Dissertation, which I submitted for examination last year, has been included in the present work. Some omissions and alterations, involving an important change of view, have been made; and nearly as much again as new matter has been added."

What this "important change" is Moore does not say. But while there is much that is different and much that is the same in the two dissertations, it seems most plausible to interpret him to be referring to his change of view regarding the Kantian answer to the question, How is *a priori* knowledge possible? In the Second Dissertation Moore unequivocally replies that the answer is *not* to be found where he thinks Kant locates it. Whereas in the First Dissertation Moore was uncritical of Kant's Copernican Revolution, well disposed to accepting the "happy thought" that in *a priori* knowledge "nothing can be attributed to the objects [of knowledge], except what the thinking subject takes out of itself," in the Second Dissertation Moore is openly distressed by the "exceedingly unfortunate suggestion" that knowledge must conform to the mind of the knower in the way Kant's Copernican Revolution requires. There is, Moore maintains, no reason to believe that "the *a priori* and the Reason" are connected in the way Kant maintains they are. Moore's object is to give the correct account of the possibility of *a priori* knowledge that eludes Kant.

Against Kant (as he understands him) Moore first argues that truth is independent of our knowledge of it. That much established, he next argues that truth is independent of mind or consciousness generally, from which he infers that the possibility of *a priori* knowledge cannot be accounted for in the way in which he thinks Kant supposes—namely, by arguing that such knowledge is involved "in our consciousness" or "in Reason." *One must look to the nature of these truths themselves, not to the nature of our minds,* in Moore's view, if one is to offer a satisfactory answer to the question, How is *a priori* knowledge possible?

Even from the preceding we can recognize how accurate Bosanquet is in his characterization of the Second Dissertation's "intellectual motive." Moore does aspire to "dissociate Truth from Knowledge," and both his case against Kant's account of the possibility of *a priori* knowledge and his case in favor of his own position clearly depend on the success of his attempt to perform this feat of dissociation. That attempt is made in the portions of the second chapter published as "The Nature of Judgment."

The Dissociation of Truth from Knowledge

Bradley is the putative stalking horse. " 'Truth and falsehood,' says Mr. Bradley (*Logic,* p. 2)," the essay begins, " 'depend on the relation of our ideas to reality' " (p. 176). Now by 'ideas' Bradley does not mean, what an empiricist would, "states of our mind." According to empiricists *what* we perceive, whenever we perceive something, are states of our own mind, variously called "sensations," "ideas," "impressions," or "perceptions." These ideas, empiricists allow, we naturally suppose correspond to or represent objects in a world external to our minds—the ordinary world of tables and chairs. But *what* we perceive, on the empiricist's theory of perception, are our ideas, which are in our minds, not tables and chairs, which are in a quite different place, the world outside our minds. If our judgments about the external world are true, they are true because our ideas correspond to or represent the way things are in this world; if they fail to do this, then they are false. Bradley for his part is no less critical of empiricism in philosophy than is Moore, and it is likely that the admiration Moore (and Russell) felt for Bradley's teachings in their philosophical youth was due as much to his criticism of empiricism as to his positive views. In any event, when Bradley writes that "truth and falsehood depend on the relation of our ideas to reality," the ideas to which he refers certainly are not those referred to by an empiricist such as Locke.

Ideas for Bradley are the "universal meanings" we use in making judgments and without which judgment of any kind would be impossible. For example, in the judgment "This rose is red," the words 'rose' and 'red' express different universal meanings. For the word 'rose' applies, not merely to the particular flower referred to in this judgment, but to *all* roses; and 'red' applies to *all* red things, not just the color of this particular flower. If we had no grasp of ideas, conceived of as universal meanings, we could not make a single judgment according to Bradley. Having secured that grasp and acquired the concomitant ability to make judgments, we then face the question of truth and falsity. The ideas (universal meanings) in our true judgments stand in a relation to reality that is lacking in the case of our false judgments. What that relation is, according to Bradley, is less important for present purposes than understanding the general structure of his thought. There are our judgments, he maintains. And there are those things our judgments are about. Truth and falsity depend upon how the two are related; truth and falsity are *relational* properties. Take away either term of the relation—take away either our judgments or the objects about which our judgments are made—and there would be nothing true. Or false. In this way, and for this reason, Bradley's position arguably presupposes that truth and falsity logically depend upon someone's making judgments. It is this feature of Bradley's position that is on the receiving end of Moore's philosophical wrath in "The Nature of Judgment."

Because the word 'idea' has such an intimate connection with talk about our mental life, and because he is intent on rescuing philosophy from its tawdry associations with psychology, Moore looks for a different word to stand for Bradley's "universal meanings." His choice is the equally unhappy one, 'concept.' As Ryle notes (p. 93), this word was soon to give way in Moore's written work to 'object' or 'notion,' and to the doublets, "object or notion" and "object or idea." To understand them we must understand it.

A concept, Moore asserts, "is not a mental fact nor any part of a mental fact" (p. 179). Rather, it is *what* we mean when, for example, we use the words 'red' and 'rose'. By way of illustration Moore offers the following example:

> When, therefore, I say "This rose is red," I am not attributing part of the content of my idea to the rose, nor yet attributing parts of the content of my ideas of rose and red together to some third subject. What I am asserting is a specific connexion of certain concepts forming the total concept "[R]ose" with the concepts "[T]his" and "[N]ow" and "[R]ed"; and the judgment is true if such a connexion is existent. Similarly when I say "The chimera has three heads," the chimera is not an idea in my mind, nor any part of such idea. What I mean to assert is nothing about my mental states, but a specific

connexion of concepts. If the judgment is false, that is not because my *ideas* do not correspond to reality, but because such a conjunction of concepts is not to be found among existents. (p. 179)

Moore here clearly implies that things (for example, his rose) are combinations or collections of concepts. This is no slip of the pen. "It seems necessary," he writes a few pages later, "to regard the world as formed of concepts" (p. 182). And, again: "All that exists is thus composed of concepts" (p. 181), some of which, like the concept Rose, are complex, while others of which, like the concept Red, are simple. Things that exist (for example, *this* rose) are combinations or collections of concepts linked with the concept of Existence. For "Existence is itself a concept" (p. 180). Things that are conceivable but nonexistent (for example, the chimera of Moore's example) are not combined with the concept of Existence. Moreover, those things that do exist, and that are comprised of concepts, are not something over and above the concepts that comprise them. There isn't some *thing*, some *substance* that possesses concepts as its attributes. Things *just are* combinations or collections of concepts, and "a concept is not in any intelligible sense an 'adjective,' as if there were something substantive, more ultimate than it. For we must, if we are to be consistent, describe what appears to be most substantive as no more than a collection of such supposed adjectives: and thus, in the end, the concept turns out to be the only substantive or subject" (pp. 192–193). To anticipate a way in which Moore will express this same point in the future, concepts (or notions, or objects) are *parts* of things, giving to things whatever substance they possess. There is no "something we know not what" that underlies a thing's properties. Things simply *are* their properties.

Moore's "dissociation" of truth from knowledge is even more complete and in its way more radical than the preceding might suggest. One way to express the thought that Moore knows that this rose is red (and Moore does express himself in this way) is to say that Moore knows that the proposition 'This rose is red,' is true. For Moore, however, there are not two different things to be known here, (*a*) the red rose and (*b*) the proposition, 'This rose is red.' There is only one truth, only one object of knowledge: this red rose. From this it is a short step to the view, which Moore openly endorses, that such things as red roses *are themselves propositions.* "An existent" [for example, this red rose], he writes, simply *is* "a proposition" (p. 183), namely, the true existential proposition, 'This rose is red.' Caird was in some ways fortunate not to have been asked to pass judgment on the Second Dissertation. "I fear Caird's hair will stand on end," Russell writes to Moore on September 13, 1898, "when he learns that an existent is a proposition." The oft-told story of Moore's nightmare, related by Keynes in "My Early Beliefs" (p. 94), in which Moore was unable to distinguish between propositions and tables, is remarkable only because it is presented as a nightmare. At least during the time Moore was actively working on the new material in his Second Dissertation, from September 1897 to August 1898, the belief that tables *are* true existential propositions is one Moore carried around with him during his most sober waking hours, not one he entertained only in the cold sweat of a bad dream.

A Platonic Realism

While certain combinations of concepts exist (as things) and have the status of true existential propositions, individual concepts (for example, Red, Rose, Exists) are not propositions. And neither do they exist. But this does not mean that individual concepts are unreal. These concepts *are*; they *have being*. But the sort of being they have precludes their having any position in space or time. They are not anywhere. Nor anywhen. Individually considered, they do not exist, where by 'exist' we mean, what Moore always means when he is precise on this point, "have being in space or time." Concepts, as "possible objects of thought" (p. 179), subsist in a realm of changeless being that has neither temporal nor spatial properties. Though they do not exist, they are not unreal.

Readers familiar with Plato's views will recognize the striking similarity between his theory of Forms and Moore's theory of concepts, a resemblance Moore mentions. For while Kant is the philosopher with whose views Moore's are "most in agreement" in the First Dissertation, and while his debts to Bradley are acknowledged in the Introductions to both dissertations, Plato seems to be the most fundamental source of inspiration. "So far . . . as a general philosophical scheme goes," Moore observes, "the standpoint here taken up seems to agree most with that of Plato," a resemblance he is proud to convey in a letter to Desmond MacCarthy dated August 14, 1898: "I have arrived at a perfectly staggering doctrine. . . . An existent is nothing but a proposition: Nothing *is* but concepts. . . . I am pleased to believe that this is the most Platonic system of modern times; though it is also not so far from Kant, as you might think at first." As is true in Plato's system, pre-eminent among the denizens of Moore's realm of concepts, as will be seen more clearly below, is the concept Good.

In order to make a judgment, Bradley had claimed, we must have a grasp of ideas, understood as universal meanings. Moore concurs. But universal meanings have a quite different status in Moore's thought. These meanings are nontemporal, nonspatial concepts that have being apart from human thought or awareness. Following Bradley, who urges that we must grasp universal meanings in order to make judgments, Moore maintains that we must grasp these concepts themselves. We must have a *direct* grasp of the concepts Rose and Red, for example, to make the judgment "This rose is red." When we think this thought, or make this judgment, it is not *our ideas* of red and rose that we are thinking of; it is these concepts *themselves*. And the same is true in the case of judgments of goodness and our grasp of the concept Good. We must directly apprehend concepts by the exercise of our mental powers; otherwise we could not do what we manifestly can do—namely, make judgments. Though concepts are "incapable of change," though they are "neither cause nor effect of [any] change" (p. 179), and though they subsist in a nonspatial, nontemporal realm inaccessible to our senses, they are not inaccessible to our minds. When in his autobiography Moore comments that his work on the Second Dissertation marked "the beginning . . . of certain tendencies in me which have led people to call me a 'Realist,' " part of what he must have had in mind are those features summarized in the preceding. Both in perception and in thinking we are directly aware of objects that have being outside our minds.

Acknowledging the peculiarity of his views—"I am fully aware how paradoxical this theory must appear," he writes, "and even how contemptible" (p. 181)—Moore believes nonetheless that he has offered a superior alternative to Bradley's theory of truth. Truth and falsity are *not* relations between "our ideas" and "reality." *Truth is a property directly possessed by true propositions.* And as for this property itself, Moore's position here parallels his more famous discussion in *Principia* regarding Good:

> A proposition is constituted by any number of concepts, together with a specific relation between them; and according to the nature of this relation the proposition may be either true or false. What kind of relation makes a proposition true, what false, cannot be further defined, but must be immediately recognised. (p. 180)

Like the concept Red, Truth turns out to be simple and indefinable.

Nonempirical Truths

The preceding omits much that a fuller exploration of "The Nature of Judgment" would be required to cover, including Moore's apparently inconsistent claims about existential propositions, which at one point (p. 190) are said to be necessarily true, at another (p. 191) possibly false. (In the remaining text of the Second Dissertation's second chapter, moreover, existential propositions also are said to be—all of them—necessarily false!) How this apparent inconsistency is to be resolved, if it can be, must be left to future scholars to decide. Here we must note another category of proposition neglected to this point. In addition to existential propositions Moore also offers some comments on the category of necessary propositions, including mathematical truths (for example, $2+2=4$). Like other propositions, mathematical propositions are combinations of concepts (for example, the concepts 2 and 4). But unlike existential propositions, which Moore identifies with "existents" (for example, this red rose), necessary propositions do not exist. Mathematical propositions in particular and necessary propositions in general have no position in space or time, nor are they inferrable from what we know about those things that do exist in space and time. "$2+2=4$ is true," Moore writes, "whether there exist two things or not. Moreover it may be doubted here whether even the concepts of which the proposition consists, can ever be said to exist. We should have to stretch our notion of existence beyond intelligibility, to suppose that 2 ever has been, is, or will be an existent" (p. 180). The distinction Moore wishes to make here is between empirical and nonempirical propositions, a distinction that he explains in terms of empirical and nonempirical concepts. "Empirical concepts are those which can exist in parts of time. This would seem to be the only manner of distinguishing them [from nonempirical concepts]. And any proposition into which an empirical concept enters may be called empirical" (p. 187).

A Summing Up

By way of summary, then, we find three distinguishable but related strands of thought in "The Nature of Judgment." The first is ontological and concerns what sorts of things have being. Moore seems to recognize at least four kinds of being. The first are those individual concepts which, considered individually, do not exist in space and time but which are capable of being instantiated in space and time in combination with other such concepts. The concepts Red, Rose, and Exists would seem to be of this kind. The second are those individual concepts which, considered individually, do not exist in space and time and which are incapable of being instantiated in space and time in combination with other concepts. Mathematical concepts (for example, the numbers 2 and 4) would seem to be of this kind. The third are those combinations of concepts of the first kind which actually exist in combination in space and time and which, when they do, are things or, what is the same, true existential propositions (for example, this red rose). The fourth are those combinations of concepts of the second kind which do not exist in space and time but subsist as nonempirical propositions in a nonspatial nontemporal realm of being (for example, the mathematical proposition, $2+2=4$). What we ordinarily understand to be things (for example, tables and chairs) are in fact combinations of concepts of the first kind and, as such, are identical with true existential propositions. Anything that has being—things, their parts, and propositions, whether existential or otherwise—will be classifiable in one of these four categories. Or so it seems.

That is the first strand. The second strand is semantic in nature and concerns how and what words mean. The sorts of being distinguished above are denoted by words or other symbols (e.g., Red is denoted by 'Red', Rose by 'Rose', 2 by 'Two', and Truth by 'Truth'). The concepts denoted by these words are these words' universal meanings, and these meanings *are*—they *have being*—even though they do not exist.

Third, and finally, there is an epistemological strand that concerns how and what we can know. In order to know that this rose is red we must be able to grasp the universal meanings or concepts Rose and Red. But we must also perceive these concepts as they are existentially combined to form this particular flower. And to do this we must perceive this combination or conjunction of concepts here and now, *not* our ideas of their combination. *What* we perceive, then, are things or the parts of things, not our ideas of the same, just as the *objects* of our thought, when we think about the meanings of words, are the meanings themselves and not our ideas of them or mere words. In perception we are directly aware of those true propositions that exist in the changing world in space and time ("perception is to be regarded philosophically," Moore states in "The Nature of Judgment," "as the cognition of an existential proposition" [p. 183]), while in thought we are directly aware of those objects (universal meanings and nonempirical truths) that have being in a changeless realm of being outside space and time.

But Still a Transcendentalist

Whatever the merits of the positions Moore sets out in "The Nature of Judgment," that paper affords us a clear view of the remarkable fertility and agility of his mind. Among the intellectual debris washed ashore by the wild currents of speculation in this paper we cannot help but find Moore's own "poor idealistic system" fashioned by him some two years earlier, at age twenty-two. Recall the main features. All that we are aware of are our ideas, which are "in us." We cannot prove but neither can we doubt that there is another world existing outside and independently of our mental life, to which our ideas when veridical correspond or which they represent. And that world, in as much as we can know anything about it at all, is "spiritual." With the Second Dissertation, the portion we know as "The Nature of Judgment" in particular, Moore puts his early affair with *this* sort of idealism behind him. While Bradley and Kant are the named advocates of the views Moore here endeavors to refute, there is more than a little reason to suppose that his principal adversary is the unnamed author of "What is matter?"

Moore's "important change of view" regarding Kant's philosophy should now be more perspicuous. Truth must *be* something since it is something to be known. That being so, its logical and ontological independence from our thought and from the structure of our minds is, for Moore, assured, and Kant's attempt to explain the possibility of *a priori* knowledge, as Moore understands this, is confuted. "If truth is something independent of knowledge and therefore of consciousness," he writes in the Second Dissertation, "[then] no theory which tries to explain the validity of necessary propositions by shewing them to be involved in knowledge or in consciousness can possibly attain its purpose." That truth *is* independent of knowledge is *the* central thesis of the Second Dissertation; it is the "dissociation of Truth from Knowledge" that Bosanquet found beyond the bounds of permissible paradox. Given this dissociation, it cannot be satisfactory to attempt to explain "the origin of necessary propositions . . . in Reason," which is what Kant attempts to do according to Moore. The necessity of such propositions, just as their truth, is a property of these propositions themselves, one that neither originates in nor is grounded by "Reason itself."

But while Moore is now in open revolt against Kant's Copernican Revolution, he remains sympathetic to Kant's Transcendentalism. "For Kant's Transcendentalism," he observes in "The Nature of Judgment," "rests on the distinction between empirical and *a priori* propositions" (p. 183), a distinction Moore believes is essential to his own philosophical enterprise in general and to his moral philosophy in particular. That distinction requires, so Moore believes, acceptance of the three strands of thought outlined above—the ontological, the semantic, and the epistemological. With these serving as philosophical backdrop the drama of the empirical and the *a priori* can be played out in an intelligible, orderly way, empirical truths reduced to combinations of universal meanings joined with the concept of Existence in the changing world in space and time, while necessary truths subsist in a changeless realm of being having neither temporal nor spatial properties. The former are known by perception, the latter by reason. How unstable this theoretical arrangement proves to be is nowhere more evident than when it is brought to bear on the aspirations of Moore's ethical philosophy.

"Who Will Shew Us Any Good?"

On the one hand there exists a world comprised of objects in space and time; on the other there is a realm of being that lacks both spatial and temporal properties. Objects in the former world come into being and pass away; they are mutable. Those in the latter world are eternal and changeless. Since Moore includes virtually the whole of the First Dissertation in the body of the Second, it seems reasonable to assume that he would not have objected to characterizing the two worlds, respectively, as phenomenal and noumenal, or, alternatively, as Appearance and Reality. For though the Second Dissertation teaches that in perception we are directly aware of things rather than our ideas—directly aware of the red rose, for example, and not of our sensations or impressions of the flower —Moore continues to accept the view that what we are aware of are things as they appear to us, not as they are in themselves. This much of the spirit of the First Dissertation permeates the Second, considered in its entirety.

The two dissertations differ, however, over the question of the relationship between Appearance and Reality. Whereas in the First Dissertation the noumenal world is said to express itself in everything that exists or occurs in the phenomenal world, the Second Dissertation's teaching is that the relation between the noumenal world (the realm of concepts and necessarily true propositions) and the world of phenomenal existence defies classification. The relation between concepts and existents is "a unique relation," a relation "which can begin or cease with a change in the subject" (that is, the existent); but while the existent can thus change from one moment to the next (for example, the red rose can change its color as it withers and dies) "the concept is neither cause nor effect of such a change" (p. 179). The notion of causality applies only within the world of existents, not between the two realms of being—the phenomenal and the noumenal. "The occurence of the relation [between concepts and existents] has, no doubt, its causes and effects, but these are to be found only in the subject" (p. 179). *How*, then, such concepts as Red and Rose are instantiated or manifested in things remains totally mysterious, given Moore's treatment of this matter in the Second Dissertation. Or, rather, given his nontreatment. The ancient problem of the One and the Many is not on Moore's agenda in this work.

The absence of an explanation of the relation between the world of existents and the realm of concepts has important implications, none of them obviously salutary, for the adequacy of the ethical theory we find in the Second Dissertation. If we were to concede to Moore the assumption that some existents are good in themselves (and reasons for disallowing this assumption will be given below) then we could agree that the criteria of objectivity and universality can be satisfied. For what properties or relations an existent thing has are determined by the concepts instantiated in or expressed by it, not by whether any one is aware of or, say, cares about what these concepts are. Thus would objectivity be guaranteed. And given that an existent thing *just is* the combination of concepts that are instantiated in it, including the concept of Existence, Moore could argue that any combination that includes the concept Good, at any one time and in any one place, must include this concept at any other time and in any other place in which this same combination of concepts recurs. Once good, always good: the criterion of universality would be met.

The ideal criterion also arguably can be satisfied by the theory we find in the Second Dissertation. By their very nature ideals are conceivable states of affairs that are better in themselves than some things that actually exist. Because in the First Dissertation Moore seems to be committed to the view that this is the best of all possible worlds, he there seems unable to account for the validity of ideals: There can be nothing better than what actually exists if what exists is the best possible. The ethical theory of the Second Dissertation is not encumbered by this Panglossian optimism. Nothing that Moore says in this work commits him to the cheerful view that this is the best of all possible worlds, and so nothing prohibits him from accepting the view that we can conceive of some nonexistent states of affairs that are better than those that actually exist. Moreover, the truth of propositions of the form 'X is good-in-itself' does not depend on the truth of propositions of the form 'X exists,' given what seem to be Moore's teachings in the Second Dissertation. For to exist, according to Moore, entails having a position in the spatio-temporal world, whereas the fundamental ethical truths, like the truths of mathematics and logic, subsist eternally in a realm of immutable being lacking both spatial and temporal properties. There again would appear to be no difficulty in Moore's accepting the validity of ideals, a success that, given the criteria being used here to interpret his development as a moral philosopher, marks an important improvement over the theory propounded in the First Dissertation.

Like the First, however, the Second Dissertation fails to satisfy the method criterion. The most Moore offers by way of a method for rationally deciding what things are good in themselves are appeals to appearance and consistency. "There does not seem any way of proving" that anything is good in itself, he writes, noting that "it is only possible to offer [a judgment of intrinsic value] in the hope that it may appear true, and further to try to produce conviction by shewing it to be more in accordance with complex propositions accepted by your opponent than other possible ones are." This is at best a small improvement on the First Dissertation, where no method was possible at all. But it is a small improvement only, if an improvement it is, since no serious effort has been made to develop a procedure or method to minimize the risks that appearances are deceiving. Let our opponent agree with our judgments as much as we wish; and let us offer as many such judgments that "appear true" as we like; unless we have found a way to minimize the possibility of error we shall lack good reason to believe that we have made any serious advance on the truth.

The Second Dissertation also is deficient when matched against the conduct criterion. As was true of the First this deficiency in the Second is not due to Moore's attempting but failing to meet this criterion. Rather, he again fails to attempt to meet it. So preoccupied is he with the metaphysical foundations of ethics, so convinced is he that the object of ethics is to know and not to do the good, and so resolute is his belief that Freedom has no essential connection with Will and so no essential connection with human action, that he does not trifle with questions concerning how we ought to act, or even with how we rationally are to decide such questions. Even were he otherwise successful in what he attempts in his Second Dissertation, therefore, Moore would have half an ethical system at best.

As it happens he is not otherwise successful. By far the most serious difficulty for his positive position is the last to be discussed: its failure to satisfy the criterion of natural goods. The First Dissertation sets forth a theory that meets this criterion with a vengeance: *Everything* in nature is good—indeed, must be good—because *everything* that exists is the logically necessary expression of Transcendental Freedom, which is absolutely good. The denizens of the noumenal world as depicted in the *Second* Dissertation, by contrast, are not assigned any logical or causal relation to the objects or events in the phenomenal world. How, then, the concepts that subsist in this latter world manage to instantiate or express themselves in the existents in the former is, as was noted earlier, a mystery that is not explained by Moore. The particular case of the concept Good, however, is worse than mysterious. What Moore says about its relation to existents seems to undermine the very possibility that any existent *can* be intrinsically good. Moore's position, in short, seems to make the existence of natural goods logically impossible.

The reasons for reaching this finding are as follows. In his Second Dissertation Moore clearly maintains that propositions that declare the intrinsic value of things are not empirical propositions, and he clearly maintains that Good is not an empirical concept. "Empirical concepts," he writes in that portion of his Second Dissertation included in "The Nature of Judgment," "are those which can exist in parts of time. This would seem to be the only manner of distinguishing them [from nonempirical concepts]. And any proposition into which an empirical concept enters may be called empirical" (p. 187). If, then, there is anything that exists that is good, Good must (somehow) be conjoined with some other concepts, including the concept of Existence. Among these other concepts, moreover, there must be at least one that is empirical, since in the absence of such a concept it is impossible for anything to exist in the natural world. And Moore clearly does want a theory that allows for the possibility of such existence. His problem is that he also maintains that "any proposition into which an empirical concept enters may be called empirical." This entails that any proposition into which Good enters, given the necessary presence of an empirical concept, is *itself* an empirical proposition. And this result is logically at odds with Moore's requirement that propositions about what things are good are necessary and *a priori*.

For if these propositions are necessary and *a priori*, they cannot be empirical. And if empirical, they cannot be necessary and *a priori*. Thus whereas the ethical theory Moore devises in the First Dissertation seems to lead to the unacceptable conclusion that everything that exists in nature is good (because everything must be), the theory he develops in the Second Dissertation seems to lead to the equally unacceptable conclusion that nothing that exists in nature is good (because nothing can be). In neither case, it seems safe to say, could Moore be permanently satisfied with the outcome. There is, indeed, a sad irony in the motto he attaches to the title page of his Second Dissertation, a motto he takes from the book of Psalms (Psalm 4, verse 7): "There be many that say: Who will shew us any good?" In view of the evident impossibility of Moore's being able to satisfy this request, given the apparently contradictory things he says about the concept Good, the motto might better serve as the Second Dissertation's epitaph.

Perhaps even as he worked on his Second Dissertation Moore had some sense that something had gone wrong. One of his recurrent quarrels with Sidgwick concerns the value of beauty, Moore affirming, Sidgwick denying that beauty in nature has intrinsic value apart from human consciousness or appreciation. At the end of the First Dissertation Moore attached a spirited critique of Sidgwick's hedonism which includes a direct challenge to Sidgwick's denial that natural beauty is intrinsically good. While much of the Second Dissertation consists of unaltered parts of the First, the critical attack on Sidgwick is noteworthy for its absence. Moreover, unlike the First, the Second Dissertation contains no considered discussion of Moore's positive views concerning what things are good. Insisting that "some necessary a priori proposition about what is good is needed as a fundamental principle of Ethics," Moore himself remains silent throughout the Second Dissertation concerning what that principle is. If the previous application of the criterion of natural goods is sound, there is a straightforward explanation for Moore's uncharacteristic reticence on this matter. Moore fails to say what things are intrinsically good because his theory prevents him from making intelligible sense of how anything could be. It is difficult to believe that Moore, as astute a thinker as he was, could have failed to realize his dilemma. Or the sad irony of the Second Dissertation's motto. One measure of the correctness of the interpretation offered here is to consider the direction in which Moore's thought turns when he next attempts to refine his ethical theory. If this interpretation is correct we should find him making a concerted effort to supply what is apparently lacking in the Second Dissertation—a concerted effort, that is, to spell out in some detail what things are intrinsically good and how we can know this. And we should also find him making a serious, self-conscious effort to explain how natural goods can exist. When we look to his next major effort in moral philosophy, the already mentioned "Elements of Ethics," we do find Moore embarked on these projects.

People in Glass Cases

Sidgwick's standard biography, *Henry Sidgwick: A Memoir*, co-edited by his brother, Arthur, and his widow, Eleanor (Nora), was published early in 1906. In addition to their recollections the book includes many of Sidgwick's own letters, diary entries, and some unpublished papers. Near the book's end we read that in May of 1900 Sidgwick consulted a London surgeon, who diagnosed him as having a terminal cancer, one that required timely surgery if he was to have any hope of prolonging his life for even a few months. For the greater part of two weeks Sidgwick told no one except his wife, quietly setting about the task of arranging the final details of his life. Toward the end of May he began to write to old friends, knowing it might be for the last time. On May 29 he writes the following to H. G. Dakyns:

> I have sad words to say, and it grieves me to think of the grief they will cause you. I learnt three weeks ago that I have an incurable complaint, . . . the fatal termination of which may, however, be averted for the time by a surgical operation, which is now arranged for Thursday. If all goes as well as possible, I shall be in bed in a nursing home in London for about three weeks; and then I am encouraged to look forward to a period of invalid life which may extend even to years, though it may be much briefer.
>
> All this is hard to bear; I shall try to bear it as a man should.
>
> I think much of old times and old friends and especially of your unfailing love and sympathy. It is through human love that I try to touch the Divine and
>
> > faintly trust the larger hope.
>
> Nora will tell you how things go with us; it is possible that you may be able to come to see me in London.
>
> Good-bye, old and dear friend,—not, I will hope, a final fare-

well, though a solemn one. Think of me in my trial: pray for me, if you are moved to prayer. Give your wife my love. (pp. 588–589)

Sidgwick survived the surgery and briefly endured a fickle convalescence. On August 13 "a decisive change for the worse showed itself," and his condition worsened rapidly. On August 20 his brother Arthur writes the following to Sidgwick's old friend Sir George Trevelyan:

> I send one line to say that we have now no hopes for Henry, but that the growing weakness, which he bears with unbroken patience and the simplest unselfish fortitude, may soon reach the natural end which he so desires.
>
> We left him on Friday, and to-day I hear only that a further change has come, and that his wife and my sister, who are there [Terling, in Essex], are simply waiting, as he is, for his release.
>
> I know your warm heart will be sorry with no common sorrow, but you must not be sorry for death to come now to him. I wish you could have seen him here (on last May 20) when he felt well, but told us that his death was certain in a short time. There were fluctuations of hope afterwards, which the doctors were probably bound to hold out to him; but he was the truer prophet. And his quiet review of his own life, briefly given to me (in the room where I write) in the simplest words, was what we can none of us forget. It was the last and best example of what he was and is—as I have known since I knew anything, and you have known for over forty years.
>
> There is no more to say, and indeed to you no need for me to say anything. You will feel as we do.
>
> I will write if and when there is a further change. You will share all our hopes for him, and we can neither of us have any fears for such as he is. (p. 598)

Sidgwick died on August 28. As the conclusion of *A Memoir* shows, he went to his grave as uncertainly as he went through his life.

> His body was buried in the village churchyard at Terling, and thus the Church of England service was used without question, although his old hope of returning to the Church of his fathers had not been fulfilled. He refrained from leaving any directions on this point; but in May 1900, when he supposed that his funeral would take place in

a town cemetery, he talked of it with his wife. If it were decided, he said, not to use the Church of England service—and not to use it was what seemed to him most in harmony with his views and actions in life—he would like to have the following words said over his grave:—"Let us commend to the love of God with silent prayer the soul of a sinful man who partly tried to do his duty. It is by his wish that I say over his grave these words and no more." (pp. 598–599)

A Memoir was more than Keynes and Strachey could endure. Or resist. In a 1906 letter to a friend, quoted by Hession, Keynes writes that the book is

> very interesting and depressing and, the first part particularly, very important as an historical document dealing with the mind of the Victorian period. Really—but you must read it yourself. He [Sidgwick] never did anything but wonder whether Christianity was true and prove that it wasn't and hope that it was. . . .
>
> I wonder what he would have thought of us; and I wonder what we think of him. And then his conscience—incredible. There is no doubt of his moral goodness. And yet it is all so dreadfully depressing—no intimacy, no clear-cut boldness. Oh, I suppose he was intimate, but he didn't seem to have anything to be intimate about except his religious doubts. And he really ought to have gotten over that a little sooner because he knew that the thing wasn't true perfectly well from the beginning. The last part is all about ghosts, and Mrs. Balfour. I have never found so dull a book so absorbing. (p. 55)

Strachey sees the publication of A Memoir as an occasion for parading his and his age's spiritual liberation. "What an appalling time to have lived!," he writes in a letter Hession quotes.

> It was the Glass Case Age. Themselves as well as their ornaments were left under glass cases. Their refusal to face any fundamental question fairly—either about people or God—looks at first sight like cowardice; but I believe that it was simply the result of an innate incapacity for penetration—for getting either out of themselves or into anything or anybody else. They were enclosed in glass. How intolerable! Have you noticed, too, that they nearly all were phy-

sically impotent? Sidgwick himself, Matthew Arnold, [Benjamin] Jowett, [Frederick] Leighton, [John] Ruskin, [George Frederick] Watts. It's damned difficult to copulate through a glass case. (p. 55)

And Moore? Moore's reactions are more compressed but not more enthusiastic. Responding to a question of his sister, Sarah, Moore in a letter dated June 29, 1906 states that he already owns a copy of Sidgwick's *Life*. "I bought it and read it last spring. I found it very interesting, but largely because I was always hoping I was going to come upon something more interesting than I ever did actually find there." In the end Sidgwick's written work, not only his lectures, could leave a weary taste in Moore's mouth. The disaffection of his earlier association with the man so many admired, the man whose wife the youthful Moore thought "very nice"— "what little she said was worth hearing, but it was little because her husband flowed continuously," he adds in a letter to his mother dated April 30, 1895—that disaffection finds no surcease in Moore's later journey through Sidgwick's *Memoir*. Whether or not it is true, as Keynes writes in a letter to Strachey (February 21, 1906), that Moore thought Sidgwick "a wicked edifactious person," it is true that Moore's estimation of Sidgwick is closer to Keynes's and Strachey's than it is to, say, F. R. Leavis's.

Sidgwick's *Memoir*, though published in 1906, is among the last shadows of Victorian thought. *Principia*, after all, had appeared three years earlier, and its "substantive moral convictions," not only the "passionate character" of its author, in Keynes's words from "My Early Beliefs," had "attracted adherents at the time of [its] publication and in the years that followed." *Principia*'s power was, Keynes continues, "not only overwhelming; . . . it was the extreme opposite of what Strachey used to call *funeste*; it was exciting, exhilarating, the beginning of a new renaissance, the opening of a new heaven on a new earth, we were the fore-runners of a new dispensation, we were not afraid of anything" (p. 82). Sidgwick and his generation had lived in glass cases. Moore had broken them. As Vanessa Bell would put it, "A great new freedom seemed about to come."

5

The Right to Believe

The Reading Party

Perspiration runs freely down his face, flushed from exertion. His hands move with frenzied abandon. Upper body swaying rhythmically, feet in a constant state of readjustment on the floor, neck quivering visibly beneath the loosened collar of his shirt, his voice is now raspy, now pure, now raucous, now plaintive. Down come the hands, with great force. Back goes the head, with a violent snap. Down again the hands, the writhing motions of his body casting grotesque shadows in the flickering candlelight. The others in the room sit in riveted attention, neither moving nor speaking, gripped by the visceral spectacle.

For spectacle it is. Moore is singing Schubert Lieder, accompanying himself on the piano. He wrings the music out of the keys. And himself. What talents he may lack, or what obstacles the shortcomings of his training may have created (his major source of instruction was his father, who began giving him lessons when Moore was three years old) are more than compensated for by the emotional intensity he brings to the music within—and beyond—his range. Possessed of a style Alan Wood labels "very enterprising," Moore is said by Wood to have had "a strong sense of rhythm and an invincible keenness which made him regard nothing as too difficult for him to tackle." Late in Moore's life Ralph Vaughan Williams, a friend from Moore's student days at Cambridge, wrote to tell his old friend that he had heard in Moore's son Timothy's playing of Chopin "a kind of dogged determination which showed great strength of character and incidentally reminded me much of his father's playing." The antiseptic quality of his published prose gave way to the outpouring of emotions, sometimes turbulent, sometimes serene, whenever he turned his hands and voice to music. Now, on this occasion, as he plays the last

121

chord, his trembling baritone barely audible after the notes have died away, his body slumps on the stool, his passion spent.

It is the Easter vacation of 1899, and Moore has organized one of his reading parties, a tradition he had initiated during the Easter vacation of the previous year and one he will honor with only two exceptions up to the outbreak of the first world war. Leonard Woolf was one of the very few Moore invited over the years. "I enjoyed these 'reading parties' enormously," Woolf recalls in *Sowing* (pp. 133–134). "I suppose we did sometimes read something, but in memory the days seem to me to have passed in walking and talking. . . . In the evenings Moore sang and played for us, and then we talked and argued again. Moore was at his best on these 'parties'; he liked everyone and was at his ease with them." This year the party is at Gunnerside, on the River Swale in North Yorkshire. Joining Moore are Charles Sangar, Robert Trevelyan, and Desmond MacCarthy. All are in their mid-twenties. All are Apostles. There are long walks along the river. The air is damp and raw. But the companionship is good. There is much talk and argument, Moore beguiling his adversaries with his pipe. "One of the pet amusements of all Moore's friends," Russell recalls in his *Autobiography*, "was to watch him trying to light a pipe. He would light a match, and then begin to argue, and continue until the match burnt his fingers. Then he would light another, and so on, until the box was finished. This was no doubt fortunate for his health, as it provided moments during which he was not smoking." And smoking *was* a challenge both to Moore's health, and his will. On April 1, 1895 he writes to his mother that he has "given up smoking." But not for long. He is still at it in 1912, when in his diary entry for March 31 we read the following (emphasis in original): "In morning look through records about *tongue*; sit and think, and finally *decide to give up smoking altogether*." That resolve was insufficient against the demands of the pipe, in whose pleasures the future Mrs. Moore was herself to join her husband for the duration of their lives. But at this earlier time, in the evenings at Gunnerside Moore plays and sings. Friendships that will last a lifetime are sealed in this idyllic time and place. What Moore calls his "very pleasant life" was underway.

A *Teacher Is Born*

That life had begun in the Fall of 1898 and included Moore's first experience as a teacher. The full title of the course he offered was "The Elements of Ethics, with a view to an appreciation of Kant's Moral Philosophy." But the title is misleading. The lectures are far less about Kant's views than they are about Moore's, a development Moore anticipated from the outset. In his opening remarks he informs his students that he "shall not enter into the details of Kant's system at all," something better "reserved for a second course next term, if the committee of this School should desire me to deliver one" (p. 1). Moore gave this second course but the lectures themselves have not survived, though a set of notes taken by his brother, Tom, together with Moore's comments, has. A full typescript of the first course of lectures remains; they are "The Elements of Ethics." These lectures were given on ten consecutive Thursday evenings. Moore took the train from Cambridge to London, there to emulate Sidgwick's reviled pedagogy by reading his prepared remarks to the assembled students of the London School of Ethics and Social Philosophy, who met at the Passmore Settlement House. A half hour's discussion, more or less, followed; then Moore returned on the last train to Cambridge.

His début in the classroom took its toll, both on the students and on the teacher. The demands on Moore were hardly inconsiderable. He wrote out his weekly lectures, each of which averages some thirty-six typed, double-spaced pages; and he did this while at the same time he was working on other projects (for example, written contributions to both the Apostles and the Sunday Essay Society). Commuting to London and back to Cambridge on the same day may have cost Moore something physically. But the largest price Moore paid was the strain "to the nerves" he experienced while giving the lectures and leading the discussion. "The delivery of an hour's lecture, followed by half-an-hour's discussion," he declares in "The Elements," "is so trying (to the nerves, I suppose I must say), that it is difficult to keep quite cool. . . . It is indeed very difficult to understand the state of mind produced by such an effort, until you have experienced it" (pp. 75–76). This strain perhaps partly explains the alacrity of Moore's response to students' questions, one student's in particular. Looking back on the second meeting Moore begins his third lecture with an apology:

> First of all, I believe I owe you a public apology for my behaviour during part of the discussion last Thursday. To one gentleman, in particular, I do owe such an apology. In the heat of the moment I certainly entertained, and implied by my words, the belief that one question which he addressed to me was not due to any serious difficulty felt by him, with regard to the matter in question. I had no right to that belief and still less right to express it. My feeling that the

question was merely a vexatious one, was indeed only momentary; but that does not excuse it. (p. 75)

Moore's remarks here speak volumes both for his character and for the passion he brought to philosophy. Doing philosophy, like playing the piano, could literally exhaust him, rendering him less in control of himself than he normally was. It is for such a temporary loss of control that he here apologizes. That he does apologize at all reveals a man whose character was not above self-reproach. How rare to find a teacher apologizing to a student. How rarer still to have one do so publicly. Nurtured on the brilliant dialectic of the Apostles, accustomed to the rarefied intellectual atmosphere of Cambridge, one can understand how easy it would have been for Moore to give his sometimes vehement tongue free rein at the expense of his inexperienced students. No doubt he had much for which to apologize. The class, which Moore tells us was not large, may never have regained whatever zeal it once had for discussing the lectures with the lecturer. After the first few lectures "The Elements" rarely records anything more about the previous week's discussion.

While we can only conjecture about how active his students were in discussion, we know that they must have found the contents of the lectures extremely difficult. Mercifully, Moore did not include much from either of his two dissertations; "The Elements" contains almost all new material. But parts of these lectures, sometimes very large parts indeed, are carried over, verbatim, to Principia. Much of this latter work's famous discussion of the naturalistic fallacy, for example, is set out in Lectures I and II. As Moore's discussion of this fallacy in Principia has befuddled generations of professional philosophers, one can only imagine—sympathetically—how incomprehensible his declarations must have been to the few amateurs who attended his lectures. "You will remember my own answer" to the question, "What does good mean?," Moore writes near the beginning of his second lecture. "My answer was that good just means good; that it is undefinable. This statement seems to have been a stumbling-block to some of you" (p. 38). A stumbling-block indeed! Slowed in the pace of his advance Moore is nonetheless undaunted by his students' lack of comprehension, resolving to "try to make myself clearer to you" (p. 38). The traditions of the Apostles and the model offered by McTaggart—the unwavering insistence on clarity, on saying exactly what one means—these exemplars seem to have taken full possession of Moore, not in the languid ambiance of Trinity College but in response to the stark gaze of his students' bewilderment. That he did not always succeed in making himself *quite* clear is no evidence against the resoluteness and sincerity of his effort to do so.

An Expanding Vision

In some respects the object of ethics as this is conceived in "The Elements" remains the same as in the two dissertations. The aim is "to be methodical and scientific" (p. 74); its "direct object . . . is knowledge and not practice" (p. 51); and its subject matter is "the general inquiry into what is good" (p. 13). But whereas before Moore was disdainful toward questions about how we ought to act, he now devotes considerable time and space to these questions. As is true of *Principia*, "The Elements" offers a general criterion or standard of right conduct. What we ought to do is what produces the best consequences. What this action is in any given case cannot be authoritatively set down without considering the details of each case, details that vary from case to case. It is not the business of ethics, considered as a science, to say what particular acts are right or wrong. That is the task of casuistry. And neither is it the business of the ethical philosopher "to give personal advice or exhortation" (p. 16). Students who came to Moore's course in the hope of being morally uplifted were informed that they had made a serious mistake.

Concomitant with Moore's emerging interest in the morality of action and the contribution the Science of Ethics can make to our quest for knowledge in this area is his growing conviction about *the* most fundamental assumption made by this science. "All that is necessary for an Ethics, and this is absolutely necessary," he writes (p. 328), "is that we should suppose that some things are *better* in themselves than others." It is by starting with this apparently meager assumption, Moore now believes, that we are led to those robust metaphysical and epistemological views we have come to associate with his name—for example, that goodness is a nonnatural, indefinable property. Ethics is the science that explains *how it is possible* for some things to be better in themselves than others.

The metaphysical theory of concepts developed in the Second Dissertation, with some important refinements, is enlisted to account for this possibility. That theory does not make an unambiguous appearance until the fifth lecture, approximately halfway through the course. It is deployed when Moore attempts to distinguish between (*a*) natural objects and properties and (*b*) nonnatural objects and properties. Natural objects (for example, this red rose) are the existents of the Second Dissertation, while natural properties (for example, the redness of the rose) are here, as they were in that earlier work, the substantial parts of these existents. Natural objects do exist in time, and natural properties can be conceived of as existing by themselves in time (p. 175). Nonnatural objects, on the other hand, do not exist in time; and nonnatural properties cannot be conceived of as existing by themselves in time. Numbers are given by Moore as an example of nonnatural objects, and intrinsic goodness is classified as a nonnatural property. Readers familiar with *Principia* will recognize that Moore's discussion here, in "The Elements," is for the most part the same as what we find in that later work (see *Principia*, pp. 40–41). Since Moore wrote the relevant passages more than three years before *Principia* was published, we have ample evidence for assuming that the distinction he draws between the natural and the nonnatural, and the terms in which he draws it, are *considered* views, not ones he dashed off in a rush to finish the manuscript of *Principia*.

In making the distinctions he makes between the natural and the non-natural Moore should not be interpreted as recanting the Platonic theory of concepts we find in the Second Dissertation. "Of *all* concepts, indeed," he writes in "The Elements" (p. 177), "it is true that they *are* whether they exist or no"—that is, whether they exist *in time* or not. "The chief significance of Plato's doctrine of Ideas," Moore explains, is that it recognizes "this peculiar kind of being which belongs to concepts as such"; what Plato calls Ideas or Forms is, Moore adds, "what I have called concepts" (p. 177). The Second Dissertation's two-tiered metaphysic of subsisting, changeless, and timeless concepts, on the one hand, and, on the other, of existing, changing objects in time—that metaphysic remains alive and well in "The Elements". At the same time the distinction between the natural and the nonnatural represents a new attempt on Moore's part to resolve a problem that plagued the Second Dissertation. As was explained above (pages 114–115), the theories developed in the Second Dissertation seem to preclude the possibility of any existent thing's being good. For to be an existent a thing must combine at least one empirical concept with the concept of Existence. But the instantiation of an empirical concept entails that the existent thing is an *empirical* proposition (a true existential proposition) whose truth can be known empirically. Our knowledge of those things that are intrinsically valuable, however, is *a priori* on Moore's view, and these propositions are necessary, not empirical. Thus the problem lying just beneath the surface of the Second Dissertation.

The distinction Moore draws, beginning in "The Elements," between natural and nonnatural properties should be read as a part of his attempt to resolve this problem. The distinction is a *distinction between kinds of concepts, not a distinction between concepts, on the one hand, and something else, on the other.* Though all concepts *are*, "there is a clear and precise distinction," Moore maintains, "between those which also can and do exist in time, and those which cannot" (p. 177). Few people have found this distinction as clear and precise as Moore does. Nevertheless, the *logical* role of the distinction is intelligible, given certain assumptions. The distinction makes it possible for Moore to attempt to offer an explanation of how it is possible for some existing things to be good in themselves—and this an explanation that is consistent with his views about our knowledge of what these things are. In order for there to be an existing thing (an existent, or a natural object, such as this red rose) some empirical concept, instantiated as a natural property, must be combined with the concept of Existence. In order, further, for some existent to be good, that thing must possess the property, intrinsic goodness. Since our knowledge of what things are good is not empirical, the *kind* of property goodness is cannot be natural. Intrinsic goodness must therefore be nonnatural. *How* existent things "have" or "possess" nonnatural properties—or natural properties for that matter—remains as unclear in "The Elements" as it was in the Second Dissertation. Still, we can understand the allure the distinction between natural and nonnatural properties had for Moore and the problem this distinction was intended to help resolve. Because our knowledge of what things are good is not empirical—and that *some* things are better in themselves than others is *the* fundamental assumption, without which a Science of Morals is not possible—Good, when it is instantiated, while it is like Red in being a property, cannot be like Red in being natural. Good must be nonnatural.

Judgments of Intrinsic Goodness

The distinction between natural and nonnatural properties also helps Moore address a problem neglected by him in the past—the problem of how to minimize the risk of error in our judgments of intrinsic goodness. Because such judgments attribute a nonnatural property to things, Moore is fully aware that they can have no empirical or naturalistic justification.

> The discarding of all naturalistic arguments involves this: That no decision with regard to what exists or happens, no decision as to the laws of happening, afford the slightest presumption that any thing

which thus exists or happens is good. The question whether it is good or not is an entirely new question: and no assertion that this or that is the tendency of human nature, or that this or that is necessary for the preservation of the state or of society, has any bearing on the moral question whatsoever. We have always still to ask is the tendency of human nature good? Is the state good? . . . [These] are the primary questions which Ethics has to answer. (pp. 300–301)

How, then, are these questions to be answered, if all naturalistic arguments are discarded? Moore anticipates the query: "This being so, how, in the last resort, can we justify our answers?" Here is his reply:

Only, as it seems to me, in the following way. We have to ask: Is it good to believe that this or that is good? And that is itself a moral question. We have to weigh the strength of our unproved belief that it is good to believe in an unproved moral judgment against that unproved moral judgment. If we do that, we have I think, the last and strongest test to which that unproved moral judgment can be submitted. (p. 301)

Moore offers a variation on this theme a few pages later when he endeavors to explain to his students that "moral goodness [is] not a mere question of belief but of rational belief, and . . . very hard . . . to come at":

In this form only, the form of rational belief, can the moral goodness, the 'faith' of Christianity be justified. It is a question not only of your feeling that such and such a thing is good, but of your feeling that this first feeling is justified, both on comparison with other feelings, and on comparison with your feeling about the need of justification. (pp. 303–304)

It is, one might say, not a question of what one believes to be good but whether one has *earned the right* to believe it that is at the heart of Moore's message to his students. It is "very hard" to do what is required if one is to satisfy oneself that one's moral beliefs are rational. Nothing less than what Moore himself has undertaken to do in "The Elements" even begins to approach the ideal requirements. Having understood, for example, that goodness is nonnatural and thus why empirical or naturalistic evidence is irrelevant to questions of intrinsic value, we are able to understand how *not* to test for the rationality of our beliefs about what things are intrinsically good. On the positive side we know, according to Moore, that only one of two contradictory moral beliefs can be true. And a third "great reason for holding one belief to be better than another, is that it is necessary." We must turn "over and over in our minds our different beliefs, [until] we find that there is one which continues in unabated force, while the others grow weaker." After we have done this, "then we have more reason to believe that that [belief] is necessary, than we have for believing that the others are so. In proportion therefore as we have done this, as we have decided on that belief which appears to us the strongest, will that belief be rational. It will be a better belief, because we shall know we can less help acting on it, whether we decide to do so or not" (pp. 306–307). And if after we have done this sort of comparison we still cannot decide which belief is rational, then we shall have to ask ourselves, "Do I believe it better to give up the search, or to continue it?" That question in its turn spawns the same process of comparison: "We must again turn these alternatives over in our mind, and if the latter seems to be the stronger, then we shall have a rational belief in the goodness of enquiry; and our continuance of it will be justified" (p. 307). If not, not. Each person must do this on his or her own. The opinions of others on matters of intrinsic value carry no weight, rationally considered. Not even the verdicts of common sense count. When the questions under consideration concern ends, concern what is good in itself, Moore sees "no ground for admitting any probability at all" that the judgments of common sense are correct (p. 311).

Too Large an Ideal

Having for the first time seriously addressed the question of how to decide which judgments of intrinsic value are rational, Moore is in a position—and this also for the first time—to say which judgments of intrinsic value he himself accepts. This he does in his final lecture, where he sketches his conception of "the Ideal." Moore's aspirations are ambitious to say the least. The Ideal, the Summum Bonum or Ultimate End as he conceives it, is "the whole, composed of everything that is good, and of every good thing in infinite amounts" (p. 333). One can anticipate why, when the dust settles, Moore will find that his reach exceeds his grasp. Whereas in his earlier work he attempted too little when it comes to saying what things are good, in "The Elements" he attempts too much.

The nature of the Ideal, Moore contends, entails that some of its constituents will be less good in themselves than others; in every case, however, whatever the comparative value of the various elements, The Ideal requires that there be an "infinite number": "The more of each good thing there is, the better" (p. 336). Again: "[The Ideal] must contain an infinite number of instances, of each distinguishable element that is positively good" (p. 339). Moreover, the *number* of such positive goods may itself be infinite (p. 340). All considered, the Ideal may consist of an infinite number of instances of an infinite number of positive goods. In the Ideal infinity may be added to infinity.

The Ideal is still more complex than these quantitative considerations might suggest. Considered as a whole, Moore insists, there is no reason to assume and good reason to deny that its value is to be fixed merely by adding together the value of its constituent parts. By way of example he offers the following:

> To take an instance: Pleasure may be admitted to be good in itself and so may consciousness; but the whole that is formed by both together, the whole of conscious pleasure, may, I think, be well maintained to have a higher degree of goodness, than could be obtained by merely adding the degree of goodness of pleasure by itself to the degree of goodness of consciousness by itself. (p. 346)

Not only is the value of the whole not fixed merely by adding together the value of the parts; Moore also thinks there is no necessary proportion between the two.

> Suppose you take a great picture and cut it up into pieces one inch square. Now each of these pieces, or some of them at all events, would have some merit in them: you would say they were the work of a great artist. But nevertheless the sum of the merits of each piece taken separately, would not be equal to the merit of the whole picture. Nor would the proportion of its merit to the sum of merits of the parts be always the same. This proportion would, I think, differ with different pictures, which might, nevertheless, taken as wholes, be themselves of equal merit. (p. 347)

The preceding in Moore's view sets forth the *formal* characteristics of the Ideal; it does not tell us *what* The Ideal is. But once we realize the nature of the (Moorean) Ideal—an infinite number of instances of an infinite number of different positive goods, all combined to make a whole of unsurpassable intrinsic value, the sum of which cannot be found merely by adding together the value of the parts—once we realize what Moore builds into his conception of *the* Ideal, we see that he understates the case when he remarks on "how hard it is to say what the Ideal is" (p. 350). More than "hard," Moore has made the task impossible.

What to do? Moore suggests to his students that they limit their attention "to those good elements of which we have in some way had experience" (p. 352). If this is done the Ideal they conceive of "will be like this world, but with all the things in it which we think bad or mere means, left out; and all that we think good, indefinitely increased in amount" (pp. 352–353). The Ideal thus conceived will not be *the* Ideal (that is, not the best possible, not the Summum Bonum); rather, it will be the best *we* can conceive of, given the limitations of our experience and our imagination. Operating within these constraints Moore is now willing to inform his students of his own views.

> In this matter, I take the common view of philosophers. I think that human minds are the best things that there are, and that these are best, when they know the truth, but also most especially when they strongly love the best—when they love other human minds, that are, in this way, like them. And of things that are not mental, I think that those which are most beautiful are the best. . . . I do think that for a mind to contemplate external beauty is better than that such beauty simply should exist. And this can only be . . . if the mind itself is the most beautiful of objects. When one mind contemplates another, then there is most beauty; but this is by no means inconsistent with its also contemplating beauty in that which is not mind. In fine, I can find no better description for the Ideal than that which Aristotle and Plato found. It is θερια or a feeling of contemplation of all that is true and beautiful and good; the contemplating mind being also in these respects like that which it is contemplating. (pp. 353–354)

Having declared his beliefs about which things "in this world I think most definitely good and the best" (p. 353) Moore tells his students that he has been "led quite unintentionally into so long a discussion of the Ideal—a discussion which is more definitely than any other part of my lectures, of the nature of which most people would call metaphysical" (pp. 354–355). He has "no great respect" for the philosophical merits of his views on these and related matters (p. 326). What he does respect are his views about the "three great steps in ethical inquiry" which he has distinguished in his lectures: the question, 'How is good to be defined?'; the question, 'What acts are right?' or, alternatively, 'What things are good as means?'; and the question, 'What things are good in themselves?' The "necessity" of these "three great steps" Moore thinks "is demonstrable" (p. 326) and has been demonstrated by him.

Loose Ends

"The Elements" reveals the remarkable pace of Moore's progress as a moral philosopher. Whatever their shortcomings, these lectures are vastly better as philosophy than either of his two Dissertations. That "independence of thought" Sidgwick had remarked upon in his comments on the First Dissertation asserts itself with increasingly vigorous clarity. The distance between *Principia* and the two dissertations is immense; it is difficult to believe that these are the products of the same mind. The distance between *Principia* and "The Elements" is considerably shorter; many of the former work's most important teachings are to be found in the latter, at least in embryonic form. Moore the teacher has become Moore the philosopher.

In "The Elements" Moore succeeds in offering an account of goodness that satisfies both the universality and the objectivity criteria. What things are good depends on what things instantiate the concept Good, and though Moore does not offer anything approaching a satisfactory account of how things manage to do this, he is very clear in his views about how they do not. Things can be intrinsically good independently of our thinking, feeling, hoping that they are. Their value is intrinsic to them; they possess their value independently of our awareness, recognition, or appreciation. When a tree falls in a forest of intrinsic value and no one is there, that does not mean that there is no intrinsic value either. True, *it is better* if someone recognizes, understands, appreciates, or loves what has intrinsic value. But there can be intrinsic goods in the absence of anyone's cognition, appreciation, and the like. Moore's views in "The Elements" thus arguably satisfy the requirement of objectivity.

That they satisfy the universality requirement also should be clear. "The good is fixed," he writes (p. 215). "If it is once good, then it is always good, and nothing can make a change in this respect." Our opinions about or our appreciation of the goodness of the same thing: these clearly can change over time. But not the presence or degree of goodness intrinsic to the thing. Notwithstanding the absence of a satisfactory account of how the goodness of good things is related to their other properties, a problem that will plague him even well beyond the publication of *Principia*, Moore's understanding of Good requires that—even if it does not fully explain how—the universality criterion is met.

Unlike either of his two dissertations, moreover, "The Elements" seems to offer an account of intrinsic value that satisfies the natural goods criterion. Contrary to the implications of the First Dissertation, not everything that exists in nature is good according to the principles of "The Elements," and contrary to the implications of the Second, these principles also allow that some good things do exist. Moreover, those things that are good are not all of equal intrinsic value. The fundamental assumption of ethics—namely, that some things are better in themselves than others—is an assumption Moore's speculations seek to explain rather than deny.

On a related matter Moore's views in "The Elements" do not render the notion of ideals unintelligible. The good that exists need not be the best possible, and though we are unable to form a complete conception of *the* Ideal (an infinite number of goods, each in infinite amounts, and so on) it does not follow either that this lofty conception of a better state of things is unintelligible or that we cannot make some progress in conceiving a better state if we set our sights a good deal lower. Moore's position allows that we can know something about what would be better than what actually exists without our having to know everything. The success of "The Elements" when tested against the objectivity, universality, natural goods, and ideal criteria compellingly demonstrates how significantly Moore's thought had matured in the few months following his receipt of his Prize Fellowship.

No less significant are the steps Moore takes in this work toward meeting both the conduct and the method criteria. What we ought to do is what produces the best consequences. That is the abstract standard of right conduct he now accepts. His challenge is to determine what conduct this is. To do this requires a serious attempt on his part to say *both* what things are good in themselves (and how we rationally can decide this) *and* what if any moral rules we should follow in our conduct. The two are intimately related. We cannot know what we ought to do if we do not know what things are good in themselves since the good we ought to produce by our acts is intrinsic good. Unhappily, Moore seems to have guaranteed that we cannot know either. The price of moral truth, it seems, is moral paralysis. "I have tried to shew you," he writes near the conclusion of "The Elements," "how impossible it is that we should know the complete end. And it is obvious at once that the doctrine of means is also incomplete. . . . It is therefore obvious that the ideal of a rational belief as to what we ought to do, is infinitely far from being attainable for us. To attain it we should have to answer all the questions I have raised, and it is irrational to believe that we can answer them" (p. 355). Pressed to the mat by the weight of his own theory, we can imagine Moore looking out into the troubled faces of his students, each wondering what has been the point of his dutiful attendance at Moore's lectures these past ten weeks. If all that Moore had succeeded in doing was to raise an impossible ideal and then declare that no one can fulfill it, how were they to decide what they ought to do? How avoid complete paralysis?

Moore anticipates their question and gives his answer:

> I think we can still say what is best in *general*. . . . Most questions of practical conduct are for the most part questions of means and not of ends. The possible effects of our choice are, in any case, very small: the amount of good attainable is whether by choice or not also very small in comparison of the ideal: we need therefore, in general ask no more than what is possible, and that we shall commonly arrive immediately at the best answer that can be given to this question, evolution guarantees us. It is only those who on the whole were best at foreseeing what will be the effect of what who could have come to survive as we have survived. (p. 356)

Knowing in general what we ought to do turns out to be rather easy. If we ask the question, 'What ought I to do here and now?' we shall "commonly arrive immediately at the best answer" without having to bother much about it; and if we press the issue and ask "How can we be sure of this?" Moore replies, "This is guaranteed by evolution." For we would not have survived in the form in which we find ourselves unless "on the whole" we shared the ability to see "what will be the effect of what."

But this will not do. What determines whether we act as we ought is not simply that our acts have effects we can foresee; it is *how good* these effects are. And our knowing how good they are, though this would be impossible without our ability to see "what will be the effect of what," is not guaranteed merely by our having this ability. In order for the ethical theory Moore offers in "The Elements" to advance toward satisfying the conduct criterion he must present a defensible method for answering questions about what things are good in themselves. He must satisfy the method criterion. This he fails to do.

As we saw earlier in the present chapter, Moore at one point discusses beliefs about intrinsic goods in psychological terms. We are to consider our beliefs about intrinsic value with a view to seeing which if any of them continue "with unabated force," which "grow weaker." The more forceful, the more necessary; the weaker, the less so. And the more necessary, the more rational. But this approach cannot verify the truth of judgments of intrinsic goodness since it runs directly contrary to Moore's adamant rejection of naturalism in ethics. Recall the passage quoted earlier: "The discarding of all naturalistic arguments involves this: That no decision with regard to what exists or happens, no decision as to the laws of happening, afford the slightest presumption that any thing which thus exists or happens is good." Even if it is true, then, that as we think about our beliefs some of them retain their "force" while others "grow weaker," this *can* only be a psychological fact about what happens when we turn these beliefs over in our minds; and that fact, like every other one, cannot afford "the slightest presumption" that the beliefs which retain their "force" are any more likely to be true than those which do not. In criticizing Kant's views about Transcendental Freedom, Moore at one point in "Freedom" charged him with mixing philosophy and psychology in ways that were symptomatic of "the too psychological standpoint above which [he] seems never to have completely risen in treating epistemological questions." The same could be said of Moore's treatment of the psychology of belief if one uses his method to verify the truth of what is believed.

We should perhaps not be surprised, therefore, to find that Moore proposes a different method of verification. "I think we can still say what is best *in general*," he writes, not only in the case of means but also in the case of ends. In the former case the truth of our judgment is "guaranteed" by "evolution." The same is true in the latter case: "In the case of ends, we have a similar guarantee. We shall not in general, be able to think that anything is good beside what other people think so. For what we think has also been determined by the course of evolution" (p. 356). Moore, it must be noted, is not merely offering a description of what *causes* our beliefs about ends; his intention is the quite different one of saying how we are able to establish what things *are best in general*. Interpreted in the manner in which he intends it, his position grievously flaunts the antinaturalistic requirements he imposes on others. If "*no* decision with regard to what exists or happens" and "*no* decision as to the laws of happening" afford "the *slightest* presumption that anything which thus exists or happens is good," then *no* decision about what the course of evolution does or does not "guarantee" can afford the slightest presumption that anything declared good by "other people" *is* good. Moore's attempts to offer a method for choosing between different judgments of intrinsic goodness dies at the hands of other, more fundamental requirements in his theory. Moreover, because his teaching concerning right action (what is good as a means) logically presupposes a rational method for resolving questions about what things are good in themselves (good as ends) the vaporous inadequacy of his attempt to confront this latter challenge undermines his teaching regarding the former.

There is some circumstantial evidence at the end of "The Elements" which suggests that Moore senses that something had gone wrong. Near the beginning Moore had boldly proclaimed that "it is not the business of the moral philosopher to give personal advice or exhortation" (another example of an idea Moore carries to *Principia*; see this latter work, p. 3). But after his ill-starred attempts to meet the conduct and the method criteria, what do we find? We find the following:

> In practical life therefore I think we should be on the whole conservative: only admitting a change in custom, where the change is slight and trivial. (p. 357)

> If the individual finds his conscience markedly against that of common sense, there is good reason why he should hesitate to follow it [that is, his conscience]. (p. 357)

> To *act* on the results of reflection is hardly ever wise. (p. 358)

> It is something important to recognise that the best of reasons can be given for *anything* whatever, if only we are clever enough: sophistry is easy, wisdom is impossible; the best that we can do is to trust to COMMON SENSE (p. 359)

More than advice, one might even read this last quotation, the final words of "The Elements," as an example of exhortation. That in the end Moore should find it necessary to eat of these forbidden fruits—that he should give advice and offer exhortation—suggests that he may have understood how weak his theory is at just those points where it needs to be strongest.

Whether this is true or not, the content of the advice and exhortation Moore offers at the conclusion of "The Elements" is of a nature we should expect, given the standard interpretation of his thought. We are not to think for ourselves, it seems: "To act on the results of reflection is hardly ever wise." The moral status quo, expressed in the rules of conventional morality, should normally be accepted without change or challenge: "a change in custom" is to be admitted "only . . . where the change is slight and trivial." The individual should "hesitate to follow" his or her own moral convictions if or as they clash with "common sense" as we find this expressed in the existing rules of conventional morality. And even the claims of independent thinking must be looked at suspiciously since "the best of reasons can be given for *anything* whatever, if only we are clever enough." If *Principia*'s teachings concerning right conduct are cut from the same morally conservative cloth we find here, then the standard interpretation wins hands down. Whether they are, and whether it does, remains to be decided. It is enough to note at this point that Moore certainly was at one time strongly inclined to accept a very conservative position concerning large-scale social change (see his remarks about changes in "social custom") and regarding the individual's right or responsibility to act and judge independently (see his remarks about acting on the basis "of reflection" or as a matter of individual "conscience"). If *Principia*'s teachings differ significantly from those we find at the conclusion of "The Elements"—and that they do will be argued below—we know that Moore could not have come to these later views without a deep, protracted struggle. In particular we know that the simple dichotomy operating just beneath the surface in "Vanity of vanities"—the obligation to abide by moral rules is grounded *either* in the dictates of God *or* in the rules of conventional morality—this simple dichotomy will have to be enriched. Moore needs a third alternative. And he will find one, embarking on his search, as we shall see shortly, soon after his demanding course of lectures in the Fall of 1899 was behind him.

The Etiology of Melancholy

Superficially considered, the circumstances of Moore's life in the Spring of 1899 would seem to be ill suited to fostering acute melancholia. His six-year Fellowship at Trinity, "a very pleasant place and a very pleasant life," had begun the previous Fall; he had completed his course of lectures at the Passmore Settlement House, written three reviews, and published two papers, "Freedom," in April 1898 and "The Nature of Judgment" in April 1899. His career as a philosopher was well launched. The Second Dissertation in general and "The Nature of Judgment" in particular sent ripples of rebellion through the philosophical community to which Moore belonged, and no one was more affected than Russell. "I have read your [Second] Dissertation," Russell writes to Moore on December 1, 1898, "[and] it appears to me to be on the level of the best philosophy I know." Those tendencies toward realism that Moore speaks of in his autobiography awakened Russell from his idealistic slumbers. It was Moore, Russell writes in "My Intellectual Development," who

> took the lead in the rebellion [against idealism], and I followed with a sense of emancipation. Bradley had argued that everything that common sense believes in is mere appearance; we reverted to the opposite extreme, and thought that *everything* is real, that common sense, uninfluenced by philosophy or theology, supposes real. With a sense of escaping from prison, we allowed ourselves to think that grass is green, that the sun and the stars would exist if no one was aware of them, and also that there is a pluralistic timeless world of Platonic ideas. The world which had been thin and logical, suddenly became rich and varied and solid.

Russell dates this rebellion against Bradley (and Hegel, Kant, and the other idealists) as 1898, which means that he must be referring to his understanding of the new ideas Moore was working out in his Second Dissertation, ultimately to be expressed in "The Nature of Judgment." Here, then, was a colossal role reversal. For it had been Russell who only a few years earlier had urged Moore to take Part II of the Moral Sciences Tripos, Russell having formed the opinion, in Moore's memorable words, that he (Moore) "had some aptitude for philosophy." And now it was Moore who was leading Russell. This was heady stuff for a young man of twenty-five.

How, then, in view of Moore's apparent good fortune at this time are we to explain the acute melancholy and nihilism of his Apostles paper "Vanity of vanities," which he delivered in April 1899, soon after returning from the reading party at Gunnerside? Part of the answer seems to lie in an unexpected development in Moore's relationship with Russell. In the Fall of 1898 Moore is leading a philosophical rebellion against idealism, with Russell assuming the role of follower. In February of 1899, however, it is Russell who is attacking, and Moore who is defending, not idealism but one of Moore's most cherished convictions.

As noted earlier Moore's First Dissertation includes an appendix entitled "Professor Sidgwick's Hedonism," in which he offers a series of objections against the views of his teacher, including an objection concerning beauty as a natural good. Sidgwick, because he believes that pleasure and pleasure alone is intrinsically good, must deny the intrinsic value of natural beauty. Moore is of another mind, maintaining that beauty in nature, even if unknown and unappreciated by a conscious being, has intrinsic value of its own. As was also noted earlier this appendix was deleted from the Second Dissertation. But Moore's criticisms of Sidgwick, including the one just noted, were reformulated in the fifth lecture of "The Elements." Here, quoting at length, is the relevant portion of that lecture:

Again, I think this same position [viz., that beauty itself is good as an end] results from another consideration. . . . If it be granted, as many would be inclined to grant, that the contemplation of beauty, at least, is better than the contemplation of ugliness; if, for instance, the pleasure resulting from such contemplation is held to be what Mill would call a 'higher' pleasure, than that which may be derived from contemplating ugliness, then I think it must follow that beauty is also in itself better than ugliness. For whenever we contemplate a thing, then there is in us and in that thing something in common. In so far as we are really contemplating a beautiful thing, the qualities, which in it are beautiful, are also present in our contemplation. Such, at least, is the commonly accepted view. And however that may be the presence of these qualities is certainly the only thing which can distinguish the contemplation of beauty from the contemplation of ugliness, if these two contemplations be considered in themselves, apart from the different states of feeling which they may excite. But, in that case, the contemplation of beauty can only be better than its opposite, in virtue of those very same qualities which are also present in the beautiful object. It is they and they only which give to it its value. . . . It would thus appear that we cannot consistently maintain even that the contemplation of beauty is better in itself than the contemplation of ugliness, that it is a higher pleasure, unless we allow that beauty alone, whether it be contemplated or not, is also better than ugliness. (pp. 162–163)

More than the students in his class at the London School of Ethics and Social Philosophy knew these words. Russell in particular was aware of them, and he subjects Moore's views to stiff criticism in a paper, "Was the world good before the 6th day?" read to the Apostles on February 10, 1899, and quoted by Levy (pp. 204–206). Russell begins as follows:

Our brother Moore has been engaged, by order of the Society, in a heroic work, involving the very highest degree of danger and difficulty. He has been endeavouring—I believe with success—to corrupt still further (an arduous task) the morals of those phenomena who frequent the shallow abyss known among the shadows as "The London School of Ethics and Social Philosophy." As the glory of God is enhanced by the damnation of the wicked, by which they are rendered still more wicked than they intended to be, so the glory of the Society is enhanced by increasing the phenomenality of phenomena. And as it is the mark of the Society to be wise and good, so it is the mark of phenomena to be foolish and wicked. Moore has been endeavouring then, to render these shadows even more foolish and more wicked than they naturally are. That this is difficult is certainly undeniable; but the difficulty seems to have been successfully overcome. . . . The danger of Moore's mission, however, was even more overwhelming than the difficulty, and has, I fear, been less effectively avoided. It is well-known that whatever is dangerous for a brother is unreal, and that contact with the unreal may entail fatal consequences. What, then, was my horror, when I discovered that these views, designed for the corruption of the non-existent, had—I shudder at the thought—infected our lamented brother himself. To free him from these dreadful toils is my purpose tonight.

The source of Moore's unsavory alliance with the phenomenal world is the idea of beauty's independent value as an end. Here is the way Russell, with a strong dose of theological jesting, describes Moore's position:

Moore contends that God, when he looked down upon the world in its early stages, was right in maintaining it to be good—that it was already good in and for itself, and would have continued so even if

God had not been looking. A world of matter alone—so says our misguided brother—may be good or bad. For it may certainly be beautiful or ugly, and beauty is better than ugliness. . . . Beauty is good *per se*, and a purely material world, with no one to contemplate it, is better if it is beautiful than if it is ugly.

Such is the argument, which, though invented for the further perdition of shadows, has alas! deceived our brother himself. Let us now endeavour to persuade him that this sophism, like the world of matter, can only be good as a means, and must never be taken as an end.

Against Moore's view Russell procedes to argue that only psychical states (that is, states of mind) are intrinsically valuable and that hedonism after all is the true theory of value.

Paul Levy argues that Moore was furious with Russell because, claims Levy, Russell misrepresented Moore's views. But there can be no serious question that in "The Elements" Moore does maintain the central view Russell attributes to him—namely, that beauty is intrinsically good, or good as an end, apart from either our contemplation or our awareness. And Russell's explicit allusion to Moore's work for the London School of Ethics and Social Philosophy supports the view that Russell is directing his remarks to that section of "The Elements" quoted at length above, though not necessarily only to that. It is not credible to follow Levy in supposing either that Russell in his paper is responding to a paper of Moore's on a different topic ("Do we love ourselves best?") read to the Apostles a week earlier or that Moore "was cross" because his views were so unpardonably distorted.

Wrong in his explanation of the importance of Russell's paper, Levy nonetheless seems to be right in judging it important in the first place. That importance is twofold. First, it represents, so far as we know, the first written criticism that passes between Russell and Moore. Not that they had never disagreed. One has only to glimpse the record of their votes at Apostles meetings to confirm how often they disagreed and over how much. Still, "Was the world good before the 6th day?" represents something new. To be on different sides of a vote is one thing; to have one's views serve as the subject of a critical paper is quite another. And to have this happen hard on the heels of one's assuming the role of "leader" in a philosophical rebellion could, one must suppose, only intensify the trauma of the event for the person on the receiving end of the criticism.

The evening of February 10, 1899 could not have been an easy one for Moore, as Levy's descriptions—Moore was "annoyed," he "*was* cross"—suggest. His happy association with Russell had been breached for the first but not for the last time. By 1903, Moore could not even bear the thought that Russell might be included in a reading party.

But that evening in February 1899, we may conjecture, was important for another reason. For what Russell highlights in his critique are the insubstantial contours of Moore's thought about intrinsic value. Moore, unlike Sidgwick, believes that beauty in nature is intrinsically good. But what are Moore's *reasons* for believing this? What *defensible method* can Moore cite to defend the superiority of his judgment over his teacher's? There is nothing philosophically weaker in "The Elements" than Moore's answers to these questions. Having himself categorically rejected each and every naturalistic argument in favor of judgments of intrinsic value, Moore in the end succumbs to the temptation, defending the superiority of some judgments over others by appealing to the "guarantee" provided by "evolution." The plain fact is, Moore had no defensible method to rely on, had no reason whatever for his beliefs about what things are good. And here is Russell, his erstwhile follower, bringing this painful fact to Moore's attention. And to the Apostles'.

"Vanity of vanities" is Moore's melancholic response. There is no rational remedy against unhappiness, he protests. Belief in God requires a leap of faith he is not prepared to make. And as for accepting the values presupposed by common sense, values that, at the end of "The Elements," he was prepared cheerfully to endorse, these, too, are without a rational foundation. "If there are reasons" for accepting the intrinsic goods affirmed by common sense, he writes, "then you ought to be able to convince yourself that it is so by direct consideration." This Moore is unable to do. He finds no rational escape from his acute unhappiness. He lives for nothing.

We understate the case if we say that Moore's confidence was shaken at this time. "Vanity of vanities" testifies to a deep, genuine spiritual crisis in his life. At this time beliefs about the goodness of ends were for him logically the same as belief in God: a matter of faith. In the confessional revelations of "Vanity of vanities" we find a man who has lost all faith, not only in God but in the value of everything. And, it seems, in himself. For Moore was ready for a fall. In his lectures to his students he had presumed to demonstrate a good deal. When the logic of his proofs made the ideal of rational belief in ethics "infinitely" unattainable, he presumed to show his students the way to escape the moral paralysis his proofs seemed to require. Russell would not allow it. "The Elements" were something of a philosophical mess. Moore must have realized this. Now, thanks to Russell, his most respected and cherished peers knew this too. *Everything* was vanity, including the pride of the author of "The Elements". The long night of Moore's soul had begun.

As we have seen from his letters to Desmond MacCarthy, that night lasted longer than a few days in April 1899. Letters to his mother as late as 1901 also suggest the dimensions of his melancholy. "I have been very lonely on the whole," he writes on September 12, 1901. And on November 14: "I seem to find it increasingly difficult to satisfy myself with anything; which sometimes makes me feel very desperate." Even a quick victory among the Apostles eluded him. Soon after reading "Vanity of vanities," Moore delivered a paper on sex (now lost, alas). "There was nothing else I could write so much about with so much interest," he writes to MacCarthy on May 30, 1899, but when the question was put to the vote, the majority disagreed with Moore. They did *not* think "self-abuse is bad *as an end*." "Just think of the question and the vote," Moore laments to MacCarthy, who was familiar with Moore's views about means and ends as these are set forth in "The Elements". Moore was astonished that the Brothers didn't *see* the intrinsic evil of self-abuse (in sexual matters presumably). Even after Moore had defended his account of intrinsic value in the face of Russell's objections, and possibly in part because of them, the Brothers could not be convinced that Moore was right. Russell had scored more than an evening's victory in debate on the evening he read "Was the world good on the 6th day?" and Moore had suffered more than a temporary defeat. He thought he knew what was not good, but he had yet to find a way to persuade others. Nor had he found a basis to justify his confidence.

The record of Moore's published and unpublished work during this period shows that he examined various escapes from this crisis in his intellectual and personal life. Notwithstanding his avowed agnosticism it would be natural for anyone with Moore's upbringing to look to religion for a safe passage out of his despair. This Moore did, as the record shows. "The Value of Religion," "Natural Theology," "Immortality," and his review of Ward's *Naturalism and Agnosticism* were all written or published after "Vanity of vanities" and before 1901. That in the end Moore found no rational substance in religious belief is not to be denied. It is the fact *that* he looks to it at all, and *when* he does, that cannot go unnoticed. If it is true, as Moore relates in his autobiography, that it was his eldest brother, Thomas, who played the largest role in converting him to agnosticism before Moore went up to Cambridge in 1892, it is Moore himself, by himself this time, who during the years 1899 to 1901 reconsecrates the grounds of his commitment.

The Happy Warrior

That other avenue of possible escape—belief in the values of common sense—is far too narrow for Moore's vastly larger aspirations at this time. In a remarkable Apostles paper of May 24, 1900, whose very title ("Is conversion possible?") is symptomatic of his spiritual unrest, Moore uses what he calls the "literary" as distinct from the "scientific" method to examine the nature and value of a mental state he calls "moral conversion." The most striking and important features of this mental state also belong to religious conversion, he maintains, except that moral conversion "is not necessarily connected with any religious ideas, with convictions about gods or saints or devils or with dreams and visions of them." Both sorts of conversion represent "a New Birth, leading to a New Life, an awakening of conscience, a conviction of sin." Dissatisfied with his initial description, Moore goes on to allow the literary method a freer reign as he attempts to describe moral conversion.

> It is indeed both a great good in itself and it secures all other goods which depend on one's own mind alone. It means a wonderful clearness of mind, wherein all things, of which you are conscious, are seen in their true proportionate values; and you are conscious of your own relation to them. It is your 'true self', of which you are conscious and you know it desires the things it sees only in proportion to their real value. And although you may be also conscious of the existence of other desires, *natural* desires, which are not so well directed—desires which have at other times almost completely occupied your mind, and have made you enjoy to do the worst of actions—you are now well assured that your true self is immensely more powerful than they are and can govern them without an effort. You see 'life steadily and whole' and can feel neither desire nor fear of what you see to be bad in it. You have no temptation to be sensual or idle, and you feel that nothing anyone can do to you could do you any harm: noone can rob you of your power to do the best that is possible under the circumstances, and hence they cannot make you feel ashamed. You have the perfect knowledge [of] what is good, which Socrates said would always make you do it, and you know

that you always will do it. But at the same time, though you are so far like the wise man of the Stoics or of Goethe, you have none of that blindness or insensibility which may disfigure him. You are not self-sufficient—not even so self-sufficient as Mr. Pater's Marius. You not only see more of what passes before you, than you can at other times; you not only see it in a clear daylight, and without a depressing or coloured atmosphere; but it also never seems to you commonplace. You are very sensitive both to what is bad and to what is good in it. You may hate and despise as strongly as ever, but without any fear; you may pity, without despising, and you may love and admire to all degrees of ardour, without being led to accept the bad along with the good. This is the Happy Warrior.

By identifying his vision of the wise man with the Happy Warrior, Moore is calling up the familiar image immortalized in Wordsworth's poem by that title. Additional allusions to Wordsworth will follow. At this point in his narrative he pauses to insist that such states really do occur and to reveal that he has experienced them himself, adding that "while we have [them], . . . I wish to suggest that we really have the powers which we seem to ourselves to have. If then we could make [this state] permanent, it would be the greatest conceivable blessing."

But is it possible to make the New Life permanent? Might we find the "true philosopher's stone" that will transform ourself and others into Happy Warriors? "Such a principle [of transformation] is one of which I have often been in search," Moore reveals, "and once I found it. One night MacCarthy and I both thought we had made the great discovery. But afterwards neither of us could remember at all what it was like, nor even how we had expressed it to one another. It had vanished as completely and as quickly, as the New Birth itself." And yet despite the record of his own failure to retain the "elixir" he seeks, Moore refuses to accept the conservative teachings of Matthew Arnold's poem "Morality":

> We cannot kindle when we will
> The fire which in the heart resides;
> The spirit bloweth and is still.
> In mystery our soul abides.
> But tasks in hours of insight willed
> May be in hours of gloom fulfilled.

Moore's contempt explodes on the page.

This is Morality; it is the Stoic doctrine, and it is not what I wish to recommend. It is undoubtedly possible to act upon a plan, of which you do not now see the bearings or the value clearly. But you will act blindly; in proportion as you act regularly, you will confirm this state of blindness; and in proportion as you are blind, you will both lack a goodness in yourself, and your actions will fail to achieve the good at which they aimed, often producing instead a result at which you would have shuddered in the hour of insight, when the spirit was blowing. Yet to persuade you to do this, to act blindly, is the object of the strenuous Morality. Its only gospel, is that you *can* do it. I doubt if it be a gospel. It is true, but not good news. It is like the gospel of 'Count 20, Fatty Coram'. You know that, if you do count 20, you will probably see clearer at the end of it than before. It is an artifice for letting Reason have her say, and you know that you can resolve to adopt it. But it involves the risk of becoming merely habitual. Instead of awakening Reason it may gradually have the effect of merely producing the same action, which she at first produced. And besides this it has the disadvantage that it is a mere artifice. To count twenty is not a great good in itself, nor are the rules of morality. You have the knowledge that you ought to act so, but you do not see the good of it. And even though the knowledge works in the sense of producing the action, it is not 'working' knowledge in the full sense of ε'νεργερά. It may, I think, be really better that so poor a knowledge should not act—that you should do nothing, except when you clearly see the good of it, on the ground that you are thus more likely to see more goods more often. At all events the temptation to wait for the Spirit is not a mark of an ignoble mind. It is not a mere temptation of the Devil, as Morality would have us think. It proceeds from the desire not to run away from him: to take the risk of yielding to his allurements, rather than to avoid them by a rule of thumb, without perceiving how poor they really are.

It is Wordsworth, not Arnold, who speaks for the New Life by offering a gospel of permanent liberation in place of the sterile, mechanical principles of "Morality."

> Serene will be our days and bright
> And happy will our nature be,

When love is an unerring light,
And joy its own security.

These lines from Wordsworth's "Ode to Duty" are "a description of the New Life" where one's acting morally is both spontaneous and joyful, not mechanical and lifeless. Wordsworth, however, because "he does not possess this Life," goes on to appeal to Duty for help. But this Duty is not the duty of "Morality." The Duty Wordsworth prays to is not the voice of *conventional* morality, not the cliché-ridden teachings with which Moore himself ended "The Elements" only a few months before, but "the voice of my own wish."

Yet not the less would I throughout
Still act according to the voice
Of my own wish; and feel past doubt
That my submissiveness was choice.
Not seeking in the school of pride
For "precepts over dignified",
Denial and restraint I prize
No farther than they breed a second Will more wise.

Wordsworth, Moore contends, "felt the New Birth when he wrote this poem," and in it "he is praying exactly for that principle, of which I am now in search"—the principle that would give one the means to make the New Life permanent.

That principle eludes Moore's grasp on this occasion. But the question remains: Is conversion possible? Is it possible to find a principle that would give us the means of rendering the New Life permanent? When put to the vote, four Brothers vote Yes. Seven vote No. Moore is in the minority, appending to his affirmative vote the sad comment: "Personally I am particularly incapable of doing so."

The Doubt

Among the major lessons to be learned from "Is conversion possible?" is how far Moore could wander off the path of common sense, not only when he turned his hand to metaphysics (this we have seen on more than one occasion in the preceding pages) but also when he turned his gaze to the substance and spirit of morality. In "Vanity of vanities," it will be recalled, Moore is unwilling to purchase his own happiness at the price of disloyalty to reason. The remedies against unhappiness recommended by common sense are duly acknowledged.

> Live virtuously and you will be happy; work hard and be unselfish and take regular exercise and be temperate, and relax yourself with those amusements which are generally held to be innocent: do all these things and you will be happy.

While he concedes that one who does these things and who abides by "the rules of common sense morality" will overcome unhappiness, Moore will not budge until he has been given *reasons* why the values affirmed by common sense are true. In that paper the value of the happiness offered by common sense is real enough; only the cost of its acquisition (disloyalty to reason) is too high. In "Is conversion possible?" the situation appears quite different. Without explicitly mentioning common sense or its values it seems clear that *the very quality* of the happiness one can achieve by following the rules offered by common sense has lost its allure. The happiness now sought ("And happy will our nature be") is of a different order altogether, spontaneous and heroic, not conventional and bland, to be secured not by such pedestrian means as taking "regular exercise and be[ing] temperate" but by the apprehension of a possibly ineffable principle that gives one the power to transform one's self permanently into a Happy Warrior. The happiness of the New Life, one might almost say, is noumenal, that of everyday life, phenomenal. Or so it seems, given the message of "Is conversion possible."

That paper's message wanders off the narrow path of common sense in yet another way. Wordsworth's "voice of my own wish" is not the voice of the plain man. It is the voice of the visionary, spoken at the apex of an exhilarating state of heightened awareness that includes both knowledge of one's "true self" and of all that is good and evil. Not possible to those who reduce morality to mechanical obedience to Moral Laws, those free spirits who would attain the New Life must be unencumbered by the weight of convention, secure enough in the immediateness of their knowledge of good and evil that they may act spontaneously. For "the life of 'chance-desires' may reveal truths, which the precepts of Morality would blind you to for ever."

But Moore's romance with a mystical happiness in "Is conversion possible?" must not be distorted. Although he believes in the reality of the mental state he calls "moral conversion," and notwithstanding the sincerity of his longing to find the "true philosopher's stone" that would make the New Life permanent, Moore shows that he is unwilling to commit himself to the real desirability of the mental state itself. "As to the goodness of the New Birth: Is it possible," he asks, "that this state of mind, with all its professions of clear and true sight and its promise of power against every temptation, merely deludes us?" Not wishing to give too much to religious belief, and required by logic not to take more for himself than he is willing to give, Moore is unable to answer, "No!" "I feel the doubt uncomfortable and certainly," he writes, adding:

> I feel it possible that the states of those, religious enthusiasts for example, whom I cannot suppose to see nothing but the truth, may be psychologically indistinguishable from mine. And, if psychologically indistinguishable, then the chief hope of my panacea vanishes.

"It is still possible," Moore allows, "that my states may really be ones in which I see nothing but the truth." But the logical chasm remains: the mere *possibility* that moral conversion is all that Moore has said it is goes no way toward showing that it *actually* is. That one might bridge this logical gap by an act of will, deliberately choosing to believe in the value of things in the absence of reason, is an option almost beneath Moore's contempt. William James, Moore supposes, had offered such an escape, enticing his followers "to say that, if we only believe the truth hard enough, the facts will some day come to be true." But the realm of normative value, no less than the world of empirical fact, is what it is, and not another thing, and in neither case can we make it what it is by choosing to believe one thing rather than another.

Sidgwick's Disciple

However "pleasant" his life was at this point, Moore was no closer to the happiness that eluded him when he wrote "Vanity of Vanities." A happy person, he there states, is one who, "whenever the question arises, whether things that we have or can get are worth having" answers "that they are." When Moore confesses that he "feel[s] the doubt uncomfortable" about the value of the mental state of moral conversion, his confidence in his convictions, about what has value, about the worth of things he can secure or that he already possesses, is still lacking. Just as Moore had argued earlier that neither common sense nor religion affords a rational passage to the happiness he seeks, so here, on this occasion, he stops short of endorsing the reasonableness of the way offered by the mystical intoxication of the Happy Warrior. What Moore was seeking and not finding in "Vanity of vanities" is the same thing he is seeking and not finding in "Is conversion possible?" To the extent that this is *happiness*, and not merely "a pleasant life," what he sought and failed to find in the former is what he sought and failed to find in the latter.

It would have been easy for those who first heard him read "Is conversion possible?" to miss Moore's expressions of doubt and distress about the value of the New Life, brief and seemingly inconsequential as these expressions appear. Possibly Strachey failed to notice them when Moore read this paper for a second time. But the doubts are there. Having painted his vision of a most uncommon state of happiness, having presented it as nobler than the sort of wooden, zestless happiness attainable by those for whom the moral life is one of habitual conformity to conventional moral rules, and having dazzled his audience with his breathless delivery, Moore yet remains unwilling or unable to affirm its value. Perhaps the New Life has no real value after all. He "feel[s] the doubt uncomfortable." Thus does he here exhibit, even if those in his audience failed to see this, the habit of indecisiveness that some would malign in his teacher, Sidgwick, whose disciple he remained in a most profound sense. "There is no doubt of his moral goodness," Keynes would write of the Sidgwick who emerges in *A Memoir*, "and yet it is all so dreadfully depressing—no intimacy, no clear-cut boldness." In Moore, on the other hand, Keynes and his contemporaries obviously thought they found another tendency. Whether this resulted from a failure on their part to heed the logic lessons that tempered Moore's enthusiasm, even in so enthusiastic a paper as "Is conversion possible?," remains to be seen. It is doubtful, however, that those lessons were wasted at a later date on the recently arrived student from Vienna, by way of Manchester, who became an Apostle on November 16, 1912, the date Moore read his paper on conversion for a third time. Ludwig Wittgenstein had an ear for logic.

The Best of Friends

Among the many friends Moore had throughout his life none was closer than Desmond MacCarthy. A number of Moore's acquaintances from his days as a student at Cambridge—Robert Trevelyan and his brother, George, for example—remark on the closeness of this friendship in their letters to Moore up to and beyond MacCarthy's death in June of 1952. At Gunnerside, in April of 1899, when Moore and MacCarthy were both in their mid-twenties, their friendship was still in its youth. But even then it was special. Although Moore himself was not "witty or humorous," Leonard Woolf recalls, "he had a fine, sensitive sense of humour. In conversation Lytton Strachey's snake-like witticisms greatly amused him. But," he continues in *Sowing,*

> the wit and humour he liked best, I think, were Desmond MacCarthy's. Desmond was half Irish and his humour had the soft, lovely charm which traditionally is characteristic of Ireland. He was a brilliant talker and raconteur, and he could make Moore laugh as no one else could. And Moore laughed, when he did laugh, with the same passion with which he pursued truth or played a Beethoven sonata. A frequent scene which I like to look back upon is Desmond standing in front of a fire-place telling a long, fantastic story in his gentle voice and Moore lying back on a sofa or deep in an armchair, his pipe as usual out, shaking from head to foot in a long paroxysm of laughter. (p. 143)

We can imagine that scene played out now, Moore having finished his evening's combat with some Schubert Lieder, the pace of the day slowed, the packing done for the trip back to Cambridge in the morning. Moore was scheduled to give a paper on April 22, soon after his return from Gunnerside. This he uncustomarily declined to do, for which omission he received the traditional Apostolic punishment: he was obliged to provide dinner for the Brothers who were able to attend. A week later, on April 29, he would read "Vanity of vanities." When the proposition that life is not worth living was put to a vote at that meeting, two Brothers joined Moore in voting no, and three voted yes: A tie. MacCarthy alone, even then Moore's most sensitive friend, perhaps understood the need to vote both ways.

6

Art as Salvation

The Interrogation

Seated stiffly at the long wooden table, the eight men comprising the Hampstead Tribunal have come to the last case on the day's docket. Even before the examinee enters, the weary examiners sense that something is different. Everywhere there are signs of a lessening of decorum, a lapse in the customary deference to which they have grown accustomed and to which they feel entitled by the stature of their position. The corridors leading to the chamber are filled with noisy people, friends of the man to be interrogated, and before them stands a not very deferential emissary, holding what is unmistakably an uninflated air cushion of the lightest blue. Perhaps as many as fifteen other supporters, rough-hewn bohemians, have dispersed themselves throughout the small courtroom and eight of the examinee's relatives, mostly brothers and sisters, no more civilized in their dress and bearing than the others, have taken up seats directly across the table from each of the examiners. When, now, there is a sudden lull in the surrounding commotion and the examiners look up to view the hero's triumphal entrance, they sense immediately that their most anxious forebodings are about to be realized.

Into the room he sweeps, tall and gaunt, haughty if ungainly in his stride and bearing. He carries a tartan traveling rug. With outstretched hands he accepts the air cushion ceremoniously presented to him by his aide, and to the utter amazement of the examiners and the knowing delight of his supporters he begins to apply to the cushion's valve the aperture which had until then been hidden amid the tangles of his audacious beard. Puff. Puff. Slowly the cushion is inflated. Puff. Puff. When the density is right the pillow is placed gently, almost solemnly on the wooden bench, and the examinee, suffering through an irascible case of the piles, lowers himself ever so gingerly onto the cushion, strategically positioned on the chair directly across from the mayor. Finally seated, he smooths out the rug which he has placed decorously across his knees. The stage is set. Lytton Strachey is ready to make his case before the Hampstead Tribunal. And the world. The history of conscientious objection has seldom if ever witnessed anything to match it.

His prepared statement is a blend of clarity and passion. Paul Levy quotes these lines in his *Lytton Strachey: The Really Interesting Question*:

> I have a conscientious objection to assisting, by any deliberate action of mine, in carrying on the war. This objection is not based on religious belief, but upon moral considerations, at which I arrived after long and careful thought. I do not wish to assert the extremely general proposition that I should never in any circumstances, be justified in taking part in any conceivable war; to dogmatize so absolutely upon a point so abstract would appear to me to be unreasonable. At the same time, my feeling is directed not simply against the present war: I am convinced that the whole system by which it is sought to settle international disputes by force is profoundly evil; and that, so far as I am concerned, I should be doing wrong to take any active part in it.
>
> These conclusions have crystallized in my mind since the outbreak of war. . . . My convictions as to my duty with regard to the war have not been formed either rashly or lightly; and I shall not act against those convictions, whatever the consequences may be.

However high Lytton's principles may have been—and there is no reason to question his absolute sincerity—his interrogation is best remembered for its low comedy, which Michael Holroyd captures in the following.

> In the course of [the examination] the military representative attempted to cause [Strachey] some embarrassment by firing a volley of awkward questions from the bench.
>
> "I understand, Mr. Strachey, that you have a conscientious objection to all wars?"
>
> "Oh no," came the piercing, high-pitched reply, "not at all. Only this one."
>
> "Then tell me, Mr. Strachey, what would you do if you saw a German soldier attempting to rape your sister?"

Lytton turned and forlornly regarded each of his sisters in turn. Then he confronted the Board once more and answered with gravity: "I should try and interpose my own body." (p. 179)

It was vintage Strachey. And vintage Bloomsbury. "At once intelligent and irreverent" in Quentin Bell's words. The members of the Hampstead Tribunal were not amused, however, and, Holroyd continues, Lytton's

> application for absolute exemption on the grounds of conscience was adjourned pending an examination by the military doctors. This examination was held only a few days later at the White City, where Lytton turned up, this time equipped with sheaves of doctors' certificates and an inventory of his medical symptoms. From eleven in the morning until half-past three in the afternoon he sat among a crowd of rowdy and promiscuous young men, silently perusing Gardner's *History of England*. But for once, in compensation for past trials, his disabilities stood him in good stead. He was rejected as medically unfit for any kind of service and formally pronounced a free man. "It's a great relief," he confessed to Ottoline [Morrell] that same evening. ". . . Everyone was very polite and even sympathetic —except one fellow—a subordinate doctor, who began by being grossly rude, but grew more polite under my treatment. It was queer finding oneself with four members of the lower classes—two of them simply roughs out of the streets—filthy dirty—crammed behind a screen in the corner of a room, and told to undress. For a few moments I realised what it was like to *be* one of the lower classes —the appalling indignity of it! To come out after it was all over, and find myself being called "sir" by policemen and ticket collectors was a distinct satisfaction. (p. 179)

Aesthetic Defecation

Strachey's sense of the dramatic and the absurd was hardly confined to his performance before the Hampstead Tribunal. If, as Holroyd observes, his "eccentricity was far more deliberate and assertive" on this occasion than it had been during an earlier examination, it remains true that Lytton had parted company with conventional dress and behavior well before his encounter with the military representatives on March 17, 1916. Even the traditions of the Apostles were not sacred in his mind, and he wasted no time in assaulting them. That assault began with his first paper, "Ought the father to grow a beard?," which he read before the Society on May 10, 1902 (quoted by Levy in *Moore*, pp. 230-231). The topic was art, more particularly whether there were any defensible limits on what art was about—on what its subject could or should be. True to his character, the position he takes is extreme: "*Anything* is capable of artistic treatment" because "the function of Art is to treat of *everything* whatever its qualities may be." The ugly. The dirty. The disgusting. Everything! "Can Baudelaire be artistic when he describes with minute detail the process of animal corruption? Or Wagner when he makes sensuality audible? Or Hogarth when he depicts the sordid and disgusting phenomena of the dissecting room?" Lytton's answer is a resounding "Yes!" and, with this much settled, he proceeds to offer his own suggestions concerning the meaning of Art:

> Personally I have always found it impossible to consider one thing apart from everything else—apart, as it were, from its content. It appears to me that the relations borne by anything to other things are nothing more than a part of itself; and reality is thus not only made up of everything in existence, but of the relations between all these things and each other. What I consider that Art does is put everything it treats into its proper position as regards reality; and what the position is it is for the Artist alone to discover—the Artist who works not by rules but by genius and an invisible flame within him.

How far this doctrine might be pushed is the next thing Strachey delights in illustrating. Think of the least likely candidate for Art—think of defecation—and Strachey's liberated artist is at the ready. How shall it be treated artistically?

> There is only one way—by finding out what relations it bears to reality. When you have done this you can treat it artistically, but only then. For me at least that mysterious and intimate operation has always exercised an extraordinary charm. I seem to see in it one of the few last relics of our animal ancestry—a strange reminiscence of the earth from which we have sprung. The thought of every member of the human race—the race which has produced Shakespeare and weighed the stars—retiring every day to give silent and incontestible

proof of his matinal mould is to me fraught with an unutterable significance. There, in truth, is the one touch of Nature which makes the whole world kin! There is enough to give the idealist perpetual cause! There—in that mystic unburdening of our bodies—that unanswerable reminder of mortality!

In commenting on this episode in Apostolic history Paul Levy writes that "Strachey scored several firsts that Saturday night—not least the destruction, in this last paragraph, of the Apostles' only remaining taboo. The brethren, even the most liberated among them, were bludgeoned into confusion by Strachey's charming assault upon their sensibilities" (p. 230).

The Lazy Fellow

Moore as it happened was absent for Lytton's maiden performance, but Levy assures us that he received detailed reports, so strong were the reactions it occasioned. In fact Strachey's views are among those examined critically by Moore in a paper he presented only slightly more than a week later to the Sunday Essay Society ("The Philosophy of Clothes," delivered on May 10, 1902). Approximately a year earlier (May 5, 1901), moreover, Moore had delivered another paper on aesthetics to the Sunday Society, this one entitled "Art, Morals, and Religion." Except for a few of his entries for *Baldwin's Dictionary*, the beginning of his review of McTaggart's *Studies in Hegelian Cosmology*, and some work on the early chapters of *Principia*, these two papers on aesthetics are what remain of Moore's written work during this time. Aesthetics, it is fair to say, was of special importance to him throughout this formative period of slightly more than a year, and it is in these two papers that we find him beginning to work his way toward a number of conclusions that find their fullest expression in *Principia*. In particular Moore here begins to understand how *radical* are the conclusions to which the logic of his argument is inexorably leading him, something later generations of readers will miss. But not Strachey. And not Keynes. And not, we may assume, the other Bloomsberries. The history of moral philosophy rests on a mistake, and ethics, considered as a science, stands in need of extensive reform. This is the conclusion Moore previously had stopped short of; it is the one toward which he is now being irrevocably drawn. Moore, the revered defender of common sense, was the radical whose time had come.

He was not an overly industrious one by his own reckoning. Beginning in 1901, Moore for a few years kept a private record of his philosophical work, both his reading and his writing, tallying the number of hours he spent on each. In the middle years of his Prize Fellowship he seems not to have been fully satisfied with the amount of work he was doing, which, in the May term of 1902, for example, came to "more than 4 hrs. for first two weeks. About 4 till May 23. Then 2 or less." It was not enough. "I am afraid I am just an idler by nature and find any work troublesome," he had written to his mother on May 26, 1895. He never felt he worked hard enough. Of his tenure as a Fellow he writes in his autobiography that, in addition to his published work, his lectures, and his progress on *Principia*,

> I wrote several papers or articles and several reviews during those six years; and I also, for most of the time, was acting, under J. S. Mackenzie, as reviewing sub-editor for English books in the *International Journal of Ethics*. Taking everything together, I think I did a respectable amount of work during my tenure of this Fellowship. *Respectable*, I think; but, I am afraid, not more than respectable. I cannot claim that during this period I worked *very* hard, nor perhaps as hard as I ought. Indeed I do not think that for any considerable period of my life I have ever worked *very* hard, except perhaps for four or five years while I was at school. The fact is that, by disposition, I am very lazy; and there is almost always something which I would much rather be doing than working: more often than not, *what* I would much rather be doing is reading some novel or some history or biography—some *story*, in fact; for stories, whether purporting to be true or avowedly mere fiction, have a tremendous fascination for me. The consequence is that I have always been having constantly to struggle to force myself to work, and constantly suffering from a more or less bad conscience for not succeeding better. This state of things seems to me so natural, that I find it difficult to believe that it is not the same with everyone; and if it were the same with everyone, it would not be worth mentioning—it would go without saying. But I have met with facts which seem to me to suggest that, unintelligible though it may seem, there are some people who don't need to struggle so hard to make themselves work as I do, and are not so constantly or strongly tempted to do something else. Perhaps such people form only a small minority; but, if there are any of them at all, it is perhaps worth mentioning that I have never, since I grew up, been one of them. Certainly during these six years [as a Fellow] I spent a very great deal of time in reading novels and in

talking to friends. But a good deal of the time spent in the latter way was by no means without profit for my philosophical work. (pp. 24–25)

One but certainly not the only example of this profit is to be found in the two essays on aesthetics Moore presented to the Sunday Essay Society.

The Science of Morals

The first, entitled "Art, Morals, and Religion," Moore refers to as "Moral Goodness" in his private record. The latter title is as revelatory as the former. In this essay Moore continues his dogged pursuit of moral goodness in the distinctive way in which he understands this notion. In his mind moral goodness is not restricted to the sort of goodness people exhibit either in their acts, intentions, or motives, or in such virtues as courage, beneficence, and justice. Rather, moral goodness is the kind of goodness that Moore believes is essential to and presupposed by morality; it is the sense in which some things are good in themselves or good as ends, the sense in which something's being good is synonymous with the idea that it ought to exist for its own sake. At least as early as the First Dissertation, if not before, Moore is wedded to this conception of moral goodness. Contrary to Kant's teaching, the "primary form" of the Moral Law, he affirms in that earlier work, does not take the form of a command. The primary form is propositional, declaring that " 'This is good' or 'this is an end-in-itself' or 'this ought to be'; the command, 'do this' is no more than a corollary from such a judgment." The Science of Morals rests on the claim that "there is an objective 'end', something which ought unconditionally to be, an absolute good." It is this conception of moral goodness that Moore continues to explore in "Art, Morals, and Religion."

In Moore's view Art, Morals, and Religion are each related to moral goodness. The terms of their respective relation are what he seeks to explain. He begins with Morals as this "science . . . [is] . . . generally understood." According to the prevailing conception the "objects" of this science are "virtues and duties." In his discussion of these two objects in "The Elements" Moore had argued against their claim as important intrinsic goods, allowing at most that some virtues or the performance of some dutiful acts might have a small amount of intrinsic value, denying in every case that their value is either great or the sole specimen of things good as ends in themselves. He goes further here.

Neither duties nor virtues, Moore contends, "are in their proper nature at all admirable or desirable; they are," he asserts, "merely necessary evils; tools for the pursuit of our own interest; things that it is expedient, convenient, and prudent to commend." These spartan declarations portend the unhappy destination Moore has in store for Morals "as this Science is generally understood." To the extent that *its* objects are duties and virtues, and given that (a) both objects are only necessary evils while (b) Ethics, properly conceived, must deal with what is intrinsically good, it follows that the prevailing conception of this Science is a muddle at best, a deceit at worst. It takes Moore approximately ten pages to reach this conclusion. But reach it he does. The Science of Ethics stands in need of radical reform.

Moore's first salvo is aimed at those unidentified thinkers who "extol [duties and virtues], in the most unguarded language, as if they possessed the highest value for their own sakes, yet, whenever they allow their thoughts to dwell on the question what is to come of it all, show an unmistakable and uniform inability to imagine that perfect bliss could be constituted solely by the everlasting exercise of virtues and performance of duties." For these thinkers—it is likely that Moore has Sidgwick and Kant in mind—in the end cannot accept the maxim that virtue is its own reward. The virtuous person *should* be happy, if not in this world then in the next. And that means, so Moore contends, that these thinkers themselves are in the end driven to accept the view that virtue is not the *only* intrinsic good. Happiness, especially when it is deserved, must count as one too.

But Moore would have us go further: Virtues and duties are not ends in themselves *at all*, a finding he supports by the following line of argument. If the world were perfectly good then whatever we did would have to be the best possible. But if whatever we did necessarily was the best possible we could never be credited either with doing our duty or with exhibiting our virtue. In the perfect world there is no room for duties and virtues. Yet such a world must contain everything that is good. If it lacks anything good in itself it would be less than the most perfect. Thus, since the most perfect world must contain everything that is good in itself, and since such a world would *not* include either duties or virtues, it follows that duties and virtues are not intrinsically good. At all. We are forced by the weight of reason, Moore believes, to conclude that "virtues and duties are tedious and worthless necessities—necessary to improve a state of things, whose vileness does not consist in their absence, into a state more tolerable, but which is constituted . . . by something very different from their presence."

Both prudent and expedient action normally are thought to be good as means, so Moore next is led naturally to consider whether duties and virtues, good only as means in his view, differ in any morally important respect from prudence and expediency. His answer is, they do not. How they differ is a matter of human psychology. Most people most of the time have a natural tendency to act with a view to their own interest. Most people most of the time do not need to be encouraged to do what they themselves desire to do. The disposition to perform acts that benefit others is different. People need to be encouraged to act in these ways, to be praised when they do and blamed or criticized when they do not. Over time the regular application of these sanctions has its desired effect, so that most people develop into individuals who can be counted upon to do their duty most of the time. It is only in those rare cases when one person's desire "appears . . . to conflict with what others desire" that duty and self-interest come into conflict: "It is this opposition of our desires to those of others, a contingency which relatively to the total number of our actions, occurs very rarely indeed, which chiefly produces the idea of alternatives." But though this sort of conflict is rare, comparatively speaking, it is frequent enough to keep the need for praise and encouragement alive.

We are not surprised therefore when Moore concludes his critical examination of duties by claiming that they "are distinguished not by any superior merit in them, but simply as actions with regard to which the desire of the majority is frequently opposed by the desire of the individual. They are singled out for praise, not because they specially deserve it, but because, being commonly done, they are things within a man's power, and the praise of them is useful. It is these actions, which we desire only because others desired them of us, to which the moral sense becomes attached." Of course if we were told the truth about this and were called upon to fulfill our duties because this is what other people want us to do, some might worry that we would fail to act dutifully even more frequently than we already do. The trick, one might say, is to encourage us to act as others want us while at the same time not telling us the truth about why we are to do so. In Moore's view this is the very trick the Science of Morals, as generally understood, is only too happy to perform. That science teaches that duties (and virtues) are good in themselves, not simply good as means to what other people want, a lesson that is "much more effective in producing the desired actions." Were we asked to give up doing what we want because others want us to do something else, some of us might wonder what gives their wants more importance than our own. If instead we are encouraged to believe that it is not a matter of our wants versus those of others, but a case of our (puny) wants versus the (noble) intrinsic goods of virtue and duty, then the claims of egoism will appear psychologically less compelling.

The preceding cannot bode well for the Science of Morals as this is generally understood. This science, Moore is now in a position to maintain, "is doubly false, first in that it singles out as desirable for their own sake what are mere necessary evils; and secondly in that even these are not better than other necessary evils—but only labours less likely to be performed. . . . So long, then, as it [that is, the Science of Morals] deals with its virtues and duties, and does not rise to the consideration of what really ought to be, and really ought to be done, it is as a science wholly abject and contemptible." In issuing this harsh judgment Moore is not suggesting that we ought to cease to encourage the performance of dutiful acts or the acquisition of virtue. "It is," he allows, "useful that we should regard with such a prejudiced favour our virtues and our duties; otherwise we shouldn't perform them and should in general do something worse. Our belief in their [intrinsic] worth is an illusion, which the preacher does well to encourage." But, claims Moore, the belief in their general usefulness is so solidly in place that it is unlikely to be destroyed if the *moral philosopher* reveals that any claim to intrinsic goodness on their behalf is false. Moore aspires to offer this revelation. The moral philosopher must teach, not preach. In the meantime Moore has a concluding message of contempt to leave with the would-be practitioners of a scientific Morals "as generally understood." Because the knowledge of the truth will do no harm, "the would-be scientific moralist who praises his virtues and his duties, cannot defend his lack of science in maintaining lies, by the plea that they are useful." That "vehemence of utterance" that characterizes some passages in *Principia* turns out to be a tendency Moore was refining all along.

Although he denounces would-be scientific moralists, Moore clearly allows for the possibility of a genuine Science of Morals. That Science would rise to consider what really ought to be and what really ought to be done—which of course Moore has been trying to do himself, most recently in "The Elements". But the mere attempt to ascend to these heights, even when the end is seen clearly, does not guarantee success, and it must be acknowledged that "The Elements," Moore's strongest effort to date, is woefully unsatisfactory. When in that work's final pages he is made to face the question of how we can justify our beliefs about what is good in itself, a version of the much maligned (by him) evolutionary ethic is trotted out and saddled with the weight of his own uncertainty. In general, we are told, the course of evolution guarantees that what most people think is good in itself, *is* good in itself. An argument of a form that Moore would have savagely attacked if deployed by another is allowed to pass unscathed here despite the fact that it flagrantly contradicts the major tenets of his earlier lectures. That most people believe that something is good provides not the slightest evidence that it is so. Moore, we may assume, understood that there is many a slip betwixt the desire to rise to the consideration of what really ought to be and its consummation.

No less unsatisfactory than the opinions of most people concerning moral goodness are appeals to the deliverances of God, a position Moore only recently had confirmed anew. Whereas Sidgwick in the end could not give up believing in a Deity though proof was lacking, Moore in time was content to be agnostic. But God's demise in Moore's life and ethical philosophy left a vacuum that needed to be filled. If God exists then there *is* something pre-eminently good in itself and unconditionally so. For God is that than which nothing better can be thought; He is that which ought to be par excellence. But God is not, Moore concludes; or rather, he finds no good reason to think that He is and none to think that He is not. We shall not (so Moore seems to believe) rise to a consideration of what truly ought to be, or what truly ought to be done, by a study of God's nature or His reputed revelations and miracles. And neither, finally, shall we make this ascent by having recourse to the visionary mysticism of the Happy Warrior, however enticing his voice might be. Despite all the allure of the state of moral conversion, Moore "feels the doubt uncomfortable" about its claims to true moral goodness. The aspirational character of Moore's philosophy seems unable to find an object in whose intrinsic goodness it can find its own reason for being.

It is during this protracted crisis in his moral philosophy that Moore discovers the object he has been looking for and the confidence to affirm his belief in its intrinsic goodness.

The Beautiful as Good

That object is art. Or, to speak more precisely, beautiful works of art. These objects, like the objects of Morality, may have an instrumental value; like virtues and duties, beautiful art may be good as a means, producing, for example, "pleasure, culture, or an imitation of itself." But these effects are not what make good art good. The goodness of art is intrinsic to the work itself. It is *its* beauty. And "what is meant by the beautiful is simply and solely that which is an end-in-itself." This is true whether the beautiful object is a work of art or a natural object (for example, a sunset).

Now Moore, we know, believes that what is good in itself ought to exist. He also believes that the objects of Morality, both duties and virtues, lack intrinsic value in themselves and are valuable only as means to what is good in itself. It might seem then that Moore is committed to a rather staggering doctrine: Morality exists for the sake of beauty in general and for the production of beautiful art in particular. Not only might this seem to be so, Moore insists that it is.

> I cannot see but what that which is meant by beautiful is simply and solely that which is an end-in-itself. The object of art would then be that to which the objects of Morals are means, and the only thing to which they are means. The only reason for having virtues would be to produce works of art.

Moore offers no argument to support the view that the beautiful is the *only* thing good in itself. But he does offer something by way of argument to support his view that the beautiful *is* good in itself. That argument turns on how beauty is to be defined. The beautiful, he asserts, *means* "that which is an end-in-itself." If not the whole, this is at least an essential part of the very meaning of the word. The truth of the claim "the beautiful is an end-in-itself" cannot be rationally doubted. The universal meaning (concept) Beauty is definable in terms of the universal meaning (concept) Good.

Here, then, Moore has found part of what he has been looking for: a *reason* to offer on behalf of his belief about what is intrinsically good. Not the revelations of God. Not the mystical state of the Happy Warrior. Not the voice of common sense. These sources of confirmation have been tried and found wanting. It is *the meaning of the word 'beautiful'* or alternatively, the concept Beauty itself that offers a reason for believing in the intrinsic value of beauty in art or nature. It is as if Moore had all along been looking in the wrong direction and then, turning around, found the argument he had been seeking right before him.

How strong this argument is, is not our concern just now. What is, is the important role it plays in the development of Moore's ethical philosophy. Moore here confidently embraces *something* as good in itself, *something* for the sake of whose existence all else is a mere means. And he does so because he thinks he has found a reason for doing so. That something is beauty, especially in art. It is by the creation of beautiful objects that we humans can make the world better. Art is the medium through which we can add to the sum of intrinsic value in the world. Virtues and duties, Moore has said, are "tedious and worthless necessities." They are "necessary to improve a state of things, whose vileness does not consist in their absence, into a state more tolerable, but which is *constituted . . . by something very different from their presence*" (emphasis added). What that "something" is now is clear. It is beauty. Morality, with all its virtues and duties, exists for the sake of Art. It is in Art that we find our true saints, our true heroes.

Moore believes the preceding has important implications for the question, What should art be about? What should be its object? "Anything and everything which is good [in itself] is a proper object of Art; and nothing else is so." This view contrasts sharply with a view we find Moore expressing in an earlier Apostles paper ("Is beauty truth?," presented October 30, 1896), where he argues that (*a*) art should represent nature and (*b*) art should be moral, illustrating the truth that the good are rewarded while the evil are punished. In that earlier vision Art exists to serve the ends of Morality. In "Art, Morals, and Religion" the reverse is true: Morality exists to serve the ends of Art.

> Art is nothing but either a representation of what ought to be, or else, itself what ought to be. . . . The function of Aesthetics will be fully performed, if it give a complete catalogue of all that ought to be; and that of Ethics, as a reformed science, if it tells us how this can be attained. The former is nothing but the Science of Ends, and the latter that of the means to it.

Especially because "Art, Morals, and Religion" finds Moore himself endorsing the intrinsic goodness of something, it is important not to exaggerate his new-found confidence. That confidence was absent in "Vanity of vanities," where everything is judged worthless, and lacking in "Is conversion possible?," where Moore felt doubts "uncomfortable." Here, in the essay under discussion, there is a glimmer of hope, a note of promise. Nevertheless, the definition of Beauty does not entail that there *is* any beauty in the world. The belief that there is requires a judgment on the part of the individual that goes beyond what words mean. *If* anything beautiful exists, *then* there is something that exists that is good in itself. That is what the definition of Beauty guarantees. Nothing more. The meanings of words cannot relieve the individual of the need to judge. But Moore, who loved stories only a little less than he loved music, is incapable of withholding his assent. There *is* beauty in art. There is *some* good in the world. Moore has climbed out from under the weight of his nihilism. His faith has been restored.

But while Moore now is ready to declare that there is some good in the world, he is no less anxious to insist that there is precious little of it. The amount of beauty produced by the pursuit of art, he declares, is "so little as to be worth nobody's attention." This world certainly is not the best possible. And even what little good there is totters on the edge of uncertainty. For while Moore here declares that some good does exist, he offers no basis for deciding that it does. At this point in his development we find a profession of faith in the existence of something good in itself but no method for assuring ourselves that we have done our rational best to minimize the chance of error in our judgment. In this respect Moore fails to find the rational faith he seeks, even while he has regained his faith in the existence of some good in the world and even while he thinks he has found a reason (the definition of Beauty) for thinking that what is beautiful is good in itself.

The moral salvation Art offers has its price. That price is Art's capacity to deceive. Using his favorite art form, music, Moore illustrates his point as follows: "Music . . . makes us believe, for the time being, that it is far more permanent and bulks far larger in the sum of things than it really does. It misrepresents the world as better than it is, as containing far more good, of the same kind, than it really does." Deceived in one respect by Art, we are not deceived in another. For no one *really* believes that all the beauty we encounter in every work of art (for example, fiction) represents something real. "Though every appreciative reader of Waverley is, in so far as it engrosses him, in the same state of mind as if the whole world had the merits of that novel; yet nobody, if you asked him, would assert that Waverley really existed." The deceitfulness of Art, though in one sense real, is in another sense transparent. What deceit there is proves to be harmless, and there is, so Moore believes, some real good in the world, though not much of it. The nihilism of "Vanity of vanities" and the skepticism of "Is conversion possible?" have each given way to a restored faith in the value of beauty, minuscule in amount in comparison to the total found by Moore, the Panglossian optimist, in the First Dissertation. But real nonetheless.

Moore's exposure to art was not untypical of his time and place. The novels of Scott and especially Jane Austen ("I do think she is much the best novelist I ever read," he writes to MacCarthy on September 19, 1896—it was not until 1941 that Moore read Proust's *Swann's Way* and Joyce's *Dubliners*), the poetry of Wordsworth and Browning, the music of Schubert and Brahms: these were the staples of his artistic diet. The French were decidedly under-represented, as was painting generally, and the variety of painting styles and subjects he encountered must have tended to be narrow. Fry's "Art-quake" after all was eight years in the future. Even so, Moore's sense of the possibilities in painting and the other visual arts was precocious. From music he had learned that artistic beauty does not depend on how accurately art depicts or represents something beyond itself. In "Art, Morals, and Religion" we see him extending the reach of this concept in a way that encompasses all the arts. In none of them does the intrinsic value of the work of art depend to any degree on how well it represents something. Intellectually, therefore, Moore was prepared for the major changes about to take place in art in the twentieth century. We are hardly surprised by Levy's observation that "Moore shared with all Bloomsbury the sense that the most important event of 1910 was the Grafton Galleries exhibition of 'Manet and the Post-Impressionists' " (p. 262), which Moore took in during December of that year. Moore's is an aesthetic that makes room for non-representational art even as it allows a place for more traditional forms. As always his feet were planted squarely in different centuries at the same time.

Religion and Goodness

Having discussed the relationship of Art and Morals to moral goodness it remains for Moore to address that of Religion. Like Art, Religion deals with objects that are good in themselves—indeed, with those "which are supposed to be, and," Moore adds, "I think, really are the best." Since Art and Religion are both directed to objects good in themselves, Moore contends that the two have the same "immediate effect upon the mind. . . . The religious emotion, is precisely that which Art produces. . . . There is, that I can see, no difference either in value or in kind between the state of mind of a religious person engaged in his devotions and that of an appreciative reader, reading, say, The Ode at a Solemn Music." Judged strictly in terms of their indistinguishable psychological effects "Religion [is] merely a subdivision of Art." Even the value Religion has as a means is shared by Art: "Every valuable purpose which Religion serves is also served by Art; and Art perhaps serves more if we are to say that its range of good objects and emotions is wider."

How, then, in view of these fundamental similarities, do Art and Religion differ? Moore anticipates the question and offers the following answer: "They are only distinguished in that the religious man thinks it necessary to assert his belief in the existence of the objects that he contemplates." The person who contemplates art, by contrast, does not share this sense of what it is necessary to assert. The appreciative reader of Waverley, for example, does not suppose that he must assert the real existence of the characters depicted in that novel in order to find them or the novel beautiful, and neither does the appreciative listener or performer of Schubert's music believe he must assert that the notes he hears or plays correspond to some "reality" beyond themselves. Art *just is* what it is, and not another thing. Those who appreciate it are content to let the matter stand there. Not so the religious believer, Moore contends. Instead of being content with enjoying the beauty of his devotions, he thinks he must

> assert his belief in the existence of the objects that he contemplates. It is often, I think, a mere assertion; implying no dishonesty, of course, but distinguished from any belief, deserving to be taken seriously, in that it merely means that he is always ready in argument and in his thoughts, to affix to a given proposition the predicate that it is true. But the emotional effect of any object upon you is produced by thinking of it, not by the thought that it is a fact or not a fact.

One need not have faith in some reality beyond the beauty before one in order to enjoy and appreciate the beauty that is there. Faith is available to the agnostic just as much as to the believer. For "faith is not a matter of what you are prepared to maintain and act upon, but of what profoundly moves and occupies your mind. And this kind of faith we all have in the objects of Art as much as any religious person in the objects of religion."

Art. Morals. Religion. Each in Moore's view has some essential relation to moral goodness, to what is good in itself. Morals, however, as generally understood is guilty of an error with regard to value, since it takes its objects, its virtues and duties, as ends in themselves when they are only good as means. Religion for its part stands convicted of an error of fact, asserting that the object of its devotions exists when in fact it does not matter whether it does or not. And Art—even Art is not entirely free from fault since it can deceive us into thinking that the world is a better place than it is. "Unless, then, we are willing to abandon the pursuit of Art," Moore contends, "I think we must admit that it is necessary and right to deceive ourselves"—to allow ourselves however momentarily to be led to believe that there is more good in the world than there is. Moore is unwilling to abandon the pursuit. Of the three—Art, Morals, and Religion—Art comes a long way first.

Art as Religion

But while Art comes first it is not possible to miss the decidedly religious color Moore gives it. Both the inner states and the outer effects occasioned by our (real) encounters with beautiful art are indistinguishable from those commonly attributed to (alleged) encounters with the Deity. Moreover, Art no less than Religion has room within it for a consuming faith. Whether we say with Moore that Religion is "merely a subdivision of Art" or with Clive Bell that "Art is a religion," the fusion of the two is unmistakable. Nor would Moore object to Bell's explanation of why and how Art is a Religion: Art "is an expression of and a means to states of mind as holy as any that men are capable of experiencing." As Gertrude Himmelfarb points out (p. 39), Art thus conceived is said to be "the distinctively modern form of religion." "It is toward art (writes Clive Bell) that the modern mind turns, not only for the most perfect expression of transcendent emotion, but for an inspiration by which to live." Moore could not have put the latter point any better. Not the end-all nor yet the be-all, Art will become inseparable from Moore's quest to find an ethic that is intellectually superior to and emotionally the equal of the theistic ethic of his youth. For Art offers an object of passionate concern. Its object—beauty—is something one can care about, something one can strive to bring into the world or encourage others to do so, something by means of which the world can be made better in just the sense in which Moore understands the notion of moral goodness: better in itself. We humans cannot create God out of the tawdry materials and limited genius we possess. We cannot create the best possible. We can only do the best thing within our capacities. Henceforth Art for Moore will be the queen of human endeavors, with a humbled Science of Morals, properly reformed, her dedicated handmaiden.

The Analysis of Beauty

As noted earlier Moore wrote a second paper on aesthetics for the Sunday Essay Society. Lacking the evangelical fervor of "Art, Morals, and Religion" this second endeavor, "The Philosophy of Clothes," shows how far his thought about Art developed in just a little more than a year. In the former paper the proper object of Art is "anything and everything that is good . . . ; and nothing else." That view is in unmistakable conflict with the view Strachey presents in "Ought the father to grow a beard?," which teaches that Art is free to treat of anything and everything, "whatever its qualities may be." For reasons soon to be disclosed Moore moves away from his earlier position and embraces something close to Strachey's. But not without putting Lytton in his proper place in passing.

The title of Moore's paper, "The Philosophy of Clothes," is inspired by Carlyle's *Sartor Resartus*, and Carlyle's aesthetic theory is taken to task at the outset. But the essay quickly moves on to consider more than Carlyle's views. The effects of a work of art are once again summarily dismissed as irrelevant to its beauty:

> A work of art is not the worse because it encourages the grossest immorality; nor is it the better because it results in the sublimist virtue. A good work of art is an end-in-itself. It has intrinsic value; and its intrinsic value can obviously only depend upon what [it] itself contains, not upon what it causes to exist.

Against those who maintain that Art must have as its subject only what is itself intrinsically valuable (and this would include the Moore of "Art, Morals, and Religion") Moore now contends that it is probable but not necessary that works of art about subjects lacking intrinsic value will themselves lack such value. Without mentioning him by name Moore's position implies that Strachey is in *principle* correct in his view about what Art may be about, and Moore himself denies that "some subjects are too filthy to be dealt with" by artists. Nevertheless, Strachey cannot be correct in his understanding of what the function of Art is or should be. To suppose as he does that Art should reveal the relationship of its subject to the rest of reality is to assign to Art a purpose over and above the creation of beauty, making works of art good or bad *as art* to the degree to which they "reveal" what the Strachian artist has "discovered." This in Moore's view is tantamount to reducing the value of Art to its utility as a means to something else, when we ought rather to celebrate its value as end in itself. For similar reasons, which he marshalls separately against each candidate, Moore rejects the view that Art is or should be "symbolic" and that its beauty or goodness consists in its power to cause emotion. Moore himself at one time held the latter view, as we see in the following passage from his Sunday Essay "Aesthetics," delivered on November 24, 1895: "I would . . . define the beautiful as that with regard to which you have a specific emotion, the nature of which [emotion] can only be discovered by looking into yourself, whenever you say that a thing is beautiful, and finding what you mean thereby." In the present essay Moore does not deny that beautiful art can occasion various emotions. How could he, given his own passionate involvement with music? He only insists that the beauty of a work of art is intrinsic to it and thus totally independent of how we respond to it emotionally.

Opposed to those who think that the "subject" is everything are those who think the same of the "treatment" offered by the artist. Beautiful art is art that "expresses perfectly." Not so, argues Moore, since to express perfectly is merely to suggest perfectly, in which case Art is once again assessed in terms of its value as a means rather than an end, good art being art that causes one to think of one thing rather than another. Good art is good *in itself* because of *its* beauty, and not for any reason beyond itself—its moral effects, its symbolism, its expressiveness, and so on. Its value stands on its own two feet, having no need of support from any other quarter. It would be easier for a camel to pass through the eye of a needle than it would be to separate Moore's position from those who advocate "art for art's sake." For what else *could* Art be, given its intrinsic value? When Clive Bell celebrates the autonomy of Art, characterizing "true art" as "completely self-consistent, self-supporting, and self-contained—constructions which do not stand for something, but . . . have ultimate value" in themselves, the views he expresses, Bloomsbury in their rich surfaces, are Moorean in their philosophical depths.

Not surprisingly, Moore is not content to let things stand at this level of analysis. Celebrate the intrinsic value of beauty in art as much as one will, it still remains to be asked if there is anything intrinsic to beautiful works of art that they all share in addition to their beauty. It is not their symbolic function. Not their expressiveness. Not their power to cause emotion. Not their subject matter. What then, if anything, is it? Moore's answer is opaque. There is, he theorizes, a happy marriage of treatment and subject in all good art: "The value of the whole always depends upon the appropriate treatment of the subject, whatever [the subject] may be: and the appropriate treatment does not mean merely what is proper to convey to us a true idea of the subject." That cannot be all that makes the treatment "appropriate" since this would make the beauty depend on the treatment's utility in conveying something beyond itself. No, claims Moore, what makes the treatment appropriate is this: that "when we contemplate it together with the subject, [the treatment] is seen to *ornament* the subject" (emphasis added).

So much clearly depends on Moore's idea of ornamentation that we must be disappointed when we turn to consider what little he has to say about it. "The relation of the ornament to what it ornaments," he writes,

> is quite different from that of the symbol to what it symbolises. When a thing is said to be an ornament, it is meant that something is added to the sum of good, by the fact that it exists as well as that which it ornaments. The whole formed of the two is always the better for the existence of both—has a greater intrinsic value; even though the ornament, if it existed by itself, might have no intrinsic value whatever. Thus, whereas a symbol is a means to the existence of something else, an ornament is a means, not to the existence of anything, but to the value of the whole formed of itself and something else.

This is so vague as to be useless. What "ornaments" a work of art adds value to it, a value the "ornament" need not possess when considered apart from what it ornaments. This tells us no more than that there is *something* (allegedly) intrinsic to a beautiful work of art that adds to its beauty even though were it to exist by itself it might have no beauty of its own. But *what* this "something" is—*what* an ornament comes to—remains just as obscure after Moore's explanation as it was before. When Moore laments that "the philosophy of Art has hitherto been almost entirely worthless" he is very near to offering a description of his own forays in this field.

This failure to achieve a reasonable level of clarity, especially given his adamant demand for clarity on the part of others, would be an irredeemable shortcoming in his theory of value in general and in his efforts to reform the Science of Morals in particular if Moore continued to maintain the view set forth in "Art, Morals, and Religion"—namely, that the beautiful is the *only* thing good in itself. If that were true, then everything would depend on his ability to make progress in aesthetic theory, the proclaimed Science of Ends. Moore will not retain this belief in the exalted status of the Science of Aesthetics for very long. By the time *Principia* is finished he is ready to give to each individual the freedom and responsibility to do the work he here assigns to the Science of Aesthetics. Decisions about what things are good in themselves are not the province of any science; they are the proper work of every individual. Each of us must decide what makes life worth living or what ends we live for. There is no guarantee that our decision will be right. Our thinking that something is good in itself does not make it so. Along with our liberty to judge for ourselves goes the terrible prospect that we might be mistaken. And no science can rescue us from the need to make this decision to declare our faith ourselves. In Moore's view the whole object of the Science of Morals, as finally conceived in *Principia*, is to demonstrate *why* this and every other science is ineradicably limited in this way. Whereof science cannot speak, thereof science must be silent.

But while Moore in time will take back the optimistic agenda he gives to Aesthetics on this occasion, the belief in the intrinsic value of beautiful objects is one he will carry with him through *Principia* and beyond. The same is true of the demand to reform the Science of Morals. That demand will continue in force, to be satisfied by Moore in Chapter Five of *Principia*, where he avoids the two falsehoods he lays at the door of those "would-be scientific moralists" under attack in "Art, Morals, and Religion." Once properly reformed, this Science will also give the individual an immense amount of liberty in deciding what *means* to use to achieve what ought to be. As we shall see when we turn to *Principia*, Moore's basic message is simple: the Science of Morals yields truths that make us free.

Returning Home

The dozen years between the composition of "The Philosophy of Clothes" and the outbreak of the first world war in 1914 were Moore's most productive period as a philosopher. Both *Principia Ethica* (1903) and *Ethics* (1912) were published, together with ten papers, some of which, most notably "The Refutation of Idealism" (1903), are of more than passing interest in the history of philosophy. During the academic terms of 1910 and 1911, moreover, Moore gave twenty lectures at Morley College "on Metaphysics," he notes in his autobiography; these are the lectures that would eventually be published as *Some Main Problems of Philosophy* (1953). The greater part of this period was spent away from Cambridge. Moore had hoped to secure a Research Fellowship after his Prize Fellowship expired. His application was unsuccessful, but it was not until 1914 that he learned something about the reasons for his failure. It was "because of unfavourable reports from the English philosopher Bosanquet," he was told, according to his diary entry for April 27, that "the older members of the Council voted against my Research Fellowship." Without knowing of Bosanquet's role in this matter until ten years after the fact, Moore's antipathy for the man had taken root even earlier. When G. F. Stout, who was then the editor of *Mind*, writes to Moore on November 1, 1903 to mention that "Bosanquet has offered himself [to review *Principia*] if I do not prefer someone else," he understates the case when he adds, "I presume this proposal does not commend itself to you." Presumably not. Even so Bosanquet did review *Principia*. The older man's assessment of the younger man's real talents seems not to have changed beyond what they were concerning Moore's Second Dissertation. "I believe Mr. Moore to have a real vocation as a critic," Bosanquet writes, "in the sense of a free lance who will make the orthodox reflect and reconsider" (p. 261). But, he adds, "whether he [i.e., Moore] has shown himself capable of dealing positively with the main burden of a great science is perhaps open to doubt" (p. 254). Bosanquet's ungenerous review is symptomatic of his lack of enthusiasm for Moore's chosen profession in general and his application for a Research Fellowship in 1904 in particular.

All of this remains unmentioned by Moore in his autobiographical account of this period of his life.

> My Fellowship elapsed at the end of September 1904. I had applied for its continuation in the form of a Research Fellowship; but election to a Research Fellowship was, and still is, a very rare and exceptional thing at Trinity, and I was not surprised that my application was refused. Nor was I, I think, at all sorry; I think I was glad to have the prospect of a change from Cambridge life. My mother and my father had both very recently died; and, owing to the facts that two of my mother's maternal uncles, both of them childless, had been rich men, and that my mother, being the only child of her mother

and having been left an orphan very early, had been almost in the place of a daughter to them, I and my brothers and sisters had now sufficient private means to enable us to live in moderate comfort without needing to earn anything. I was therefore in a position to go on working at philosophy, which was what I wanted to do, without a Fellowship and without needing to try to obtain any paid employment. The only question was where I should live. Having ceased to be a Fellow, and having no official post in the University, I should not be able any longer to live in College; and I did not like the idea of living at Cambridge in lodgings after having spent so many years in College. (pp. 25–26)

As it happened R. A. Ainsworth, a younger, intimate friend of Moore's (he was six years Moore's junior), recently had been appointed to a lectureship in Greek at Edinburgh University. Among Moore's special followers, Ainsworth was, in Leonard Woolf's terms, Moore's "lieutenant." Like Moore a graduate of Dulwich College, Ainsworth's record at Kings exceeded even that of his revered mentor's at Trinity: a first in Classics Part I in 1900 and, in 1902, a first in *both* Classics Part II *and* Moral Sciences Part II. Moore personally nominated Ainsworth for membership in the Apostles, which he officially joined in November 1899. It is Ainsworth to whom Moore refers without naming him in the following passages from his autobiography:

[A] close friend of mine had been recently appointed to a post on the teaching staff of Edinburgh University; I was anxious to be near him, and also Edinburgh had a romantic attraction for me, chiefly owing to its association with Scott and his novels, which I loved and was in the habit of reading again and again. We decided that I should move to Edinburgh, and that we should take an apartment there together. We found one which suited us admirably, at the bottom of a huge forbidding building of dark grey stone on the south side of Buccleuch Place just opposite to George Square where Scott's father had lived at the time when Scott was a boy. At the back our house looked clear out towards the Meadows, with no houses intervening. We lived there for three years and a half, and I was not at all disappointed with Edinburgh: it still seemed to me very romantic, and I became very fond of it.

In the spring of 1908, however, my friend had to move to London, having been appointed to a post in the Board of Education; and it happened that at the same time two of my sisters [Hettie and Nellie] wished to set up house together somewhere near London and wished that I should join them. After house hunting in a good many different directions in the neighborhood of London, we found a house on The Green, at Richmond, Surrey, which we thought would suit us. The Green has a good deal of charm, with the row of red-brick Georgian houses called "Maids of Honour" Row, along one side of it, and the still older red-brick palace in which Elizabeth died in its far corner. Our house moreover looked out behind over the old Deer Park. I lived at Richmond, as I had at Edinburgh, for three years and a half, and I became very fond of Richmond also. (p. 26)

Later in 1908, their respective moves complete, Ainsworth married Moore's youngest sister, Sarah.

Of this period of seven years away from Cambridge Moore recalls that he "worked at philosophy as hard as, though no harder than, I had worked during the six years of my Fellowship" (p. 27). In the Spring of 1911, thanks in part to the political maneuvering of Keynes and the timely vacancy of a position, Moore was presented with the opportunity to return to Cambridge as a lecturer in either logic or psychology. Unfortunately he had little interest in teaching the former and no competence to teach the latter, when psychology is viewed as an empirical science. Moore's masterful solution was to reform the nature of psychology as this was offered in Part I of the Moral Sciences Tripos. If psychology was to be a part of the philosophy curriculum, it should not, he proposed, be approached as an "empirical science at all . . . but [as] something which might fairly be said to belong to the Philosophy of Mind" (p. 29). The dilemma was solved to everyone's satisfaction. When on May 11, 1911 Moore received a telegram from McTaggart informing him that he (Moore) had been elected to the lectureship, Moore was pleased to be returning to his real home. He would teach with distinction at Cambridge for the next twenty-eight years until his compulsory retirement, aged sixty-five, in 1939.

Political Acts

Throughout the first world war Moore offered his "psychology" lectures at Trinity and continued to write and publish philosophy on a regular basis. That a war was being waged was a fact that initially failed to make a strong impression on him. A not unrepresentative specimen from the early days of the war is the following (from his diary, August 15, 1914): "Sat. Lazy in morn.: New Statesman. Walk by Cotton path to Burton Rd.: buy flowers. *Hall* between Murray and How; Brown opp.; talk a little—bats in Library. Sing. Think of definition." Once the reality of the war did compel his recognition, it had a special fascination for him. In a letter to Desmond MacCarthy, dated November 15, 1914, for example, he writes that

> I don't understand people being really *miserable* about the war; though I rather admire people who are, and feel rather ashamed that I can't be. I believe, really and truly, it gives me much more pleasure than pain, simply because I am so interested in it; and though I do truly believe that war is horrible, and though, if I could, I would arrange that there should never be any, I can't really *feel* miserable about it, though no doubt I should if I saw the horrible things. But, so far as I can gather, Russell does really *feel* miserable, and so does Sanger, and a few others. But I think most people are much more like me.

Among his colleagues at Cambridge and his friends and associates generally the war was predictably divisive. McTaggart, whose loyalty to institutions was among his ruling passions, was a staunch supporter of Britain's involvement, as were virtually all of the older Cambridge fellows. Many (but certainly not all) of the younger men, including more than a fair share of the younger Apostles, were against the war for reasons of conscience, and of these some, like Strachey, were against *this* war without opposing war in general. In the early months of the war Moore found himself in the middle, having not decided whether he did or did not believe in the morality or wisdom of British involvement. On January 20, 1915, however, after having spent the previous day talking the issue over with MacCarthy, he came out against the war and became one of the founding members of the Cambridge branch of the Union of Democratic Control (UDC), an organization which, though not pacifistic, had political ideals that the likes of McTaggart found less than appropriately patriotic. When in November of this same year the Council of Trinity College (the same group that would remove Russell from his lectureship eight months later) refused to allow a private meeting of the UDC in the rooms of the renowned mathematician J. E. Littlewood, a veritable tempest broke out, with Moore assuming an unfamiliar political role. Much of the November 27 issue of the *Cambridge Magazine* is given over to a lively discussion of the controversy, including, so the accompanying editorial notes with detectable pride, "a contribution from the author of *Principia Ethica.*" Here in full is Moore's first and only published venture into the world of politics. He titled it "Suggestions for the Council of Trinity College."

Dear Sir,

The spirited action, on the part of the Council of Trinity College, which you had the privilege of announcing on your first page last week, must have given great encouragement to all true patriots. It gives ground for a confident hope that the Council of this great College may be relied on to adopt at once any further measures on the same lines, of which the need may be pointed out to them. Two such measures have occurred to me. Both, it will be seen, are fully in harmony with the spirit in which they have already acted; we may, therefore, rest assured that the rare qualities of heart and head, which must have prompted the admirable decision of last week, will cause them to embrace with enthusiasm these two further opportunities for beneficent activity, when once they see how unanswerable are the arguments which (as I flatter myself) I have been able to adduce in their favour.

The two measures which I wish to suggest, as plainly enjoined by their duty to their Country and their College in this trying time, are as follows:

I. That they should at once make the following orders—

"That no meeting of the Cambridge University Moral Science Club is to be held within the precincts of the College."

The urgency of this measure will be evident from the fact that, as I write, a meeting of the Club in question is actually announced to be held in the rooms of a *Fellow* of the College on Friday next, November 26. And anybody who is acquainted with the objects both of the Moral Science Club and of the Union of Democratic Control, will see at once that the same dangerous consequences are to be apprehended from a meeting of either body. The Council is, perhaps, not so well-informed with regard to the Club as it *evidently* is with regard to the Union, and may not, therefore, have realised how dangerous to the patriotism of young men the meetings of this

Club may be, and what a serious effect they may have upon recruiting. But it is, in sober earnest, possible that young English men should, at one of its meetings, be urged to believe a proposition as that *the greatest good of humanity as a whole ought, in cases of conflict, to be preferred to that of their own countrymen!* Now it is, I know, arguable that, in times of peace, an enlightened College should, in the interests of freedom of thought, allow such a proposition to be discussed within its precincts, *even* at a private meeting; but the risk to patriotism is obvious, and, in times of war, it is surely evident that such a dangerous liberty must be utterly abolished. The experience of the Council may, perhaps, lead them to think that nothing that is said at any meeting connected with a subject for examination, can possibly be taken seriously by any undergraduate. But I can assure them, from personal knowledge, that this rule does not hold quite invariably. It is actually the case, incredible as it may seem, that the practical views of undergraduates have, in some cases, been seriously influenced by the study of Moral Science, in spite of the fact that it is an examination subject. Action, therefore, against the Moral Science Club is just as necessary as was action against the Union of Democratic Control. And the usefulness of such action would undoubtedly be greatly enhanced, if the Council would again take care to communicate their decision to the Press, even before announcing it to the Fellow concerned. Such a vigorous and prompt proceeding, following upon the similar action which they took last week, will unquestionably raise to a still higher pitch the reputation they have already earned for patriotism, liberality of mind, and courtesy; and they may expect to see the increased confidence of the public reflected in the increased number of parents who will be anxious to send their sons to a College so wisely governed.

2. The other measure, which I wish to suggest, is on exactly the same lines, and I need not elaborate the arguments in its favour. It is that the Council should forthwith suspend all services in the College Chapel until the conclusion of the war. The absolute necessity for this measure, in the interests of recruiting and of national unity, is obvious. It is necessary, because at services of the Christian churches young men are liable to have brought to their notice maxims quite as dangerous to patriotism as any which they will hear at a meeting of the Union of Democratic Control or of

the Moral Science Club. I need only give one single instance. The maxim "*Love your enemies; do good to them that hate you,*" actually occurs in one of the books habitually read in Churches. Here, again, it may, of course be argued that nobody ever takes seriously what they hear in Church. But I can again assure the Council, from personal knowledge, that this is not absolutely *always* so. There really is *some* risk that an undergraduate may (however illogically) draw practical conclusions, unfavorable to the patriotic action which the times require, from such a maxim as that which I have quoted. In view of the action which the Council have already taken, we may, I think, feel a quiet confidence, that they will at once take the further steps necessary to secure that no undergraduate shall, within the walls of the College, run the very *smallest* risk of being perverted by such principles.

> Yours faithfully,
> G. E. MOORE

Trinity College.
November 23.

"Great encouragement to all true patriots," "two further opportunities for beneficent activity," "incredible as it may seem . . . the practical views of undergraduates have, in some cases, been seriously influenced by the study of Moral Sciences"—these unexpected specimens of Moorean bitterness are of an order in which a Shaw might take pride. As uncharacteristic as the letter is in some respects, it is vintage Moore in others—clear, coherent, a little labored in its style, the familiar demand for consistency in thought and action. The senior Fellows on the College Council did not fail to read Moore's contribution to the debate filling the pages of the *Cambridge Magazine*. Moore's diary reveals that "Ward was chuckling over it": "A pretty good roasting!," Ward is reported to have said, "he is obviously pleased." For his part Moore was terribly worried about how the letter would be received. On the day of its publication he notes that he is "really afraid and in a fever." This was not a case of misplaced anxiety. For though Ward may have chuckled, the majority of the senior Fellows did not find Moore's adventure into the world of political satire amusing. The mathematician G. H. Hardy informed Moore that "what angered Council most" was Moore's letter, a revelation that "sets [Moore] to thinking whether I did wrong to write it." His temporary relief came when, as he records in his diary for that day (December 18, 1915), he goes to Hardy's rooms "to look for Monist." As things turned out, Moore's first adventure in this realm would be his last.

Though Moore did not contribute any more written work to the debate over the war his political activity was not exhausted. His opposition to the war heightened in the next few months, and after conscription was introduced he played an active role in counseling younger men regarding how they might present their case, especially if that case rested, as in Strachey's it did, on selective conscientious objection. Moore in fact was of invaluable assistance to Strachey in the latter's presentation to the Hampstead Tribunal. And in a venture reminiscent of his youthful experience on the promenade at the beach Moore went so far as to hand out anti-war literature to commuters at the Cambridge railway station. This brush with a new form of evangelicalism seems not to have been as traumatic as the earlier one.

For all his outward opposition Moore was inwardly unsettled. In March of 1916, now forty-three, he records in his diary that he had been "afraid lately that they may raise age of compulsion to 45: can't help thinking a good deal of what would happen to me . . . depressed." Paul Levy goes on to chronicle the gradual unwinding of Moore's opposition to the war:

> His spirits had been low for some time; he had been dissatisfied with his lectures, and the month before, he noted on 14 February that, "on walk feel as if I can hardly bear it—should go mad: but easier when I allow myself to go on thinking." Once, even earlier, on 7 December 1915, Moore had noted with unconscious humour: "Feel very incapable of thinking, so read *Mind*." By late March 1916 then, Moore was justifiably worried about being conscripted, and had to confess to himself that he was also afraid; on the 26th he felt 'rather afraid of Zeppelins: altogether depressed and worried' and on the 31st, he was distressed by the partial blackout in hall at nine o'clock, which he took as a sign of the approach of Zeppelins, for which he waited about "listening in my rooms". Then there was the discomfort of having to mix with officers at dinner in hall, where champagne was always served when some of their number left Trinity for their new assignments. This was the most painful and difficult time Moore had in his whole life. Finally the man who had counselled so many younger men about conscientious objection decided that he himself

was not a conscientious objector, and this gave him relief. On 19 April 1916 Moore recorded in his diary: "Have reconciled myself to idea of military service, and feel much happier." He was, in fact, never called up. (p. 289)

Since he was never called up, we do not know how much more doubt and confusion, fear and depression that event would have occasioned. Nor do we even know if Moore continued to feel "much happier" throughout the remaining years of the war. His diary breaks off during 1916, and his later diaries were destroyed. Given his history of unsettledness about English and his own involvement in the war up to April 19, 1916, it would not be surprising if Moore had further bouts of uncertainty and depression. His Bloomsbury followers and his erstwhile friend, Russell, were united in their fierce opposition to the war. The generation of Moore's surviving teachers was represented by the no less passionate support of McTaggart. It remained for Moore to attempt to serve both masters. If justice was done and Sidgwick's shade enjoyed the happy adventure of invisibly frequenting the rooms of Trinity, he must have smiled knowingly at his prized student's chronic indecisiveness at this time on the issue of the war. And envied him his renewed faith in the modern religion—Art.

7

The Autonomy of Ethics

A Student Again

🐌 D.A.T. Gasking and A. C. Jackson, two of Wittgenstein's former students, recreate the scene:

> When you entered his room for a lecture, you found some fifteen or twenty wooden chairs and one deck chair facing the fireplace, before which stood a black anthracite stove. To the right below the window a trestle table with papers. On the mantlepiece a low-powered bulb on a retort stand. Behind you a bookcase with two or three books. Wittgenstein stood waiting, occasionally glancing at a watch which he pulled out of his breast pocket. A short, slightly built man in grey trousers, open-necked shirt and suede golfing jacket. His face was ruddy and very deeply lined, the eyes sharp blue and the hair (in the thirties) brown and curly. The audience would consist of all those who were taking the Moral Sciences tripos seriously, about the same number of those who had recently taken the tripos, one or two other undergraduates, a philosophy don, perhaps a maths don, one or two research students from overseas.

On this occasion the philosophy don is Moore, now fifty-nine. It is the May term of 1933. Wittgenstein is lecturing on language. Or, rather, he is *thinking* about language. Desperately. In silence.

The room is still. Not a person moves. Wittgenstein stares intently out of the window overlooking the large Whewell's Court, the pinnacles of King's College Chapel visible above the random angles of tiled Cambridge roofs. His hands move plaintively. His face is austere. Ideas rule his life. When they come in torrents, as they sometimes do, he darts about the small room, propelled by the excitement of a new image, animated by

183

the power of a novel analogy, his resonant voice demanding unqualified attention. As Norman Malcolm, another of Wittgenstein's students, recalls in his *Memoir*, Wittgenstein's "whole personality was commanding, even imperial" (p. 24), even—perhaps especially—during his prolonged silences, when his mind turned ruthlessly in upon itself. On such occasions, which were not infrequent, Wittgenstein might break the spell of collective concentration by painfully exclaiming to his students, "This is hard as *hell*!" Ward's no less unhappy declaration made to Moore some forty years earlier—Denken ist schwer!—had taken on a life of its own.

Malcolm knew and respected Moore. But even Moore in Malcolm's view was not "pursued and tormented by philosophical difficulties to the degree that Wittgenstein was. I imagine that after a few hours of work Moore could stop and turn his attention to other matters." By Moore's own account, of course, *his* problem was to turn his attention to philosophy *at all*, so lazy was he by inclination, so predisposed to find agreeable mental absorption in one story or another. Not Wittgenstein. In the *Philosophical Investigations*, on which he worked from 1936 to 1949 and which, at his request, was published after his death, Wittgenstein writes that "the real discovery is the one that makes me able to break off doing philosophy when I want to." Wittgenstein, Malcolm believes, never made that discovery.

In the May term of 1933 Wittgenstein is a Research Fellow of Trinity College, having received a five-year fellowship in December 1930. After his fellowship expires he will spend a year living in seclusion in Norway, beginning the *Investigations*. Returning to Cambridge in 1937 he will in time assume Moore's professorship when the latter steps down in 1939. Though he was a controversial figure it was unthinkable not to appoint him. The philosopher C. D. Broad, neither an intimate nor an admirer of Wittgenstein's, thought that refusing him the chair would have been like refusing Einstein a chair in physics. Wittgenstein is said to have respected Broad for his fairness.

After World War II Wittgenstein will spend varying amounts of time in Ireland, the United States, Vienna, Oxford, and Norway before returning to Cambridge. On April 27, 1951 he will fall violently ill from the prostate cancer that had been diagnosed less than two years earlier. Two days later he will die, age sixty-two, working on philosophy almost to the last. To his doctor's wife, who saw him through his last night, he is reported to have said, "Tell them I've had a wonderful life!" Malcolm interprets 'them' to mean Wittgenstein's closest friends, adding:

When I think of his profound pessimism, the intensity of his mental and moral suffering, the relentless way in which he drove his intellect, his need for love together with the harshness that repelled love, I am inclined to believe that his life was fiercely unhappy. Yet at the end he himself exclaimed that it had been 'wonderful'! To me this seems a mysterious and strangely moving utterance. (p. 81)

A Puzzled Look

Wittgenstein had spent an earlier period of his life (1912–1913) in Cambridge. Writing in *Mind* at the time of Wittgenstein's death, Russell recalls the beginnings of their sometimes volatile relationship.

> When I made the acquaintance of Wittgenstein, he told me that he had been intending to become an engineer, and with that end in view had gone to Manchester. In the course of his studies in engineering he had become interested in mathematics, and in the course of his studies in mathematics he had become interested in the principles of mathematics. He asked people at Manchester (so he told me) whether there was such a subject, and whether anyone worked at it. They told him that there was such a subject and that he could find out more about it by coming to me at Cambridge, which he accordingly did. (p. 30)

Russell's initial impressions were not propitious:

> Quite at first I was in doubt as to whether he was a man of genius or a crank, but I very soon decided in favor of the former alternative. Some of his early views made the decision difficult. He maintained, for example, at one time that all existential propositions are meaningless. This was in a lecture room, and I invited him to consider the proposition: "There is no hippopotamus in this room at present." When he refused to believe this, I looked under all the desks without finding one; but he remained unconvinced. (p. 30)

Wittgenstein's mastery of mathematical logic was rapid. But though he worked energetically he seemed in Russell's view not to be getting anywhere. And he was, besides, "not easy to deal with," as Russell's later account in *The Listener* attests:

He used to come to my rooms at midnight and, for hours, he would walk backwards and forwards like a caged tiger. On arrival, he would announce that when he left my rooms he would commit suicide. So, in spite of getting sleepy, I did not like to turn him out. On one such evening, after an hour or two of dead silence, I said to him, "Wittgenstein, are you thinking about logic or about your sins?" "Both," he said, and then reverted to silence. However, we did not only meet at night. I used to take him on long walks in the country round Cambridge. On one occasion I induced him to trespass with me in Madingley wood where, to my surprise, he climbed a tree. When he had got a long way up, a gamekeeper with a gun appeared and protested to me about the trespass. I called up to Wittgenstein and said the man had promised not to shoot if Wittgenstein got down within a minute. He believed me, and did so.

Uncertain of what to make of his tempestuous pupil, Russell asked Moore his opinion. Moore's answer, recorded in Russell's piece in *Mind*, is now legendary: "Moore replied, 'I think well of him indeed.' When I enquired the reason for his opinion, he said it was because Wittgenstein was the only man who looked puzzled at his [Moore's] lectures" (p. 31).

Moore's judgment proved to be characteristically insightful, and Russell himself eventually was able to record his own admiration:

Getting to know Wittgenstein was one of the most exciting intellectual adventures of my life. In later years there was a lack of intellectual sympathy between us, but in early years I was as willing to learn from him as he from me. His thought had an almost incredible degree of passionately intense penetration, to which I gave wholehearted admiration.

Wittgenstein's effect on Russell's life is only hinted at here. The teacher's motivation to do serious work in philosophy was destroyed by the trenchant critical insights of the pupil. In a letter to Lady Ottoline Morrell in 1916, included in his *Autobiography*, Russell asks, "Do you remember that at the time [that is, June 1913] . . . I wrote a lot of stuff about Theory of Knowledge, which Wittgenstein criticized with the greatest severity? His criticism . . . was an event of first-rate importance in my life, and affected everything I have done since. I saw he was right, and I saw I could not hope ever again to do foundational work in philosophy. My impulse was shattered, like a wave dashed to pieces against a breakwater" (p. 57).

When Moore first met Wittgenstein he was immediately struck by his brilliance. These are his recollections from his autobiography, published in 1942:

> In 1912 I became acquainted with Wittgenstein. During the first year in which he was at Cambridge he attended my lectures on Psychology; but it was only during the next two years that I got to know him at all well. When I did get to know him, I soon came to feel that he was much cleverer at philosophy than I was, and not only cleverer, but also much more profound, and with a much better insight into the sort of inquiry which was really important and best worth pursuing, and into the best method of pursuing such inquiries. (p. 33)

Although it is true that Wittgenstein attended his lectures on psychology Moore fails to divulge how unsatisfactory Wittgenstein found them. In a 1912 letter to F. A. Hayek, Wittgenstein's cousin, Moore writes that

> at the beginning of the October term 1912, he came again to some of my psychology lectures; but he was very displeased with them, because I was spending a great deal of time in discussing Ward's view that psychology did not differ from the Natural Sciences in subject-matter but only in point of view. He told me these lectures were very bad—that what I ought to do was to say what I thought, not to discuss what other people had thought; and he came no more to my lectures.

Unlike Russell, whose will to do foundational work in philosophy was destroyed by Wittgenstein's criticisms, Moore was more resilient. That "independence of thought" Sidgwick remarked upon seems to have made it possible for Moore to recognize Wittgenstein's quickness and profoundness, and to accept his pupil's dismal estimation of his lectures, without requiring that he attempt to modify or abandon his own slow, labored way of doing philosophy. If, as F. R. Leavis recalls Wittgenstein's having said, "[Moore] shows you how far a man can get with absolutely no intelligence whatever," this perhaps proves nothing so much as how over-rated "intelligence" can be.

Despite Wittgenstein's absenting himself from Moore's lectures the two continued to see a good deal of one another. Both attended Russell's lectures on the foundations of mathematics, and both were regular participants at the weekly meetings of the Moral Sciences Club. A third, less fruitful setting was Wittgenstein's predictably turbulent history as an Apostle. However noumenal the other members may have found those Saturday evening meetings, Wittgenstein surely must have judged them more than a little unreal.

Russell in this case proved to be more prescient than the others. There was no doubting Wittgenstein's being temperamentally ill-suited to the Society's degraded condition at this time in Russell's view. The others—Keynes and Strachey in particular—thought otherwise and saw in Russell's protestations a not very thinly veiled anxiety at the prospect of having to share his prized pupil with the other Brothers. Possibly even to *lose* him! Whatever Russell's motives, his judgment was eminently correct. If Wittgenstein found Moore's lectures "very bad," it is hardly surprising that he found discussions with the youngest Brothers—"schoolgirlish" and "frivolous" about sex in general and their own homosexuality in particular, according to Paul Levy—absolutely worthless. Even the possibility of Moore's occasional visit was not enough to convince Wittgenstein to continue attending. Moore had reread his paper "Is conversion possible?" at Wittgenstein's first meeting. This is the paper in which Moore first extols the goodness of moral conversion, as personified by the Happy Warrior, only in the end to confess his own doubt and uncertainty. At best one can meekly speculate about Wittgenstein's reactions to Moore's intoxicated portrait of the mystical Warrior. A common opinion is that Moore's philosophy left "[not] a trace of influence" on Wittgenstein's. This would lead one to suppose that Wittgenstein probably was unimpressed.

The Disciple

Moore's sense of corporate identity was more robust than Wittgenstein's. The Dedication in *Principia* is generous both in its sentiments and its scope.

DOCTORIBUS AMICISQUE CANTABRIGIENSIBUS

DISCIPULUS AMICUS CANTABRIGIENSIS

PRIMITIAS

D.D.D.

AUCTOR

Anyone confident enough of Moore's friendship was free to feel included. Strachey did. "It was very pleasant to be able to feel that one came into the Dedication," he wrote to Moore on October 11, 1903, just after finishing *Principia*. Presumably all the Apostles felt the same pleasure. Certainly the traditional Apostolic insistence on clarity sounds forth like a clarion call in the book's opening paragraph. It is as if a Saturday evening meeting is about to begin.

> It appears to me that in Ethics, as in all other philosophical studies, the difficulties and disagreements, of which its history is full, are mainly due to a very simple cause: namely to the attempt to answer questions, without first discovering precisely *what* question it is which you desire to answer. I do not know how far this source of error would be done away, if philosophers would *try* to discover what question they were asking, before they set about to answer it; for the work of analysis and distinction is often very difficult: we may often fail to make the necessary discovery, even though we make a definite attempt to do so. But I am inclined to think that in many cases a resolute attempt would be sufficient to ensure success; so that, if only this attempt were made, many of the most glaring difficulties and disagreements in philosophy would disappear. At all events, philosophers seem, in general, not to make the attempt; and, whether in consequence of this omission or not, they are constantly endeavouring to prove that 'Yes' or 'No' will answer questions, to which *neither* answer is correct, owing to the fact that what they have before their minds is not one question, but several, to some of which the true answer is 'No,' to others 'Yes.' (p. vii)

Not even McTaggart could have crafted a more Apostolic beginning.

Having proclaimed the need for clarity Moore next proceeds to explain how he has tried to satisfy it.

> I have tried in this book to distinguish clearly two kinds of question, which moral philosophers have always professed to answer, but which, as I have tried to shew, they have almost always confused both with one another and with other questions. These two questions may be expressed, the first in the form: What kind of things ought to exist for their own sakes? the second in the form: What kind of actions ought we to perform? I have tried to shew exactly

what it is that we ask about a thing, when we ask whether it ought to exist for its own sake, is good in itself or has intrinsic value; and exactly what it is that we ask about an action, when we ask whether we ought to do it, whether it is a right action or a duty. (pp. vii–viii)

A clear grasp of the meaning of one's questions bears fruit when one turns to consider the nature of possible answers.

But from a clear insight into the nature of these two questions, there appears to me to follow a second most important result: namely, what is the nature of the evidence, by which alone any ethical proposition can be proved or disproved, confirmed or rendered doubtful. Once we recognise the exact meaning of the two questions, I think it also becomes plain exactly what kind of reasons are relevant as arguments for or against any particular answer to them. It becomes plain that, for answers to the *first* question, no relevant evidence whatever can be adduced: from no other truth, except themselves alone, can it be inferred that they are either true or false. We can guard against error only by taking care, that, when we try to answer a question of this kind, we have before our minds that question only, and not some other or others; but that there is great danger of such errors of confusion I have tried to shew, and also what are the chief precautions by the use of which we may guard against them. As for the *second* question, it becomes equally plain, that any answer to it *is* capable of proof or disproof—that, indeed, so many different considerations are relevant to its truth or falsehood, as to make the attainment of probability very difficult, and the attainment of certainty impossible. (p. viii)

From the outset we sense Moore's growing maturity as a thinker. The language is measured: Thought is being dissected; things are what they are, and it is not for us to rejoice or complain. A sense of confidence is detectable between the lines: Moore has a firm grasp of where *Principia* leads us; notwithstanding his remarks at the end of the Preface where he says that he is "painfully aware that [the book] is full of defects," one cannot help thinking that he believes it is full of truth as well. The book itself is an exercise in science—the Science of Morals, or, simply, Ethics—and foremost among Moore's intentions is that of clarifying what this Science is, both its nature and its limitations. In this respect Moore continues to carry out, this time on a large scale, his ambition to reform the Science of Morals, a project that on a small scale he had begun in "Art, Morals, and Religion." The objects of the Science of Morals, as generally understood, are duties and virtues. Moore's reform will put them in their place. A properly conceived Ethics will allow room for both, but neither duties nor virtues will occupy the position of prominence generations of moral philosophers, from Aristotle to Bradley, have accorded them. Moore, then, clearly *is* a moral reformer in one sense. He aspires to exorcise the spell the ethics of duties and virtues has had on the human mind, a spell cast on Sunday by preachers and throughout the week by those who should know better—"would-be scientific moralists."

The True Object of Ethics

Moore's reformist aspirations regarding the Science of Morals presuppose a clear conception of what this Science is, beginning with what it should be about. At least as early as a review published in 1899 Moore begins to argue in print that Ethics must deal with a notion that belongs to it and it alone. That notion is Good, understood as the property shared by all and only those things that are good in themselves, or that have intrinsic value, or that ought to exist or are worth having for their own sakes. In his review of Fred Bon's *Ueber das Sollen und das Gute: eine begriffsanalytische Untersuchung* Moore chastises Bon for having "omitted to notice the only notion which really serves to distinguish Ethics from any other study. What this is *called* matters no more than Herr Bon thinks it matters. What is important is that there is a perfectly distinct meaning, of which he says not a word, that I should prefer to denote by the name 'good' " (p. 421). Moore's conviction that Ethics has a unique object to study actually predates his review of Bon's book. Among his unpublished work the opening pages of the First Dissertation, for example, begun some three years before this review, are no less insistent that Ethics studies an object that is not studied by any other science.

Moore's steady conviction about the autonomy of Ethics—its logical independence from any other science when it confronts its most basic question, the question about the nature of Good—that conviction has obvious Kantian roots. For Kant Ethics fundamentally is concerned with what ought to be done. And what ought to be done is in his view logically independent of what is done. Moore accepts the spirit while altering the letter of Kant's position. Good is not the object of any empirical or natural science, including psychology, and propositions about what things are intrinsically good are logically distinct from propositions about any fact that any natural science might discover. But in opposition to Kant Moore maintains that the unique object of Ethics—Good—itself has no essential connection with volition, whether human or otherwise. For Kant there could be nothing of intrinsic value in a world lacking volition. For Moore there can be, the intrinsic value of beauty in nature being perhaps the clearest example. This difference echoes throughout the pages of *Principia*. Whereas for Kant the fundamental principle of Ethics takes the form of a command (the so-called categorical imperative), for Moore the fundamental principle takes the form of a proposition, declaring that something *is* good, *not* that some act ought to be done. But despite the differences, which are many and profound, Moore's kantianism is alive and well in *Principia*, something in evidence as early as the Preface, where he writes the following:

> One main object of this book may, then, be expressed by slightly changing one of Kant's famous titles. I have endeavoured to write 'Prolegomena to any future Ethics that can possibly pretend to be scientific.' In other words, I have endeavoured to discover what are the fundamental principles of ethical reasoning; and the establishment of these principles, rather than of any conclusions which may be attained by their use, may be regarded as my main object. (p. ix)

Moore has answered the fundamental questions of the Science of Morals. The objects of this Science, as *generally* conceived, are duties and virtues. The object of Ethics, *properly* conceived, is Good. How, then, may we account for the pervasive misunderstanding concerning the object of Ethics on the part of would-be scientific moralists?

One possibility is that these thinkers assume that Good *is the same thing* as doing one's duty, or that Good *is the same thing* as virtue. If that were so these thinkers would naturally suppose that in studying duties or virtues they were studying that unique object that defines their Science. As a preliminary to his attack on the prevailing views about the relationship of the Science of Morals to conduct, which he develops in Chapter Five, Moore first addresses the more fundamental question about the relationship of Good to other things. Is Good identical with Virtue? Is Good identical with the performance of a dutiful act for duty's sake? Is Good identical with anything other than itself? That is *the* fundamental question of Ethics. Moore's famous answer to these questions is everywhere the same. It is, No.

The Naturalistic Fallacy

The "naturalistic fallacy" is the name Moore gives to any attempt to identify Good with something other than itself. Since its christening a veritable industry devoted to the study of this fallacy has come into being, and if there is anything that has kept Moore's name alive in moral philosophy up to now it is his contribution to the debate over whether there is such a thing as the "naturalistic fallacy" and, if so, what it is. It will not be possible but neither would it be desirable to attempt to canvass this extensive secondary literature on this occasion. And the same is true even of Moore's own varied characterizations of this fallacy. The present examination is limited to highlighting the role played by Moore's position regarding the naturalistic fallacy when this is viewed against the backdrop of *Principia*'s central theoretical purpose: the reform of the Science of Morals.

In maintaining that Good is not identical with anything except itself (or, as he frequently expresses this point, that Good is indefinable) Moore is not saying that nothing *is* good. On the contrary he carries into *Principia* his newly recovered confidence that beauty in art and nature is good in itself and offers an expansive inventory of the best things we know or can imagine in that work's final chapter. Because all intrinsically good things, despite their many differences, are alike in being good in themselves, Moore believes that they must all possess or share the same property: intrinsic goodness. Ethics must fix the nature of this shared property. That is the point from which this Science must begin.

In *Principia* Moore sometimes refers to Good as a notion or object, and sometimes as an idea. These are the proxies noted by Ryle for the vocabulary of 'concepts' that characterizes both the Second Dissertation and the portion of it published under the title "The Nature of Judgment." In those earlier works concepts are universal meanings. The meaning of 'red' is the concept Red; of 'rose,' the concept Rose; and so on. There is in every case only one universal meaning though there may be many instances—many red things, but only one concept, Red; many roses, but only one concept, Rose; and so on. Moore in *Principia* continues to operate with this ontology of meanings in the background, so that when he insists that the *object* of Ethics is Good, he means that Ethics must start with an examination of this particular concept, object, notion, or, in other words, this particular universal meaning. Accordingly, by claiming that Good is indefinable Moore does not mean that the English word 'good' lacks a dictionary definition. He means that the universal meaning of the word 'good'—the concept, notion, object, or idea that this word, or its equivalent in any natural language, names, denotes, or signifies—cannot be defined. The *notion* Good is not identical with any notion other than itself.

Those "tendencies towards Realism" Moore initially exhibits in "The Nature of Judgment" also are carried over into *Principa*. In opposition to that "poor idealistic system" of his youth Moore now holds that in sense perception we are directly aware of the properties of things, not our (mental) "impressions" of these properties. And in thought we are directly aware of universal meanings (notions, concepts, and the like), not our (mental) "ideas" of them. When two people see a red rose, they both see the same thing. And when two people think about the meaning of 'red' or 'rose,' they both think about the same things too: namely, Red and Rose. The situation is no different in the case of our thought about the universal meaning of 'good.' Representative of Moore's "realistic tendencies" regarding Good is the following:

> Everyone does in fact understand the question 'Is this good?' When he thinks of this, his state of mind is different from what it would be, were he asked 'Is this pleasant, or desired, or approved?' It has a distinct meaning for him, even though he may not recognize in what respect it is distinct. Whenever he thinks of 'intrinsic value,' or 'intrinsic worth,' or says that a thing 'ought to exist,' he has before his mind the unique object—the unique property of things—which I mean by 'good.' Everybody is constantly aware of this notion, although he may never become aware at all that it is different from other notions of which he is also aware. (pp. 16–17)

It is the *notion* Good—of which, Moore confidently proclaims, "everybody is constantly aware"—that is indefinable. Like the notions Yellow and Truth, which are simple and unanalyzable (this is the teaching of "The Nature of Judgment"), the notion Good has "no parts," is "simple," and so is "unanalyzable" or "indefinable."

In general, then, although there may be and in Moore's view there are many different things that are good in themselves, there is nothing that is good in itself because of the universal meanings of words. Expressed alternatively, one can say that in his view there is no proposition of the form 'X is good' that is true because of its meaning—except, of course, the proposition 'Good is Good.' Following traditional Kantian usage one may say that all significant true propositions of the form 'X is good' are synthetic; none is analytic. For in order to be the latter such a proposition would have to be true because of its meaning alone. And that can never be the case if Moore is right in maintaining that Good is not identical with anything except itself. That at least a large part of what Moore thinks is at stake in his discussion of the naturalistic fallacy is captured by the preceding is confirmed by the following passage, where he again expresses himself in Kantian terms:

> But, if we understand the question [What is Good?] in this sense, my answer to it may seem a very disappointing one. If I am asked 'What is good?' my answer is that good is good, and that is the end of the matter. Or if I am asked 'How is good to be defined?' my answer is that it cannot be defined, and that is all I have to say about it. But disappointing as these answers may appear, they are of the very last importance. To readers who are familiar with philosophic terminology, I can express their importance by saying that they amount to this: That propositions about the good are all of them synthetic and never analytic; and that is plainly no trivial matter. And the same thing may be expressed more popularly, by saying that, if I am right, then nobody can foist upon us such an axiom as that 'Pleasure is the only good' or that 'The good is the desired' on the pretence that this is 'the very meaning of the word.' (pp. 6–7)

Moore offers a variety of arguments in support of his view that Good is indefinable. Whatever their respective strengths or weaknesses the implication is always the same: A certain form of inference is illicit. To make this clearer suppose we construct a column for the universal meaning Good.

Column 1

The Universal Meaning, Good

- ought to exist for its own sake
- is good in itself
- is worth having for its own sake
- is intrinsically valuable

And suppose a second column is constructed in which things judged to be good in themselves are listed.

Column 2

Things That Are Good in Themselves

- pleasure
- knowledge
- friendship
- beauty

The logical implication of Moore's arguments against attempts to define Good is simply this: one can never validly infer that something belongs in Column 2 on the basis of reflecting only on what is in Column 1. All that can be found in Column 1 is that Good is Good, or that Good means what ought to exist for its own sake, or what is worth having for its own sake, or what has intrinsic value. What one can never find or validly infer is what things these are.

Moore's position is perfectly general, applying to every proposed definition of Good. Whether that definition is offered in terms of some psychological state (for example, 'Good is identical with pleasure'), some biological tendency (for example, 'Good is identical with whatever is more evolved'), or some supersensible existent (for example, 'Good is identical with what is willed universally by the noumenal self'), the error is always the same. Something (Good) that is not identical with anything other than itself is being treated as if it were identical with something else, or, alternatively, results that can only be found in Column 2 are being treated as if they could themselves be found in, or validly inferred from a study of what is found in, Column 1.

If such confusion were confined to only a few thinkers Moore might be charged with raising an unnecessary fuss. In fact the confusion is of epidemic proportions in his view. Virtually every would-be scientific moralist commits the naturalistic fallacy along the way to "establishing" one or another favorite set of rules of duty or virtue. Only Sidgwick seems to have managed to escape the disease. That anonymous reviewer in the *Guardian* (April 24, 1904) captures well the dimensions of Moore's curative campaign when he writes that "Mr. Moore's mission . . . takes the form of assuring almost all other philosophers since the world began . . . have never even conceived the problem of ethics correctly, much less solved it." The "gross absurdities" of Aristotle, Kant, "and other triflers" are swept "into the waste-paper basket," along with Christianity, leaving "no one outside that useful receptacle except a fragment of Henry Sidgwick and himself, a result which may be gratifying to the University of Cambridge but must be distressing to the rest of the world." Sidgwick is spared because he recognizes that Good is indefinable. The rest of the practitioners of the Science of Morals in Moore's view stand justly condemned.

Most of *Principia*'s first four chapters, almost a full two-thirds of the book, is devoted to the explanation and detection of the naturalistic fallacy. It is slow going, to say the least, "a bare and bleak book, a little low in tone, not nearly as exciting," Leonard Woolf writes of *Principia* in the *Times Literary Supplement*, "as it [was] to the youthful Keynes when he wrote to [a friend] on October 7, 1903, 'I have been reading Moore's *Principia Ethica*, which has been out a few days—a stupendous and entrancing work, *the greatest* on the subject.' " Keynes evidently had an appetite for fine analysis not shared by the *Guardian*'s reviewer.

Or by Virginia Woolf. One particularly important argument Moore deploys against proposed definitions of Good has come to be called the Open Question Argument. He characterizes this argument by stating that "whatever definition [of Good] be offered, it may be always asked, with significance, of the complex so defined, whether it is itself good." To make his meaning clearer Moore offers an example.

> To take, for instance, one of the more plausible, because one of the more complicated, of such proposed definitions, it may easily be thought, at first sight, that to be good may mean to be that which we desire to desire. Thus if we apply this definition to a particular instance and say 'When we think that A is good, we are thinking that A is one of the things which we desire to desire,' our proposition may seem quite plausible. But, if we carry the investigation further, and ask ourselves 'Is it good to desire to desire A?' it is apparent, on a little reflection, that this question is itself as intelligible, as the original question 'Is A good?'—that we are, in fact, now asking for exactly the same information about the desire to desire A, for which we formerly asked with regard to A itself. But it is also apparent that the meaning of this second question cannot be correctly analysed into 'Is the desire to desire A one of the things which we desire to desire?': we have not before our minds anything so complicated as

the question 'Do we desire to desire to desire to desire A?' (pp. 15–16)

We recognize this as the passage Virginia refers to in her struggle to "climb" Moore: "One sentence, a string of 'desires' makes my head spin with the infinite meaning of words unadorned." Virginia misleads only in that she suggests that this sentence is somehow exceptional.

The Nonnaturalness of Good

Nowhere is "the infinite meaning of words unadorned" more apparent than in Moore's discussion of what makes Good nonnatural. As a result of his determined effort to be systematic, Moore attempts to introduce rigor and precision into his analysis by resurrecting the distinction, first made five years earlier in "The Elements," between the natural and the nonnatural. Hardly a word has been changed from that earlier discussion in the following passages in *Principia*:

> By 'nature,' then, I do mean and have meant that which is the subject-matter of the natural sciences and also of psychology. It may be said to include all that has existed, does exist, or will exist in time. If we consider whether any object is of such a nature that it may be said to exist now, to have existed, or to be about to exist, then we may know that that object is a natural object, and that nothing, of which this is not true, is a natural object. Thus, for instance, of our minds we should say that they did exist yesterday, that they do exist to-day, and probably will exist in a minute or two. We shall say that we had thoughts yesterday, which have ceased to exist now, although their effects may remain: and in so far as those thoughts did exist, they too are natural objects.
>
> There is, indeed, no difficulty about the 'objects' themselves, in the sense in which I have just used the term. It is easy to say which of them are natural, and which (if any) are not natural. But when we begin to consider the properties of objects, then I fear the problem is more difficult. Which among the properties of natural objects are natural properties and which are not? For I do not deny that good is a property of certain natural objects: certain of them, I think, *are* good; and yet I have said that 'good' itself is not a natural property. Well, my test for these too also concerns their existence in time. Can

we imagine 'good' as existing *by itself* in time, and not merely as a property of some natural object? For myself, I cannot so imagine it, whereas with the greater number of properties of objects—those which I call the natural properties—their existence does seem to me to be independent of the existence of those objects. They are, in fact, rather parts of which the object is made up than mere predicates which attach to it. If they were all taken away, no object would be left, not even a bare substance: for they are in themselves substantial and give to the object all the substance that it has. But this is not so with good. If indeed good were a feeling, as some would have us believe, then it would exist in time. But that is why to call it so is to commit the naturalistic fallacy. It will always remain pertinent to ask, whether the feeling itself is good; and if so, then good cannot itself be identical with any feeling. (pp. 40–41)

The distinction Moore makes for a second time between natural and nonnatural properties is no less a "stumbling-block" in 1903 than it was in 1898, and it must be said at this point—though not only at this one— that Leonard Woolf greatly exaggerates the simplicity of Moore's thought when, writing in *Sowing*, he states that Moore "did not require us to accept any . . . intricate, if unintelligible, intellectual gymnastics of a Platonic . . . [or] . . . Kantian . . . nature," or that Moore's voice was unwaveringly "the more divine voice of common-sense." (pp. 147–148) Moore's conception of nonnatural properties is extremely unclear and does require some rather elaborate "intellectual gymnastics"—and these of a decidedly Platonic nature. As is true of "The Elements" and even of some earlier work, Moore in *Principia* maintains that Good *is* despite the fact that Good does not exist. This is perhaps clearest in his discussion of metaphysics.

What, then, is to be understood by 'metaphysical'? I use the term . . . in opposition to 'natural.' I call those philosophers preeminently 'metaphysical' who had recognised most clearly that not everything which *is* is a 'natural object.' 'Metaphysicians' have, therefore, the great merit of insisting that our knowledge is not confined to the things which we can touch and see and feel. They have always been much occupied, not only with that other class of natural objects which consists in mental facts, but also with the class of objects or properties of objects, which certainly do not exist in time, are not therefore parts of Nature, and which, in fact, do not *exist* at all. To this class, as I have said, belongs what we mean by the adjective 'good.' It is not *goodness*, but only the things or qualities which are good, which can exist in time—can have duration, and begin and cease to exist—can be objects of *perception*. But the most prominent members of this class are perhaps numbers. It is quite certain that two natural objects may exist; but it is equally certain that *two* itself does not exist and never can. Two and two *are* four. But that does not mean that either two or four exists. Yet it certainly means *something*. Two *is* somehow, although it does not exist. And it is not only simple terms of propositions—the objects *about* which we know truths—that belong to this class. The truths which we know about them form, perhaps, a still more important subdivision. No truth does, in fact, *exist*; but this is peculiarly obvious with regard to truths like 'Two and two are four,' in which the objects, *about* which they are truths, do not exist either. It is with the recognition of such truths as these—truths which have been called 'universal'—and of their essential unlikeness to what we can touch and see and feel, that metaphysics proper begins. Such 'universal' truths have always played a large part in the reasonings of metaphysicians from Plato's time till now; and that they have directed attention to the difference between these truths and what I have called 'natural objects' is the chief contribution to knowledge which distinguishes them from that other class of philosophers—'empirical' philosophers—to which most Englishmen have belonged. (pp. 110-111)

Moore's Platonism clearly remains intact. And this, coupled with his tendencies toward Realism, enables him to assume that we have direct dealings with the world of universal meanings. Whenever we think about what words mean, what we think about are subsisting concepts, notions, and the like. In contrast to the majority of English philosophers, who have been empiricists and who teach that what we perceive or think of are our own ideas (contents in our separate minds), Moore marches to two foreign drummers. He is both a platonist and a realist.

But notwithstanding both the largely favorable things Moore writes about metaphysicians and his remarks about Good in this context, it would be a mistake to suppose that the alleged nonnaturalness of Good could possibly be captured by one or another metaphysical account of this notion. 'Metaphysical', it is true, is a term Moore uses in opposition to 'natural'. And 'nonnatural' also is opposed in its meaning to 'natural'. But that does not make 'metaphysical' and 'nonnatural' the same. On the contrary, 'nonnatural' is no less opposed to 'metaphysical' than it is to 'natural'. 'Nonnatural', in other words, means "any property that is *neither* natural *nor* metaphysical." Perhaps Moore would have been less easily misunderstood if he had retained the idea that Good has a *transcendental* meaning and referred to the property of something's being good as a transcendental rather than a nonnatural property. In any event, because his explanations of these various kinds of property are unclear, his account of Good remains opaque. Moore's failure to secure the requisite clarity on these matters is one of *Principia's* major weaknesses.

This weakness aside, it is reasonably clear what Moore is trying to do if we view his critical discussions of various naturalistic and metaphysical definitions of Good against the larger reformist aspirations he brings to *Principia's* pages. Some of those who offer definitions of Good define it in terms of one or another natural fact—for example, a psychological state, such as pleasure, or a biological tendency, such as whatever is more evolved—facts that are in principle discoverable and confirmable by the natural sciences, including psychology. Others offer strikingly different definitions, identifying Good with something that is not natural—for example, with whatever can be universally willed by the noumenal self—such things that, if they do exist, cannot even in principle be discovered or confirmed by any natural science, including psychology. Definitions of the former sort are naturalistic definitions. Those of the latter, metaphysical. Despite their differences, both have this much in common in Moore's view: Both *are* definitions of Good. And their implications are in one fundamental respect the same. If a definition of either type could conceivably be correct it would follow that the Science of Morals would lose its autonomy. And if that happened, Moore implies, the *Science of Morals itself* could pose a grave threat to the autonomy of individual moral agents.

Threats to Autonomy

Naturalistic definitions of Good destroy the autonomy of Ethics, reducing this Science to a branch of one or another of the natural sciences, including psychology. If Good is identified with some empirically verifiable biological tendency (say, what is more evolved) Ethics becomes a branch of biology. If Good is defined in psychological terms (say, whatever anyone prefers) Ethics becomes a branch of psychology. And so on. In every case Ethics loses that "question of its own" Moore unflaggingly insists defines this Science. At the most abstract level, then, Moore's sometimes vehement denunciation of naturalistic definitions of Good reflects his passionate commitment to viewing Ethics as an independent Science. The fundamental error committed by those who define Good in naturalistic terms is a purely intellectual error, resulting from a failure to recognize that Ethics is what it is, and not another thing.

But at another level it is the autonomy of individuals that is lost or diminished if one or another naturalistic definition of Good is accepted. Our freedom to judge intrinsic values would be the first casualty. If Good means "whatever is more evolved," for example, then that's that. There would be no room—there *could* be no room—for individual judgment about *what sorts of things ought to exist for their own sakes.* That would be settled: All and only those things that are more evolved would fall into this category. The meanings of words would take over the work of the value judgments of individuals, and the determination of what things actually are good would be the business of those most qualified to decide what things actually are more evolved. In this case biologists would become our authorities.

A second, no less troubling threat to individual autonomy and judgment concerns what a naturalistic ethic could imply concerning human conduct. What we ought to do, Moore maintains, is what produces the best results. In his view this is what 'ought' means—at least this is his view in *Principia.* Suppose this definition of 'ought' in terms of Good is accepted. And suppose further that "best results" is interpreted in terms of some naturalistic definition of Good—say, "whatever is more evolved." Then what each of us ought to do is act in those ways that will bring about whatever results are more evolved. And that, again, would be that. There could be no room for individuals to wonder whether this is so. There could be no place for individual judgment about the different kinds of things that might make a right act right. These matters, too, would be beyond dispute settled once and for all by the meanings of words. Individuals could no more intelligibly wonder whether they ought to do what will produce more evolved results than they can now intelligibly wonder whether a cube can have more than twelve edges. Once again, moreover, an elevated class of moral experts would evolve. If moral values are reduced to biological facts, biologists would be in a privileged position to decide what is right and wrong.

A third assault on individual autonomy posed by naturalistic definitions of Good is bound up with the sanctions such definitions would authorize. Any ethical system that recognizes a list of rules of duty also authorizes the use of sanctions in the form of various rewards and punishments to encourage compliance. Naturalistic ethics therefore will have sanctions as part of their moral baggage. The possible threat to individual autonomy again is clear. People should be rewarded for acting as they ought and punished to varying degrees for failing to do so. Suppose Good is defined naturalistically as "whatever is more evolved." Then the basis for the social institutions of rewards and punishments would be settled, would be fixed. There could be no reasoning about it, no room for individual judgment. The meaning of words again would decide these matters, and decide them in ways against which the individual would be powerless to lodge a meaningful complaint. The very *vocabulary* for doing so would have been taken away.

The situation is no different in the case of virtues. If these are defined naturalistically, as dispositions to do what is defined as Good, the same assaults on autonomy, both on the Science of Morals and on individual judgment and conduct, will be in the offing. In Moore's unbending hostility toward naturalistic definitions of Good we see a defense, not only of the autonomy of Ethics but also of the autonomy of the individual.

The situation is essentially the same if Good is defined in metaphysical terms. Suppose it is defined as "what the noumenal self wills universally." Then decisions about what things are good become the province of metaphysics, and the Science of Morals, having lost "its question," will have lost its autonomy as well. Similarly lost is room for individuals who lack expertise in metaphysics. These people could not even *wonder* whether what the noumenal self wills universally is good. The very meanings of words, given this definition, would make this impossible. Rather than representatives of a natural science (say, biology) emerging as the priestly class of moral authorities, metaphysical definitions of Good would elevate the likes of Bradley and McTaggart to this high office. The autonomy of Ethics is the first casualty of metaphysical definitions of Good; the autonomy of the individual is the second.

When Moore's arguments against metaphysical and other sorts of definitions of Good are viewed in this larger perspective, *Principia*'s kantianism can be seen more clearly. That work's fundamental theoretical question is, How is a Science of Morals possible? Moore's answer in part is, Only if its object, Good, is not identical with any other *kind* of notion. For if it were identical with some other kind of notion, Ethics would become absorbed by the kind of science that routinely studies notions of this other kind—a natural science if Good is defined in naturalistic terms, the science of metaphysics if Good is defined metaphysically. If, however, Good is not identical with any other kind of notion, then Good cannot be defined either in naturalistic or in metaphysical terms, and the autonomy of the Science of Morals is assured.

But the autonomy of Ethics could be assured without having to deny that Good is definable. Perhaps Good can be defined *nonnaturalistically*. In that case Ethics would not be in danger of being absorbed by either a natural science or metaphysics. *Its* autonomy would remain intact. But not the autonomy of the individual, especially the autonomy to judge what has intrinsic value. Suppose Good were defined as some x; and suppose x is nonnatural. Then individuals could no more intelligibly wonder whether x is good than they can wonder whether a cube can have more than twelve edges. And neither could they agree that something is x and then go on intelligibly to ask whether it is good—or question the deliverances of "experts" in the Science of Morals. It is not simply the nonnaturalness of Good that is crucial for Moore's purposes, all considered. It is the *uniqueness* of Good that is. Good simply is what it is, and not another thing, not even another nonnatural thing. That is what Moore's arguments are meant to show. At the deepest level it is the autonomy of individual judgment about what has intrinsic value, not the autonomy of the Science of Morals, that is at issue and that Moore relentlessly seeks to defend. *Individuals* must judge for themselves what things ought to exist, what things are worth having for their own sakes. No natural science can do this. No metaphysical system can do this. Not even the Science of Morals can do this. Every attempt to take this freedom (and this responsibility) away from the individual rests on the same kind of fallacy—the (so-called) naturalistic fallacy. The *raison d'être* of Ethics is to prove that there are some things—and these the most important things in human life—that no science can prove. Fundamentally *Principia* is a book about the limits of all science, including the Science of Morals. This is a message the members of Bloomsbury could hardly have missed.

The Severest Critic

In the early 1920s a series of severe criticisms were raised against Moore's treatment in *Principia* of the naturalistic fallacy and related matters. These criticisms are summarized in a paper by Casimir Lewy. "Good is Good, and nothing else whatever" is said to be "either merely trivial or else obviously false" (p. 294). The *Principia* account of natural properties is characterized as "hopelessly confused" (p. 295). The thesis that Good is indefinable is judged to be of far less importance and far more doubtful than it is there supposed to be. And the use of the word 'fallacy' is challenged (p. 297) because that word properly applies only to errors people make when they infer one thing from another, not, as this word is used in *Principia*, when they confuse one thing with another. These are among the best-informed criticisms of *Principia*. They are not Lewy's. Instead Lewy is recounting Moore's own telling criticisms of *Principia*.

Moore had contemplated adding a lengthy, revised Preface to the second edition of *Principia*, which was issued in 1922. This he never completed, but an unfinished draft exists. Presumably the task of finishing it took on larger proportions than he had assumed at the start. The actual Preface to the second edition intimates how very large those proportions were.

> This book is now reprinted without any alteration whatever, except that a few misprints and grammatical mistakes have been corrected. It is reprinted, because I am still in agreement with its main tendency and conclusions; and it is reprinted without alteration, because I found that, if I were to begin correcting what in it seemed to me to need correction, I could not stop short of rewriting the whole book. (p. xii)

When Moore writes that he is "still in agreement with its main tendency and conclusion" at least part of what he means is that he continues to believe in the autonomy of the Science of Morals, a conviction that was to bend at a later period of his life. But not break. What the unfinished and still unpublished draft of the new Preface shows, Lewy notes, "is that many of the criticisms made of Moore's treatment of the naturalistic fallacy and related matters in the 1930s and 1940s were fully anticipated by him many years earlier" (p. 297). When Moore encountered these criticisms raised by others he must have felt as if he were meeting a shadow of his former self.

Hedonism

Of all his predecessors in Ethics Moore believes that only Sidgwick recognizes that Good is indefinable. Yet Sidgwick embraces hedonism, the view that pleasure and pleasure alone is good in itself. Sidgwick's great merit in Moore's view is that he does not attempt to defend hedonism by *defining* Good as pleasure. He avoids the naturalistic fallacy. And yet he is a hedonist. Moore is not. What are Moore's reasons for diverging from his teacher's views, views that, as we know from his first Apostles paper, Moore himself once accepted?

Moore's arguments against Sidgwick are set forth in Chapter Four. The greater part of this chapter is devoted to a critique of Sidgwick's fellow utilitarian, Mill. The language, both in the sections devoted to Mill and in those that focus on Sidgwick, is the most strident in the book. Mill is said to be guilty of "as naïve and artless a use of the naturalistic fallacy as anybody could desire," and his attempt to explain how the intrinsic value of virtue meshes with his hedonism is characterized as "contemptible nonsense." Sidgwick in turn is credited with reaching an "absurd conclusion" and with offering "flimsy arguments." And the basis on which he argues for his hedonism is deemed "quite ridiculous." He also is characterized at one point as a thinker who "strains at a gnat and swallows a camel." The vituperativeness of the language is perhaps an index of the importance in Moore's mind of putting some distance between himself and his utilitarian forebears. For he does not want to be thought of as "just another utilitarian."

The language aside, Moore's criticisms of Sidgwick are representative of his energetic if not always well-directed critical aim. His mind is relentlessly on the lookout for the intellectual gnats he thinks are made to do the work of camels. For example, Sidgwick is charged with failing to distinguish between pleasure and the consciousness of pleasure. (Moore at this time believed that pleasure could exist apart from consciousness.) This failure on Sidgwick's part allegedly undermines his hedonism. For it is not, Moore insists, the *mere existence* of pleasure that has a large claim to having intrinsic value; it is the consciousness of it. And that fact, once admitted, opens the floor to the consideration of other complex wholes. If it is the complex state of affairs comprised of pleasure plus consciousness that has a serious claim to having intrinsic value, and not merely the pleasure itself, might it not be that there are *still more complex wholes*—states of affairs that include, for example, true belief, contemplation, admiration, and love—that are even better? Moore thinks there are, and he finds Sidgwick's attempts to defend hedonism against a pluralistic view of intrinsic goods "flimsy." Moreover, not only is it true that the value of these wholes does not consist only in their pleasure, it is also true that the value of these wholes cannot be determined merely by summing the value of their parts. In making this claim Moore is of course reaffirming the notion of organic unities that first finds clear expression in "The Elements." Judgments of value are *far* more difficult—one might even say, literally, *incalculably* more difficult—than hedonism would have us believe.

The reaffirmation of the doctrine of organic unities is not the only case where Moore incorporates ideas and, sometimes, whole passages from "The Elements." The same is true of his discussion of natural and nonnatural properties, for example. And true, too, in the case of his long-standing disagreement with Sidgwick over the intrinsic value of beauty. First appearing in the Appendix to the First Dissertation, only to be excised from the Second, and then to be resurrected in "The Elements," the presence of this debate in Moore's ethical writings during this period is a litmus test of his confidence both as a philosopher and as a person who finds life worth living. Russell's 1899 attack on Moore's views regarding beauty contributed to that crisis in his philosophy and personal life we find expressed in the melancholic pages of "Vanity of vanities." And it is the reaffirmation of the intrinsic value of beauty in "Art, Morals, and Religion" in 1901 that signals that his quest for a value to believe in has come full circle. This crisis resolved, we are not surprised to find Moore for a third time challenging Sidgwick's hedonism by appealing to the intrinsic value of beauty.

As a hedonist Sidgwick is committed to the view that beauty in nature, apart from the pleasure humans may take in perceiving it, has no intrinsic value. The claims of such things as beauty to having intrinsic value are "put out of court" by Sidgwick's views. Moore initiates his challenge by asking, "Is this exclusion justified?," to which he answers as follows:

> I cannot think it is. 'No one,' says Prof. Sidgwick, 'would consider it rational to aim at the production of beauty in external nature, apart from any possible contemplation of it by human beings.' Well, I may say at once, that I, for one, do consider this rational; and let us see if I cannot get any one to agree with me. Consider what this admission really means. It entitles us to put the following case. Let us imagine one world exceedingly beautiful. Imagine it as beautiful as you can; put into it whatever on this earth you most admire—mountains, rivers, the sea; trees, and sunsets, stars and moon. Imagine these all combined in the most exquisite proportions, so that no one thing

jars against another, but each contributes to increase the beauty of the whole. And then imagine the ugliest world you can possibly conceive. Imagine it simply one heap of filth, containing everything that is most disgusting to us, for whatever reason, and the whole, as far as may be, without one redeeming feature. Such a pair of worlds we are entitled to compare: they fall within Prof. Sidgwick's meaning, and the comparison is highly relevant to it. The only thing we are not entitled to imagine is that any human being ever has or ever, by any possibility, *can*, live in either, can ever see and enjoy the beauty of the one or hate the foulness of the other. Well, even so, supposing them quite apart from any possible contemplation by human beings; still, is it irrational to hold that it is better that the beautiful world should exist, than the one which is ugly? Would it not be well, in any case, to do what we could to produce it rather than the other? Certainly I cannot help thinking that it would; and I hope that some may agree with me in this extreme instance. The instance is extreme. It is highly improbable, not to say, impossible, we should ever have such a choice before us. . . . I admit, of course, that our beautiful world would be better still, if there were human beings in it to contemplate and enjoy its beauty. But that admission makes nothing against my point. If it be once admitted that the beautiful world *in itself* is better than the ugly, then it follows, that however many beings may enjoy it, and however much better their enjoyment may be than it is itself, yet its mere existence adds *something* to the goodness of the whole: it is not only a means to our end, but also itself a part thereof. (pp. 83–85)

Moore does not suppose that he has *proven* that the unseen beautiful world is good in itself. Like Sidgwick, Moore thinks that no evidence can be given in support of a judgment of intrinsic value. Our decision must be the verdict, to use Sidgwick's words quoted by Moore in *Principia* (p. 92), of our "intuitive judgment after due consideration of the question when fairly placed before it." There is no argument to be given for or against one verdict or another. There is only the judgment itself, hanging suspended in the universe, so to speak, without any support from anything other than itself. Such judgments are ultimate judgments both in the logical sense that they cannot be inferred from any proposition(s) more basic than themselves and in the psychological sense that they provide the materials out of which individuals can create answers to the question, What makes life worth living?

That is a question no science, not even the Science of Morals when properly reformed, is able to answer. Each person must answer this question individually. There are no moral "experts," whether dressed in the gowns of science or the robes of religion. The autonomy of Ethics ensures the autonomy of the individual's judgments of intrinsic value. The limits of reason make room for the commitments of faith. Sidgwick's great merit in Moore's view is that he sees this. His major defect is that he embraces a monistic moral faith: Only one thing is good in itself, and that is pleasure. With his background in the classics Moore is temperamentally at home in a polytheistic universe. There are many goods, not only one. If this belief makes the moral universe more complicated than Sidgwick's monism implies, that is no reason for choosing simplicity if the price is losing truth. Moore makes this point in the Appendix to his First Dissertation, stating that "the adoption of pleasure as our standard, merely for the sake of having some system, would, if it happened not to be the true one, as I have seen no reason for thinking that it is, lead us only into systematic error." The individual must make a leap of faith into the uncertain universe of intrinsic value not once but many times. The early chapters of *Principia* attempt to wrest this freedom from every science—and from every god— and to give it to its rightful bearer: the individual. Among the views that meet an untimely end in the wake of *Principia*'s onslaught are those youthful speculations of the author of "The Elements." Our judgments about what things are good in themselves, that work teaches, are in general "guaranteed" to be correct because this is "determined by the course of evolution." Small wonder that Moore in *Principia* sometimes vents his spleen with special satisfaction in his discussions of evolutionary ethics. In some ways—though not of course in all ways—his main target is his own earlier views. Few things are so reviled as the sins of our youth.

Whether successful or not, Moore's indefatigable effort to defend the freedom of the individual to judge what is valuable in itself is one part of *Principia*'s enduring greatness. At a time when the natural sciences were everywhere on the march, when what was thought to be known was increasingly filtered through the conceptual sieves of Darwinism and Freudianism, and when a cheery optimism taught that the sciences could teach us everything of importance and give us the technology to secure it, Moore stands steadfast, determined to ensure that the moral freedom individuals had only recently grasped from the weakened clutches of an all but deceased religious tradition would not be stolen by the eager hands of evangelical scientists. How well Virginia Woolf understood this. Beneath those heavy lines, weighed down by "the infinite meaning of words unadorned," buried amid the burdensome details about nonnatural properties and the naturalistic fallacy, she detects a man who is "so humane." Few have understood the essential spirit of the author or his work as well.

Three Tests

The account of Good Moore offers in *Principia* satisfies the three relevant criteria of adequacy applied throughout the present work. Because he continues to maintain that Good, when it is instantiated, is a nonnatural property of those things that are good in themselves, Moore likewise continues to satisfy the objectivity criterion. What things *are* good depends on what things possess this property; and what these things are in no way depends upon what we think, feel, or, say, hope about them. On Moore's view a state of affairs can be good and no one need notice or care.

The universality criterion also is met. The theme "Once good, always good" is played again and again throughout *Principia*, beginning in the first chapter, where Moore states that judgments of intrinsic value, "if true at all, . . . are all of them universally true" (p. 23), and continuing into the last chapter, where he sets forth his own view about what these good things are. Intrinsic goodness is just that—a kind of goodness that is intrinsic to those things that possess it and thus unalterable so long as these things themselves remain the same. To put the same point more abstractly, if a given thing, A, is intrinsically good, and if, in addition to its intrinsic value, A possesses properties x, y, z, then anything else like A in these same respects—that is, anything else that possesses these (and only these) same properties in the same combination—must likewise be intrinsically valuable. And equally so. Regardless of when or where this occurs.

Similarly successful is Moore's account of Good when assessed against the natural goods criterion. Nothing in his views precludes the possibility that things that exist in space and time—in nature—can be good in themselves. Moore in fact believes that there are many such things rather than just one. And he also believes that some good things are better than others —sometimes, as in the case of natural beauty, even apart from any human awareness or appreciation. That Moore's attempt to explain how his account of Good meets these three criteria encounters major difficulties —for example, the nature of the relationship between a thing's goodness and its other properties is not sufficiently explained in *Principia*, which leaves Moore's treatment of universality incomplete—that this is so does not entail that Moore's account of Good fails to satisfy the three criteria at hand. On these counts Moore is successful. But on these counts he had been successful before, in "The Elements." As we shall see in the next two chapters, another part of the enduring greatness of *Principia* is how well it fares when the remaining criteria of adequacy are applied.

Moore's Wobble

Wittgenstein's influence on twentieth-century thought is enormous. Though he published very little in his lifetime—the much celebrated *Tractatus Logicus Philosophicus* appeared in an English translation in 1922, and one paper, "Some Remarks on Logical Form," came out in *Mind* in 1929 —the combined impact of his posthumously published writings and the evangelical careers of his students, both before and after his death, have combined to make him one of the most influential philosophers of the twentieth century. Moore was unclear about whether and, if so, how his own work in philosophy had been influenced by Wittgenstein's. Of the *Tractatus* he says in his autobiography that "I read it again and again, trying to learn from it. It is a book which I admired and do admire extremely. There is, of course, a great deal in it which I was not able to understand; but many things I thought I did understand, and found them most enlightening" (p. 33).

Wittgenstein himself in time came to reject the major teachings of the *Tractatus* and it is his later views, those he began to develop after his return to Cambridge in 1929, to which Moore is referring when he writes that Wittgenstein had developed "a method quite different from any which I have ever used—a method which he himself uses successfully, but which I myself have never been able to understand clearly enough to use it myself" (p. 33). What this "method" is Moore does not say. And only a fool would attempt to do so in a few words. But that "method" made Ward's somber counsel obsolete in Wittgenstein's view. M. O'C. Drury, who attended Wittgenstein's lectures and talked with him frequently, recalls the following conversation from 1949.

Drury: James Ward used to say "Denken ist schwer."

Wittgenstein: Yes, that must have been a frequent remark of his. Moore quoted him as saying that. But I wouldn't say now "Thinking is hard." There is I believe a stage in philosophy where a person feels that. This material I am working at [in the *Investigations*] is as hard as granite but I know how to go about it.

Moore by contrast seems never to have progressed beyond the stage where Ward's dictum applies, perhaps in part because of the power of Wittgenstein's ideas, ideas which, Moore relates, "certainly had the effect of making me very distrustful about many things which, but for him, I should have been inclined to assert positively" (p. 33).

Among the things Moore "should have been inclined to assert positively" it seems likely that some concern how words mean what they mean. These are among the near obsessional concerns that hounded Wittgenstein throughout his life, and at least part of what marks the difference between the so-called "early Wittgenstein" and the "later Wittgenstein" are the changes his views undergo on these matters. In the *Tractatus* language requires *names*, which are understood as "simple signs." Because they are simple, they are not composed of other signs (as is, for example, the phrase "the present Queen of England.") What these names name are *objects*, and, like the signs that name them, objects are absolutely simple. They have no parts. For every simple sign, therefore, there exists a corresponding simple object. And the *meaning* of each simple sign is the object that it names.

Wittgenstein later repudiated this view of meaning, and Moore was among the first to know that and why he did. As Moore recounts this, Wittgenstein spent a good deal of time during his lectures in the 1933 academic year explaining how words mean what they mean. Among the more important "mistakes" to be avoided in this quarter, Moore records in his notes on Wittgenstein's lectures, is the view that "a word is related to its meaning in the same way in which a proper name is related to the 'bearer' of that name." Moore continues:

He gave as a reason for holding that this is false that the bearer of a name can be ill or dead, whereas we cannot possibly say that the meaning of the name is ill or dead. He said more than once that the bearer of a name can be "substituted" for the name, whereas the meaning of a word can never be substituted for that word. He sometimes spoke of this . . . mistake as the view that words are "representative" of their meanings, and he held that in no case is a word "representative" of its meaning, although a proper name is "representative" of its bearer (if it has one). He added in one place: "The meaning of a word is no longer for us an object corresponding to it."

Nothing but trouble awaits a philosopher who thinks of meanings as "objects"—something Wittgenstein knew firsthand from his own "bewitchment" by language during his *Tractatus* period.

Among those philosophers possibly "bewitched" by language in this way is the Moore one meets in *Principia*. In the particular case of the word 'good,' for example, what Moore is interested in is not what the *Oxford English Dictionary* says it means, but whether the *object* the word 'good' names—the universal meaning, Good—is definable or analyzable. Moore could not have failed to see the connection between Wittgenstein's attack on the naming theory of meaning and his (Moore's) own views about what words mean. It is not implausible to suppose that the former's attack on this theory of meaning is one of those things that gave the latter occasion to be "distrustful" of his own beliefs.

That Moore did come to distrust his beliefs about Good is shown in *The Philosophy of G. E. Moore* in his reply to criticisms raised by Charles L. Stevenson. In that volume Stevenson chooses to concentrate on the word 'right' rather than 'good,' but Moore in his reply suggests that what Stevenson says about 'right,' if it is true in that case, would be true of 'good' too. Stevenson's essential point is simple. Whenever two people express what appear to be two contradictory ethical judgments, the one saying "Abortion is always right," for example, the other saying "Abortion is not always right," there is no genuine contradiction. What separates the two people are differences in their attitudes toward abortion, not differences in their beliefs about abortion. 'Right' (and 'wrong') are not the names of characteristics or properties that acts do or do not possess. Rather, these words function to express our emotions and to influence those of others. They have "emotive," not "cognitive" meaning. If Stevenson's views are correct in the case of 'right,' then, Moore reasons, they are just as correct in the case of 'good,' 'evil,' and the like. These words, too, would not name characteristics or properties, and so not name nonnatural characteristics or properties.

Are Stevenson's views correct? That is the question Moore is compelled to address. Nothing less than the autonomy of the Science of Morals hangs in the balance. The nonnatural or transcendental character of Good, for the neglect of which Herr Bon was roundly chastised by the youthful Moore, threatens to go up in smoke. Are Stevenson's views correct? Moore's famous answer in his "Reply" bears the familiar marks of honest Sidgwickian indecision.

> I must say again that I am inclined to think that "right," in all ethical uses, and, of course, "wrong," "ought," "duty" also, are . . . not the names of characteristics at all, that they have merely "emotive meaning" and no "cognitive meaning" at all: and, if this is true of them, it must also be true of "good," in the sense I have been most concerned with. I am *inclined* to think that this is so, but I am also inclined to think that it is not so; and I do not know which way I am inclined most strongly. (p. 554)

In his later years, J. N. Findlay assures us, Moore "definitely came out of this particular wobble, and *was* more inclined to believe once more in the unique nonnatural character of goodness." In the end the autonomy of Ethics triumphed. But it is likely that the cause of his 1942 "wobble" was not limited to the considerations marshalled by Stevenson. None of Wittgenstein's students in 1933 is likely to have been more attentive than Moore.

A Two-Way Street

To suggest that Wittgenstein may have influenced Moore is hardly revolutionary. Who could have avoided the great thinker's powers? But to suggest that the influence was reciprocal—that Moore contributed something to Wittgenstein's thought—that is less likely to go down without a quarrel. Wittgenstein himself seems to speak powerfully against the suggestion. Recall his remarks about Moore's lack of "intelligence" and his displeasure at Moore's lectures. His response to *Principia*, moreover, was anything but positive, as we see in this letter to Russell dated from June 1912:

> I have been reading a part of Moore's *Principia Ethica* (now please don't be shocked), I don't like it at all. (Mind you, quite *apart* from

disagreeing with most of it.) I don't believe—or rather I am sure—
that it cannot dream of comparing with Frege's or your own works.
. . . Moore repeats himself dozens of times, and what he says in three
pages could—I believe—easily be expressed in half a page. *Unclear*
statements don't get clearer by being repeated!!

The very *style* of the two thinkers seems to militate against Moore's moving Wittgenstein's thought off its natural course. In the whole of *Principia*
there is not one memorable line—except, perhaps, its motto: "Everything
is what it is, and not another thing." And *that* is taken from Bishop Butler.
Whereas in Wittgenstein's case—here we have a great stylist, a true crafts-
man of the quotable: "Night is the architect's friend." "If a lion could
speak, we would not understand him." "Whereof one cannot speak,
thereof one must be silent." These are sentences out of which a writer's
literary immortality can be made. When Moore's appetite for "the infinite
meaning of words unadorned" is placed alongside Wittgenstein's near
poetry, it is difficult not to agree with von Wright, that there is not "a
trace of an influence of Moore's philosophy on Wittgenstein."

But there clearly is more than a trace. There is something of "The
Nature of Judgment" reverberating throughout the propositions of the
Tractatus. The very ideas Wittgenstein himself was most violently to
repudiate in later life—that words mean what they name—is at the heart
of that classic early paper of Moore's, the one that liberated Russell from
his bondage to idealism. No one can read that paper and not be struck by
how Moore's theory of meaning, with its simple concepts on the one
hand, and its complex concepts on the other, reappears in the ontology of
Wittgenstein's *Tractatus*. And there is, besides, a hint of a Moorean influence in that work's insistence that Good is "transcendental." We under-
estimate the stature of Moore both as a person and as a profound thinker
if we fail to see the many traces of his influence, even on those—perhaps
especially on those—who would seem to be above it.

Perhaps even those few encounters Moore and Wittgenstein had as
Apostles were not without their effect. Recall the state of moral conversion as Moore describes it in "Is conversion possible?" It involves "a
wonderful clearness of mind"—you are conscious of your "true self"—
"and you feel that nothing anyone can do to you could do you any harm."
Wittgenstein's "mysticism" is better known than Moore's, but perhaps
we are not entirely wrong to suggest that the former's may have been given

some impetus by the latter's. When Malcolm records that Wittgenstein "once read a paper on Ethics" in which he revealed that "he sometimes . . . had the experience of feeling *absolutely* safe. I mean," Wittgenstein declares, "the state of mind in which one is inclined to say 'I am safe, nothing can injure me *whatever* happens'" (p. 70), do we not detect, perhaps, just a trace of the Happy Warrior?

8

The Liberator

A Visit of State

🪶 "Bunga-bunga. Hmmm. Bunga-bunga. Hmmm."

"He says, 'The cannon are quite big. Bunga-big.' "

"Bunga-ubda."

"Yes."

"What did he say?"

"He said, 'The cannon are quite big. True.' "

"Ah, yes. True."

"Yes. Indeed."

"Ta bat ubda bunga. Hmmm."

"What did he say?"

"He said, 'Many boats.' "

"Well, he's right about that, what say?"

"Yes. He is. Quite right."

An awkward silence reigns as the men on board regard one another with polite but intense curiosity. "Shall we go below deck, then?" the Admiral inquires.

"Yes, of course," the interpreter replies, gesturing toward the open doorway. The Abyssinian Emperor and the other members of his entourage nod approvingly. Into the bowels of the ship they go.

The Abyssinian Emperor in fact is Anthony Buxton, a friend of Adrian Stephen's from their Cambridge student days. Buxton, Adrian, and two other Cambridge friends, Guy Ridley and Horace Cole, are embarked on the second hoax of their career, this one involving the British Navy in general and the *Dreadnought*, the flagship of the British fleet anchored off Weymouth, in particular. (An earlier hoax in which Cole disguised himself as the Sultan of Zanzibar, complete with accompanying suite, had

217

fooled the mayor of Cambridge). The year is 1910, the same year as Roger Fry's first Post-Impressionist Exhibition. With Thoby's death in 1906, Vanessa's marriage to Clive in 1907, and the move by Virginia and Adrian from Gordon Square to Fitzroy Square, Bloomsbury is in what Leon Edel calls its "third phase." In another year Virginia and Adrian Stephen, Duncan Grant, Maynard Keynes, and Leonard Woolf all will be living in the same house at 38 Brunswick Square. Bloomsbury will be in full flower. On this occasion it is represented by two of its more illustrious members.

The pranksters earlier had sent a telegram to the Admiral, apprising him of the impending arrival of the Abyssinian Emperor, accompanied by a representative of the Foreign Office (played by Cole), an interpreter (Adrian), and the Emperor's entourage. The entire troupe had met at the Stephen house in Fitzroy Square to dress and run through the plot. Cole wore an English gentleman's top hat and tail coat, and Adrian, who wore a bowler hat and greatcoat, was disguised by making his face appear sunburned and by wearing a false beard and moustache. The requirements for the Emperor and the others were more demanding. They were outfitted in brilliantly colored Eastern robes, billowy silken creations that flowed to the ground and flapped in the sea breeze. Their faces were blackened, and false beards and moustaches were added. Duncan Grant's dark eyes peered out from under his exotic turban. But it was the other member of the Emperor's retinue who was the most remarkable. The future author of *The Voyage Out*, replete with beard and moustache, made low, gruff noises to sound masculine. Virginia Stephen-cum-Woolf, in Eastern drag. Small wonder that Henry James would find the company Virginia and Vanessa were keeping "deplorable." How could Leslie Stephen's daughters have got themselves mixed up with the likes of Clive Bell and Duncan Grant, he wondered. "Tell Virginia," he writes in a letter to a mutual friend (quoted by Edel, p. 132), "tell her—how sorry I am that the inevitabilities of life should have made it possible even for a moment that I would allow any child of her father's to swim out of my ken." It was one of Henry James's unsuspected blessings that he was not on board the flagship *Dreadnought* when the Abyssinian Emperor and his company arrived.

When they arrived—having been met at the Weymouth train station by a naval officer in full uniform, escorted along a red carpet through the depot, driven in cabs to the harbor, and ferried out to the ship on board a small steam launch—when they arrived, the fleet's band, unable to locate the music for the Abyssinian national anthem, played what seemed to be the next best thing, the anthem of Zanzibar. How fitting, Adrian thought. The Admiral's chief officer, as it happened, was a cousin of the Stephens; and another officer of the *Dreadnought* was among Adrian's circle of acquaintances. But neither Adrian's nor Virginia's true identity was detected —despite a few near catastrophes. Duncan's moustache began to come unglued; but Adrian deftly forced it back in place. And in their anxiety to shower welcome upon their honored guests the officers pressed the Abyssinians to join them in their mess. Adrian recalls that he "was too afraid of the effect on our make-up" and contrived to find an excuse "on the grounds that the religious beliefs of Abyssinia made it impossible for the Royal family to touch food unless it was prepared in quite special ways." Most threatening of all was the matter of language. Buxton and Adrian had crammed a few Swahili phrases into their heads. So long as Adrian was required to translate Buxton's "bunga-bunga's" all went rather smoothly. Problems arose when the Admiral wanted Adrian to translate from the English into Abyssinian for the benefit of the Emperor's enlightenment. Adrian recounts his ordeal:

> The first thing to do was to inspect the Guard of Honour, and this put the first strain on my powers of interpretation. There were two kinds of marines in the guard, and some of them had blue uniforms and some red, some were, I think, artillery and some infantry. The Admiral explained this to me and told me to pass it on to the Emperor. For a moment I boggled at this, I could not think what to say. 'I am afraid it will be rather hard to put that into Abyssinian, sir,' I said. 'However, I'll try.' 'Entaqui, mahai, kustufani,' I started, addressing Anthony Buxton, and whether those were real Swahili words learnt from the grammar, or whether they were invented on the spur of the moment, I don't remember, but they have stuck in my memory ever since. If they were real Swahili they were the only native African words that any of us used, and I could get no further. I don't find it easy to speak fluent gibberish impromptu, and I was again in something of a difficulty. I must somehow produce something that would not be too jerky, and too unplausible. After a pause I began again as follows: 'Tahli bussor ahbat tahl aesque miss. Erraema, fleet use . . .' and so on. My language may have sounded a bit odd, but at any rate I could be fluent enough. When I was a boy I had spent years on what is called a classical education, and now I

found a use for it. It was the habit in the middle forms of my school to learn by heart the fourth book of Virgil's *Aeneid* as 'repetition.' I was able, therefore, to repeat whole stretches of it, and I knew a good deal of Homer in the same way. I was provided by my education, then, with a fine repertory of nonsense and did not have to fall back entirely on my own invention.

The hoax was complete. The British Navy had played the fool.

This was a role neither the Navy nor Parliament enjoyed. When the story of the hoax adorned the front page of the *Mirror*—Adrian believed Cole broke the pact of silence—official outrage had its day. First the Navy, in the person of Adrian's and Virginia's cousin, required the restitution of its tarnished honor. Cole was ceremoniously tapped six times with a cane. Duncan received two ceremonial taps. The rest apparently none. That much justice done, politicians demanded a pound more. "Inquiries were made in the House of Commons," Edel observes, with "one member wanting to know whether 'the joke was a direct insult to His Majesty's flag.' The answer was not given, but the First Lord simply said he hoped he would not be asked to go into a matter 'which is obviously the work of foolish persons.' Later," Edel continues, "the House was told 'no flags were hoisted or salutes fired, and no special train was ordered by the Admiral'" (p. 168). The political outrage soon exhausted itself. But the episode obliged the Navy to tighten its regulations involving visitors. Virginia, looking back on the caper some years later, luxuriates in her icy sense of patriotism. "I am glad," S. P. Rosenbaum quotes her as writing (p. 33), "to think that I too have been of help to my country." Unknowingly blessed for a second time, Henry James, the consummate Englishman, went to his grave without having to feel the chill of Virginia's contempt for "British tradition."

Although the immediate sensation surrounding the *Dreadnought* hoax was short-lived, the event had its lingering effects. The hard-core Cambridge presence did not go unnoticed and in some quarters was seen as a symptom of the general deterioration of that University's once high standards. A university that had earlier produced the likes of Sidgwick could now claim Lytton Strachey as one of its more illustrious sons. As for the public's memory, Bloomsbury's involvement in the escapade outlived Cambridge's. When Buxton's, Ridley's, Adrian's, and Cole's parts in the prank were forgotten, Duncan Grant's and Virginia's were not. This rude assault on English customs and institutions came to symbolize the prevailing conception of Bloomsbury's character and values. Bloomsbury was everywhere against "the old" and for "the new"—in art, fiction, biography, economics. And not less so (and perhaps more) in the private recesses of their day-to-day lives. The "Establishment" and conventional morality had no hold on them. They may not have been liked, but they were watched. For they were liberated. And it was Moore's new philosophy that was responsible.

The Standard Interpretation

The standard interpretation of that philosophy runs directly counter to the suggestion that it is in any way responsible for Bloomsbury's open disdain for conventional morality. The people who were Bloomsbury obviously thought they were living as they ought—or in any event that they were not doing anything wrong in living as they did. They were not amoralists. The vocabulary of ethics and the desire to use it judgmentally did not drop out of their lives even if the pressure to conform to what they viewed as stodgy, suffocating expectations about "proper behavior" did. To attribute any deserved influence to Moore in this regard therefore presupposes both that Bloomsbury took his teachings regarding right and wrong seriously and that they could reasonably think that their way of life was consonant with those teachings. (One must say "reasonably" because, whatever else may be said about Bloomsbury, they certainly were not fools.) It is precisely in both these respects that the standard interpretation challenges claims to influence made on behalf of Moore's teachings. That interpretation maintains that Moore offers a defense of conventional morality: In general, we are always to follow the prevailing rules of our society. Why? Because, limited as we are in our knowledge of the future consequences of our acts, we are more likely to do what is right by following conventionally encrusted rules than we are if we make an exception in our own case. After all, does not Moore himself write in *Principia* that "there is . . . a strong probability in favour of adherence to an existing custom, even if it be a bad one"? (p. 164) Small wonder that Russell early on would regret what he characterizes as the "unduly Conservative and anti-reforming" tenor of Moore's teachings in practical ethics.

So insipid are Moore's views in practical ethics supposed to be that it would come as something of a relief to learn that he really was not much interested in questions about the morality of conduct. Mary Warnock suggests as much in her *Ethics Since 1900*. Of the final two chapters of *Principia* she writes as follows:

> These two chapters have had very little influence indeed upon the subsequent course of moral philosophy; it is, however, worth remarking that Moore has perhaps been more frequently misrepresented than most other moral philosophers, and this is largely due to the neglect of these two chapters. Chapter Five of *Principia Ethica* is entitled 'Ethics in relation to Conduct.' At the beginning of it, Moore summarizes the course of the argument so far (p. 142). He has first, he says, tried to show what the adjective 'good' means; he has then discussed various proposed self-evident principles of ethics. The conclusion of this second step was negative, namely that neither pleasure nor any non-natural object was the sole good. The final step in the argument of the book is to deal positively with the question, What things are good? But this final step is postponed till the last chapter. In the present chapter he declares his intention of dealing with a quite separate question, namely What ought we to do? It will be seen therefore, that on Moore's own admission, this chapter is outside the main course of the argument, and it is fairly clear that he is far less interested in this question about conduct than in the more general question about what is good.

Had his development as a moral philosopher been arrested before or during his two dissertations or at the conclusion of "The Elements," it might be true that Moore was "far less interested" in questions about right conduct than he was in questions about what things are good. But his growth did not stop there. The task of reforming the Science of Morals made the chapter on "Ethics in Relation to Conduct" absolutely essential, not one that stood "outside the main course of the argument." Moore himself is quite clear on this matter, as can be seen even as early as *Principia*'s Preface, where, in a passage quoted in part in a previous chapter, he characterizes his aspirations:

> One main object of this book may, then, be expressed by slightly changing one of Kant's famous titles. I have endeavoured to write 'Prolegomena to any future Ethics that can possibly pretend to be scientific.' In other words, I have endeavoured to discover what are

the fundamental principles of ethical reasoning; and the establishment of these principles, rather than of any conclusions which may be attained by their use, may be regarded as my main object. I have, however, also attempted, in Chapter VI, to present some conclusions, with regard to the proper answer of the question 'What is good in itself?' which are very different from any which have commonly been advocated by philosophers. (p. ix)

One of *Principia*'s chapters *is* set off from the rest, as standing outside Moore's "main object." But *not* Chapter Five. Moore clearly implies that that chapter contains some of the fundamental principles of ethical reasoning it is his main object to identify and defend. To view Chapter Five in the way Warnock does is to miss part of what Moore himself clearly implies is most important in *Principia*'s pages. Less a side show, Chapter Five is one of *Principia*'s main events.

The Greater Reform

In "Art, Morals, and Religion" Moore had argued that the Science of Morals (Ethics) stands in need of reform. As generally understood, this Science is doubly false, teaching in the first place that the fulfillment of duty or the exercise of virtue are good as ends, when each is only good as a means, and teaching in the second place that the fulfillment of duty or the exercise of the so-called moral virtues is morally superior to other forms of rational behavior (self-interested and expedient conduct in particular) which also are good as means. For a preacher to extol these falsehoods as if they were true may have some utility, Moore concedes, but he refuses to allow the "would-be scientific moralist, who praises his virtues and his duties," the defense that his system can "lack science" because his "lies . . . are useful."

Given the small compass of that earlier paper Moore is only able to trace the broad outlines of the sort of reform he aspires to bring to his Science, when applied to conduct. In the more expansive setting of *Principia*'s fifth chapter he has the opportunity to fill in the details. And he does. The object of Ethics is truth, whether useful or not. Moore intends to get it. As that anonymous reviewer in the *Guardian* saw, Moore is "a man with a mission." That mission is to liberate his readers from those chains of lies by which both preachers and would-be scientific moralists would keep them in bondage.

Not all practitioners of Ethics, as this Science is generally conceived, agree about everything. Some emphasize the performance of duty. Others the acquisition of virtue. Those who belong to the former group agree that every individual is bound by the same principles of duty; they differ over *what* these principles are. And those who belong to the latter group agree that every individual ought to develop the same virtues; they differ over *what* these virtues are. What both approaches have in common is their shared insistence on strict universality. Once right (or virtuous), always right (or virtuous). For everyone. At all times. In all places. There is little moral breathing room for the individual. Morally speaking, everyone ought to do or be the same, each person performing and avoiding all and only those acts that everyone else ought to perform or avoid, or acquiring or avoiding all and only the same set of virtues. Individual differences, when they are permitted, are allowed only if the demands of morality do not apply. Whether the ethic be one of duty or virtue, the essence of the moral life is uniformity. In the following representative passage Moore makes it clear both that he sees the ethics of duties and virtues in these terms, and that he aims to do better:

> The most that can be said for the contradictory principles which are urged by moralists of different schools as universal duties, is, in general, that they point out actions which, for persons of a particular character and in particular circumstances, would and do lead to a balance of good. It is, no doubt, possible that the particular dispositions and circumstances which generally render certain kinds of action advisable, might to some degree be formulated. But it is certain that this has never yet been done; and it is important to notice that, even if it were done, it would not give us, what moral laws are usually supposed to be—rules which it would be desirable for every one, or even for most people, to follow. Moralists commonly assume that, in the matter of actions or habits of action, usually recognised as duties or virtues, it is desirable that every one should be alike. Whereas it is certain that, under actual circumstances, and possible that, even in a much more ideal condition of things, the principle of division of labour, according to special capacity, which is recognised in respect of employments, would also give a better result in respect of virtues. (pp. 165–166)

This does not read like a man intent upon demanding unbridled conformity to the demands of conventional morality. And it shouldn't. Nothing could be further from Moore's actual intentions. The point of those very few universal requirements he does defend is not to force everyone into the same moral lock-step as they march through their separate lives. These few requirements are necessary to make room for the vastly larger number of cases where individuals, liberated from the morality of rules, are free to decide for themselves what they ought to do.

Two Levels of Analysis

Part of the reason Moore's views concerning practical ethics have been so often misunderstood seems to lie in a failure to understand that he carries out two quite different levels of analysis in Chapter Five. As we should expect from the passage just quoted, one of the objects of his critical attention is the Science of Morals itself—and, along with this, some of its "would-be practitioners." In keeping with the overarching aims of *Principia* Moore here intends to define the limits of this Science when it is applied to questions about the morality of conduct, just as in earlier chapters he has endeavored to establish its limits in the case of judgments of intrinsic goodness. In the latter case Ethics, like every other science, is itself incapable of establishing what is good. In the former case the practitioners of Ethics must radically temper their claims to knowledge. When this Science's resources are brought to bear on questions of right conduct Moore argues that there is nothing that can be known with certainty about our duties, strictly conceived, and very little that can be known about them even when we approach them in a less demanding way. What *is* conservative in relation to conduct, then, according to Moore, is *the Science of Morals: Its* legitimate powers are very limited indeed. At the very most it can justify universal compliance to a very few rules. And these rules are ones that *already* are generally observed. It is largely because of their failure to recognize the limits of their Science that would-be scientific moralists, with their extensive lists of universal duties and virtues, many of which are not part of the existing moral code, offer lies in the guise of truth.

Moore offers three reasons why Ethics is likely to fail if its practitioners offer rules of duty or sets of virtues that are not part of the already existing moral conventions of a given society:

> In the first place, (1) the actions which they advocate are very commonly such as it is impossible for most individuals to perform by any volition. It is far too usual to find classed together with actions,

which can be performed, if only they be willed, others, of which the possibility depends upon the possession of a peculiar disposition, which is given to few and cannot even be acquired. It may, no doubt, be useful to point out that those who have the necessary disposition should obey these rules; and it would, in many cases, be desirable that everybody should have this disposition. But it should be recognised that, when we regard a thing as a moral rule or law, we mean that it is one which *almost everybody can* observe by an effort of volition, in that state of society to which the rule is supposed to apply. (2) Actions are often advocated, of which, though they themselves are possible, yet the proposed good effects are not possible, because the conditions necessary for their existence are not sufficiently general. A rule, of which the observance would produce good effects, if human nature were in other respects different from what it is, is advocated as if its general observance would produce the same effects now and at once. In fact, however, by the time that the conditions necessary to make its observance useful have arisen, it is quite as likely that other conditions, rendering its observance unnecessary or positively harmful, may also have arisen; and yet this state of things may be a better one than that in which the rule in question would have been useful. (3) There also occurs the case in which the usefulness of a rule depends upon conditions likely to change, or of which the change would be as easy and more desirable than the observance of the proposed rule. It may even happen that the general observance of the proposed rule would itself destroy the conditions upon which its utility depends. (pp. 160–161)

What needs to be emphasized is that Moore is not here defending blind conformity to social custom on the part of individual moral agents. His point is a very different one—namely, that *the Science of Morals* is limited in what it can do by way of challenging or changing social custom. "One or another of these [three] objections," he goes on to observe, "seems generally to apply to proposed changes in social custom, advocated as being better rules to follow than those now actually followed; and, for this reason, *it seems doubtful whether Ethics* can establish the utility of any rules other than those generally practiced" (p. 161, emphasis added). Moore does not infer from this either that (*a*) all existing rules have utility or that (*b*) each individual ought to abide by every existing rule. His concern here is *not* with what individuals ought to do, or with how they should decide this but rather with putting the Science of Morals in its proper place. In terms of a positive contribution to questions about what our duties are, the best it can do is to make the case for everyone's following "a very few" of the rules that are generally observed. To attempt anything more than this is to attempt too much. In particular, to draw up a list of rules of duty or virtue other than those that are generally observed, and to argue that these *new* rules ought to be followed by everyone —to do this is to tilt at windmills. There is no reason to look forward to success and at least three sorts of reason—those previously identified by Moore—to expect failure. When properly reformed, therefore, we see that the Science of Morals lacks the wherewithal to change existing social customs by justifying the introduction of entirely new rules.

That is the first strand of analysis Moore weaves through the pages of Chapter Five. The second, though related to the first, is distinct from it. It concerns the domain of individual moral autonomy and how this domain is defined by the Science of Morals. According to Moore, the principles of this Science can be used to make a plausible case in favor of universal compliance to certain rules even when—indeed, perhaps especially when —the individual is most tempted to make an exception for himself or herself. Very few in number, these rules are presupposed by *any* existing society, given the world as we know it. So the Science of Morals does offer principles that in Moore's view justify the imposition of certain limits on everyone's behavior. At the same time, however, the very same principles that underwrite these universal limits on individual behavior also provide the basis for that extensive individual liberty, both in conduct and judgment, that Moore's own practical ethic allows and encourages. Just as the Science of Morals cannot rationally justify general adoption of a *new* set of rules, so it cannot rationally defend uniform conformity to the *old* set of rules that define the conventional morality of one's society. It is precisely these limits of Ethics, when it comes to establishing what *everyone* ought to do or what virtues *everyone* ought to acquire, that open up the vast area of individual discretion Moore wants to protect from the moral imperialism that characterizes those would-be scientific moralists who use their "science" to call for the establishment of a "new" set of rules or who offer a blanket defense of the "old" set. Moore's fundamental point is that in the vast percentage of cases the individual does—and should—get along just fine without trying to conform to *any* rule, *old or new*. In this respect, though not only in this one, Moore's practical ethic is far from being "conservative," or "anti-reformist," or "a feeble concession to conventional morality." To present him as one who fits these descriptions is to perpetuate a widespread but altogether groundless interpretation of his views. Mary Warnock is right: Moore has "been more frequently misrepresented than most moral philosophers," and nowhere more so than in the present context. How much of this misrepresentation would have been avoided by attending carefully to the two quite different strands of analysis Moore offers in Chapter Five it is impossible to say. One can understand how someone might infer that Moore believes that we ought always to follow the rules of conventional morality because the Science of Morals lacks the wherewithal to defend the introduction of new rules. The important point to recognize is that this *is* an inference born of confusion. What the individual ought to do, and what the Science of Morals can do, are quite different things. From the fact that this Science cannot muster the needed defense of a new set of rules it simply does not follow that the individual must always abide by the old ones.

The Limits of Ethics When Applied to Conduct

Some of the details of Moore's argument may now be considered. In terms of sheer concentration, rigor, precision, and analytical power, the fifth quite likely is *Principia*'s best chapter. That it is largely ignored and misunderstood is that book's finest irony. Even here it will not be possible to do full justice to Moore's tour de force. Enough will be said to make his reformist aspirations clearer.

Part of Moore's effort to establish the limits of Ethics is made easier by his understanding of the meaning of such key concepts as Right, Ought, Duty, and the like. On his view " 'right' does and can mean nothing but 'cause of a good result' " (p. 147), while "our 'duty,' " he insists, "can only be defined as that action, which will cause more good to exist in the Universe than any other possible alternative" (p. 148). And again: "The assertion 'I am morally bound to perform this action' " is said to be "identical with the assertion 'This action will produce the greatest possible amount of good in the Universe' " (p. 147). Moore thinks these claims are "demonstrably certain." Representative of his supporting arguments is the following:

> It is plain that when we assert that a certain action is our absolute duty, we are asserting that the performance of that action at that time is unique in respect of value. But no dutiful action can possibly have

unique value in the sense that it is the sole thing of value in the world; since, in that case, *every* such action would be the *sole* good thing, which is a manifest contradiction. And for the same reason its value cannot be unique in the sense that it has more intrinsic value than anything else in the world; since *every* act of duty would then be the *best* thing in the world, which is also a contradiction. It can, therefore, be unique only in the sense that the whole world will be better, if it be performed, than if any possible alternative were taken. And the question whether this is so cannot possibly depend solely on the question of its own intrinsic value. For any action will also have effects different from those of any other action; and if any of these have intrinsic value, their value is exactly as relevant to the total goodness of the Universe as that of their cause. It is, in fact, evident that, however valuable an action may be in itself, yet, owing to its existence, the sum of good in the Universe may conceivably be made less than if some other action, less valuable in itself, had been performed. But to say that this is the case is to say that it would have been better that the action should not have been done; and this again is obviously equivalent to the statement that it ought not to have been done—that it was not what duty required. (pp. 147–148)

Against those who might object that social justice, for example, is of no less importance than the amount of good brought into the world by our actions, Moore has an answer:

'Fiat iustitia, ruat caelum' can only be justified on the ground that by the doing of justice the Universe gains more than it loses by the falling of the heavens. It is, of course, possible that this is the case: but, at all events, to assert that justice *is* a duty, in spite of such consequences, is to assert that it is the case. (p. 148)

What is true of the duty of justice is true in every other case. When, for example, the assertion is made that we have an absolute duty not to murder, what this means is that "that action, whatever it may be, which is called murder, will under no circumstances cause so much good to exist in the Universe as its avoidance" (p. 148).

Looking back on these claims almost forty years after the publication of *Principia*, Moore in his autobiography acknowledges some changes in his thinking. In his review of *Principia*, Moore recalls, Russell "pointed out that it was very paradoxical to say that 'This is what I ought to do' is merely a short way of saying 'The Universe will be a better Universe if I do this than if I were to do instead anything else which I could do'" (p. 558). Moore concedes the paradox and indicates that he now thinks the two statements are logically equivalent, not identical. In *Principia*, however, Moore uniformly analyzes the meaning of Duty, Right, Wrong, and Obligation in terms of what is productive of intrinsic good. The Science of Morals is related to questions of conduct because its unique object, Good, is part of the definition of concepts that are used in the moral assessment of conduct. Accordingly, if this Science is to offer any rationally grounded principles for determining what our duties are or how we ought to act, it must systematically inquire into how our conduct is related to the production of intrinsic good. This Moore proceeds to do. His initial objective is entirely negative: He aims to show that, strictly speaking, we can never know what our duties are.

Against those who maintain that moral laws, such as 'Do no murder,' are "self-evident," which if true would entail that we can know what our duties are, Moore's reply is simple: No moral law is self-evident. The very meanings of such concepts as Duty, Right, Wrong, and the like, tied as they are in his view to the production of intrinsic good, entail that we must first investigate what is productive of such good before we can possibly know what is right, wrong, and so on. And which acts *are* productive of intrinsic good is an open question, one that must be approached by examining what the actual consequences of our acts are, not one that can be answered by armchair appeals to what is supposed to be "self-evident."

Once this much is conceded, it does not take long to realize how absolutely hopeless is the task of ever knowing what our duties are, when Duty is strictly interpreted.

> In order to shew that any action is a duty, it is necessary to know both what are the other conditions, which will, conjointly with it, determine its effects; to know exactly what will be the effects of these conditions; and to know all the events which will be in any way affected by our action throughout an infinite future. We must have all this causal knowledge, and further we must know accurately the degree of value both of the action itself and of all these effects; and must be able to determine how, in conjunction with the other things in the Universe, they will affect its value as an organic whole. And not only this: we must also possess all this knowledge with

regard to the effects of every possible alternative; and must then be able to see by comparison that the total value due to the existence of the action in question will be greater than that which would be produced by any of these alternatives. But it is obvious that our causal knowledge alone is far too incomplete for us ever to assure ourselves of this result. Accordingly it follows that we never have any reason to suppose that an action is our duty: we can never be sure that any action will produce the greatest value possible. (p. 149)

What, then, can the Science of Morals contribute to our knowledge of our duties, when Duty is interpreted strictly? Moore's answer is in keeping with *Principia*'s overarching goal of reforming this Science. Contrary to those would-be scientific moralists, whose unbridled optimism about our knowledge of duty he seeks to rein in, Moore's position is simple. And devastating. Strictly speaking, this Science can never tell us what our duties are.

A Humbler Task

Given the impossibility of knowing our duties, strictly conceived, Moore next considers whether Ethics might be assigned "a humbler task." Suppose we limit attention to those very few alternatives likely to occur to people in daily life when faced with decisions about what they should do. May we not then be able to say which of these alternatives is right, which wrong? Moore's answer is the same: No. Even when the field of alternatives is narrowed in this way, "no sufficient reason has ever yet been found for considering one action more right than another" (p. 152). And this for a simple reason. Because the effects of any act may continue to be felt into the indefinite future, because the value of these effects determine the morality of the act, and because our knowledge of these effects is limited to the immediate or near future, we simply do not know of any given act whether its total consequences are better than those that would have resulted from some other act that we may have thought about doing and that we might have performed. *If* we could know that the distant effects of an act never will, or are never likely to, alter the value of its immediate or near effects, *then* we could possibly know which acts are right, which wrong. But we cannot know that the antecedent is true. "That this [antecedent] is justified must be shewn before we can claim to have given any reason whatever for acting in one way rather than another" (p.

153). Since this assumption has not been and cannot be justified, it follows, given Moore's own assumptions, that we cannot possibly know which acts are right, which wrong, even when Ethics is given the "humbler task" Moore has described.

Moore is more optimistic about the chances of success if the task is made humbler still by limiting attention to those very few alternative actions that are likely to occur to people and generally produce a greater total of intrinsic good in the immediate future. If attention is limited in this way, the notion of Duty is somewhat relaxed. But in the nature of the case a relaxed interpretation of Duty is the best the Science of Morals can handle. Thus relaxed, we can, Moore thinks, offer a "defense of most of the rules most universally recognized by Common Sense" (p. 156). As it happens, Moore believes that Common Sense recognizes "*very few*" such rules (p. 165), so the defense he offers covers only "*most*" of "*a very few*" rules—hardly a large number, it seems fair to say. Clearly, there is no blanket endorsement of conventional morality in the offing. Even those "very few" rules that can be defended could conceivably lose their binding force in the future if all or most people came to have different desires than they have at present. To illustrate his point, Moore again considers the prohibition against murder. The pessimist thinks "human life is on the whole evil," a belief that in Moore's view has never been either proven or refuted. Still, most of his contemporaries are not pessimists and desire to go on living. And this is enough for the *present* prohibition against murder. Murder *is* to be avoided because "the majority of mankind will not agree to it, but will persist in living." Moore elaborates upon his defense as follows:

> When, therefore, we say that murder is in general to be avoided, we only mean that it is so, so long as the majority of mankind will certainly not agree to it, but will persist in living. And that, under these circumstances, it is generally wrong for any single person to commit murder seems capable of proof. For, since there is in any case no hope of exterminating the race, the only effects which we have to consider are those which the action will have upon the increase of the goods and the diminution of the evils of human life. Where the best is not attainable (assuming extermination to be the best) one alternative may still be better than another. And, apart from the immediate evils which murder generally produces, the fact that, if it were a common practice, the feeling of insecurity, thus

caused, would absorb much time, which might be spent to better purpose, is perhaps conclusive against it. So long as men desire to live as strongly as they do, and so long as it is certain that they will continue to do so, anything which hinders them from devoting their energy to the attainment of positive goods, seems plainly bad as a means. And the general practice of murder, falling so far short of universality as it certainly must in all known conditions of society, seems certainly to be a hindrance of this kind. (pp. 156–157)

Moore sketches the same kind of defense in behalf of "most of the rules most universally enforced by legal sanctions, such as respect for property" (p. 157). Roughly speaking, then, rules necessary for the respect of property (including in particular the prohibition against theft) and those necessary for the respect of the person (including in particular the prohibition against murder) are justified, given the relaxed standards of justification Moore is using. In the case of these rules, common sense morality and the law speak with one voice. Not so in the case of some of the other rules "most commonly recognized by Common Sense, such as industry, temperance and the keeping of promises." In this case Moore implies that though the law does not punish violations, it is nonetheless true that everyone ought to be encouraged to be industrious, temperate, and to keep their promises. "Industry," he writes, "is a means to those necessaries, without which the further attainment of any great positive goods is impossible; temperance merely enjoins the avoidance of those excesses, which, by injuring health, would prevent a man from contributing as much as possible to the acquirement of these necessaries; and the keeping of promises greatly facilitates cooperation in such acquirement" (p. 157).

What all these rules have in common is their usefulness, when generally observed, in making it possible for people "to preserve and propagate life" and to satisfy "the desire for property." These particular desires seem to Moore to be embedded in "any known state of society," seem to him to be "so universal and so strong," that he is led to infer that "it would be impossible to remove them." The satisfaction of these desires makes a stable society—*any* stable society—possible. The obligation to abide by those rules grounded in these desires can therefore be known without our having to know what things truly are good in themselves. *Whatever* these things might be, we shall not be able to produce much of them without a stable society. The few rules Moore has enumerated therefore "can be recommended as a means to that which is itself only a necessary condition for the existence of any great goods" (p. 158). Moore believes that the obligatoriness of following these rules is truly universal: If the kind of "proof" he offers is sound, then no exceptions should be permitted. Everyone ought *always* to keep a promise, ought *always* to avoid murder, ought *always* to act temperately, and so on.

Not all moral rules, certainly not even all those claimed on behalf of Common Sense, are so firmly rooted in desires at once so strong and universal. Many human desires are alterable in a variety of ways, and any rule that is connected with a malleable desire may itself change without posing any threat to the stability of society. Whether such a rule *should* remain in force thus depends on which things *are* great goods, which great evils. If the general observance of such a rule does produce the most good, then the Science of Morals, having been properly reformed and assigned its "humbler task," can offer its defense; if not, not. Moore, in short, is so far from offering a blanket endorsement of conventional morality that he assigns to the practitioners of the Science of Morals the task of ferreting out those rules that *are* generally observed but that are *not* productive of good consequences. Ethics *does* have a role to play in the effort to reform the existing rules of morality, by using its principles either to modify or to abolish them. Moore uses "most of the rules comprehended under the name of Chastity" to illustrate his point.

> These rules are commonly defended, by Utilitarian writers or writers who assume as their end the conservation of society, with arguments which presuppose the necessary existence of such sentiments as conjugal jealousy and paternal affection. These sentiments are no doubt sufficiently strong and general to make the defence valid for many conditions of society. But it is not difficult to imagine a civilised society existing without them; and, in such a case, if chastity were still to be defended, it would be necessary to establish that its violation produced evil effects, other than those due to the assumed tendency of such violation to disintegrate society. (p. 157)

The Science of Morals is not the handmaiden of the existing moral status quo, not the docile servant of every expectation of conventional morality. It has its reformist powers. But those powers are quite limited, something would-be scientific moralists frequently fail to take into account. For Moore, however, these limits are no less important for what they entail about the scope of individual moral freedom than for what they tell us about widespread misconceptions regarding the legitimate powers of the Science of Morals. This becomes clearer when he next turns to consider how individuals should decide what they ought to do.

How Individuals Should Decide

The results of Moore's examination of the Science of Morals have important implications for how individuals should decide what they ought to do. There is a broad sweep of possibilities here, ranging from cases where "it is certain that in a large majority of cases the observance of a certain [that is a certain, established] rule is useful" (p. 162) to cases where it is certain that general observance is genuinely harmful. In the former case—but only in the former case—Moore recommends that everyone always follow the rule.

> If it is certain that in a large majority of cases the observance of a certain rule is useful, it follows that there is a large probability that it would be wrong to break the rule in any particular case; and the uncertainty of our knowledge both of effects and of their value, in particular cases, is so great, that it seems doubtful whether the individual's judgment that the effects will probably be good in his case can ever be set against the general probability that that kind of action is wrong. Added to this general ignorance is the fact that, if the question arises at all, our judgment will generally be biassed by the fact that we strongly desire one of the results which we hope to obtain by breaking the rule. It seems, then, that with regard to any rule which is *generally* useful, we may assert that it ought *always* to be observed, not on the ground that in *every* particular case it will be useful, but on the ground that in *any* particular case the probability of its being so is greater than that of our being likely to decide rightly that we have before us an instance of its disutility. In short, though we may be sure that there are cases where the rule should be broken, we can never know which those cases are, and ought, therefore, never to break it. (pp. 162-163)

The key words here are the first four: "if it is certain." A defense of such certainty must meet the demands imposed by the Science of Morals, and Moore has been at pains to explain how very difficult it is to meet them. It is not true that every rule that is generally observed is one whose general utility is thereby established. The question of general utility and general observance are logically distinct, and it is only in those rare cases where (*a*) a rule is generally observed and (*b*) the general utility of the rule *is certain* (that is, we know that compliance with it is productive of most good, in the short run, in the vast majority of cases) that Moore recommends unbroken compliance. In the nature of the case there are, he thinks, *very few rules* that meet these conditions. Some rules that would be useful *if* everyone observed them fail to impose a duty on the individual because not everyone will observe them. Some rules that people do generally observe fail to impose a duty on the individual because general observance of the rule lacks the requisite utility. And some rules that are generally useful and that are generally observed fail to impose a duty on the individual because we lack the requisite certainty. As Moore (almost grudgingly) observes in his summary of Chapter Five, "it may be possible to prove that a few of the commonest rules of duty are true," adding that even these are true "*only* in certain conditions of society, which may be more or less universally presented in history" (p. 181). Do not murder. Keep your promises. Do not steal. A few such rules of this familiar sort, without whose general observance Moore believes a stable society is impossible, are always to be observed, even when we are tempted to make an exception in our own case. And a very few virtues—Moore mentions only prudence, temperance, and industry—are to be universally encouraged for the same reasons. But certainly not *all* the duties, and not *all* the virtues, recommended by would-be scientific moralists. And not *all* those rules or virtues enshrined in conventional morality. Not even all those duties and virtues commended by "Common Sense." Only "*most* of the rules *most universally recognized* by Common Sense" pass muster. And these, when totalled, turn out to be—only "a very few."

No one who carefully examines the details and subtlety of Moore's argument to this point will be tempted to saddle him with the standard interpretation. His is not a conservative call to acquiesce before, not a "feeble concession to," the demands of conventional morality. That a form of behavior is generally expected of one and generally regarded as "right and proper" does not show that anyone is morally obliged to conform. Moore personally did not like to be told what his duties were, however indirectly, as the following humorous excerpt from his diary for July 4, 1911 illustrates: "On Monday croquet with Oliver, then with Logan. Sit with Mrs. Russell, Mrs. Worthington and Logan, while four play tennis: then find discussion going on about duty to talk: then play piano alone." Moore became renowned for his long periods of silence as he grew older. His silence was his business, not other people's. If he knew anything he knew there was no duty to talk, whatever others might say.

He also valued individual liberty greatly, however little he explicitly addressed this topic in his published work. "I do think it very important that people should be left as free as possible to choose for themselves what they should do," he writes to his son, Timothy, on June 29, 1937, "even if the result is that they often choose wrong." Characterizing "a belief in Liberty" as "a belief that there are certain kinds of right action that it is not right for other people to *compel* you to do: that everybody ought to be left free to choose whether he will do them or not," Moore goes on to make it clear that he is on the side of liberty and against compulsion. This was not a belief he came to late in life. A careful reading of *Principia* reveals that this is one of that work's central teachings.

Whatever might be conventionally expected of one, and whatever the accompanying means of compulsion, some rules that are part of conventional morality (for example, those associated with chastity) can lack the required justification. And it is, in his view, the rigorous application of the correct principles of ethical reasoning, those established in a reformed Science of Morals, that will determine whether the required justification is at hand. True, those who practice this Science are limited in what they can do by way of making changes in the rules of conventional morality. Though their Science has the power to modify or abolish old rules, it lacks the potential to introduce new ones. But these limitations on what this Science can do are not to be lamented. On the contrary, these very limitations highlight why the individual in Moore's view has an enormous range of individual freedom and discretion in morally deciding how to behave. It is precisely because this Science can do so little that the individual is both free and required to do so much.

That this interpretation of *Principia*, stridently at odds with the standard interpretation because of its emphasis on the freedom of the individual to operate outside of rather than to conform to the demands of conventional morality—that this interpretation is the correct one must be evident to anyone who would take the time to read its pages. By way of example, witness this specimen of Moore's "defense of conventional morality": "The extreme improbability that any general rule with regard to the utility of an action will be correct seems . . . to be the chief principle which should be taken into account in discussing how the individual should guide his choice" (p. 165). In other words, because the Science of Morals can establish (at best) that *very few rules* ought always to be followed, and given that there are many rules urged upon us both by the defenders of conventional morality and by would-be scientific moralists, it is far more probable that we should *not* conform to a given rule than it is that we should do so. Indeed, "almost all actions," Moore insists, "are not even covered by rules which are generally observed and whose utility is known." An enlightened ethic in relation to conduct thus will encourage rich diversity between individuals, not bland sameness. On this matter, recall the passage quoted above:

> Moralists commonly assume that, in the matter of actions or habits of action, usually recognised as duties or virtues, it is desirable that every one should be alike. Whereas it is certain that, under actual circumstances, and possible that, even in a much more ideal condition of things, the principle of division of labour, according to special capacity, which is recognised in respect of employments, would also give a better result in respect of virtues. (pp. 165–166)

To encourage diversity among individuals is not to answer the question, How should we decide what we ought to do when, as is true in the vast majority of cases, it is improbable that we should follow a rule? Moore replies as follows:

> It seems, therefore, that, in cases of doubt, instead of following rules, of which he is unable to see the good effects in his particular case, the individual should rather guide his choice by a direct consideration of the intrinsic value or vileness of the effects which his action may produce. (p. 166)

This, however, is only part of an answer. Which among the possible good effects should we aim at: The immediate or the distant? Those that will affect strangers or those that will affect friends? Moore anticipates the need to complete his reply. In general we ought to aim at goods affecting oneself and "those in whom one has a strong personal interest" rather than to "attempt a more extended beneficence" (pp. 166–167); and in general we also ought to try to secure goods that are in "the present" rather than to seek goods that are in the more distant future. Both points of general instruction are defended in terms of their probability of success.

We are *less* likely to secure a good in the future than we are in the present, and we are *more* likely to obtain goods for those (ourselves included) for whom we are more concerned than for those for whom we are concerned less. "Egoism," Moore proclaims, "is undoubtedly superior to Altruism as a doctrine of means: in the immense majority of cases the best thing we can do is to aim at securing some good in which we are concerned [that is, concerned either for ourselves personally or for those in whom we have a 'strong personal interest'], since for that very reason we are far more likely to secure it" (p. 167). Precisely because we already want the outcome more than other possibilities, we are more likely to act in a sensible, determined way to get it. And thus more likely to succeed.

Contrary to such would-be scientific moralists as Kant, the supposed *ethical* distinction between "duty" and "interested action" breaks down. Both are good as means. They differ—and here Moore reiterates points first made in "Art, Morals, and Religion"—in that duties are useful acts people may be tempted to avoid, so that it is particularly useful to praise their performance and blame their violation. In this way people are encouraged to act "as duty requires." But there is no good reason to maintain that performing our "duties," understood as compliance with rules that are generally observed and whose utility is certain, is morally superior to acting in ways that promote our self-interest. In the vast majority of cases we act as we morally ought by doing what is in our self-interest, properly conceived. For what we *morally ought* to do is more encompassing than what we have a *moral duty* to do. *Sometimes* what we morally ought to do is our (and everyone else's) moral duty. Sometimes, that is, we (and everyone else) ought to conform to rules that are generally observed and whose utility is certain. But at other times—and this is true almost all the time—what we morally ought to do is what promotes *our* interests, what secures for us and those we care about a full plate of what is good. To act in this way is no less to do what we morally ought than when we do what duty requires. " 'Duties' are not, in general, more useful or obligatory than interested actions" (p. 171). The only difference is that because people are less inclined to do their duty than to pursue their self-interest, it is both more necessary and more useful to praise them when they do what duty requires, and to blame them when they fail to do so.

How far Moore is from endorsing those views attributed to him by advocates of the standard interpretation should now be clear. There are, he thinks, a *very few* rules that people ought always to follow. (Not even all the rules commended by Common Sense qualify: only "*most* of those *most universally* recognized by Common Sense" are accepted, and even then Moore concedes only that the requisite type of justification "*may* be possible" [p. xxii].) *Almost all* our decisions will have to be decided without relying on general rules: in almost all cases "*rules of action* should not be followed at all" (p. xxiii). In *all* such cases individuals should guide their choice "by a direct consideration of the effects which the action may produce," *not* by reference to the expectations of conventional morality. In *these* cases one in general ought to do what one thinks will promote one's own interests, where these interests are understood to include the interests of those in whom one has a strong personal interest. And of the goods to be aimed at, the more immediate are generally to be preferred to the more distant. *In short, in virtually all our activities in our day-to-day life we are at liberty to operate without worrying much over whether we are doing "what duty requires."* So long as we do not pursue evil ends or violate those few rules of duty necessary for the stability of any society (for example, no murder and no theft), we act as we morally ought if we act with an eye to increasing our store of what is good in this world and sharing this with those for whom we care most—our family and friends. To limit the scope of our moral concern in this way, shunning the much-proclaimed obligatoriness of "a more extended beneficence," is not arbitrary. It has reason, discovered, articulated, and defended by a reformed Science of Morals, on its side.

The Philosopher's Stone

It was just such a liberation of the self from the habitual drudgery of conventional morality, heavy with the burdens of conforming to a proliferation of rules of duty, that Moore celebrated in "Is conversion possible?" "You see 'life steadily and whole,'" he writes there, adding that "noone can rob you of your power to do the best that is possible under the circumstances, and hence they cannot make you feel ashamed. . . . Though you are so far like the wise man of the Stoics or of Goethe, you have none of that blindness or insensibility which may disfigure him. You are not self-sufficient." The opposite of those who unthinkingly follow the morality of the herd, the liberated self, as personified in Wordsworth's Happy Warrior, does not act from habit, enslaved to unquestioned and rationally indefensible rules of duty. Awakened to "Reason" and launched on "the New Life," the Happy Warrior acts according to his own lights, according to "[his] own wish." Recall Wordsworth's poem:

Yet not the less would I throughout
Still act according to the voice
Of my own wish; and feel past doubt
That my submissiveness was choice.
Not seeking in the school of pride
For "precepts over dignified",
Denial and restraint I prize
No farther than they breed a second Will more wise.

There is more to life than "denial and restraint," and no need to offer a 'dignified' defense of one's seeking to go beyond negation. Life can be fun without being evil. One can act on one's own, "according to the voice of [one's] own wish," without thereby doing something wrong and without having to feel "ashamed."

In that earlier essay Moore had confessed to his doubt and uncertainty about the intrinsic value of the mental state of the mystical Happy Warrior. He worried about whether this state could be psychologically distinguished from "the states of those, religious enthusiasts, for example, whom I [Moore] cannot suppose to see nothing but the truth." He understood that if the two states are psychologically indistinguishable, then any claim to value on behalf of the Happy Warrior's mental state could not be any stronger than a similar claim made on behalf of the mental state of these religious enthusiasts. And though the New Life for these latter enthusiasts is no less a matter of faith than is true in the case of their counterparts who follow in the Happy Warrior's wake, Moore was unable to accept the equal intrinsic value of the two mental states. For the latter includes, he thought, the apprehension of what is true, whereas the former does not. The insuperable challenge he faced—and faced honestly—was to distinguish between the two mental states in a way that would make the attribution of value in the case of moral conversion, and its denial in the case of religious conversion, nonarbitrary. This he was unable to do.

Principia's fifth chapter is Moore's creative way out of this impasse. The question that occasioned his doubt and uncertainty is recast. In the earlier essay the question concerned the intrinsic value of a particular state of mind—namely, the mystical state of the Happy Warrior. Second only to his doubts about the intrinsic value of this state was Moore's painful inability to find the means to produce this state, either in himself or in others. The true "philosopher's stone" eluded him. The possible moral liberation of the individual seemed to end in failure.

In *Principia* Moore sees his way clear to a less mystical but no less liberating outcome. *One can argue one's way to freedom.* One does not have to wait for the occurrence of a fickle, ineffable intoxication. It does not require mystical insight in order to make the case for following "the voice of my own wish" instead of following those rules of duty preachers and would-be scientific moralists are only too happy to impose on everyone. And neither does it require a proof of or even faith in the intrinsic value of the Happy Warrior's mental state. There is a kind of moral conversion that is possible this side of mysticism. Conversion from a way of life in which one unthinkingly observes putative "rules of duty" to one in which Reason is awakened and, without shame, one responds creatively and joyfully to the promptings of one's "own will"—*this* sort of moral conversion can be produced by philosophical argument. And Moore (we may assume) believes he has found the means to produce it. He has uncovered the true philosopher's stone. Those who would join him in his discovery and conversion to "the New Life" need only follow the rigorous path he blazes in *Principia*'s fifth chapter. Moore offers, not a potion, not a set of mystical exercises, not a diet of denial and restraint, but an *argument* that sets his readers free. Small wonder that Strachey would respond to that chapter by exclaiming "Glory Hallieluiah!" or that he would fix "the beginning of the Age of Reason" as the date on which *Principia* was published. As Moore hoped to show, and as Strachey thought he had, it was Reason that had the power to break the chains of lies by which both would-be scientific moralists and preachers would bind us. "The truth," Strachey proclaims, ". . . is really upon the march . . . : henceforth who will be able to tell lies one thousand times as easily as before?" He read *Principia* well. Strachey had a firm grasp of the philosopher's stone. He was one of the first of Moore's converts. But far from the only one.

Another Test

In Chapter Five Moore for the first time offers a serious account of ethics in relation to conduct, one that enables him to satisfy the conduct criterion. "The Elements" at best offers an unsettled and unstable approach to questions of right and wrong, duty and obligation. Somehow "the course of evolution" is supposed to "guarantee" that "in general" what people of "Common Sense" think right, is right. And the same is happily (and mysteriously) supposed to be true in the case of what is wrong. But all this is more a case of the youthful Moore's public wish-fulfillment than it is one in which he presents a well-crafted position. That last lecture Moore gave to the students of the London School of Ethics and Social Philosophy is woefully inadequate. And yet its very inadequacy makes Moore's performance in *Principia*'s fifth chapter all the more remarkable. There is no intimation in that earlier work of the nature of the views he will develop in the later one. And no reason to look forward to his meeting with much success when he turns his hand to questions about ethics in relation to conduct. So accustomed had Moore been to restricting his attention to the metaphysical foundations of Ethics that it would have been natural for him to be at his weakest when he begins to explore how the Science of Morals is related to our conduct in the real world.

But Moore is not at his weakest in this regard. He is at his strongest. Chapter Five includes a standard by reference to which the ethics of conduct may be appraised, and Moore goes to considerable length to show how to apply it. Whereas before his work in Ethics could not satisfy the conduct criterion, his theory in *Principia* does. He may not offer the correct standard, but he does succeed in offering one. In the short span of five years, the period between his work on "The Elements" and the publication of *Principia*, we see Moore's amazing growth as a moral theoretician. Shortly before he died Sidgwick had been told (mistakenly) that Moore had published a book called *The Elements of Ethics*. In fact "The Elements" had been accepted for publication by Cambridge University Press. But despite the strenuous work he had put into preparing the lectures in the first place and in revising them for publication (on which task he worked off and on for two years), and notwithstanding the desirability of having a book to his credit given his hopes of landing a research position at the end of his Prize Fellowship, Moore ultimately decided against having "The Elements" published. Sidgwick had not read these lectures. But in a letter to a friend, cited by Jerome Schneewind, after first expressing surprise at the news that Moore has published a book, he goes on to add that he has no doubt that "The Elements" will be "acute" though lacking in "insight." "So far as I have seen his work," Sidgwick writes, "his *acumen*—which is remarkable in degree—is in excess of his *insight*." It is one of the sad truths of the not always convivial and sometimes strained relationship between Sidgwick and Moore that the teacher went to his grave without having seen his student's magnum opus. One wonders what Sidgwick would have thought of his earlier assessment of Moore's ability after reading *Principia*. He had not the benefit of knowing the Moore we do.

Bloomsbury's Conduct

Moore's teachings in Chapter Five of *Principia* could not have been lost on those attentive readers who were already familiar with the major tendencies of his thought at this time—in particular, his developing interest in reforming the Science of Morals. In a letter to MacCarthy, for example, dated November 19, 1902, almost a full year before *Principia*'s publication, Moore requests that Desmond return his copy of "Art, Morals, and Religion" because he thinks "a piece of it will go into my book." Part of that reform on which Moore was embarked involves breaking this Science free from mistaken connections with other sciences, both natural and metaphysical. That is the work of the first four chapters, where Moore tirelessly makes the case both for the uniqueness of the concept, Good, and for the autonomy of Ethics. But another part of his reform involves defining the limits of this Science *after* its autonomy has been secured. Nothing would be more natural than to suppose that an autonomous Science of Morals is at liberty to promulgate wearisome lists of duties and virtues, each incumbent upon everyone, at all times, and in all places. Given its autonomous status, no other science could challenge its claims. What else could?

Moore could. And does. A further reform must come *from within* this science itself. Because in his view such notions as Duty, Right, Obligation, and the like are necessarily tied to the notion, Good, ethics must consider what is right, what is dutiful, and so on. But because of how these notions are related to Good, he believes the limits of knowledge in this quarter are severe. We do not know very much about what is productive of good. And this must chasten the enthusiasm of each and every practitioner of Ethics. That Science must be appropriately "humbled." When it is, Moore believes its practitioners are only slightly better able to say what acts are duties than they are able to say what things are good. On the latter point Ethics can prove nothing; on the former it can prove (at best) that a very few rules impose duties. Nothing in the one case. A few things in the other. Not a very impressive showing.

When properly understood, however, the results *are* impressive. Immensely so. By severely limiting the number of duties and virtues the Science of Morals can identify and defend, Moore offers an ethical system that aspires to prick the inflated pretenses of would-be scientific moralists, one that justifies the necessity of the *individual*'s moral judgment and freedom. What this Science loses, the individual gains. That is the principal message of *Principia* generally and of Chapter Five in particular. This it is that occasioned Strachey's "Glory Hallieluiah!" As was so often true, in this case Lytton spoke well for all those who would be Bloomsbury. But perhaps it is Vanessa who captures best what they took from Moore. When she writes that "a great new freedom seemed about to come," she pays proper homage to Moore the liberator.

For Bloomsbury practiced what *Principia* preaches, not only (as many commentators have noted) in its acceptance of *Principia*'s pronouncements about what things are good in themselves, but also this work's major themes concerning what sort of person we ought to be and how we ought to live. Each member of Bloomsbury in his or her own way worked at acquiring those "private" virtues Moore commends: prudence, temperance, industry. There was not a slackard in the crowd. Not one who recklessly threw his or her life away through willful over-indulgence in one vice or another. Though God was dead in Bloomsbury, the work ethic of their largely Protestant upbringings was alive. Moore's celebration of those virtues the members already were determined to pursue and in time were in large measure to possess could hardly have failed to elicit their happy approval. Not beneficence. Not charity. Not civic-mindedness. Not justice. Not patriotism. Not self-sacrifice. Not any of those "social virtues" that would-be scientific moralists applauded and that Bloomsbury by its cliquish aloofness tended largely to disdain. The virtues of Bloomsbury are *Principia*'s virtues. They are the virtues of the self first, not the virtues of the citizen.

But not only *Principia*'s virtues, that book's entire practical ethic permeates Bloomsbury's moral approach to living. How ought we to decide what to do, if we are to act as a legitimate, scientific ethic requires? *Principia* offers its justification of a (very) few rules: Do not murder. Do not steal. Do not break your promises. Bloomsbury could not have asked for more sanguine universal prescriptions. Murder was not on their social agenda. Nor the theft of another's property. And neither was any serious meddling with the existing social structure, the one that enabled the Bloomsberries to work at perfecting their several crafts while the servants did the housework. Theirs was an anarchy of the bedroom, not the streets. Bloomsbury had everything to lose and little to gain in a state of society where one's property rights were not respected. How reassuring to learn that everyone had a moral duty not to steal. The stability of society, which was necessary for everything else, required nothing less. Or so Moore claims. And as for the keeping of one's promises and the speaking of truth generally—well, that was certainly required between friends. Perhaps, however, the groundless pomposity of certain persons and institutions needed to be exposed now and again, even if this meant an occasional deceit. Lies about Abyssinian emperors were perhaps nothing when compared with the shallow depravity of those whose appetite for foolish customs were unmasked by false beards. While Moore himself may have differed with some members of Bloomsbury over the complete list of rules requiring universal compliance, there was very little room for disagreement, really, since there were very few rules to begin with. And even if they did disagree with Moore over the status of one rule or another, they could still agree with him concerning *how* they should decide which rules (if any) to accept, which to reject.

This was a liberty Moore himself was determined to preserve and encourage. His object in Chapter Five, announced in *Principia*'s Preface, is "to discover the fundamental principles of ethical reasoning; and the establishment of these principles, rather than any conclusions which may be attained by their use, may be regarded as my main object" (p. ix). In Chapter Five itself, moreover, Moore states that he does "not propose to enter upon [a defense of those few rules he accepts] in detail"; his primary concern is a different one—namely, "to point out what seem to be the chief distinct principles by the use of which [any defense] can be made" (p. 156). That is Moore's principal business: To establish the correct principles of ethical reasoning. And that is what his followers could take from him without having to accept all that he arrived at when *he* used these principles. To be a Moorist did not require anything like the compulsory recitation of the Thirty-nine Articles.

But Moore's influence goes deeper still. That passage in *Principia* in which Moore extols the virtue of Egoism over Altruism as a means of producing good—that passage more than any other captures the essence of Bloomsbury's ethic. We are to act to increase our share of what is good, including in our range of concern those persons "in whom [we have] a strong personal interest." Loyalty to friends comes before loyalty to country. The patriotism of a McTaggart is dead. The friendship of a Forster is alive. We have no *duty* to attempt to cultivate "a more extended beneficence". In general we do best if we keep to ourselves and our friends, mindful, of course, that we are not to commit murder or steal—even in the company of strangers. That cool aloofness that is synonymous with the name Bloomsbury is a predictable outgrowth of Moore's teachings when taken seriously by intelligent people who belong to the leisure class. Leon Edel is both right and wrong when he states that "the ethical side of Moorism . . . touched the young men [that is, the Cambridge core of Bloomsbury] less than the philosophical sanction given them to assert themselves, to shake off old rigidities, to be homosexual if they wished, to scoff at the dying—the dead—Victorians" (p. 37). Right in ascribing this liberating influence to Moore, Edel is wrong only in thinking that the influence is somehow distinct from Moore's "ethical side." Moore's "ethical side" *is* a declaration of individual liberty, not, as the standard interpretation supposes, a dreary call to acquiesce in the face of "old rigidities." The Bloomsberries took this teaching into themselves. They were doing exactly what Moore taught they ought to do: Above all else they pursued their self-interest, where that interest is understood to include the enrichment of the lives of those for whom one has special affection. In those cases where some members of the group contributed their time and energy to a more extended beneficence, they did no wrong if their special talents led them there. But others in the group had no duty to follow their lead. It was the great mass of people—too much involved in the unproductive affairs of social justice, too frequently in pursuit of a hopelessly extended beneficence, too much in bondage to a morality of rule worship, too little in control of their individual destinies—it was the great mass of humanity who failed to carve out an approach to life that could be defended by a truly scientific ethic. The barbarians outside Bloomsbury did not live as they ought. The Bloomsbury elect did. The people who were Bloomsbury are nothing if not the visible expression of Moore's ethic in relation to conduct.

An End to the Battle

The preceding helps minimize the real differences between Keynes and Leonard Woolf regarding Moore's influence. Judged superficially, the two seem to offer widely divergent recollections, in Keynes's words, of "the individual's duty to obey general rules." Keynes states that "we claimed the right to judge every case on its merits," "repudiat[ing] entirely customary morals, convention and traditional wisdom" (p. 97). "We recognized no moral obligation on us, no inner sanction, to conform or to obey" (p. 98). Woolf's memory seems to differ. It is not true, he writes in *Sowing*, that he and his fellows "neglected all that Moore said about 'morals' and the rules of conduct." By way of evidence against Keynes, he offers the following:

But Moore himself was continually exercised by the problems of good and bad as means of morality and rules of conduct and therefore of the life of action as opposed to the life of contemplation. He and we were fascinated by questions of what was right and wrong, what one *ought* to do. We followed him closely in this as in other parts of his doctrine and argued interminably about the consequences of one's acts, both in actual and imaginary situations. Indeed one of the problems which worried us was what part Moore (and we, his disciples) *ought* to play in ordinary life, what, for instance, our attitude *ought* to be towards practical politics.

Who, then, is right—Keynes or Woolf? The answer seems to be, "Sometimes both, and sometimes neither." To begin with, there is far less actual difference than there appears to be. Everything that Woolf actually says about Moore's interest in questions about right conduct is perfectly consistent with what Keynes says about the individual's duty to obey general rules. Woolf says, for example, that "Moore himself was continually exercised by the problems of . . . rules of conduct, . . . questions of what was right and wrong." From this it does *not* follow that Moore claimed that anyone has a duty "to observe general rules." Indeed, we know that Moore himself said nothing so loose as this. And even the examples Woolf gives are consistent with the general tenor of Keynes's remarks. To ask (as Woolf says they did) what Moore ought to have done vis-à-vis the political world, for example, is not to ask what *general rule* he ought to have followed. *Whatever* Moore's duty was in this case, assuming he had one, it presumably was not to be decided by appeal to some general rule of obligation. To discuss such questions as *this one*, therefore, is not at odds with Keynes's claim that "we entirely repudiated a personal liability to obey general rules."

Perhaps, however, Woolf means something different than what he actually says. Perhaps he means that he and Moore's other followers accepted Moore's views concerning the *specific* topic of the individual's duty to follow general rules. If this is what Woolf means, then we know Moore's view. We have a duty to follow a rule if and only if it is generally observed and its utility is certain. *That* is Moore's view. It *seems* not to be Keynes's. But one must be careful even here. One could accept Moore's view, that one has a duty to follow a rule in such a case, and still maintain, as Keynes does, that "we recognized no moral obligation on us . . . to conform or obey." This is consistent if what one means by "moral obligation" is what Keynes evidently means by it—namely, an "inner sanction."

For it is perfectly possible *both* that Keynes had a duty to follow a rule *and* that he did not feel an "inner sanction" to do so.

But Keynes *does* recall that he and his peers "repudiated entirely customary morals, convention and traditional wisdom." And Woolf? Woolf is less than clear on this matter. "Moore himself was continually exercised by the problems of good and bad as means of morality and rules of conduct," he insists. True. But this in no way entails that Moore cherished "customary morals, convention and traditional wisdom." For Moore could be much exercised by questions of right and wrong and not think that the answers were to be found merely by consulting custom, convention, or tradition. In fact Moore in *Principia* never argues that a successful appeal to any one of these sources is either necessary or sufficient for deciding what is right or wrong. That all three (custom, convention, tradition) can easily involve rules whose general observance no longer is useful shows that a successful appeal to any one of them is not sufficient to prove that we ought to follow a given rule. And while it is unlikely that the Science of Morals ever will be able to defend the introduction of an entirely new rule, binding at all times on all people, at least in a given society, almost all of our moral decisions must be made without reference to any rule, old or new, which shows that a successful appeal to tradition and the like is not a necessary condition for determining what is right. In a certain sense, then, even Moore "repudiated" the grounds of duty Keynes mentions and Woolf feels compelled to try to defend. An uncritical acceptance of "customary morals, convention and traditional wisdom" is not part of the Happy Warrior's standard repertoire. Neither is it of Moore's.

Still, Keynes does declare, in an unqualified way, that "we claimed the right to judge every case on its merits." And that does seem to be another claim Woolf wishes to answer by suggesting that Moore was of another mind. Well, Moore was of another mind in one sense, but not in another. For Moore does argue that there are only "a very few" rules which everyone ought always obey. And Keynes might be supposed to be denying this. When he writes that "we claimed the right to judge every case on its merits," what he means is that they recognized no case in which a sufficient reason for acting in a given way was that it was called for by a general rule—even a rule that was generally observed and whose utility was certain. Moore thought otherwise. And that's what Woolf remembers, it may be claimed.

Now, this does constitute a genuine difference in what the two older men remember, so that here we seem to be compelled to choose between them. If so, then Keynes's own testimony decides the issue in favor of

Woolf's. As Skidelsky ably demonstrates, Keynes's unpublished work, written in the aftermath of *Principia*'s publication, offers an insight into Keynes's competing loyalties. With Edmund Burke, Keynes saw the need for social stability—the duties of citizenship. But with Moore, as understood by Keynes, he saw the importance of cultivating the quality of one's own experience. "Moore and Burke," Skidelsky writes: "Keynes's life was balanced between the two sets of moral claims. His duty as an individual was to achieve good states of mind for himself and for those he was directly concerned with; his duty as a citizen was to help achieve a happy state of affairs for society. The two claims he thought of as logically independent of each other. He attached greater priority to the first than to the second, except when he thought the state was in danger" (p. 157).

And that, perhaps, is the finest irony. Precisely where Keynes thinks his loyalty to Moore is compromised—in those cases where the stability of the state comes before one's private moral enterprise—his loyalty to the deeper teachings of Moore are tightened rather than relaxed. The stability of the state *is* absolutely essential, *is* a prerequisite for everything else, in Moore's view, as it is in Keynes's (and in Burke's). It is just that in Moore's view the justified limits on individual freedom required for this stability are themselves very limited. In the end there are, he thinks, only a "very few" rules whose universal observance is required if society—any society—is to be stable. For the rest of our lives we are at liberty to decide what is best on our own, and to act accordingly. The much heralded virtues of the citizen, though possibly useful, are unnecessary. It is enough that people do not rob, do not assault, do not kill. *Why* they limit their behavior in these socially useful ways is far less important than that they do so.

Keynes, as Skidelsky shows, argued for nothing less, but also for nothing more. Keynes seems to have thought that he was parting company with Moore on these morally substantive matters. A careful reading of *Principia*, however, especially the fifth chapter, reveals that Keynes's own thought echoes the conclusions Moore reaches there, which is why we may assume that both men took some pleasure in the successful hoax played on the Navy by Virginia Woolf, Duncan Grant, and the others. The stability of the state was not in jeopardy, only the inflated pretenses of petty men dressed in stiff uniforms of faded power. Had the Abyssinian Emperor presented a gift copy of *Principia* to the British Admiral, it would have been the perfect gesture: Vintage Bloomsbury! But vintage Moorism, too.

9

The More Beautiful

Little Swarming Selves

🐝 "I have called this faith a religion," Keynes intones, looking up momentarily from his prepared remarks,

and some sort of relation of neo-platonism it surely was. But we should have been very angry at the time with such a suggestion. We regarded (inquiries into what things are good) as entirely rational and scientific in character. Like any other branch of science, it was nothing more than the application of logic and rational analysis to the material presented as sense-data. Our apprehension of good was exactly the same as our apprehension of green, and we purported to handle it with the same logical and analytical technique which was appropriate to the latter. Indeed we combined a dogmatic treatment as to the nature of experience with a method of handling it which was extravagantly scholastic. Russell's *Principles of Mathematics* came out in the same year as *Principia Ethica*; and the former, in spirit, furnished a method for handling the material provided by the latter. Let me give you a few examples of the sort of things we used to discuss. (p. 86)

Maynard's audience consists of the assembled members of the Memoir Club. It is the Summer of 1938, "the summer before Munich," as Quentin Bell would later remind everyone. The surviving members of Bloomsbury (Strachey was the first to die, in 1932, followed two years later by Fry) are gathered to hear Keynes's paper, "My Early Beliefs." Just three years before her own death, Virginia will refer to Keynes's effort as "very translucent, . . . very formidable." He is retracing his intellectual lineage from the

251

time of his arrival at Cambridge. In addition to Bloomsbury's "old guard" and a few non-Bloomsbury guests, the younger generation, the children of the original members, are listening. Keynes had wondered out loud whether the new members of the Club knew anything about the religion he and his contemporaries had taken from Moore: "Even if the new members of the Club know what the religion was (do they?), it will not do any of us any harm to try and recall the crude outlines" (pp. 82–83). The examples he now gives are intended to suggest the style and substance of their spiritual exercises.

If A was in love with B and believed that B reciprocated his feelings, whereas in fact B did not, but was in love with C, the state of affairs was certainly not so good as it would have been if A had been right, but was it worse or better than it would become if A discovered his mistake? If A was in love with B under a misapprehension as to B's qualities, was this better or worse than A's not being in love at all? If A was in love with B because A's spectacles were not strong enough to see B's complexion, did this altogether, or partly, destroy the value of A's state of mind? Suppose we were to live our lives backwards having our experiences in the reverse order, would this affect the value of our successive states of mind? If the states of mind enjoyed by each of us were pooled and then redistributed, would this affect their value? How did one compare the value of a good state of mind which had bad consequences with a bad state of mind which had good consequences? In valuing the consequences did one assess them at their actual value as it turned out eventually to be, or their probable value at the time? If at their probable value, how much evidence as to possible consequence was it one's duty to collect before applying the calculus? Was there a separate objective standard of beauty? Was a beautiful thing, that is to say, by definition that which it was good to contemplate? Or was there an actual objective quality 'beauty', just like 'green' and 'good'? And knowledge, too, presented a problem. Were all truths equally good to pursue and contemplate?—as for example the number of grains in a given tract of sea-sand. We were disposed to repudiate very strongly the idea that useful knowledge could be preferable to useless knowledge. But we flirted with the idea that there might be some intrinsic quality— though not, perhaps, quite on a par with 'green' and 'good' and 'beautiful'—which one could call 'interesting', and we were prepared to think it just possible that 'interesting' knowledge might be better to pursue than 'uninteresting' knowledge. Another competing adjective was 'important', provided it was quite clear that 'important' did not mean 'useful'. Or to return again to our favourite subject, was a violent love affair which lasted a short time better than a more tepid one which endured longer? We were inclined to think it was. But I have said enough by now to make it clear that the problems of mensuration, in which we had involved ourselves, were somewhat formidable. (pp. 86–87)

The "religion" of Keynes and his contemporaries at Cambridge, he had remarked earlier, was one that

> closely followed the English puritan tradition of being chiefly con-cerned with the salvation of our own souls. The divine resided within a closed circle. There was not a very intimate connection between 'being good' and 'doing good'; and we had a feeling that there was some risk that in practice the latter might interfere with the former. But religions proper, as distinct from modern 'social service' pseudo-religions, have always been of that character; and perhaps it was a sufficient offset that our religion was altogether unworldly—with wealth, power, popularity or success it had no concern whatever, they were thoroughly despised. (p. 84)

Nevertheless, despite this renunciation of the goods of the world and notwithstanding a certain wobble about the intrinsic value of enjoyment, this "did not prevent us from laughing most of the time. . . . We enjoyed supreme self-confidence, superiority and contempt towards the rest of the unconverted world" (p. 91). All this—and more—they had gotten from *Principia*. And nothing less had the Cambridge-core of Bloomsbury moved with them to that famous London neighborhood. "It seems to me looking back," Maynard proclaims, something of the original zeal still present in his words, "that this religion of ours was a very good one to have grown up under" (p. 92). They had been spared Marx, and escaped Freud.

Not everyone agreed. Among the more famous dissenters was D. H. Lawrence. Lawrence met only two of Bloomsbury's original cast: Keynes and Duncan Grant. But he also met Russell when, in 1914, he visited Russell in the latter's rooms at Trinity, where Keynes joined them. It made a lasting impression on him. Lawrence was repulsed, a feeling that was reinforced the following year when David Garnett, who would soon join Grant at the Charleston farm, paid a visit to Lawrence and his wife Frieda. Accompanying Garnett was Frances Birrell, at that time a close associate of Bloomsbury. Garnett recounts part of their visit as follows:

Lawrence had disappeared to work after breakfast and Frankie and I were joined by Bertie Farjeon, his wife Joan, and his sister Eleanor and Margaret Radford and we all sat happily gossiping and roasting in the sun. It was only the 17th of April but it was as hot as midsummer. We were happy and little suspected that trouble might be brewing as we first talked, and then played, with a gnome-like Saleeby child. Our high spirits lasted all day. After the Farjeons and Margaret had departed for London Frankie talked, and I talked and I think Frieda laughed a lot at supper and looked as though she would have kissed us for being so noisy. But slowly I became aware that Lawrence was silent and that something dreadful was going on inside him. He was in the throes of some dark religious crisis and seemed to shrink in size with the effort of summoning up all his powers, all his spiritual strength. The muscles knotted and he became smaller—but he said nothing. Frieda, however, had observed what was going on. I said we were tired and that I had a long day's walk in front of me. Then Frankie and I took our candles and retired to our little rooms.

I was, actually, rather tired but I was kept awake by angry and incessant whispering in the next room which sounded most sinister. At last, however, Lawrence stopped and I soon dropped off. Suddenly, in the middle of the night, I was woken by a series of bangs and tumbles and strangulated sounds. I sat up and realized that someone was blundering about outside the door of my room. I lit a candle and investigated. Frankie was standing, swathed in a pair of thick flannel pyjamas, in the passage, dumb and obviously in great distress. He pointed to his mouth and in the light of the candle I saw it was open and choked with a large object. His tongue had swollen to an enormous size. I shoved the handle of my toothbrush into his mouth and he winced and gave nasal moans. Then Frieda, followed by Lawrence, came in and stared at us in astonishment. I explained matters and discussed doctors, poultices and fomentations with Frieda. There was a quiet, triumphant certainty in Lawrence's manner. He had prayed for deliverance to his Dark Gods and they had sent this mysterious sign, blasting his enemy in what had hitherto seemed his strongest organ. For a little while, Frieda and I tortured Frankie, one of us holding the candle, while the other tried to insert teaspoonfuls of almost boiling water into his mouth. Finally we pushed him off to bed and he was glad to escape from us. I had discovered by that time that his temperature was normal and went off to sleep encouraged to hope that he would last till next day, when I could take him to a doctor.

Morning came at last and, to the astonishment of us all, Frankie's tongue had resumed its normal size and functions. It was neither larger nor smaller than usual. Frieda and I contented ourselves with giving him a big dose of salts. (pp. 367–368)

It was more than Lawrence could bear. In a letter to Ottoline Morrell, posted soon after the visit and reproduced in Garnett's *The Flowers of the Forest*, he writes the following:

We had David Garnett and Francis Birrell here for the week-end. When Birrell comes, tired and a bit lost and wandering-I love him. But, my God, to hear him talk sends me mad. To hear these young people talk really fills me with black fury: they talk endlessly, but endlessly—and never, never a good thing said. They are cased each in a hard little shell of his own and out of this they talk words. There is never, for one second, any outgoing of feeling and no reverence, not a crumb or grain of reverence. I cannot stand it. I will not have people like this—I had rather be alone. They made me dream of a beetle that bites a scorpion. But I killed it—a very large beetle. I scotched it and it ran off—but I came on it again, and killed it. It is this horror of little swarming selves I can't stand. (p. 368)

Evidently Lawrence felt the same "horror of little swarming selves" in Birrell's company as he had in that of Keynes's and Grant's. And perhaps he had encountered the same "endless talk" in the presence of the latter men that he had met in his meeting with Garnett and Birrell. In the case of Moore the situation was predictably different. When the two found themselves seated next to one another at dinner in hall, neither could think of anything to say. Moore's similar encounter years later with Vanessa at Charleston had its precursor.

Lawrence wrote a second letter, also dated April 19, 1915, this one to

Garnett, whose father, Edward, was an editor who had helped Lawrence at the outset of the latter's career. Lawrence may have felt something approaching a paternal interest in the young man. His counsel is direct.

> Never bring Birrell to see me any more. There is something nasty about him like black beetles. He is horrible and unclean. I feel I should go mad when I think of your set, Duncan Grant and Keynes and Birrell. It makes me dream of beetles. In Cambridge I had a similar dream. . . . But it came full upon me in Keynes and in Duncan Grant. And yesterday I knew it again in Birrell—you must leave these friends, these beetles. Birrell and Duncan Grant are done for forever. Keynes I am not sure—when I saw Keynes that morning in Cambridge it was one of the crises of my life. It sent me mad with misery and hostility and rage. (p. 369)

Garnett was angered by Lawrence's letter: "He seemed to me mad and determined to interfere in my life. I therefore decided not to see him again. It was a great loss, for I loved both Lawrence and Frieda—especially Frieda" (p. 369).

Lawrence was not alone in being "mad with misery and hostility and rage." He found a notable ally in the controversial literary critic F. R. Leavis, who took repeated satisfaction in publicly attacking the "Cambridge-Bloomsbury *milieu*." This "coterie," which in his view had succeeded in destroying much of what had been best in English culture, he traces back to Keynes's arrival at Cambridge.

> We can see it to have been a significant moment in the history, not only of Cambridge, but of modern English culture, when, at the turn of the century, at the time of Keynes's going up to King's from Eton, the coterie had its start, and the character of the *milieu* began to define itself. It might be asked why the coterie should have been so inferior. Without offering to explain in any ultimate sense, one may say something about the nature and conditions of the inferiority. The group of young men, mainly King's and Trinity . . . , a group having in its connection with the famous 'Society', intimate contacts at more senior levels, and a continuity with an illustrious intellectual tradition, obviously contained some real distinction as well as a good deal of academic—and academic-social—brilliance. But there is

something about the constitutive ethos of the *milieu* that the intellectual distinction and the continuity from the past make the more ominous. We have it here, in Keynes's attitude to a representative great Cambridge man of the immediate past (the letter is dated 1906)

> Have you read Sidgwick's Life? Very interesting and depressing. . . . He never did anything but wonder whether Christianity was true and prove that it wasn't and hope that it was. . . .
> I wonder what he would have thought of us; and I wonder what we think of him. And then his conscience—incredible. There is no doubt about his moral goodness. And yet it is all so dreadfully depressing—no intimacy, no clear-cut boldness.

We can guess well enough what Sidgwick would have thought of Lytton Strachey. And an *élite* of young Cambridge minds that could find the ethos of Lytton Strachey more congenial than that of Henry Sidgwick was certainly a significantly new thing. (p. 397)

F. R. Leavis assigns some role to Moore in bringing about the change in English culture he so deeply laments. "Moore was, in his very limited way," Leavis states, "a disinterested and innocent spirit" (p. 398). His disinterest and innocence, we are told, "made him the more irresistibly the very sanction they [that is, the Apostolic core of the *milieu*] needed" (p. 398). Moore, it seems, was a leader in spite of himself. Or at least in spite of his ideas. It was his character (his innocence, his disinterested spirit), not his thought, that made him an irresistible sanction. It is little wonder that a man who underestimates Moore so much should understand the extent of and the reasons for his influence so little.

Once Again, the Ideal

In his memoir Keynes celebrates the evangelical impact of *Principia*'s sixth chapter, "The Ideal," on the Cambridge-core of Bloomsbury. In that chapter Moore again faces the daunting challenge of identifying the major types of intrinsic value. His previous effort, made in the last chapter of "The Elements," had ended in disaster. The Ideal (or Summum Bonum) consists of an infinite amount of a possibly infinite number of different kinds of things each of which is more or less good in itself. To describe this Ideal, Moore says, is "hard." He should rather have said "impossible."

He wisely does not set himself so large a task in *Principia*, limiting his reach on this occasion to identifying only the major types of intrinsically good and intrinsically evil things "which we know or can imagine." And although beauty, whether in art or nature, is included, Moore no longer claims, as he had in "Art, Morals, and Religion," that it is the only thing good in itself.

This last chapter Moore clearly views in some ways as standing outside *Principia*'s argumentative core. Part of the reform he calls for in the Science of Morals is a move away from the promulgation of rules of duty and virtue and toward a consideration of what things are good in themselves. That call was issued in "Art, Morals, and Religion," and it is heard again in *Principia*. In that former essay, when beauty is viewed as the only intrinsic good, aesthetics is declared to be the "Science of Ends," with an unfinished agenda of requests: What kinds of beauty are there? And what are their respective degrees of intrinsic value? In *Principia*, where a pluralistic view regarding intrinsic values is defended, the practitioners of ethics are called upon to make themselves useful. "Judgments of intrinsic value have this superiority over judgments of means," Moore writes,

> that, if once true, they are always true, whereas what is a means to a good effect in one case, will not be so in another. For this reason the department of Ethics, which it would be most useful to elaborate for practical guidance, is that which discusses what things have intrinsic value and to what degree; and this is precisely that department which has been most uniformly neglected, in favor of attempts to formulate rules of conduct. (p. 166)

Moore seeks to rectify this imbalance by discussing what things have intrinsic value and in what degree. This is a part—indeed, *the* most important part—of practical ethics, as Moore understands this department of his Science.

That this is Moore's view is clear as early as the Preface, where, in a passage already quoted in part on two previous occasions, he writes the following:

> One main object of this book may, then, be expressed by slightly changing one of Kant's famous titles. I have endeavoured to write 'Prolegomena to any future Ethics that can possibly pretend to be

scientific.' In other words, I have endeavoured to discover what are the fundamental principles of ethical reasoning; and the establishment of these principles, rather than of any conclusions which may be attained by their use, may be regarded as my main object. I have, however, also attempted, in Chapter VI, to present some conclusions, with regard to the proper answer of the question 'What is good in itself?' which are very different from any which have commonly been advocated by philosophers. I have tried to define the classes within which all great goods and evils fall; and I have maintained that very many different things are good and evil in themselves, and that neither class of things possesses any other property which is both common to all its members and peculiar to them. (pp. ix–x)

One chapter is set off from the rest, only this is not, as it is sometimes thought to be, Chapter Five. It is Chapter Six. The first five chapters, Moore implies, contain his views concerning the correct principles of ethical reasoning. The last chapter, by contrast, is less theoretical and more directly practical in tone and conception. The determination of what things are good in themselves is "the most useful to elaborate for practical guidance," far more useful than the "attempts to formulate rules of conduct." Why Moore would view things in this way should be clear once we remind ourselves of his reformist aspirations. For since on his view we almost always must decide what we ought to do independently of what moral rules prescribe, and since Duty, Right, Obligation, and related notions are defined in terms of what is productive of intrinsic value, it follows that in almost all our decisions, "instead of following rules, . . . the individual should rather guide his choice by the direct consideration of the intrinsic value or vileness of the effects which his action may produce" (p. 166). In *Principia*'s first five chapters Moore has labored to secure the liberty of the individual to decide and judge autonomously. In Chapter Six he does something quite different. He offers practical guidance by sharing *his* vision of the best things "we know or can imagine." But more important than his vision is the model he offers of how we are to decide these matters. The method to be used is more important than the results obtained, something Moore himself insists upon near the conclusion of "The Ideal." "I am content," he writes, "that the results of this chapter should be taken as illustrating the method which must be pursued in answering the fundamental question of Ethics, and the principles that must be observed, than as giving the correct answer to that question" (p. 223). Viewed philosophically, it is the how, not the what, that matters most.

Moore's Method

Once we have been liberated from those false systems of ethics that demand universal compliance to long lists of rules of duty and virtue, nothing would be more natural than to have our "free Spirits" blow in every direction at once, deaf to the voice of reason. Viewed in this perspective we see that Moore could not have made it more difficult for himself. Unless he were willing—which of course he was not—to allow that any judgment of intrinsic value is the equal of any other, that there is nothing that can be said in favor of some that cannot equally be said in favor of all, Moore was obliged to face the challenge of providing some rationally defensible basis for choosing to accept some judgments over others. His problem arises because he seems to have undermined every possibility of success. Judgments of intrinsic value are ultimate, both in the sense that they are the ones by which we decide what makes our life worth living and in the sense that no direct evidence can be given for them. And it is this latter feature that seems to doom Moore to failure if he attempts to offer any reason for trusting more in some judgments of this sort than in others.

He had faced this challenge on at least two previous occasions. One was that memorable meeting of the Apostles when Moore read his missing paper on sex and met with defeat in his attempt to persuade the Brothers that self-abuse was intrinsically bad. He found the vote "really astonishing" and thought that MacCarthy, who was familiar with "The Elements of Ethics," would share his amazement. "The Elements" itself is the second place Moore had addressed the major challenge he now faced in *Principia*. MacCarthy's familiarity with these lectures could only have left him more confused than edified. For in the final lecture of "The Elements," after previously offering a sustained critique of naturalistic ethics, Moore confronts the questions, "What things are good in themselves? And how may we rationally choose between various answers?" His reply to this latter question is vulnerable to the same kind of argument he had earlier marshalled against naturalistic accounts of Good. "In general" we can be assured that we know what things are good in themselves, he submits, if what we think is in harmony with what "other people think":

"For what we think has . . . been determined by the course of evolution" (p. 356). But what we think, even if it is harmonious with the thoughts of others, does not by itself support the view that we think rationally or truly, or even that we probably do so; and appeals to "the course of evolution" in this quarter only thicken a philosophical plot already gone wrong. Unless we have independent reason to believe that what "the course of evolution" leads us to believe is, or is likely to be, correct or rational, the appeal to "evolution" is logically illicit. To suppose that some things are good because evolution leads most of us to believe that they are grievously flaunts Moore's stern requirement that we avoid naturalism in ethics. In *Principia* he is more careful to practice what he preaches.

Moore's avenue of escape from his apparent dilemma is to be found in his so-called "method of isolation." The very conception of intrinsic value, once properly grasped, rationally obliges us to approach questions about what things are good in themselves in one way—and in one way only. Those persons who do approach them in this, the right way, who make use of the appropriate method, minimize their chance of error. By having a maximally clear understanding of the meaning of the question they are asking, they do all that rationally can be done to increase the likelihood that their judgment will be right. By contrast, those who do not understand the question well or who fail to rely on the appropriate method for answering it increase the likelihood of being mistaken. We can, then—or so Moore apparently believes—have a rationally defensible basis for thinking that some judgments of intrinsic value are more likely to be correct than others, even though no direct evidence can be given in support of any judgment of this sort. The basis for selection is the appropriate use of the appropriate method. Part of the enduring splendor of "The Ideal" is the display of disciplined passion Moore brings to his live demonstration of how to do this. He teaches by example. Keynes and the others learned, and learned well.

Those things that are good in themselves do not depend on anything else for their value. That is part of what it means to say that their value is intrinsic. If these things were the only things that existed, if they existed in absolute isolation from everything else, they would not be any less good than they are when they exist as they now do—in ways that connect them with other existing things. Things that actually exist are causally related, either as causes or as effects of one another. Intrinsically good things are no exception. Because it is possible that things having intrinsic value are causally linked with things that are themselves indifferent or evil, and because our judgments of value about the objects to which they are causally linked might color or influence our judgment about these good things themselves, it is essential in Moore's view that we not think about a thing's causes or effects when we ask whether it is intrinsically good. Questions about the intrinsic value of works of art show how real this problem is. More than a few people have been led to deny that a work of art has intrinsic value because the work leads to (is causally implicated in the occurrence of) immoral behavior. Not Moore. "A work of art is not the worse," we have seen him aver, "because it encourages the grossest immorality." Nor is the converse inference any more to be accepted. No work of art "is better because it results in the sublimest virtue." As Moore states in "Art, Morals, and Religion," "a good work of art is an end-in-itself. It has intrinsic value; and its intrinsic value can obviously only depend upon what [it] itself contains, not upon what it causes to exist." Or what causes it.

Whenever we ask whether something is good in itself, therefore, we must concentrate our attention on it and it alone. We must practice *Principia*'s method of isolation, a method Moore describes as follows:

> In order to arrive at a correct decision . . . it is necessary to consider what things are such that, if they existed *by themselves*, in absolute isolation, we should yet judge their existence to be good; and, in order to decide upon the relative *degrees* of value of different things, we must similarly consider what comparative value seems to attach to the isolated existence of each. (p. 187)

By using this method we are able to "guard against two errors, which seem to have been the chief causes which have vitiated previous conclusions" about what things are good in themselves.

> By employing this method, we shall guard against two errors, which seem to have been the chief causes which have vitiated previous conclusions on the subject. The first of these is (1) that which consists in supposing that what seems absolutely necessary here and now, for the existence of anything good—what we cannot do without—is therefore good in itself. If we isolate such things, which are mere means to good, and suppose a world in which they alone, and nothing but they, existed, their intrinsic worthlessness becomes apparent. And, secondly, there is the more subtle error (2) which consists

in neglecting the principle of organic unities. This error is committed, when it is supposed, that, if one part of a whole has no intrinsic value, the value of the whole must reside entirely in the other parts. It has, in this way, been commonly supposed, that, if all valuable wholes could be seen to have one and only one common property, the wholes must be valuable solely *because* they possess this property; and the illusion is greatly strengthened, if the common property in question seems, considered by itself, to have more value than the other parts of such wholes, considered by themselves. But, if we consider the property in question, *in isolation*, and then compare it with the whole, of which it forms a part, it may become easily apparent that, existing by itself, the property in question has not nearly so much value, as has the whole to which it belongs. Thus, if we compare the value of a certain amount of pleasure, *existing absolutely by itself*, with the value of certain 'enjoyments,' containing an equal amount of pleasure, it may become apparent that the 'enjoyment' is much better than the pleasure, and also, in some cases, much worse. In such a case it is plain that the 'enjoyment' does *not* owe its value *solely* to the pleasure it contains, although it might easily have appeared to do so, when we only considered the other constituents of the enjoyment, and seemed to see that, without the pleasure, they would have had no value. It is now apparent, on the contrary, that the whole 'enjoyment' owes its value quite equally to the presence of the other constituents, *even though* it may be true that the pleasure is the only constituent having any value by itself. And similarly, if we are told that all things owe their value solely to the fact that they are 'realisations of the true self,' we may easily refute this statement, by asking whether the predicate that is meant by 'realising the true self,' supposing that it could exist alone, would have any value whatsoever. Either the *thing*, which does 'realise the true self,' has intrinsic value or it has not; and if it has, then it certainly does not owe its value solely to the fact that it realises the true self. (pp. 187–188)

Rationally speaking, therefore, we *can do something* to minimize the chance of error in making judgments of intrinsic value, even while it is true that no direct evidence can be offered for or against any judgment of this sort. We must consider things in absolute isolation. Then we must decide what we think is true: Does the thing have intrinsic value or not?

Would it be worth having purely for its own sake? And if it has such value, to what degree? In every case "the sole decision must rest with our reflective judgment" (p. 197).

The Best of the Good

Having described the appropriate method, Moore now is in a position to show how to use it. He is confident that those who have understood him and who use the method of isolation will agree with his judgment. No more the painful differences about whether "self abusive sex" is an end in itself.

> If, now, we use this method of absolute isolation, and guard against these errors, it appears that the question we have to answer is far less difficult than the controversies of Ethics might have led us to expect. Indeed, once the meaning of the question is clearly understood, the answer to it, in its main outlines, appears to be so obvious, that it runs the risk of seeming to be a platitude. By far the most valuable things, which we know or can imagine, are certain states of consciousness, which may be roughly described as the pleasures of human intercourse and the enjoyment of beautiful objects. No one, probably, who has asked himself the question, has ever doubted that personal affection and the appreciation of what is beautiful in Art or Nature, are good in themselves; nor, if we consider strictly what things are worth having *purely for their own sakes*, does it appear probable that any one will think that anything else has *nearly* so great a value as the things which are included under these two heads. (pp. 188–189)

This much, Moore believes, is noncontroversial—"a platitude." What is not either noncontroversial or platitudinous is where this finding takes us.

> This simple truth may, indeed, be said to be universally recognised. What has *not* been recognised is that it is the ultimate and fundamental truth of Moral Philosophy. That it is only for the sake of these things—in order that as much of them as possible may at some time exist—that any one can be justified in performing any public or private duty; that they are the *raison d'être* of virtue; that it is they—these complex wholes *themselves*, and not any constituent or charac-

teristic of them—that form the rational ultimate end of human action and the sole criterion of social progress: these appear to be truths which have been generally overlooked. (p. 189)

Moore here enlarges the class of intrinsic goods that justify morality, understanding by 'morality' the required performance of any duty or the display of any virtue. In "Art, Morals, and Religion," where beauty was said to be the only thing good in itself, morality is said to exist for the sake of the creation and appreciation of what is beautiful. And for that alone. In *Principia*, where beauty is no longer judged to be the only intrinsic good, the justification of morality is more expansive. The performance of duties and the exercise of virtue are to be commended, when they are, because they are necessary means for making society—*any* society—stable; and it is only if we live in a stable society that we are likely to have much chance of creating or appreciating beauty, whether in art or in nature, and of forming and taking pleasure in our friendships. Morality is the foundation of the possible proliferation of things good in themselves; the few rules of duty and virtue Moore recognizes are justified, if they are, only because they are necessary "in order that as much of them [that is, the admiring contemplation of beauty and the pleasure of friendship] may at some time exist" (p. 189). As Desmond MacCarthy makes the point, "Morality was either a means to attaining those goods of the soul or it was nothing—just as the railway system existed to bring people together and to feed them, or the social system that as many 'ends' as possible should be achieved." In this respect, though certainly not only in this one, MacCarthy understood Moore perfectly.

Complex Values

Far from being simple, the major kinds of intrinsic goods Moore identifies are "highly complex organic unities," wholes whose intrinsic values are not to be discovered merely by adding the value of the several parts. For the various parts of a highly valuable whole may have no or little value in themselves. How this is possible and that it is true are the points Moore next moves on to demonstrate.

Concerning the matter of complexity first, Moore maintains that the goods he has identified all contain at least the following distinguishable parts. Each contains some feeling or emotion; and each includes a cognition and belief. For example, in the case of the admiring contemplation of a beautiful object we are able to distinguish the mere cognition of the object from the appreciation of it, where by 'appreciation' is meant "an appropriate emotion towards the beautiful qualities which [the person] cognises" (p. 190). And there is, besides, the belief in the beauty of the object that stands apart, in analysis, both from the cognition of the object and the feeling of an appropriate emotion. In the best of cases, moreover, that belief is true: the object for which one feels appreciation *is* beautiful. In general, then, the admiring contemplation of a beautiful object includes (*a*) a person's cognition of the object, (*b*) that person's belief in the object's beauty, (*c*) the feeling of an appropriate emotion toward that object's beauty, (*d*) the truth of that person's belief in the beauty of the object, and so (*e*) the existence of an object that *is* beautiful both in the way in which it is believed to be beautiful and in the manner in which it is appreciated. It is this whole state of affairs, including both the state of mind of the person who appreciates the object and the object itself, that, so to speak, exudes intrinsic value. For Moore this is one of the best things we know or can imagine.

Some things are even better. If the beautiful object is itself capable of cognition, belief, and the like (that is, if the beautiful object is itself another person); if this person *in turn* also cognizes, appreciates, and believes truly in the beauty of the first person (if, that is, there is a mutual appreciation that holds between two beautiful persons); and if, finally, this mutual appreciation of their beauty is also accompanied by personal warmth, affection, or love, *then* we have a highly complex organic unity that is, for Moore, even better than one that is comprised of the (mere) admiring contemplation of a beautiful object. An *even better* whole would be comprised of the admiring contemplation of the beauty of the whole just described—"the contemplation of such contemplation" (p. 204). One can readily see how the recognition of one specimen of intrinsic value could father a family of ever-increasingly complex and more valuable relations. Perhaps it is the love of all that is good, including the love of love itself, that Moore would accept as the logical limit of what can be valued for its own sake. Those who read *Principia* and miss its "mysticism" read its surfaces and miss its depths.

No less important for Moore than a partial listing of those things that are good in themselves are his reminders that these complex organic unities can contain parts of no or little value in themselves and that the value of these wholes is not fixed by adding the value of the parts. In earlier discussions in *Principia* where he challenges Sidgwick's hedonism,

Moore maintains that the mere existence of beauty, apart from anyone's awareness of it, is good in itself. But the intrinsic value of such beauty is not very great in Moore's view, which leads him to concede that "Prof. Sidgwick was so far right . . . that such mere existence of what is beautiful has value, so small as to be negligible, in comparison with that which attaches to the *consciousness* of beauty" (p. 189). And yet this difference in the value of this whole is not to be located merely in the intrinsic value of consciousness. So far as consciousness itself is concerned, Moore believes that it, too, has a value that is negligible.

What is true of the mere existence of beauty or the mere existence of consciousness is true of all the other separate parts that go to comprise the highly complex intrinsic goods we know or can imagine. Not only is this true of the great unmixed goods (the admiring contemplation of a beautiful object and the pleasures of human intercourse, goods that contain nothing evil or ugly as one of their parts); it is also true of those things that, though intrinsically good, do contain such elements. Goods of this latter type Moore calls "mixed goods," a class that includes deserved retributive punishment. For though this whole includes at least two evils —namely, the wickedness of the criminal and the pain of the punishment —the whole comprised of them, when the punishment fits the crime and is deserved, is intrinsically good on the whole.

As for the greatest evils we know or can imagine, they are in some respects the opposite of the greatest goods. The enjoyment or admiring contemplation of things that are themselves either ugly or evil are great evils, as is the hatred of what is beautiful or good. A third great evil is pain, or suffering, which is far worse in itself in Moore's view than its opposite, pleasure, is good in itself.

Gone, then, is the methodological simplicity of Sidgwick's hedonism. Whereas Sidgwick could attempt a systematic synthesis of all of morality by recognizing only one intrinsic value, pleasure, Moore is cast adrift in a sea of value pluralism. There are many different sorts of things that are good in themselves, some of which are unmixed goods, others of which are mixed. And there are many different things that are intrinsically evil. A world in which this was not true would be a simpler one in which to do what is right. In such a world as Sidgwick's, where pleasure is the only good, it is pleasure and pleasure alone whose existence we should concern ourselves with, when we deliberate about what we ought to do. And though even then it would be no simple matter to know what is right, this would be vastly simpler in Sidgwick's moral universe than in Moore's.

But truth is not necessarily allied with simplicity, and "to search for 'unity' and 'system,' at the expense of truth," Moore insists, "is not, I take it, the proper business of philosophy, however universally it may have been the practice of philosophers" (p. 222).

Moral Therapy

Keynes, Leonard Woolf, and others who have tried their hand at recounting *Principia*'s influence are unable to do full justice to that book's power. Nowhere perhaps is this more obvious than in their several attempts to convey the restrained passion of its final chapter. Recall Keynes's celebration of it:

> The New Testament is a handbook for politicians compared with Moore's chapter on 'The Ideal'. I know no equal to it in literature since Plato. And it is better than Plato because it is quite free from *fancy*. It conveys the beauty of the literalness of Moore's mind, *un*fanciful and *un*dressed-up. Moore had a nightmare once in which he could not distinguish propositions from tables. But even when he was awake, he could not distinguish love and beauty and truth from the furniture. They took on the same definition of outline, the same stable, solid, objective qualities and common-sense reality. (p. 94)

Some of these features of "The Ideal" can be suggested by a summary of its major themes. But no summary can do justice to the passionate concentration one encounters there. Moore's beliefs burn through the pages. He clearly thinks he has come upon truths that are the most important in the world.

And yet, for all that, Moore is less inclined to maintain that he is right in the conclusions he reaches than he is to insist that he has gone about things in the right way. "[I] am content," he writes, "that the results of this chapter should be taken rather as illustrating the method which must be used in answering the fundamental question of Ethics, and the principles which must be observed, than as giving the correct answer to that question" (p. 223). And what an illustration he offers! By way of example, consider the following passage, where Moore inquires into the value of a particular kind of complex whole:

> The question I am putting is this: Whether the *whole* constituted by the fact that there is an emotional contemplation of a beautiful ob-

ject, which both is believed to be and is *real*, does not derive some of its value from the fact that the object *is* real? I am asking whether the value of this whole, *as a whole*, is not greater than that of those which differ from it, *either* by the absence of belief, with or without truth, *or*, belief being present, by the mere absence of truth? I am not asking *either* whether it is not superior to them as a means (which it certainly is), *nor* whether it may not contain a more valuable *part*, namely, the existence of the object in question. My question is solely whether the existence of its object does not constitute an addition to the value of the whole, quite distinct from the addition constituted by the fact that this whole does contain a valuable part. (p. 197)

In some ways Moore's answer, whatever it might be, must come as an anticlimax. One is inclined to think that the power lies in getting the question right, not in getting the right answer. When Moore announces that the use of his method helps guard against error, who could doubt him after seeing him use it so impressively himself?

And so it is that Keynes and his contemporaries at Cambridge, uplifted by *Principia*'s teachings, could take seriously such questions as whether the fact that A loves B "because A's spectacles are not strong enough to see B's complexion" alters the value of the organic whole of which the love of A for B forms a part. Because the value of such wholes likely will vary with the presence of true belief, A's false belief about B's looks does not bode well as a contribution to the value of that whole, all considered. One can imagine the dialectical heights to which bright young men like Keynes and Strachey could soar, given the indefinite complexity of the wholes into whose intrinsic value they were at liberty to inquire. But not carelessly. Everywhere there was an insistence on clarity. On precision. On saying exactly what one means and not answering a question until every ounce of ambiguity and vagueness had been wrung out of it. Moore's "famous poser" was in the air. McTaggart would have been pleased. But not Lawrence.

This diet of questions about questions is not offered by Moore as an end in itself. It has direct and profound implications on how we ought to live. Except in a very few cases what we ought to do, he believes, is what will bring about the best consequences in the immediate present or the near future, for ourselves and for those for whom we care. Not to have clear thoughts about what is good is not to know what we morally ought to do. It is a dangerous ignorance, one that affords would-be scientific moralists the opening they need to weigh the individual down with their heavy lists of duties and virtues. To play the sort of parlor axiology Keynes describes and Moore's position encourages opens the mind to new possibilities, frees it from dumb habit. It is a form of moral therapy in which any number can take part. If those who participated sometimes did so for the fun of it, they could not have long forgotten its serious point. The thought of Moore's distress, if he were to discover them being silly or playing at being shrewd, would not allow disingenuousness for very long.

A Formal Adequacy

Principia marks the first time Moore satisfies the complete set of criteria of adequacy used throughout the present work to interpret his development as a moral philosopher. The universality criterion ("Once good, always good"), met as early as the First Dissertation, is met again in *Principia*. The deeper metaphysical foundations of this universality remain opaque. In no small measure this is because the relationship between the concept or notion Good and the other properties of good things (their so-called natural properties) remains obscure. That relationship is not causal. But neither is it logical. Moore had wrestled (unsuccessfully) with the problem of explaining the relationship between the noumenal and the phenomenal world in both his dissertations. The problem of explaining the relationship between Good and a thing's natural properties is a lingering shadow of that darker metaphysical mystery. He will approach it directly in a later paper, "The Conception of Intrinsic Value," and again in his "Reply" to his critics. But an adequate solution always will elude him. What he knew (or what he thought he knew) is that things that are once intrinsically good are always so. What he did not know (and never thought he did) is how to explain this.

The objectivity criterion also is satisfied. Those things that are intrinsically good possess their value in themselves, independently of whether we happen to notice this and of how we feel about them. Moore's tendencies toward realism are in full flower in *Principia*. We are directly aware of things themselves, not our ideas of them, both in perception and in thought. What we perceive is the red flower, not our own sensations or perceptions of a rose, and what we are aware of when we reflect on the intrinsic value of the pleasures of friendship is the value of that complex whole, not our own idea or impression of its value. How we can be mistaken in our perceptual or value judgments is a problem Moore insufficiently considers in *Principia*. But that it is a problem for him at all is in part a consequence of his steadfast insistence that those things that are good, just as those flowers that are red, themselves have certain properties apart from our knowing or caring.

Success likewise characterizes the application of the natural goods criterion. Unlike the First Dissertation, with its happy message that this is the best of all possible worlds (evil having been proven to be unreal) *Principia*'s teachings are not zealously optimistic. No enthusiastic claims are made about how much good exists, only that we know that some does. And unlike the Second Dissertation, which seemed to rest on principles that made the existence of natural goods impossible, *Principia*'s principles, despite the opacity of the relationship between natural and nonnatural properties, at least do not negate their possible existence. Once having granted this, moreover, that work seems to contain nothing which entails that all good things must be equally good. When Moore judges that some things are better than others, there is no reason to think that he must be mistaken.

Principia also satisfies the ideal criterion. Because Moore does not claim that this is the best of all possible worlds he is at liberty to conceive of ways in which it can be improved. Some things that do exist are not as good as some things that might. Indeed, the entire justification of morality, understood as a system of rules of duty to which everyone ought to conform, is that it makes a stable society possible; and the rational justification for calling for a stable society is that this makes it possible for more intrinsic good to come into the world, especially in the form of friendships and the creation and appreciation of beauty. This world could be better than it is, and it would be better if there were more and deeper friendships, more and deeper appreciation of beautiful objects. Moore is not Pangloss. But neither is he Schopenhauer.

In these respects *Principia* demonstrates Moore's steady progress as a moral philosopher. When assessed in terms of the criteria *Principia* satisfies, both dissertations are seen to contain major flaws, and *Principia*'s successes in these respects only serve to highlight the earlier failures. But these same successes characterize "The Elements." And yet this set of lectures, even granting their status as a sort of proto-*Principia*, are vastly inferior to *Principia* itself. How then shall we account for the latter's clear supremacy?

The answer lies in the application of the two remaining criteria: the conduct and the method criteria. In "The Elements" Moore makes a number of declarations about what is right and wrong, and why, something he had not done in either of his dissertations. But he offers no serious or well-developed theory of right conduct in those lectures. There is nothing remotely comparable to *Principia*'s fifth chapter—no sustained, careful critique of those would-be scientific moralists who get pummeled by Moore in that chapter, for example. Moore came late to an interest in Ethics in relation to conduct, so convinced had he been that Ethics must be "pure theory." When he finally does turn his attention to conduct, his system nears completion. With *Principia* he enters the mainstream of Western moral philosophy.

Far and away the most serious problem facing Moore concerned how to answer questions about intrinsic value. Is there a rational method for answering the fundamental question of Ethics: What things are good in themselves? Nothing in "The Elements" is weaker than Moore's lame answer to that question, the answer that certain beliefs about what things are good in themselves are "guaranteed by evolution." Whatever we may or should say about the merits of *Principia*'s method of isolation, a plausible case can be made for the claim that it satisfies the formal requirement imposed by the method criterion. Here, at last, Moore offers a method for answering the fundamental question of Ethics. With this method in hand he is in a position to show how to use it. Certainly a part of *Principia*'s enduring greatness results from the skill and drama with which he does so.

Rational Faith

But *Principia* is more than the scene of Moore's fulfillment of a set of abstract criteria. It is his sustained answer to a set of questions, some philosophical, some personal, that had demanded his attention at least since his initial presentation of "Vanity of vanities" on April 24, 1899— and, judging from his letters, especially those to MacCarthy, even before then. Principal among these questions is the one Moore answers in *Principia*'s last chapter: What things are good in themselves? What things are worth having for their own sakes? In "Vanity of vanities" he answered that nothing is good in this sense and that we therefore "live for nothing." He gave these answers because he thought no reason could be given to support the values assumed either by common sense morality or by theism. That no reason can possibly be given in support of *any* judgment of intrinsic value, not just those presupposed by common sense morality and theism, is one of *Principia*'s most important teachings; it is a direct consequence of Good's status as simple and unique. No natural science can provide evidence for what is worth having for its own sake. And no metaphysical system can either. If, then, no reason can possibly be given for or against any judgment of this kind, the deeply troubling personal problem Moore faced—how to recover his lost moral faith—seems to grow more difficult, not simpler.

The intoxicated vision of the Happy Warrior offered one means of escape. The mystical Warrior sees all that is good and all that is evil—sees at a glance, one might say, The Ideal as this is formally presented in "The Elements." All in the blink of an eye. Because his knowledge is direct and noninferential, it is not impossible that he should know what is good given Moore's view that Good is simple and unique. The allure of the mystical Warrior was real enough, and Moore was sorely tempted. As a secular icon Wordsworth's celebrated hero combined for Moore the inspiring image of the individual's doing battle with the oppressive demands of conventional morality (he is a *Warrior*) and the optimistic message that the individual will emerge triumphant (he is *Happy*). But Moore was uncertain. When he expressed his doubts about the intrinsic value of the Happy Warrior's mental state he did so because he lacked rational confidence in the belief that Wordsworth's hero "sees" only what is true. In the end Moore is too much the rationalist to find cognitive absolution in the universal mystical wisdom of the noble warrior.

But if neither the work of reason as we find this in the natural sciences and metaphysics nor the all-embracing insights of the mind as we find this personified in the mystical triumph of the Happy Warrior is an adequate avenue to a renewal of his moral faith, where was Moore to turn? His solution, set forth in *Principia*, consists in his attempt to find a rational niche between the excessive mysticism of the Happy Warrior and the fallacious reasoning that in his view characterizes every naturalistic and metaphysical ethical system. These latter systems offer reasons for what is good in itself. But because no reasons can be offered they stand condemned. The mystical Warrior, because he offers no reasons for his judgments of intrinsic value, avoids this condemnation. But because he allows no rational check against his claims to knowledge it is not rational to accept them. The rational niche Moore thinks he finds between these two discredited approaches is his method of isolation. Unlike the fallacious reasoning that characterizes naturalistic and metaphysical ethical systems, this method does not purport to offer any evidence to support judgments of intrinsic value. It does not legitimize inferences of the form "This is pleasant therefore it is good" or "This is willed by the noumenal self therefore it is worth having for its own sake." What this method does offer, when joined with a precise understanding of the question one is asking, is a rational means of minimizing the chances that one is mistaken. We are more likely to be correct in our judgments of intrinsic value if we have a precise understanding both of the question we are asking and of the kind of value into whose existence we are inquiring. But that we do employ this method is itself *no evidence* that the judgments we make when doing so are true. In this way Moore's method of isolation avoids committing the kind of fallacy that in his view all naturalistic and metaphysical ethical systems, save Sidgwick's, commit.

This method also avoids the dangers endemic to a rationally unrestrained mysticism of the sort we find personified in the Happy Warrior. Ours is not to reason why the Warrior says what he says about what is good. He simply "sees" it—all of it—at a glance. But so do those "religious enthusiasts" whom Moore cannot suppose to have a corner on the truth. Without any rational check on the deliverances of the mystically intoxicated we cannot have any reason to accept the deliverances of some in preference to those of others. Moore's method of isolation is his attempt to mediate rationally between such conflicting judgments. If those people who announce their visions of value are confused about Good, muddled about the precise question they are asking, liable to mistake the causes or effects of something for what is intrinsic to it, or are in other ways the victim of careless thinking, then we have no reason to suppose that they know what they are talking about. And, so, no reason to assume that what they say is true. Those persons, on the other hand, who are not confused or muddled in these ways, and who have done all that rational beings can possibly do to prepare themselves for answering the questions of intrinsic value, are less likely to be in error. Appeal to the appropriate method is the rational check on such judgments, the test of reason every mystical pronouncement must satisfy. It does not follow that the judgments of those who are rational in the required ways are true. They may be false. What is true is that these people have done the best anyone can possibly do to make the best judgment about what is best. And no one can or should be required to do more than this. Or less. Those who meet the demands of reason by employing the method of isolation may see only the nuts and ball bearings of the universe of value—may see it only piece by piece rather than in its entirety, after the fashion of a more enthusiastic mysticism. But they are more likely to see things as they are, not as they imagine them to be.

Thus does Moore satisfy his earlier demand that *reasons* be given when it comes to questions of ultimate values. But the logical role of the reasons he offers in *Principia* differs from the one depicted in "Vanity of vanities." If by 'reasons' one means 'evidence,' which is what Moore seems to have meant in that earlier paper, then *Principia*'s counsel is stern: No reason can possibly be given in support of any judgment of intrinsic value. But if by 'reasons' one means "ways to minimize the possibility of error," then reasons can be offered. And Moore has offered them. A place for reason has been found. *After* one has done all that a rational person can do to prepare oneself for answering a question of intrinsic value, then one either "sees" or one does not "see" that the whole in question is good. And how good it is. A place for "mysticism" remains. Moore's bold adventure lies in his attempt to marry the apparently irreconcilable claims of reason, on the one hand, and mysticism, on the other.

The emphasis placed here on Moore's tendencies toward mysticism (or "intuition") should not obscure the ways in which *Principia* is of a piece with the history of his concern with a number of more technical problems in Ethics. The nonnatural (or Transcendental) character of Good, for example, initially proclaimed in his First Dissertation, continues to make its presence felt, serving to ground both the possibility of a Science of Morals and the synthetic a priori status of judgments of intrinsic value. Perhaps these ideas, which remain a stumbling block for many, were less a hurdle for Moore because he was so much in the grip of a confident realism, both in his theory of our perception of the natural properties of things and in his theory of the mind's apprehension of their nonnatural properties. Realism in either quarter encounters enormously difficult theoretical problems. In the future Moore will attend to some of them, especially in the case of sense perception. Whatever his record of success, if we grant him those tendencies toward realism bubbling up between the lines of *Principia* we are able to view the positions he develops in this work as his answers to questions that had overwhelmed him during an earlier period of his life. What Moore sought was a rational faith. And that is what in *Principia* he thinks he finds.

Moore's "Religion"

The renewal of that faith marks the vindication of values Moore himself associated with the theistic ethic of his youth. Those values, we know from "The Value of Religion," are principally two: first, the comfort we take in the knowledge that someone cares for us and, second, the valuable emotional element involved in the contemplation of what we think is "most truly and perfectly good." In that earlier paper Moore had announced that there were "plenty" of really existing "good objects," including presumably many specimens of the two just mentioned. That confidence could not long endure. Before *Principia* was published the most Moore had offered by way of an answer to his demand for reasons for thinking that some things are good in themselves was the infamous appeal in "The Elements" to the "guarantee" provided by "evolution." With the publication of *Principia*, its method of isolation, and the larger backdrop of its insistence on precision, those comfortable values of his youth are on more stable ground. We are not surprised that when, in *Principia*'s final chapter, Moore turns to the extra-scientific task of saying what things he himself thinks are pre-eminently good in themselves, the goods he cites are near relatives of the two he associates with religion. By turning his mind to what is beautiful in art and nature, the infidel can have his full share of the valuable emotion the theist takes in his devotions. And the infidel can also take comfort in the knowledge that he has friends who care for him, however mortal he and they might be. The moral faith Moore bequeathed to his disciples thus is (to use Keynes's word) a "religion" not only in the sense that it shares in Moore's view certain crucial logical properties with belief in God (neither one's moral nor one's religious faith can have any evidence offered on its behalf; both are logically independent of any matter of fact); it is also a "religion" in the sense that both religious and moral faith share a common fund of values (both include the presence of someone who cares and also the caring for something beyond one's self). That the identities of the one who cares and of the something to care about differ (in both cases it is God for the theist while for the infidel it is a friend in the former case and beauty in the latter) is less important than that the two kinds of faith have the same kind of ultimate values in common. Moore offers a faith that can satisfy the natural human longing for a worthy object of belief. And he does so without having to follow either Sidgwick or Kant in postulating a perfect Deity.

A person's moral faith, for Moore, is more than the affirmation of propositions about what things are good in themselves. In "Vanity of vanities" the quest for reasons to support judgments of intrinsic value was treated as inseparable from questions about human happiness. A happy person is one who "whenever the question arises, whether things that we have or can get are worth having . . . [answers] . . . that they are." A person is unhappy to the extent that he is unable to answer affirmatively. With his rational faith in the value of things he has or can get restored, Moore achieves the happiness that had eluded him despite his "very pleasant life." Now in possession of his method of isolation, Moore may be understood as a man who thinks he has found the best—indeed, the only—method for judging what is best. A place for reason *has* been found. In so doing he has fought his way to happiness without sacrificing his commitment to reason. He is a man who is happy *and* who has a right to be. In his own way the Moore we find in *Principia* is the true Happy Warrior.

A Fair Measure

No student of Bloomsbury denies that Moore influenced those who comprised that group. Many question why and how he did, and opinion is divided over how salutary his influence was. F. R. Leavis and his wife, Q. D. Leavis, are among Bloomsbury's severest critics. The latter nurtured a special fondness for heaping critical abuse on Virginia Woolf. S. P. Rosenbaum characterizes Q. D. Leavis's review of *Three Guineas* as "a ferocious attack" on Virginia, one filled with personal bile (Virginia is ridiculed for being childless, for example). F. R. Leavis's is hardly less contemptuous of Bloomsbury's personalities and values. He resolutely aligns himself on the side of Lawrence, with his "working class culture," and against the "swarming selves" who comprised "the Cambridge-Bloomsbury coterie." When Keynes in his memoir looks back nostalgically to the Cambridge of his youth, dominated by the values of Moore's "religion," Leavis is all but speechless. "Still in 1938," F. R. Leavis writes,

> [Keynes] takes [these values] seriously; he sees them, not as illustrating a familiar undergraduate phase which in any case should be left behind as soon as possible, and which the most intelligent men should escape, but as serious and admirable—even, it would seem, when cultivated well beyond undergraduate years. And that is what seems to be most significant about [Keynes's] Memoir, and most revelatory of the Cambridge-Bloomsbury ethos. (p. 391)

Once a Moorite, always a Moorite. That is Keynes's message. And that is the message Leavis, in company with Lawrence, most despises. In his

1914 visit to Cambridge "what Lawrence heard," Leavis contends, "was the levity of so many petty egos, each primed with conscious cleverness and hardened in self-approval" (p. 394). He had encountered the same lamentable shallowness in Duncan Grant and his friends: "They talk endlessly, but endlessly—and never, never a good thing said. They are cased each in a little hard shell of his own and out of this they talk words. There is never for one second any outgoing of feeling and no reverence, not a crumb or grain of reverence: I cannot stand it." Neither can Leavis.

Both cannot be quite right. In view of what we know about the Cambridge of Keynes and the Bloomsbury of Strachey, Leonard Woolf, and the others, it cannot be quite right to say that "there is never for one second any outgoing of feeling." Lawrence (and Leavis) may not have cared for these people, but Keynes and Strachey, for example, certainly cared for one another. That Keynes and, by implication, others of his ilk did not care for Lawrence—with his "ignorant, jealous, irritable, hostile eyes" (p. 103)—may well be true. *He* may not have received "any outgoing of feeling." But that was not true of the relations among the members of the "Cambridge-Bloomsbury coterie" themselves.

Reverence, on the other hand, they did lack. Lawrence was right about that, and so was Wittgenstein. "We lacked reverence," Keynes writes, "as Lawrence observed and as Ludwig with justice also used to say—for everything and everyone" (p. 99). What remained for them to revere? Certainly neither the barren God nor the oppressive morality of their Victorian predecessors. The Cambridge Moorites saw themselves as having made a clean break from the past and as being in fundamental ways divorced from the present. The roots of this separation from the larger reality of their time and place Leavis fixes in the Cambridge of Keynes and Strachey, the Apostolic milieu Beatrice Webb laments in a September 19, 1911 letter to Lady Courtney:

> I am sorry now that Bertie [that is, Bertrand Russell] went to Cambridge—there is a pernicious set presided over by Lowes Dickinson, which makes a sort of ideal of anarchic ways in sexual questions— we have, for a long time, been aware of its bad influence. . . . The intellectual star is the metaphysical George Moore with his *Principia Ethica*—a book they all talk of as "The Truth"! I never can see anything in it, except a metaphysical justification for doing what you like and what other people disapprove of!

Russell, too, comments on what (in his view) Moore's views came to when distorted by the likes of Keynes and Strachey:

> The tone of the generation ten years junior to my own was set mainly by Lytton Strachey and Keynes. It is surprising how great a change in mental climate those ten years had brought. We were still Victorians; they were Edwardians. We believed in ordered progress by means of politics and free discussion. The more self confident among us may have hoped to be leaders of the multitude, but none of us wished to be divorced from it. The generation of Keynes and Lytton did not seek to preserve any kinship with the Philistine. They aimed rather at a life of retirement among fine shades and nice feelings, and conceived of the good as consisting in the passionate mutual admiration of a clique of the elite. This doctrine, quite unfairly, they fathered upon G. E. Moore, whose disciples they professed to be.

Russell, like both Lawrence and Leavis, cannot be quite right in what he says. The creation and appreciation of beauty, of fundamental importance to Moore and his followers, is noteworthy for its absence in Russell's catalogue of Apostolic values, and the industry that characterizes the lives of Keynes and Strachey, for example, hardly seems conducive to "a life of retirement." But there was an elitist tendency that grew out of the Cambridge of Keynes and Strachey and into the reality known as Bloomsbury. And something of the values that took root there is hinted at by Russell's description. Strachey, Keynes, and the others worked not only to create beauty, know truth, and cultivate friendships. They also aspired to enjoy and contemplate the fruits of their labor. Together. In these respects they not only professed to be, they were disciples of Moore.

That discipleship was expressed in other terms Russell and Beatrice Webb found less than uplifting. Sexual relations between the two sexes certainly are better as a means of propagating the species than homosexual alliances. But intrinsic values have an independent logic of their own; they are to be assessed apart from the past and the future. And when they are, both Strachey and Keynes had little difficulty in discovering that Moore's method, rigorously applied, yields a decisive vindication of the higher sodomy. Paul Levy remarks on the enthusiasm of Strachey in particular, "trumpeting his view of good states of mind all around Cambridge" (p. 238). No one within earshot could doubt that Strachey found in *Principia* the philosophical justification of his well-known homosexuality. That the Beatrice Webbs of the world would not be converted by the force of Moore's logic, he never doubted. "It's madness of us to dream," he writes to Keynes in April 1906, "of making dowagers understand that feelings are good, when we say in the same breath that the best ones are sodomitical."

What dowagers did not understand, Moore did. He could not have been ignorant of the truths Strachey, Keynes, and others found as a result of their finest application of his method. Yet nowhere in Moore's surviving correspondence or in his diaries is there a hint that he disapproved or that he ever sought to correct the vindication of homosexuality others gained from his work. And the same is true concerning the absence of any challenge to Keynes's memoir. Levy must surely be right in suggesting that "the explanation of Moore's silence [soon after *Principia*'s publication]— and much later, when he read Keynes's 'My Early Beliefs'—is that he did not then object to this use being made of his work, and had no very strong inclination to discourage it" (p. 238). That this is likely to be true is far more certain than why it is.

One possible explanation is that Moore himself had found the same truths as Strachey and Keynes. Whatever in the end we should make of his relationship with A. R. Ainsworth, the fact remains that not long after *Principia*'s publication Moore did move to Edinburgh to live with him, an arrangement that was to last for almost four years, when for different reasons both men moved to different parts of London. Moreover, we also know from Moore's own record of their pre-Edinburgh relationship that he had a special fondness for Ainsworth. By way of example, we find the following diary entries for 1899–1900. "Ainsworth. Elected Michaelmas Term. Comes to see me, when I am in bed with influenza at beginning of Lent Term. Walk to Ely with Crompton, Dakyns and him in May Term: hold his hand." For 1900–1901: "Lent Term. Speak out to Ainsworth." For 1903: "Come up January 3 to meet A.: he stays two nights: very affectionate: important Sunday night." Russell for his part fixes the point of Moore's (in Russell's view) personal degeneration at the time of his serious involvement with Ainsworth. In her *Diary* Virginia Woolf records Russell's remarks to her on February 23, 1924.

> "When he first came up to Cambridge, . . . Moore was the most wonderful creature in the whole world. His smile was the most beautiful thing I have ever seen. We believed in Berkeley" (perhaps). "Suddenly, something went wrong with him; something happened

to him and his work. *Principia Ethica* was nothing like so good as his Essay on Judgment. He was very fond of Ainsworth. I don't know what happened—it ruined him. He took to putting out his tongue after that. You" [that is, Virginia] "said he had no complexes. But he's full of them. Watch him putting his tongue round his mouth" (pp. 293–294).

Despite this evidence (including letters from Ainsworth which speak of his desire "to reach three hundred miles and kiss you [Moore]," for example), all of which is of course circumstantial, Levy is confident that Moore and Ainsworth in time discovered that they were just very good friends and that the full extent of their physical relationship was exhausted on that one occasion when the two held hands. This may be true. But it is conjectural at best. What is not conjectural is that Moore had a particularly close relationship with Ainsworth, one that, whether or not it included acts of physical intimacy beyond the holding of hands, at least must have awakened in Moore the realization that it was possible for two men to love one another in more than a Platonic fashion. This would help explain why he never objected, so far as we know, to the very public conclusions Strachey reached as a result of his strenuous application of Moore's method. And if others urge that it surely is impossible that Moore himself might ever have been anything more than Ainsworth's very good friend since the latter after all did go on to marry Moore's sister (a desperately unhappy marriage, as it happened, one that ended in divorce) it would not be irrelevant to remind them of Moore's position. If in Bloomsbury all the couples were triangles, it cannot be impossible that Bloomsbury's prophet found himself a part of one.

Whatever the truth may be about Moore's relationship with Ainsworth, the public use made of his teachings by Strachey in particular more than vindicated the worries expressed by some of *Principia*'s early reviewers. Found to be "of immoral tendency" by one (*Oxford Magazine*, February 10, 1904), that work was judged to be positively dangerous by another (*Notes on British Theology and Philosophy*, April, 1904). Moore's views, this reviewer urges, "give an irrational cast to ethics which is hardly to be commended. . . . If Mr. Moore's [views] . . . were ever to have the slightest chance of currency, ethics would be in danger of becoming a science of the visionary, imaginary, and unreal." And, it should be added, of the iconoclast. And who could challenge the judgment of another? Who could offer any reason against the judgments of Lytton Strachey on behalf of the higher sodomy? Moore's teachings abolished the giving of direct reasons, of evidence, for or against any and every judgment of intrinsic value. There was only the method of isolation on which to rely, and that was a method available to everyone, to the Lytton Stracheys of the world as much as, and no less than, to those who were experts in one or another science, whether natural or metaphysical. The judgments of the Stracheys of the world could no longer be dismissed because of who they were or what they said. Moore's teachings at least made this much certain.

That certainty was power in Strachey's hands. Along with Keynes, Strachey exerted a profound influence on his generation, among and beyond the Apostles. F. R. Leavis is unable to understand how so great a change in the *milieu* of Cambridge, personified in the person of Lytton Strachey, could have transpired so quickly. "Can we imagine," he asks, "Sidgwick or Leslie Stephen . . . being influenced by, or interested in, the equivalent of Lytton Strachey? By what steps, and by the operation of what causes, did so great a change come over Cambridge in so comparatively short a time?" (p. 395). Moore is assigned some credit for effecting the change. Moore was "in his very limited way, a disinterested mind and innocent spirit," and it was this combination of character traits, certainly not his practical ethics, that made him in Leavis's view "the more irresistibly the very sanction they [that is, the Moorites] needed" (p. 398). In these few words Leavis epitomizes the gross misconception of Moore so common among those who have sought to understand him and explain his influence. "A *disinterested* mind"? One has only to think of the passion that accompanies the assault on truth in *Principia*'s pages. "An *innocent* spirit"? One has only to recall the depths of despair Moore reaches in his quest for a rational faith, a way out from under the oppressive demands of morality, as portrayed by Matthew Arnold, and toward the courage and confidence to act according to the promptings of "his own wish." And all this "in his *very limited way*"? Can this possibly be true of the man who aspired to do nothing less than reform the Science of Morals with a view to reclaiming for the individual the freedom to judge and to choose? No, Leavis like so many others describes an imaginary Moore, not the Moore who was. The Moore who was is a Promethean figure. He stole fire from the gods. That is what, in their several ways, his disciples took from him. One may wish they had not. But the fact is, they did.

There is no simple answer to the question Leavis asks: "By what steps, and by the operation of what causes, did so great a change come over Cambridge in so comparatively short a time?" Perhaps there is no knowable answer at all. One thing at least we do know. We shall not approach the truth here so long as we remain captive to one or another mythological conception of Moore. The possibility remains that he had a far greater influence in effecting the change Leavis grieves. And that he was influential for far different reasons than Leavis and others suppose. A small installment on making the case for this possibility has been offered in these pages.

The More Beautiful

Moore was in Cambridge on the evening Keynes read "My Early Beliefs." Wittgenstein had by then returned and in 1939 would assume the post made available by Moore's retirement. Ahead lay the second world war, Moore's American sojourn, and his wobble regarding the nature of Good. Later, in 1951, he would receive the Order of Merit, the highest civilian honor given to a British citizen. During his conversation with the King, Moore mentioned Wittgenstein. He was astonished to learn that the King had never heard of him. The two cultures that separated Vanessa Bell from Asquith evidently remained intact.

That Moore was at home in Cambridge when Keynes presented his paper was hardly unusual. Throughout his life he kept his distance from Bloomsbury. The close friend of some members (MacCarthy in particular) it was not his custom or style to be around them when they were many. He never attended one of Bloomsbury's Thursday evening "at-homes," for example, nor any meeting of the Memoir Club, and he would not have functioned well if he had. Leonard Woolf, who came as close to idolizing Moore as anyone, found that

> Moore was never easy to talk to. . . . It was extremely difficult to live up to his extraordinary simplicity and integrity, which were combined with great intellectual power. Talking with him one lived under the shadow of the eternal, though silent, question: "What exactly do you mean by that?" It is a menacing question, particularly when you know that muddle and not knowing "exactly what you mean by *that*" will cause Moore almost physical pain which he will show involuntarily in his eyes. (p. 41)

As early as 1905 Keynes writes to Leonard that "He [Moore] is too remote for ease or intimacy" (p. 138). "I seem to know him by description only," he writes to Strachey (January 25, 1906), "and he lives with Socrates [and] Shakespeare" (p. 138). Even MacCarthy, as loquacious and confident a man as Moore ever met, in his full maturity prevailed upon Moore not to attend a lecture he was scheduled to deliver because the mere fact of Moore's presence would have been too intimidating: MacCarthy would not have been able to speak. No, Moore would not have been a comfortable addition to the gatherings in Bloomsbury. His increasing tendency toward reticence coupled with his power to stop the speech of others in the throat would have combined to make Bloomsbury's sometimes celebrated icy silences only longer and more severe. Moore knew his place, and kept it.

He also knew his virtues, and these did not consist in playing the guru to a mainly younger generation anxious to find the means to show their adulation. Another sort of man might easily have been corrupted, might easily have stopped growing in his own way, according to his own tastes and vision, and rested content with where and who he was. Or with where and who his disciples told him he was. The final measure of the man and his commitment to his philosophy is how he lived and what he lived for. Industry, temperance, prudence: these virtues Moore worked at perfecting in his own life, as he had enjoined others to do in theirs. Perhaps he never *really* worked as hard as he should have. Perhaps he was *better* at prudence and temperance than he was at industry. It is true that his published corpus is not large and that he never wrote another book even half as large as *Principia*. But Moore was not as lacking in industry as he would have us believe. In addition to his published writings and his classes, on which he worked very hard indeed, he also gave decades of service to the journal *Mind* as its editor. In this capacity he contributed an immense amount of time and energy that never were reflected in his own output but which did find tangible if indirect expression in the high quality of that journal during his tenure as its editor.

But there were other virtues Moore cultivated. In *Principia* he writes approvingly of rich diversity among people, each with his or her own special talents. Against those "moralists [who] commonly assume that, in the matter of actions or habits of actions, usually recognized as duties or virtues, it is desirable that everyone should be alike," he claims that "it is certain that . . . the principles of the division of labour, according to special capacity, which is recognized in respect of employment, would also give a better result in respect of virtues" (pp. 165–166). Moore had certain "special capacities" that he developed. He became an object-lesson in how to live by *Principia*'s principles in ways that went well beyond the unwavering insistence on clarity and precision. *Principia*, which liberated so many, also liberated him. For he was not by temperament a leader of men (which does not entail that he therefore was a follower). His special capacities were those of the surgeon, not the trail blazer. His mind was a scalpel, not a machete. Having himself made the case for the moral propriety of the individual's developing "special capacities," he was free to do so himself. Those capacities are the ones Moore worked diligently at developing both before and after the publication of *Principia*, the ones we find, for example, in those *sui generis* essays he writes for the next forty years or so. They are no less works of art for the weight of their rigor and analysis. Moore gave to the literature of philosophy a voice as unmistakably his own as Virginia Woolf gave to the novel. A few sentences are enough for the knowledgeable reader to recognize that Moore is being read. The perfection of a style is no less hard in philosophy than elsewhere. Perhaps more so.

The perfection of that style was mastered more beyond Ethics than within that Science. Except for a few essays of a mostly technical nature after the publication of *Ethics* in 1912, the never completed Preface to the second edition of *Principia*, and the relevant portions of his "Reply" to his critics in 1942, Moore made no further direct contribution to moral philosophy during his lifetime. The task of writing philosophy always was painful to him. Not only was he always tempted to do something else, he became increasingly dissatisfied with what he produced. Keynes captures Moore's tortured encounter with his sense of philosophy's demands in a letter to Strachey, quoted by Skidelsky, dated March 16, 1906. "Only a passionate sense of duty," Keynes writes, "could persuade him [Moore] to produce [his paper on 'Objects of Perception']. When one reads some philosophy, the pleasure of the writer is obvious. But this is not like that. It is wrung out, squeezed with pain and contortion through a constipated rectum" (pp. 137–138). Strachey offers his own variation on the theme of cerebral constipation in a January 2, 1908 letter to Moore. "How shocking that you should still be so constipated! Why isn't there a purgative," he asks, "for the mind? But you know you really do take too dark a view of your achievements! Only consider the rest of mankind, and especially the rest of philosophers." The achievements of "the rest of philosophers" were no consolation for Moore. MacCarthy had solicited an essay on Hume from him for inclusion in the *New Quarterly*. Along with his essay Moore sends a letter (dated March 29, 1909) in which he castigates his "miserable performance": "It's not easy to understand; it's childish; it's awkward; and all the points are very badly made. I should be ashamed to think of anybody reading it as mine." He would be happy, he tells Desmond, if MacCarthy was able "to find something else."

Moore's inability at this time to take any satisfaction in his philosophy was even more intense in the particular case of his work in Ethics. Leonard Woolf recreates a week in Dartmoor spent with Moore and Strachey during the summer of 1911. ("Constipation" seems to be the favored metaphor of the day as we see in this passage from *Beginning Again*.)

> In the morning Lytton used to sit in one part of the garden, with a panama hat on his head, groaning from time to time over his literary constipation as he wrote *Landmarks in French Literature* for the Home University Library; in another part of the garden sat Moore, a panama hat on his head, his forehead wet with perspiration, sighing from time to time over his literary constipation as he wrote *Ethics* for the Home University Library. Lytton used to complain that he was mentally constipated because nothing at all came into his mind, which remained as blank as the paper on his knees. Moore on the contrary said that his mental constipation came from the fact that as soon as he had written down a sentence, he saw either that it was just false or that it required a sentence to qualify it which would require another sentence to qualify the qualification. This, as we pointed out to him, would go on ad infinitum, and the 60,000 words which he had bound himself to write on ethics for the Home University Library would, after he had written a first sentence which was not 'just false', consist of an infinite series of qualifications to it only cut short by the fact that the publishers would not print more than 60,000 words. (pp. 41–42)

When in time *Ethics* was finished, we find many of *Principia*'s main themes in a new key. But there are notable exceptions, including the absence of any explicit reference to the "naturalistic fallacy" as well as any detailed exploration of the distinction between natural and nonnatural properties. There are important developments, however, especially concerning the definitions of Right, Obligation, and related notions. Whereas in *Principia* Moore had held that these notions were definable in relation to Good, he abandons this position in *Ethics*. What is right *is* what produces at least as much intrinsic good as any other alternative, but Right is not *definable* in these terms. The insistence on clarity, one of *Principia*'s hallmarks, is no less in evidence in *Ethics*, and the concluding paragraph of this latter book, where Moore offers the last of "two final remarks," is representative of its style and substance.

The other final remark is that we must be very careful to distinguish the two questions (1) whether, and in what degree, a thing is *intrinsically* good and bad, and (2) whether, and in what degree, it is capable of adding to or subtracting from the intrinsic value of a whole of which it forms a part, from a third, entirely different question, namely (3) whether, and in what degree, a thing is *useful* and has good *effects*, or *harmful* and has *bad* effects. All three questions are very liable to be confused, because, in common life, we apply the names 'good' and 'bad' to things of all three kinds indifferently: when we say that a thing is 'good' we may mean either (1) that it is intrinsically good or (2) that it adds to the value of many intrinsically good wholes or (3) that it is useful or has good effects; and similarly when we say that a thing is bad we may mean any one of the three corresponding things. And such confusion is very liable to lead to mistakes, of which the following are, I think, the commonest. In the first place, people are apt to assume with regard to things, which really are very good indeed in senses (1) or (2), that they are scarcely any good at all, simply because they do not seem to be of much *use*—that is to say, to lead to *further* good effects; and similarly, with regard to things which really are very bad in senses (1) or (2), it is very commonly assumed that there cannot be much, if any, harm in them, simply because they do not seem to lead to *further* bad results. Nothing is commoner than to find people asking of a good thing: What *use* is it? and concluding that, if it is no use, it cannot be any good; or asking of a bad thing: What harm does it do? and concluding that if it *does* no harm, there cannot be any harm *in* it. Or, again, by a converse mistake, of things which really are very useful, but are not good at all in sense (1) and (2), it is very commonly assumed that they *must* be good in one or both of these two senses. Or again, of things, which really are very good in senses (1) and (2), it is assumed that, because they are good, they cannot possibly do harm. Or finally, of things, which are neither intrinsically good nor useful, it is assumed that they cannot be any good at all, although in fact they are very good in sense (2). All these mistakes are liable to occur, because, in fact, the degree of goodness or badness of a thing in any one of these three senses is by no means always in proportion to the degree of its goodness or badness in either of the other two; but if we are careful to distinguish the three different questions, they can, I think, all be avoided.

The tenets of *Principia*'s Ideal remain. Only the passion of the author is missing.

"*The Author of* Principia Ethica"

Moore was acutely dissatisfied with *Ethics* not only while he worked on it but after he had finished that slender volume. "I'm afraid it is rather a failure," he writes to his sister Nellie after receiving the proofs on March 15, 1912. In an earlier letter (September 22, 1911), sent shortly after the manuscript had gone to the publisher, he conveys the same dismal estimation to his sister. "I am afraid it is a bad failure; but I haven't time to try to mend it now."

The reaction of the book's reviewers could not have lifted his spirits. Writing in *The Journal of Philosophy* (April 10, 1913), Walter B. Pitkin, while registering his cheerful agreement "with Mr. Moore's pluralistic objectivism," goes on to note that he "does not admire the mode of its presentation," particularly the way in which everything is "presented abstractly and illumined with no simple empirical illustrations." Harold P. Cook in his review in *Mind* (October 1913) is no less unhappy. The book, the second in the Home University Library series (Russell's classic *The Problems of Philosophy* was the first), is supposed to be for nonprofessionals. Mr. Cook voices his doubts about its chances of reaching them. "The uninstructed reader, . . . I think, will have a great difficulty in detecting the fundamental questions at issue and bearing them clearly in mind in virtue of so many, so subtle distinctions, so continuous a flow of dialectic."

Ethics, it is fair to say, all but fell stillborn from the press. Except for a handful of unenthusiastic reviews in learned journals of philosophy, the book attracted no notice in the world of ideas. And unlike the passionate, effusive letters Moore received from friends when *Principia* was published (recall Strachey's being "carried away"), the surviving correspondence includes not so much as a word of congratulation from any of his followers concerning *Ethics*. R. C. Trevelyan, a friend and fellow Apostle from Moore's student days at Cambridge, does write to Moore on September 14, 1912 to acknowledge receipt of a copy of the book Moore had sent. "I intend probably to read it on my voyage," he writes. But there is no further word to show that he did. The notice taken of *Ethics* is perhaps captured best by the editor of the *Cambridge Magazine*. In 1915, three years after *Ethics* was published, Moore's previously discussed "Suggestions for the Council of Trinity College" appeared in that magazine. Moore is identified as "the author of *Principia Ethica*." *Ethics* might never have been written as far as the editor was concerned. His blindness was representative of the age. *Ethics* was lost in *Principia*'s lingering shadows. And it would remain so.

Even in Bloomsbury, Moore's tortured progress on *Ethics* was well known to his followers before the week he spent at Dartmoor with Woolf and Strachey. In the Spring of 1911 Moore had arranged a reading party at Lulworth, in Dorset. MacCarthy and Strachey were included. The latter's *Landmarks in French Literature* was underway, and Moore already had embarked on *Ethics*. Together the two would endure the pain of their creative constipation. Their respective books in some measure would be the products of their shared ordeal. Yet Strachey seems not so much to have disliked Moore's *Ethics* as to have ignored it. In this as in so many other ways Strachey's response epitomized the response of Bloomsbury generally. Given Moore's own low opinion of that work, who among his followers would have dared to think otherwise?

But perhaps there is another explanation. We know that the neglect showered upon *Ethics* by the Bloomsberries did nothing to diminish the esteem in which they held its author. After his return to Cambridge in 1911 Moore once again had more frequent contacts with some of the group's members, usually on an individual basis, something the outbreak of the first world war intensified. Especially before the dawn of England's involvement, occasions for relaxation and fellowship remained, Moore beguiling anyone within earshot with his "enterprising style" at the piano and with the remarkably moving power of his voice. The neglect of *Ethics* did not alter the radius of his personal friendships or lessen their intensity. If his followers paid no attention to that book, perhaps this was because any praise of it might seem to detract from the importance of their "Bible" —*Principia*. Every religion knows its sacrilege.

The Final Irony

Despite his original dissatisfaction Moore in time came to view *Ethics* in a different light. *Principia* had made him a famous man; it had helped change the moral outlooks and lives of countless people. By contrast *Ethics* caused not a ripple of popular attention; its main claim to fame was that it was written by "the author of *Principia Ethica*." However much of a "failure" Moore may have thought *Ethics* was when he completed it, he shows that he is more sanguine when he surveys it in his autobiography. *Ethics*, he writes, "I myself like better than *Principia Ethica*." And if we ask why, Moore is ready with an explanation. It is because *Ethics* seems to him "to be much clearer and far less full of confusions and invalid arguments." Moore both taught and embodied the virtue of independence of mind. He would not publicly favor more what he privately admired less, even if the world was against him. Even in the case—especially in the case—of his own work. *Ethics* was not so much as mentioned by Keynes during his legendary presentation to the Memoir Club. But *Ethics* was "the more rational" in Moore's view, and, so, "the more beautiful." Of the two books, *Ethics* and *Principia*, it is the former that is more worthy of admiring contemplation. But it was in the latter that Moore first argued for those very principles by which he sought to assign *Ethics* pride of place. In some ways, then, Moore no less than Leonard Woolf and John Maynard Keynes, for example, remained a lifelong student of *Principia*, even when he placed his other work above it. Perhaps this final irony will serve to remind others of that book's uncommon power and importance, when properly understood.

References

Material quoted in the body of the present work is listed here alphabetically, according to the author's last name, chapter by chapter. When multiple references are made to the same work in a particular chapter, the page numbers appear in parentheses in the body of the text.

Chapter 1

Annan, Noel. *Leslie Stephen: His Thought and Character in Relation to His Time*, p. 125. Cambridge, Mass.: Harvard University Press, 1952.

Bell, Clive. "Notes on Bloomsbury," p. 89. In S. P. Rosenbaum, ed., *The Bloomsbury Group* (Toronto: University of Toronto Press, 1975). Originally published in Bell, *Old Friends: Personal Recollections* (London: Chatto and Windus, 1956).

Bell, Vanessa. "Notes on Bloomsbury," p. 82. In S. P. Rosenbaum, ed., *The Bloomsbury Group* (Toronto: University of Toronto Press, 1975).

Edel, Leon. *Bloomsbury: A House of Lions*, p. 46. New York: Avon Books, 1980.

Harrod, R. H. *The Life of John Maynard Keynes*, p. 76. New York: Macmillan, 1951.

Himmelfarb, Gertrude. "From Clapham to Bloomsbury: A Genealogy of Morals," p. 40. *Commentary* 79, no. 2 (Feb. 1985).

Keynes, John Maynard. Letter to Lytton Strachey, Feb. 21, 1906, p. 134. Quoted in Robert Skidelsky, *John Maynard Keynes*, Vol. I: *Hopes Betrayed, 1883–1920* (London: Macmillan, 1983).

———. "My Early Beliefs." In *Two Memoirs* (New York: Augustus M. Kelley, 1949).

Leavis, F. R. "Keynes and Currency Values," p. 398. In S. P. Rosenbaum, ed., *The Bloomsbury Group* (Toronto: University of Toronto Press, 1975). Originally published in *Scrutiny* 18 (June 1951).

Levy, Paul. *Moore: G. E. Moore and the Cambridge Apostles.* Oxford: Oxford University Press, 1981.

MacDonald, Hugh. Letter to G. E. Moore, May 23, 1948. The Moore Papers, Cambridge University Library.

Moore, G. E. "An Autobiography," p. 11. In Paul A. Schilpp, ed., *The Philosophy of G. E. Moore* (New York: Tudor, 1952).

————. *Ethics,* pp. 131–132. London: Oxford University Press, 1958.

————. *Principia Ethica,* p. 189. Cambridge, Eng.: Cambridge University Press, 1960.

————. "A Reply to My Critics," p. 667. In Paul A. Schilpp, ed., *The Philosophy of G. E. Moore* (New York: Tudor, 1952).

Russell, Bertrand. *The Autobiography of Bertrand Russell,* Vol. I: 1872–1914, pp. 94–95. Boston: Little, Brown, 1967.

————. Letter to G. E. Moore, October 10, 1903. The Moore Papers, Cambridge University Library.

Skidelsky, Robert. *John Maynard Keynes,* Vol. I: *Hopes Betrayed, 1883–1920.* London: Macmillan, 1983.

Spalding, Francis. *Vanessa Bell,* p. 125. New Haven, Conn.: Tichnor and Fields, 1983.

Strachey, Lytton. Letter to G. E. Moore, Oct. 11, 1903. The Moore Papers, Cambridge University Library.

————. Letter to Leonard Woolf, p. 239. Quoted in Paul Levy, *Moore: G. E. Moore and the Cambridge Apostles* (Oxford: Oxford University Press, 1981).

Woolf, Leonard. *Beginning Again: An Autobiography of the Years 1911–1918,* p. 25. New York: Harcourt Brace Jovanovich, 1964.

————. *The Journey Not the Arrival Matters: An Autobiography of the Years 1939 to 1969,* p. 48. New York: Harcourt Brace Jovanovich, 1966.

————. *Sowing: An Autobiography of the Years 1880 to 1904.* New York: Harcourt Brace Jovanovich, 1966.

Woolf, Virginia. *The Diary of Virginia Woolf,* ed. Anne Olivier Bell, Vol. I: 1915–1919, p. 155. New York: Harcourt Brace Jovanovich, 1977.

————. *The Letters of Virginia Woolf,* ed. Nigel Nicholson. New York: Harcourt Brace Jovanovich, 1975.

Chapter 2

Ayer, A. J. *Russell and Moore: The Analytic Tradition,* p. 138. Cambridge, Mass.: Harvard University Press, 1971.

Broad, C. D. "Introduction." In J. M. E. McTaggart, *Some Dogmas of Religion* (London: Edward Arnold, 1930).

Dickinson, Goldsworthy Lowes. *McTaggart.* Cambridge, Eng.: Cambridge University Press, 1931.

Forster, E. M. "What I Believe," p. 66. In Forster, *Two Cheers for Democracy* (London: Edward Arnold, 1939).

Levy, Paul. *Moore: G. E. Moore and the Cambridge Apostles.* Oxford: Oxford University Press, 1981.

Moore, G. E. "An Autobiography." In Paul A. Schilpp, ed., *The Philosophy of G. E. Moore* (New York: Tudor, 1952).

————. "The Elements of Ethics, with a View to an Appreciation of Kant's Moral Philosophy." The Moore Papers, Cambridge University Library.

————. "Immortality." The Moore Papers, Cambridge University Library.

————. "In What Sense, If Any, Do Past and Future Time Exist?," p. 240. *Mind* n.s. 6 (April 1897). Reprinted in Tom Regan, ed., *G. E. Moore: The Early Essays* (Philadelphia: Temple University Press, 1987).

————. Letters to Desmond MacCarthy, June 19, 1898, April 26, 1899, Feb. 18, 1900, and Feb. 24, 1900. The Moore Papers, Cambridge University Library.

————. Letter to Mrs. MacCarthy, Aug. 22, 1900. The Moore Papers, Cambridge University Library.

————. "Shall we take delight in crushing our roses?" The Moore Papers, Cambridge University Library.

————. "The Value of Religion." *International Journal of Ethics* 12 (Oct. 1901). Reprinted in Tom Regan, ed., *G. E. Moore: The Early Essays* (Philadelphia: Temple University Press, 1987).

————. "Vanity of vanities." The Moore Papers, Cambridge University Library.

Russell, Bertrand. *The Autobiography of Bertrand Russell*, Vol. I: *1872–1914*. Boston: Little, Brown, 1967.

————. Letter to Alys Pearsall Smith, Feb. 10, 1894, p. 127. Quoted in Paul Levy, *Moore: G. E. Moore and the Cambridge Apostles* (Oxford: Oxford University Press, 1981).

Sidgwick, Henry. In Arthur Sidgwick and Mrs. E. M. Sidgwick, comps., *Henry Sidgwick: A Memoir* (London: George Allen and Unwin, 1906).

Skidelsky, Robert. *John Maynard Keynes*, Vol. I: *Hopes Betrayed, 1883–1920*. London: Macmillan, 1983.

Toulmin, Stephen. Review of Paul Levy, *Moore: G. E. Moore and the Cambridge Apostles*, p. 29. *The New Republic*, Aug. 30, 1980.

Chapter 3

Bosanquet, Bernard. "Report." The Moore Papers, Trinity College Library.

Caird, Edward. "Report." The Moore Papers, Trinity College Library.

Moore, G. E. "An Autobiography." In Paul A. Schilpp, ed., *The Philosophy of G. E. Moore* (New York: Tudor, 1952).

————. "Certainty." In Moore, *Philosophical Papers* (New York: Collier, 1962).

_____. *Commonplace Book, 1919–57*, ed. Casimir Lewy. London: George Allen and Unwin, 1962.

_____. "A Defence of Common Sense." In Moore, *Philosophical Papers* (New York: Collier, 1962).

_____. First Dissertation. The Moore Papers, Trinity College Library.

_____. "Freedom." *Mind* n.s. 7 (April 1898). Reprinted in Tom Regan, ed., *G. E. Moore: The Early Essays* (Philadelphia: Temple University Press, 1986).

_____. "Kant's Idealism." *Proceedings of the Aristotelian Society* n.s. 4 (1903–1904). Reprinted in Tom Regan, ed., *G. E. Moore: The Early Essays* (Philadelphia: Temple University Press, 1987).

_____. Letters to Henrietta Sturge Moore, March 12, 1893, Feb. 18, 1896, and Aug. 26, 1897. The Moore Papers, Cambridge University Library.

_____. "What End?" The Moore Papers, Cambridge University Library.

_____. "What is belief in God?" The Moore Papers, Cambridge University Library.

_____. "What is matter?" The Moore Papers, Cambridge University Library.

Moore, Tom. *Boomerang*. The Moore Papers, Cambridge University Library.

Russell, Bertrand. Letter to Alys Pearsall Smith, Feb. 10, 1894, p. 127. Quoted in Paul Levy, *Moore: G. E. Moore and the Cambridge Apostles* (Oxford: Oxford University Press, 1981).

Sidgwick, Henry. "Report." The Moore Papers, Trinity College Library.

Warnock, G. J. *English Philosophy Since 1900*, p. 10. New York: Oxford University Press, 1966.

Chapter 4

Bell, Vanessa. "Notes on Bloomsbury," p. 82. In S. P. Rosenbaum, ed., *The Bloomsbury Group* (Toronto: University of Toronto Press, 1975).

Bosanquet, Bernard. "Report." The Moore Papers, Trinity College Library.

Hession, Charles H. *John Maynard Keynes: The Man Who Revolutionized Capitalism and the Way We Live*. New York: Macmillan, 1984.

Keynes, John Maynard. "My Early Beliefs," p. 94. In *Two Memoirs* (New York: Augustus M. Kelley, 1949).

Moore, G. E. "An Autobiography." In Paul A. Schilpp, ed., *The Philosophy of G. E. Moore* (New York: Tudor, 1952).

_____. First Dissertation. The Moore Papers, Trinity College Library.

_____. Letter to Desmond MacCarthy, Aug. 14, 1898. The Moore Papers, Cambridge University Library.

_____. Letter to Daniel Moore, Jan. 30, 1895. The Moore Papers, Cambridge University Library.

_____. Letter to Henrietta Sturge Moore, April 30, 1895. The Moore Papers, Cambridge University Library.

————. Letter to Sarah Moore, June 29, 1906. The Moore Papers, Cambridge University Library.

————. "The Nature of Judgment." *Mind* n.s. 8 (April 1899). Reprinted in Tom Regan, ed., *G. E. Moore: The Early Essays* (Philadelphia: Temple University Press, 1987).

————. "The Relation of Reason to Moral Action, and of Ignorance to Moral Responsibility: The Intellectual Virtues." The Moore Papers, Cambridge University Library.

————. Review of Leon Brunschvicg, *La Modalité du Jugement*, p. 555. *Mind* n.s. 6 (Oct. 1897).

————. Second Dissertation. The Moore Papers, Trinity College Library.

Russell, Bertrand. Letter to G. E. Moore, Sept. 13, 1898. The Moore Papers, Cambridge University Library.

Ryle, Gilbert. "G. E. Moore's 'The Nature of Judgment.'" In Alice Ambrose and Morris Lazerowitz, eds., *Moore: Essays in Retrospect* (London: George Allen and Unwin, 1970).

Sidgwick, Henry. In Arthur Sidgwick and Mrs. E. M. Sidgwick, comps., *Henry Sidgwick: A Memoir* (London: George Allen and Unwin, 1906).

Chapter 5

Keynes, John Maynard. Quoted in Charles H. Hession, *John Maynard Keynes: The Man Who Revolutionized Capitalism and the Way We Live* (New York: Macmillan, 1984), p. 55.

Levy, Paul. *Moore: G. E. Moore and the Cambridge Apostles.* Oxford: Oxford University Press, 1981.

Moore, G. E. Diary. The Moore Papers, Cambridge University Library.

————. "The Elements of Ethics, with a View to an Appreciation of Kant's Moral Philosophy." The Moore Papers, Cambridge University Library.

————. "Freedom." *Mind* n.s. 7 (April 1898). Reprinted in Tom Regan, ed., *G. E. Moore: The Early Essays* (Philadelphia: Temple University Press, 1987).

————. "Is conversion possible?" The Moore Papers, Cambridge University Library.

————. Letters to Desmond MacCarthy, Sept. 19, 1896, and May 30, 1899. The Moore Papers, Cambridge University Library.

————. Letters to Henrietta Sturge Moore, April 1, 1895, Sept. 12, 1901, and Nov. 14, 1901. The Moore Papers, Cambridge University Library.

————. "Vanity of vanities." The Moore Papers, Cambridge University Library.

Russell, Bertrand. *The Autobiography of Bertrand Russell*, Vol. I: *1872–1914*, p. 86. Boston: Little, Brown, 1967.

————. "My Intellectual Development," p. 12. In Paul A. Schilpp, ed., *The*

Philosophy of Bertrand Russell (Evanston, Ill.: Library of Living Philosophers, 1946).

———. "Was the world good before the 6th day?," p. 249. Quoted in Paul Levy, *Moore: G. E. Moore and the Cambridge Apostles* (Oxford: Oxford University Press, 1981).

Vaughn Williams, Ralph. Letter to G. E. Moore, April 26, no year. The Moore Papers, Cambridge University Library.

Wood, Alan. *Bertrand Russell: The Passionate Sceptic*, p. 80. New York: Simon & Shuster, 1958.

Woolf, Leonard. *Sowing: An Autobiography of the Years 1880 to 1904.* New York: Harcourt Brace Jovanovich, 1966.

Chapter 6

Bell, Clive. Quoted in Himmelfarb, Gertrude. "From Clapham to Bloomsbury: A Genealogy of Morals." *Commentary* 79, no. 2 (Feb. 1985).

Bell, Quentin. Quoted in Himmelfarb, Gertrude. "From Clapham to Bloomsbury: A Genealogy of Morals." *Commentary* 79, no. 2 (Feb. 1985).

Bosanquet, Bernard. "Report." The Moore Papers, Trinity College Library.

Himmelfarb, Gertrude. "From Clapham to Bloomsbury: A Genealogy of Morals." *Commentary* 79, no. 2 (Feb. 1985).

Holroyd, Michael. *Lytton Strachey: A Critical Biography*, Vol. II. New York: Holt, Rinehart and Winston, 1968.

Levy, Paul. *Lytton Strachey: The Really Important Question and Other Papers*, p. xiii. New York: Conrad, McCann and Geoghegan, 1973.

———. *Moore: G. E. Moore and the Cambridge Apostles.* Oxford: Oxford University Press, 1981.

Moore, G. E. "Aesthetics." The Moore Papers, Cambridge University Library.

———. "Art, Morals, and Religion." The Moore Papers, Cambridge University Library.

———. "An Autobiography." In Paul A. Schilpp, ed., *The Philosophy of G. E. Moore* (New York: Tudor, 1952).

———. Diary. The Moore Papers, Cambridge University Library.

———. First Dissertation. The Moore Papers, Trinity College Library.

———. Letters to Desmond MacCarthy, Sept. 19, 1896, and Nov. 15, 1914. The Moore Papers, Cambridge University Library.

———. Letter to Henrietta Sturge Moore, May 26, 1895. The Moore Papers, Cambridge University Library.

———. "The Philosophy of Clothes." The Moore Papers, Cambridge University Library.

———. "Suggestions for the Council of Trinity College," *Cambridge Magazine*, Nov. 27, 1915.

Stout, G. F. Letter to G. E. Moore, Nov. 1, 1903. The Moore Papers, Cambridge University Library.

Strachey, Lytton. "Ought the father to grow a beard?," pp. 274–275. In Paul Levy, *Lytton Strachey: The Really Important Question and Other Papers* (New York: Conrad, McCann and Geoghegan, 1973).

––––––. Statement Before the Hampstead Tribunal, pp. 271–272. In Paul Levy, *Lytton Strachey: The Really Important Question and Other Papers* (New York: Conrad, McCann and Geoghegan, 1973).

Chapter 7

Drury, M. O'C. "Conversations with Wittgenstein," p. 173. In Rush Rhees, ed., *Ludwig Wittgenstein: Personal Recollections* (Towota, N.J.: Rowman and Littlefield, 1981).

Findlay, J. N. "Some Neglected Issues in the Philosophy of G. E. Moore," p. 75. In Alice Ambrose and Morris Lazerowitz, eds., *Moore: Essays in Retrospect* (London: George Allen and Unwin, 1970).

Gasking, D. A. T., and A. C. Jackson. "Wittgenstein as a Teacher," p. 50. In K. T. Fann, ed., *Ludwig Wittgenstein: The Man and His Philosophy* (New York: Dell, 1967).

Leavis, F. R. "Memories of Wittgenstein," p. 64. In Rush Rhees, ed., *Ludwig Wittgenstein: Personal Recollections* (Towota, N.J.: Rowman and Littlefield, 1981).

Levy, Paul. *Moore: G. E. Moore and the Cambridge Apostles.* Oxford: Oxford University Press, 1981.

Lewy, Casimir. "G. E. Moore on the Naturalistic Fallacy." In Alice Ambrose and Morris Lazerowitz, eds., *Moore: Essays in Retrospect* (London: George Allen and Unwin, 1970).

Malcolm, Norman. *Ludwig Wittgenstein: A Memoir.* London: Oxford University Press, 1958.

Moore, G. E. "An Autobiography." In Paul A. Schilpp, ed., *The Philosophy of G. E. Moore* (New York: Tudor, 1952).

––––––. Appendix to the First Dissertation. The Moore Papers, Trinity College Library.

––––––. "Is conversion possible?" The Moore Papers, Cambridge University Library.

––––––. Letter to F. A. Hayek, p. 265. Quoted in Paul Levy, *Moore: G. E. Moore and the Cambridge Apostles* (Oxford: Oxford University Press, 1981).

––––––. *Principia Ethica.* Cambridge, Eng.: Cambridge University Press, 1960.

––––––. "A Reply to My Critics." In Paul A. Schilpp, ed., *The Philosophy of G. E. Moore* (New York: Tudor, 1952).

_____. Review of Fred Bon, *Ueber das Sollen und das Gute: eine begriffsanaly-tische Untersuchung* p. 421. *Mind* n.s. 8 (July 1899).

_____. "Wittgenstein's Lectures in 1930–33," p. 255. In Moore, *Philosophical Papers* (New York: Collier, 1962). Originally published in *Mind* 63 (1954).

Russell, Bertrand. *Autobiography*, Vol. II: *1914–1944*. London: Allen and Unwin, 1968.

_____. "Ludwig Wittgenstein." In K. T. Fann, ed., *Ludwig Wittgenstein: The Man and His Philosophy* (New York: Dell, 1967). Originally published in *Mind* 60, no. 239 (1951).

_____. "Philosophers and Idiots," p. 32. In K. T. Fann, ed. *Ludwig Wittgenstein: The Man and His Philosophy*. New York: Dell, 1967. Originally published in *The Listener*, Feb. 10, 1955.

Strachey, Lytton. Letter to G. E. Moore, Oct. 11, 1903. The Moore Papers, Cambridge University Library.

Von Wright, Georg Henrik. "Biographical Sketch," p. 15. In Norman Malcolm, *Ludwig Wittgenstein: A Memoir* (London: Oxford University Press, 1958).

Wittgenstein, Ludwig. *Ludwig Wittgenstein: Letters to Russell, Keynes and Moore*, ed. G. H. von Wright, p. 9. Ithaca, N.Y.: Cornell University Press, 1974.

_____. *Philosophical Investigations*. New York: Macmillan, 1953.

Woolf, Leonard. "G. E. Moore and the 'Principia Ethica,'" *Times Literary Supplement*, Aug. 28, 1953.

_____. *Sowing: An Autobiography of the Years 1880 to 1904*. New York: Harcourt Brace Jovanovich, 1966.

Woolf, Virginia. *The Letters of Virginia Woolf*, ed. Nigel Nicholson, p. 340. New York: Harcourt Brace Jovanovich, 1975.

Chapter 8

Bell, Vanessa. "Notes on Bloomsbury," p. 82. In S. P. Rosenbaum, ed., *The Bloomsbury Group* (Toronto: University of Toronto Press, 1975).

Edel, Leon. *Bloomsbury: A House of Lions*. New York: Avon Books, 1980.

Keynes, John Maynard. "My Early Beliefs." In Keynes, *Two Memoirs* (New York: Augustus M. Kelley, 1949).

Moore, G. E. "Art, Morals, and Religion." The Moore Papers, Cambridge University Library.

_____. "An Autobiography." In Paul A. Schilpp, ed., *The Philosophy of G. E. Moore* (New York: Tudor, 1952).

_____. Diary. The Moore Papers, Cambridge University Library.

_____. "The Elements of Ethics, with a View to an Appreciation of Kant's Moral Philosophy." The Moore Papers, Cambridge University Library.

_____. "Is conversion possible?" The Moore Papers, Cambridge University Library.

———. Letter to Desmond MacCarthy, Nov. 19, 1902. The Moore Papers, Cambridge University Library.

———. Letter to Daniel Moore, Jan. 30, 1895. The Moore Papers, Cambridge University Library.

———. Letter to Timothy Moore, June 29, 1937. The Moore Papers, Cambridge University Library.

———. *Principia Ethica*. Cambridge, Eng.: Cambridge University Press, 1960.

Rosenbaum, S. P., ed. *The Bloomsbury Group*. Toronto: University of Toronto Press, 1975.

Russell, Bertrand. Letter to G. E. Moore, Oct. 10, 1903. The Moore Papers, Cambridge University Library.

Sidgwick, Henry. Quoted in Jerome Schneewind, *Sidgwick's Ethics and Victorian Moral Philosophy* (Oxford: Clarendon Press, 1977), pp. 16–17.

Stephen, Adrian. *The 'Dreadnought' Hoax*, pp. 36–37. Portions reprinted in S. P. Rosenbaum, ed., *The Bloomsbury Group* (Toronto: University of Toronto Press, 1975). Originally published London: Hogarth Press, 1936.

Strachey, Lytton. Letter to G. E. Moore, Oct. 11, 1903. The Moore Papers, Cambridge University Library.

Warnock, Mary. *Ethics Since 1900*, 3rd ed. Oxford: Oxford University Press, 1978.

Woolf, Leonard. *Sowing: An Autobiography of the Years 1880 to 1904*, pp. 148–149. New York: Harcourt Brace Jovanovich, 1966.

Chapter 9

Bell, Quentin. *Bloomsbury*, p. 74. London: Weidenfeld and Nicolson, 1968.

Cambridge Magazine, Nov. 27, 1915.

Cooke, Harold P. Review of *Ethics*. *Mind* n.s. 22 (Oct. 1913): 553.

Garnett, David. "Lawrence and Bloomsbury." In S. P. Rosenbaum, ed., *The Bloomsbury Group* (Toronto: University of Toronto Press, 1975). Originally published in Garnett, *The Flowers of the Forest* (London: Chatto and Windus, 1955).

Keynes, John Maynard. Letters to Lytton Strachey, Jan. 25, 1906, and March 16, 1906. Quoted in Robert Skidelsky, *John Maynard Keynes*, Vol. I: *Hopes Betrayed, 1883–1920* (London: Macmillan, 1983).

———. Letter to Leonard Woolf, 1905. Quoted in Robert Skidelsky, *John Maynard Keynes*, Vol. I: *Hopes Betrayed, 1883–1920* (London: Macmillan, 1983).

———. "My Early Beliefs." In Keynes, *Two Memoirs*. New York: Augustus M. Kelley, 1949).

Lawrence, D. H. Letter to David Garnett, April 19, 1915, p. 369. In David Garnett, "Lawrence and Bloomsbury," in S. P. Rosenbaum, ed., *The Blooms-*

bury Group (Toronto: University of Toronto Press, 1975). Originally published in Garnett, *The Flowers of the Forest* (London: Chatto and Windus, 1955).

———. Letter to Ottoline Morrell, April 19, 1915, p. 369. Quoted in David Garnett, "Lawrence and Bloomsbury," in S. P. Rosenbaum, ed., *The Bloomsbury Group* (Toronto: University of Toronto Press, 1975). Originally published in Garnett, *The Flowers of the Forest* (London: Chatto and Windus, 1955).

Leavis, F. R. Selections from "Keynes, Lawrence and Cambridge." In S. P. Rosenbaum, ed., *The Bloomsbury Group* (Toronto: University of Toronto Press, 1975). Originally published in Leavis, *The Common Pursuit* (London: Chatto and Windus, 1953).

———. Selections from "Keynes and Currency Values." In S. P. Rosenbaum, ed., *The Bloomsbury Group* (Toronto: University of Toronto Press, 1975). Originally published in *Scrutiny* 18 (June 1951).

Levy, Paul. *Moore: G. E. Moore and the Cambridge Apostles*, p. 238. Oxford: Oxford University Press, 1981.

MacCarthy, Desmond. Selections from *Portraits I*, p. 30. In S. P. Rosenbaum, ed., *The Bloomsbury Group* (Toronto: University of Toronto Press, 1975). Originally published London: Putnam, 1931.

Moore, G. E. "Art, Morals, and Religion." The Moore Papers, Cambridge University Library.

———. "An Autobiography." In Paul A. Schilpp, ed., *The Philosophy of G. E. Moore* (New York: Tudor, 1952).

———. Diary. The Moore Papers, Cambridge University Library.

———. "The Elements of Ethics, with a View to an Appreciation of Kant's Moral Philosophy." The Moore Papers, Cambridge University Library.

———. *Ethics*, pp. 154–155. London: Oxford University Press, 1958.

———. Letter to Desmond MacCarthy, March 29, 1909. The Moore Papers, Cambridge University Library.

———. Letters to Nellie Moore, Sept. 22, 1911, and March 15, 1912. The Moore Papers, Cambridge University Library.

———. *Principia Ethica*. Cambridge, Eng.: Cambridge University Press, 1960.

———. "The Value of Religion," p. 98. *International Journal of Ethics* 12 (Oct. 1901). Reprinted in Tom Regan, ed., *G. E. Moore: The Early Essays* (Philadelphia: Temple University Press, 1986).

———. "Vanity of vanities." The Moore Papers, Cambridge University Library.

Pitkin, Walter B. Review of *Ethics*, p. 223. *Journal of Philosophy*, April 10, 1913.

Russell, Bertrand. *The Autobiography of Bertrand Russell*, Vol. I: *1872–1914*. Boston: Little, Brown, 1967.

———. Letter to Virginia Woolf, Feb. 23, 1924, pp. 293–294. In Virginia Woolf, *The Diary of Virginia Woolf*, ed. Anne Olivier Bell, Vol. II: *1920–1924*. New York: Harcourt Brace Jovanovich, 1980.

Strachey, Lytton. Letter to John Maynard Keynes, April 1906, p. 238. Quoted in Paul Levy, *Moore: G. E. Moore and the Cambridge Apostles* (Oxford: Oxford University Press, 1981).

————. Letter to G. E. Moore, Jan. 2, 1908. The Moore Papers, Cambridge University Library.

Trevelyan, R. C. Letter to G. E. Moore, Sept. 14, 1912. The Moore Papers, Cambridge University Library.

Webb, Beatrice. Letter to Lady Courtney, Sept. 19, 1911, p. 372. In Sidney and Beatrice Webb, *The Letters of Sidney and Beatrice Webb*, ed. Norman Mackenzie, Vol. II: *Parnership, 1892-1912* (Cambridge, Eng.: Cambridge University Press, 1978).

Woolf, Leonard. *Beginning Again: An Autobiography of the Years 1911-1918.* New York: Harcourt Brace Jovanovich, 1964.

Virginia Woolf, *The Diary of Virginia Woolf*, ed. Anne Olivier Bell, Vol. II: 1920-1924, pp. 293-294. New York: Harcourt Brace Jovanovich, 1980.

Index

Aesthetics, 157, 159, 165, 173, 258
Ainsworth, R. A., 175, 176, 280, 281
Annan, Noel, 23
Apostles, The, 33, 34, 35, 36, 38, 39,
    40, 67, 70, 71, 72, 80, 123, 124, 140,
    141, 155, 156, 157, 165, 174, 188,
    215, 260. *See also* Cambridge Conver-
    sazione Society
Appearance, 77, 80, 81, 82, 83, 84, 85,
    92, 111
Aristotle, 131, 191, 197
Arnold, Matthew, 119, 145, 146, 282
Art, 163, 164, 165, 166, 168, 169, 170,
    171, 172, 182
"Art-quake," 167
Asquith, H. H., 9, 13, 283
Ayer, A. J., 40

Beauty, 115, 131, 139, 140, 142, 163,
    164, 165, 166, 169, 171, 192, 193,
    207, 208, 258, 264, 265, 267
Bell, Angelica, 5
Bell, Clive, xi, 4, 5, 6, 8, 9, 15, 20, 21, 22,
    169, 171
Bell, Julian, 5
Bell, Quentin, 5, 251
Bell, Vanessa, 3, 4, 5, 6, 7, 13, 21, 22,
    119, 218, 255, 283
Berkeley, Bishop George, 73, 74, 75, 76,
    78, 81, 82, 280
Birrell, Frances, 254, 255
Bloomsbury, xi, xii, xiii, xiv, 3-10, 221,

245-250, 257, 277-283; Moore's
    influence on, 20-28, 245-250,
    277-283
Bon, Fred, 191, 214
Boomerang, 90
Bosanquet, Bernard, 68, 69, 70, 101, 103,
    110, 174
Bradley, F. H., 68, 76, 80, 90, 98, 99,
    100, 103, 104, 106, 107, 110, 191,
    203
Broad, C. D., 30, 60, 71, 184
Brooke, Rupert, 33
Brunschvicg, Leon, 101
Burke, Edmund, 250
Butler, Bishop, 215
Buxton, Anthony, 217, 219, 220

Caird, Edward, 87, 89, 105
Cambridge Conversazione Society, 32, 41.
    See also Apostles, The
Cambridge Magazine, 178, 180, 289
Cambridge University Moral Science
    Club, 178, 179, 180, 188
Carlyle, Thomas, 170
Cezanne, Paul, 6
Charleston farm, 5, 9, 21, 254, 255
Cole, Horace, 217, 218, 220
Common Sense, 65, 66, 67, 68, 91, 92,
    98, 142, 144, 148
Concepts, 104, 105, 106, 125, 126, 193
Conduct criterion, 58, 89, 113, 132, 135,
    136, 242, 243, 271

Cook, Harold P., 288
Council of Trinity College, 31, 177, 178, 179, 180
Crampton, Davis, 35n

Dakyns, H. G., 116
Davis, Theodore, 35n
Dickinson, Goldsworthy Lowes, 30, 59, 278
Dickinson, Violet, 15
Dreadnought, 217–220, 250
Drury, M. O'C., 211, 212
Duties and virtues, 164, 165, 169, 192, 196
Duty (defined), 228, 230–235

Edel, Leon, 14, 218, 247
Egoism, 239, 246
Eliot, T. S., 7
Ely, Dorothy, 13
Empiricism, 78, 79, 103, 200
Ethics, 84, 160, 165, 189, 190, 191, 193, 202, 204, 205, 223, 224, 225, 227, 232, 234, 275
Evils, 267

Faith, 276
Findlay, J. N., 214
First world war, 176, 177, 181
Forster, E. M., 31, 246
Freedom, 82, 83, 85, 86, 87, 88. *See also* Transcendental Freedom
Freud, Sigmund, 253
Fry, Roger, 4, 5, 6, 8, 9, 22, 33, 167, 218, 251

Garnett, David, 5, 8, 254, 255, 256
Garnett, Edward, 256
Gasking, D. A. T., 183
Gauguin, Paul, 6
God, belief in, 142. *See also* Religion
Goethe, J. W., 145, 240
Good, 84, 85, 88, 101, 106, 112, 114, 115, 125, 159, 168, 191, 192, 194, 195, 196, 198–214, 244, 270, 273, 274, 275, 283
Goods: mixed, 267; unmixed, 267
Gore, Canon, 96
Grant, Duncan, 5, 6, 7, 8, 9, 218, 219, 220, 250, 253, 254, 255, 256, 278

Hampstead Tribunal, 145, 148, 150, 163, 188, 216, 240, 241, 249, 273, 274, 277
Hardy, G. F., 180, 181
Harrod, Sir Roy, 15
Hayek, F. A., 187
Hedonism, 39, 44, 139, 141, 205, 206, 207, 266, 267
Hegel, G. W. F., 30, 72, 76, 91, 100, 138
Hession, Charles H., 95, 118
Himmelfarb, Gertrude, 23, 169
Holroyd, Michael, 154, 155
Hume, David, 46, 98, 285
Hutchinson, Mary, 5

Ideal, the, 25, 26, 129, 130, 131, 133, 257, 261, 268, 273, 288
Ideal criterion, 58, 88, 112, 133, 271
Idealism, 70, 72, 75, 76, 77, 78, 81, 110, 139, 194, 215
Immortality, 40, 41, 52, 55, 76

Jackson, A. C., 183
James, Henry, 218, 220
James, William, 149
Jowett, Benjamin, 119

Kant, Immanuel, 46, 52, 78, 79, 80, 81, 82, 85, 87, 90, 95, 99, 101, 102, 103, 106, 110, 122, 123, 135, 138, 159, 160, 192, 197, 222, 239, 276
Keynes, John Maynard, xi, xii, 3, 5, 6, 7, 8, 9, 14, 17, 18, 19, 20, 22, 23, 24, 25, 26, 27, 33, 39, 70, 95, 106, 118, 119, 150, 157, 188, 197, 218, 247, 248, 249, 250, 251, 253, 255, 256, 257, 261, 268, 269, 270, 276, 277, 278, 279, 280, 282, 283, 285, 290

Lawrence, D. H., 253, 254, 255, 256, 269, 277, 278, 279
Lawrence, Frieda, 254, 255, 256
Leavis, F. R., 8, 25, 119, 187, 256, 257, 277, 278, 279, 282
Leavis, Q. D., 277
Leighton, Frederick, 119
Levy, Paul, 13, 26, 27, 40, 61, 140, 141, 142, 154, 156, 157, 167, 181, 279, 280, 281
Lewis, Wyndham, 6

Lewy, Casimir, 204, 205
Littlewood, J. E., 178
Locke, John, 78, 79, 103
London School of Ethics and Social
Philosophy, 40, 123, 140, 141, 243
Lotze, Rudolf Hermann, 90
Lowell, James Russell, 95

MacCarthy, Desmond, xi, 5, 6, 7, 8, 33,
42, 55, 122, 143, 150, 260, 265, 272,
283, 284, 285, 286, 289
MacCarthy, Mary, 8
MacDonald, Hugh, 26
Mackensie, J. S., 158
McTaggart, J. M. E., 29, 30, 31, 32, 33,
36, 38, 40, 59, 60, 61, 68, 71, 72, 76,
100, 124, 157, 176, 177, 180, 189,
203, 246, 269
Malcolm, Norman, 184, 216
Marsh, Eddie, 35n
Marx, Karl, 253
Matisse, Henri, 6
Memoir Club, 7, 251, 252, 283, 290
Method criterion, 58, 89, 113, 133, 135,
136
Method of isolation, 261, 262, 264, 269,
272, 273, 274, 276, 277
Mill, John Stuart, 74, 139, 206
Moore, Daniel, 36
Moore, G. E.: early religious beliefs,
37–38; idealism, 70–78; literary style,
90; melancholy, 41–44, 137–151;
"mysticism," 148, 215, 266, 275;
nihilism, 41–44; views of religion,
37–52
  Apostles' papers: "Do we love ourselves
  best?," 141; "Is beauty truth?," 165;
  "Is conversion possible?," 144, 147,
  148, 150, 165, 188, 215, 240; "Shall
  we take delight in crushing our
  roses?," 39; "Vanity of vanities,"
  41–44, 46, 54, 55, 60, 137, 138,
  142; "Was the epistle of straw?," 40;
  "What end?," 39, 70; "What is belief
  in god?," 40, 67; "What is it to be
  wicked?," 40; "What is matter?," 41,
  70, 72–77, 110
  Books: *Commonplace Book*, 91; *Ethics*,
  xv, 11, 16, 57, 173, 285, 286, 287,
  288, 289, 290; *The Philosophy of*

G. E. *Moore*, xv, 213; *Principia Ethica*,
  xii, xiii, xiv, xv, 16, 18, 19, 20, 21,
  23, 24, 27, 42, 43, 44, 56, 57, 125,
  126, 136, 137, 157, 158, 162, 173,
  174, 178, 188–211, 214, 221, 224,
  225, 228–240, 245, 246, 247, 250,
  258–272, 273, 275, 277, 282, 284,
  288, 289, 290; *Some Main Problems
  of Philosophy*, 174
  Dissertations: First Dissertation, 78, 80,
  81–92, 98, 101, 102, 106, 111, 112,
  113, 114, 115, 132, 133, 139, 159,
  167, 191, 207, 209, 270, 271, 275;
  Second Dissertation, 68, 69, 70, 81,
  91, 99, 100, 101, 102, 103, 106,
  107, 108, 111, 112, 113, 114, 115,
  116, 125, 126, 127, 133, 138, 139,
  174, 193, 271
  Lectures: "The Elements of Ethics," 41,
  50, 51, 116, 123, 124, 125, 126,
  128, 129, 132, 133, 134, 135, 136,
  137, 139, 141, 142, 143, 147, 159,
  162, 198, 199, 207, 209, 222, 242,
  243, 257, 260, 271, 272, 273, 276
  Letters: to Desmond MacCarthy, 42,
  106, 167, 177, 244, 286; to
  Desmond MacCarthy's mother,
  55–56; to Moore's father, 98; to
  Moore's mother, 90, 94, 97, 119,
  143, 158; to Sarah Moore, 119; to
  Cambridge Magazine, "Suggestions
  for the Council of Trinity College,"
  178–180, 289
  Published papers: "Are the Materials of
  Sense Affections of the Mind," 11;
  "A Defence of Common Sense," 40,
  65; "Freedom," 78–87, 113, 135,
  138; "Immortality," 143; "Mr.
  McTaggart's 'Studies in Hegelian
  Cosmology,'" 40; "The Nature of
  Sensible Appearances," 11; "Objects
  of Perception," 285; "The Refutation
  of Idealism," 173; "A Reply to My
  Critics," 12, 214, 285; "Some
  Judgments of Perception," 11; "The
  Status of Sense Data," 11; "The
  Value of Religion," 40, 41, 44–56,
  77, 143, 275
  Sunday Essay Society papers: "Aes-
  thetics," 171; "Art, Morals, and

Moore, G. E., (*continued*)
　Religion," 157, 159–170, 173, 191,
　207, 223, 239, 244, 258, 261, 265;
　"Immortality," 41; "Natural
　Theology," 40; "The Philosophy of
　Clothes," 157, 170–173; "Religious
　Belief," 40
Moore, Hettie, 176
Moore, Nellie, 176, 288
Moore, Sarah, 176
Moore, Sturge, 90
Moore, Thomas, 143
Moore, Timothy, 237
Moral conversion, 144, 163, 188
Moral law, 85
Moral Science Club. *See* Cambridge
　University Moral Science Club
Morals, 167, 168, 169. *See also* Ethics;
　Science of Morals
Morrell, Ottoline, 155, 186, 255
Myers, F. W. H., 94

Natural goods criterion, 57, 88, 114, 115,
　133, 210, 271
Naturalism, 135, 261
Naturalistic fallacy, 124, 193–198, 286

Objectivity criterion, 57, 88, 112, 132,
　210, 270
Objects: natural, 125, 126; nonnatural,
　125, 126
Omega workshops, 4
Open question argument, 197
Organic unities, 207, 263, 265
Ornament, 172

Paradox of analysis, 12, 13
Passmore Settlement House, 123, 138
Pater, Walter, 145
Pitkin, Walter B., 288
Plato, 106, 126, 131, 200, 268
Post-Impressionism shows, 4, 5, 6
Principia Ethica, reviews of, 18–20. *See
　also* Moore, G. E., Books, *Principia
　Ethica*
Prize Fellowship, 69, 90, 100, 133, 158,
　174, 176, 243
Properties: metaphysical, 199–200, 201;
　natural, 125, 126, 127, 199, 201, 205,
　286; nonnatural, 125, 126, 127,

198–199, 200, 201, 203, 214, 275,
　286
Propositions, 105, 107; existential, 108,
　109, 111, 126; necessary (*a priori*),
　108, 110, 111

Realism, 100, 107, 138, 194, 200, 270,
　275
Reality, 77, 80, 81, 82, 83, 85, 87, 88,
　92, 111
Religion, 167, 168, 169, 276. *See also*
　Moore, G. E., views of religion
Richmond, Sir William, 6
Ridley, Guy, 217, 220
Right (defined), 228, 286
Rosenbaum, S. P., 277
Ruskin, John, 119
Russell, Bertrand, xi, 23, 25, 29, 30, 31,
　32, 34, 36, 37, 38, 59, 61, 66, 100,
　103, 106, 140, 141, 142, 143, 177,
　180, 185, 186, 187, 188, 207, 214,
　215, 221, 229, 251, 253, 278, 279,
　280, 288
Ryle, Gilbert, 61, 101, 104, 193

Sangar, Charles, 35n, 122
Sargent, John Singer, 6
Schneewind, Jerome, 243
Schopenhauer, Arthur, 271
Science of Morals, xii, xiii, 77, 125, 127,
　160, 161, 162, 170, 173, 190, 191,
　192, 193, 201, 203, 204, 205, 209,
　213, 222, 223, 225, 226, 227, 228,
　230, 231, 232, 234, 235, 237, 238,
　240, 243, 244, 249, 258, 275, 282
Sidgwick, Arthur, 116, 117
Sidgwick, Eleanor, 116
Sidgwick, Henry, xi, 34, 71, 90, 93, 94,
　95, 96, 97, 100, 114, 116, 119, 123,
　132, 139, 142, 149, 150, 160, 163,
　180, 187, 196, 197, 205, 206, 207,
　208, 209, 220, 243, 257, 266, 267,
　276, 282
Skidelsky, Robert, 19, 23, 24, 33, 34,
　250, 285
Smith, Alys Pearsall, 36
Society for Psychical Research, 94
Socrates, 144
Sodomy, 39
Solipsism, 73, 74, 75, 77, 78, 81

Standard interpretation, 23–26, 137, 221, 236, 237, 239, 247
Stein, Gertrude, 14
Stephen, Adrian, 7, 217, 218, 219, 220
Stephen, Leslie, 7, 218, 282
Stephen, Thoby, 7, 9, 218
Stephen, Vanessa. See Bell, Vanessa
Stephen, Virginia. See Woolf, Virginia
Stevenson, Charles L., 213, 214
Stoics, 15, 145, 146, 240
Stout, G. F., 69, 71, 72, 174
Strachey, Lytton, xi, xii, xiv, 4, 6, 8, 9, 15, 16, 17, 18, 19, 24, 25, 33, 39, 118, 119, 150, 151, 154, 155, 156, 157, 170, 177, 181, 188, 189, 242, 245, 251, 257, 269, 278, 279, 280, 281, 282, 284, 285, 288, 289
Sturge, Henrietta, 36
Sunday Essay Society, 41, 123, 157, 159, 170, 171
Sydney-Turner, Saxon, 20

Time, 32, 38, 59, 60, 80
Toulmin, Stephen, 33
Transcendental Freedom, 114, 135. See also Freedom
Transcendentalism, 110
Trevelyan, Robert, 122, 150, 288
Trevelyan, Sir George, 117, 151
Trinity Essay Society, 40
Truth, 107, 110

Union of Democratic Control (UDC), 177, 178, 179
Universality criterion, 57, 88, 112, 132, 133, 210, 270
University of Michigan, 91

Van Gogh, Vincent, 6
Von Wright, G. H., 215

Ward, James, 71, 91, 100, 143, 180, 184, 187, 212
Warnock, G. J., 67, 68, 70
Warnock, Mary, 222, 223
Watts, George Frederick, 119
Webb, Beatrice, 13, 278, 279, 280
Wedgewood, Ralph, 35n
Whitehead, Alfred North, 33
Wittgenstein, Ludwig, xi, 150, 183, 184, 185, 186, 187, 188, 211, 212, 213, 214, 215, 216, 278, 283
Woolf, Leonard, xiii, 5, 6, 7, 8, 9, 13, 14, 15, 16, 18, 20, 21, 22, 23, 24, 26, 27, 33, 122, 151, 175, 197, 199, 218, 247, 248, 249, 250, 268, 278, 283, 289, 290
Woolf, Virginia, xi, 3, 7, 9, 15, 20, 21, 22, 23, 33, 197, 198, 210, 218, 219, 220, 250, 277, 280, 281, 285
Wordsworth, William, 145, 146, 147, 148, 240, 273

Made in the USA
Monee, IL
25 October 2021